ANALECTA BIBLICA

INVESTIGATIONES SCIENTIFICAE IN RES BIBLICAS

105

analecta biblica - 105

BENJAMIN FIORE, S.J.

Canisius College, Buffalo

The Function of Personal Example in the Socratic and Pastoral Epistles

ROME
BIBLICAL INSTITUTE PRESS
1986

ISBN 88-7653-105-X

© Iura editionis et versionis reservantur

PRINTED IN ITALY

GREGORIAN UNIVERSITY PRESS
BIBLICAL INSTITUTE PRESS
Piazza della Pilotta, 35 - 00187 Rome, Italy

For My Mother and Father

Acknowledgments

I am particularly grateful to Mr. Abraham J. Malherbe for his encouragement and guidance, which coaxed the initial idea for this dissertation into full development. Whatever of value is to be found in these pages I unhesitatingly ascribe to the alchemy of his direction. The baser materials are the products of my own apprentice efforts.

Thanks are also due to the other Yale faculty, Nils A, Dahl (now retired), Carl H. Holladay (now at Emory U.), Luke T. Johnson (now at the U. of Indiana), Wayne A. Meeks, and Bentley Layton, for their interest and suggestions.

The abiding support and assistance of my family, of my fellow students and Jesuit confreres in New Haven, and of my friends and associates at Assumption Church in Woodbridge were inestimable in seeing me through the ups and downs of research and writing.

In the preparation of the manuscript, Dr. Rose-Ann Martin worked wonders drawing the final typed copy out of the preliminary drafts. Fr. John J. Jennings, S.J. lent a sharp eye to the proofreading and Mrs. Lynne Glair proved invaluable in the final stages of typing and correction. To all of these I offer sincerest thanks, as well as to the New York Province of the Society of Jesus for making the whole project possible *ad majorem Dei gloriam*.

BENJAMIN FIORE, S.J.

New Haven
May, 1982

The indices, transliterations, and text corrections for the present edition were prepared with the help of Mrs. Veronica Caldwell, Misses Loraine Laidlaw and Margaret Hillery, and Fr. James J. Shanahan, S.J.

Buffalo
January, 1984

Table of Contents

Abbreviations

Abbott-Smith	Abbott-Smith, G. *A Manual Lexicon of the New Testament*
Abh. sächs. Ges. Wiss.	*Abhandlungen des sächsischen Gesellschaft der Wissenschaften*
AJP	*American Journal of Philology*
An Bib.	*Analecta Biblica*
ANRW	*Aufstieg und Niedergang der römischen Welt*
APF	*Archiv für Papyrusforschung*
ATR	*Anglican Theological Review*
BAG	Bauer, Arndt, Gingrich. *A Greek-English Lexicon of the New Testament and Other Early Christian Literature*
BDF	Blass, Debrunner, Funk. *A Greek Grammar of the New Testament and Other Early Christian Literature*
BET	Beiträge zur biblischen Exegese und Theologie
BEvT	Beiträge zur evangelischen Theologie
Bib.	*Biblica*
BTB	*Biblical Theology Bulletin*
BZ	*Biblische Zeitschrift*
BZNW	Beihefte zur ZNW
CBQ	*Catholic Biblical Quarterly*
CJ	*Classical Journal*
ConNT	*Coniectanea neotestamentica*
CPh	*Classical Philology*
CQ	*Classical Quarterly*
CR	*Classical Review*
ETR	*Etudes théologiques et religieuses*
Exp. Tim.	*Expository Times*
FRLANT	Forschungen zur Religion und Literatur des Alten und Neuen Testaments
G & R	*Greece and Rome*
HNT	Handbuch zum Neuen Testament
HSPh	*Harvard Studies in Classical Philology*
HUCA	*Hebrew Union College Annual*
JAC	Jahrbuch für Antike und Christentum
Jahr. f. cl. Phil.	*Jahrbücher für classische Philologie*
JBL	*Journal of Biblical Literature*
JHPh	*Journal of the History of Philosophy*
JHS	*Journal of Hellenic Studies*
JR	*Journal of Religion*
JRH	*Journal of Religious History*
JTS	*Journal of Theological Studies*
KBW	Katholisches Bibelwerk

Kl. Pauly	*Der Kleine Pauly: Lexikon der Antike*
LCL	Loeb Classical Library
Leipz. Stud.	*Leipziger Studien zur klassischen Philosophie*
LSJ	Liddell-Scott-Jones. *A Greek-English Lexicon*
MH	*Museum Helveticum. Revue Suisse pour l'Étude de l'Antiquité classique*
Mnemos.	*Mnemosyne*
NovT	*Novum Testamentum*
NovTSup	Novum Testamentum, Supplements
NTS	*New Testament Studies*
OCD	*Oxford Classical Dictionary*
Philol.	*Philologus*
PW	Pauly-Wissowa. Real-Encyclopädie der klassischen Altertumswissenschaft
RAC	*Reallexikon für Antike und Christentum*
RB	*Revue biblique*
*RGG*³	*Die Religion in Geschichte und Gegenwart: Handwörterbuch für Theologie und Religionswissenschaft.* 3rd rev. ed.
RHE	*Revue d'histoire ecclésiastique*
RhM	*Rheinisches Museum für Philologie*
RNT	Regensburger Neues Testament
SANT	Studien zum Alten und Neuen Testament
SBL	Society of Biblical Literature
SBLSBS	SBL Sources for Biblical Study
SBS	Stuttgarter Bibelstudien
ScrB	*Scripture Bulletin*
ST	*Studia theologica*
TAPA	*Transactions of the American Philological Association*
TDNT	Kittel. *Theological Dictionary of the New Testament*
TLZ	*Theologische Literaturzeitung*
TZ	*Theologische Zeitschrift*
UNT	Untersuchungen zum Neuen Testament
WUNT	Wissenschaftliche Untersuchungen zum Neuen Testament
YCS	*Yale Classical Studies*
Zerwick–Grosvenor	Zerwick, Max and Mary Grosvenor. *Grammatical Analysis of the Greek New Testament.* vol. 2. Rome: Biblical Institute, 1979.
ZNW	*Zeitschrift für die neuestestamentliche Wissenschaft*
ZTK	*Zeitschrift für Theologie und Kirche*

Chapter I

The Genre of the Pastoral Epistles:
A Survey of the Scholarship

The genre and purpose of the Pastoral Epistles have long puzzled the letters' interpreters, who have agreed on one or other reading of the message of the letters even when they disagreed about the letters' Pauline authenticity. In fact, the question of authorship does not logically precede that of genre and purpose.[1] Rather, the analysis of the form and intent of the letters from internal evidence would have to be complemented by hypotheses as to compatible historical situations. Perhaps then Paul or his double might emerge from the shadows. In any event, the question of authorship will not be dealt with here, and the form and purpose of the letters will be treated later in this study. The next few pages will simply survey representative scholarly opinion about the genre and purpose of the letters, in order to isolate those categories which will illuminate the formal analysis of the letters in the following sections.

I. Three Approaches to Explaining the Pastorals

It is noteworthy that most commentators present a presumed historical situation first, into which they place the Pastorals and from which they conclude to the letters' purpose. The commentators perceive the letters' purpose under one of three headings: (A) polemic defense, (B) ecclesiastical discipline, (C) traditional instruction. Little formal analysis of the genre is undertaken. The discussion of these options to explain the purpose of the Pastorals will (1) lay out the proposed historical situations and the purposes presumed for the letters as they confront those circumstances. (2) It will then call attention to the general classifications of genre. (3) The function perceived for Timothy and Titus will be brought out, as well as the reaction expected of the community.

---

[1] M. Dibelius and H. Conzelmann, *The Pastoral Epistles,* Hermeneia, trans. P. Buttolph and A. Yarbro (Philadelphia: Fortress, 1972) 1.

A. Polemic Defense

(1) The false teaching threatening the community lurks in the shadows of the letters' indefinite accusations. Nonetheless, F.C. Baur and his followers [2] emphasized the letters' polemic within their understanding of early church history. By their reassertion of the Pauline tradition, the Pastorals met the opponents on two opposing fronts: Marcion's anti-Jewish distortion of Paul and the Judaizers' anti-Pauline traditionalism. Harrison [3] labels the false teachers less precisely as ascetics and libertines, but he agrees with the first group in seeing concern for community structure in the letters as the other weapon against heresy; that is, along with their reaffirmation of Pauline teaching. The cautious opinion that the Pastorals seem to be confronting a form of Gnosticism still in its Protean forms [4] is about all that the statements in the letter explicitly suggest.

In general, (2) defense of the community's belief and practice and reaffirmation of the authentic (some read Pauline) tradition is the concern of the letters for those taking this view. (3) If the letters are authentic, then Timothy and Titus are being alerted to the danger of false teaching. If not, then Timothy and Titus become transparent figures through which the leaders of the latter-day community see themselves and their responsibilities in the crisis situation of their church.

---

[2] F.C. Baur, *Die sogenannten Pastoralbriefe der Apostel Paulus* (Stuttgart/Tübingen: J.G. Cotta, 1835) 56-58, 75-76, 86-88; H.J. Holtzmann, *Die Pastoralbriefe* (Leipzig: Wilhelm Engelmann, 1880) 1-6; W.M.L. de Wette, *Kurze Erklärung der Briefe an Titus, Timotheus und die Hebräer* (Leipzig: Weidmann, 1847) 3, 25, 62, 118 ff. R. Schwarz, *Bürgerliches Christentum im Neuen Testament? Eine Studie zu Ethik, Amt und Recht in den Pastoralbriefen,* Österreichische Biblische Studien 4 (Klosterneuburg: Österreichisches Katholisches Bibelwerk, 1983) appeared after this study was completed but explains the aim of example and paraenesis in light of the letters' polemic context.

[3] P.N. Harrison, *The Problem of the Pastoral Epistles* (Oxford: Oxford University, 1921) 9-10.

[4] C.K. Barrett, *The Pastoral Epistles in the New English Bible* (Oxford: Clarendon, 1963) 12-19; B.S. Easton, *The Pastoral Epistles* (New York: Charles Scribner's Sons, 1947) 1-8; and for a variation on this, i.e. an original, general, anti-gnostic first redaction, later reworked in an anti-Marcionite direction, see A. Loisy, *Remarques sur la littérature épistolaire du Nouveau Testament* (Paris: Emile Nourry [J. Thiébaud], 1935) 114-25 and *The Origins of the New Testament*, trans. L.P. Jacks (New York: Macmillan, 1950) 279. See also: W. Mangold, *Die Irrlehren der Pastoralbriefe* (Marburg: Elwert, 1856); W. Lütgert, *Die Irrlehre der Pastoralbriefe,* Beiträge zur Förderung Christlicher Theologie, 8 (Gütersloh: C. Bertelsmann, 1909); H. Binder, "Die historische Situation der Pastoralbriefe," in *Geschichtswirklichkeit und Glaubensbewährung,* Fest. F. Müller, ed. F.C. Fry (Stuttgart: Evangelisches Verlagswerk, 1967); U.B. Müller, *Zur frühchristlichen Theologiegeschichte; Judenchristentum und Paulinismus in Kleinasien an der Wende vom ersten zum zweiten Jahrhundert n. Christus* (Gütersloh: Gerd Mohn, 1976); J. Massyngberd Ford, "Proto-Montanism in the Pastoral Epistles," *NTS* 17 (1970-71) 338-46; M. Rist, "Pseudepigraphic Refutations of Marcionism," *JR* 22 (1942) 39-62.

This understanding of the Pastoral Epistles, however, is subject to serious questioning. The identity of the opponents, the content of their teaching, and the nature of the polemical situation are not clearly specified or elaborated.[5] Moreover, the polemical charges, while a consistent feature of all three letters, never dominate any one of the letters. Perhaps, then, the comments on false teachers do not characterize the letters as polemic or apologetic in genre but stand together with other features as formal elements of a broader class of literature.

The proponents of a polemical reading of the letters move from the hints of a crisis in teaching and belief, to a designation of a likely historical situation, and from there to a characterization of the letters. Unfortunately, this hypothesis goes begging for a study of the form.

B. *Ecclesiastical Discipline*

In the second approach, some scholars focus on the form of the letters and try to understand them from the perspective of church discipline. (1) A combination of the statements of purpose within the letters[6] and of external evidence like the title "Pastoral"[7] and comments in ancient witnesses[8] allows others[9] to consider

---

[5] The opponents are sometimes named, 1 Tim 1:20; 2 Tim 2:17; 4:14; but their relationship to the community and the contents of their teaching is generally unspecified, 1 Tim 1:3; 2 Tim 2:17 ff., Titus 1:10; they do not know the law, 1 Tim 1:7; they are immoral, 1 Tim 6:3 ff.; 2 Tim 3:2 ff.; Titus 1:16; they teach a false asceticism, 1 Tim 4:3; Titus 1: 14-15; they are wrong about the resurrection, 2 Tim 2:18; they teach false knowledge, 1 Tim 6:20-21; Titus 1:16. Others are not named at all but are only described in stock terms.

[6] 1 Tim 3:14-15 is most often cited along with the special instructions after the greetings: 1 Tim 1:2 ff. and Titus 1:5 ff. for re-establishing community conduct and structures or organizing them where they are not yet established. The qualifications for office holders (bishops in 1 Tim 3:1-7, elders in Titus 1:5-9, deacons in 1 Tim 3:8-13, widows in 1 Tim 5:3 ff.), regulations for community procedures (in prayer, 1 Tim 2:1-2, 8; in teaching, 1 Tim 2: 11-12; in judgment, 1 Tim 5:19 ff.; for salaries, 1 Tim 5: 17-18; for care of the needy, 1 Tim 5:8-10; for authorizing officials, 1 Tim 4:14), and general rules of conduct (for the community, Titus 3:1-2, 8, 14; for elders, Titus 2:2; for older women, Titus 2:3-5; for women, 1 Tim 2:9-10; for young men, Titus 2:6; for slaves, 1 Tim 6:1-2; Titus 2:9-10; for the rich, 1 Tim 6:9 ff.), as well as the admonitions about false teachers (identifying them, 1 Tim 1:20a; 2 Tim 1:15; 2:17; 4:10, 14-15; characterizing their teaching and conduct, 1 Tim 1:6-9; 4:1-3; 6:3-5; 2 Tim 2:18; 3:2-8; 4:3; Titus 1:10; suggesting avoiding them, 1 Tim 1:20b; 4:7; 2 Tim 2:16; 2:23; Titus 3:9, or directly challenging them, 1 Tim 1:3-4; Titus 1:11-16; 3:10-11) fill out these introductory remarks. Other recommendations and prescriptions look directly to Timothy and Titus and their particular duties (1 Tim 1:18; 4:6-7, 11-16; 5:1-2; 6:3, 11, 14, 20; 2 Tim 1:8; 2:1-3, 14-15, 22; 3:14; 4:2, 5; Titus 2:1, 7, 15).

[7] The title "Pastoral" as a general description for all three letters was introduced by Paul Anton in 1753 in his *Abhandlungen der Pastoralbriefe,* as G. Wohlenberg, *Die Pastoralbriefe* (Leipzig: A. Deichert [Georg Böhme], 1906) 68-69, points out. C. Spicq, *Saint Paul: Les*

the letters as instructions on church discipline or order. (2) 1 Timothy and Titus reveal Paul in the midst of his missionary career; 2 Timothy finds him imprisoned and even looking to his death. Those who approach the letters in this way [10] eventually trace in them a double, but complementary, route: 1 Timothy and, to a lesser extent, Titus mark out a path of community order with lists of qualifications for office and codes of conduct; 2 Timothy is Paul's exhortation that Timothy be faithful to his office, encouraged by Paul's own career in this his last testament.

(3) As "church order" documents, the letters' interest would rest in the community. Timothy and Titus would be the transmitters of regulations issued and authorized by their apostolic "father," whether they are the disciples and co-workers of Paul or figures of any church official. In the second instance, another dimension is added to the regulations for officials, and even to those for the community, in this "fleshed out" model of true Christian service and conduct.[11] The community and its officials, then, would find in these letters an outline of their roles and expected behavior, as well as a demonstration of these in the practice to which the addressees are exhorted. Obedience and conformity are called for and, perhaps, imitation too.

Epîtres Pastorales, 4 rev. ed., 2 vols. (Paris: Gabalda, 1969) 1:31, also mentions D.N. Berdot along with Anton when discussing the origin of the title. Wohlenberg, 69, questions the appropriateness of the title for two reasons: the letters are not only about community officials or pastors, nor are the addressees with their extraordinary powers simply community leaders. In a more general sense, however, Wohlenberg accepts the title and agrees with Anton who justified the title because he saw in the letters "divine instruction for all church servants and the true original of a church constitution established according to God's sense," as cited by H. Koelling, *Der erste Brief Pauli an Timotheus* (Berlin: Hugo Rother, 1882) 3. Loisy, *The Origins*, 272, restricts the pastoral instruction to the institution of a system of government for better resistance to heresy, but Anton saw the letters as "a living mirror of the right direction of a whole Christian community in all sorts of circumstances."

[8] Wohlenberg, 67, cites the Muratorian Canon which says of the Pastorals and Philemon that "pro effectu et dilectione, in honorem tamen ecclesiae catholicae, in ordinationem ecclesiasticae disciplinae sancti-[read signi-] ficatae sunt." He also finds that Tertullian, *Contra Marc.* 5.21, says that the letters are *de statu ecclesiastico*. And referring to the pastor himself, Augustine, *Doctr. Christ.* 4.16, says, "Quas tres apostolicas epistolas ante oculos habere debet, cui est in ecclesia doctoris persona imposita." These few witnesses, however, are not satisfying, even to Wohlenberg.

[9] In addition to the authors cited in note 8, see also T. Zahn, *Introduction to the New Testament*, 3 vols., trans. J.M. Trout et al. (New York: Charles Scribner's Sons, 1909) 2:29-33, 43; A. Loisy, *Remarques*, 114; *The Origins*, 272; *Les Livres du Nouveau Testament* (Paris: Emile Nourry, 1922) 204; J. Weiss, *Die Briefe Pauli an Timotheus und Titus* (Göttingen: Vandenhoeck & Ruprecht, 1894) 29; J. Wagenmann, *Die Stellung des Apostels Paulus neben den zwölf in den ersten zwei Jahrhunderten*, ZNW Beiheft 3 (Giessen: A Töpelmann, 1926) 97-99; J. Wegscheider, *Die Briefe des Apostels Paulus* (Göttingen: Johann F. Röwer, 1810) 36-37.

[10] Wohlenberg, 70-73; Zahn, 29-30; Loisy, *Les Livres*, 214, 221; Weiss, 9-10, 29.

[11] Wohlenberg, 69-70; Koelling, 2-3.

Once again, the explanation offered is problematic. The tenuous line stretched between the "church order" material of 1 Timothy and Titus and the exhortation to fidelity in office of 2 Timothy does not offer a firm footing for this interpretation. First of all, the relation between the church order form and the exhortation-testament forms is not clearly worked out. And so, the division of the material into two types of letters is not explained under the designation church order. Then, too, the church structure in 1 Timothy, with its bishop, elders, deacons, and widows, is more elaborate than Titus' Cretan churches, with mention only of elders. An hypothesis of two stages of church development attempts to reconcile this discrepancy.[12] The qualifications for office are not specific to Christianity, nor to the particular office, and the obligations and duties are equally vague. The same is true in large part for the conduct expected of the community members, with the net result that the church order is neither explicitly church nor definitively order. Moreover, the parallels noted between the roles of Timothy and Paul in 2 Timothy [13] and the call for Timothy to imitate Paul in that letter [14] amplify what is heard, though more faintly, in 1 Timothy and Titus.[15] Furthermore, community order is not the other side of the coin which has the challenge of false teaching on its face, because 2 Timothy has the challenge but presents a different response.[16] If

---

[12] Unless accompanied by a defense of Pauline authorship, this hypothesis would rest on the unusual situation whereby the letters apply to newly evolved church structures inconsistently (see H.F. von Campenhausen, *Ecclesiastical Authority and Spiritual Power in the Church of the First Three Centuries,* trans. J.A. Baker (Stanford: Stanford University, 1969) 105-9. See also A. Sand, "Anfänge einer Koordinierung verschiedener Gemeindeordnungen nach den Pastoralbriefen" in *Kirche im Werden: Studien zum Thema Amt und Gemeinde in Neuen Testament,* ed. J. Hainz (Munich: Ferdinand Schöningh, 1976) 215-37; P. Wendland, *Die hellenistisch-römische Kultur in ihren Beziehungen zu Judentum und Christentum: Die urchristlichen Literaturformen* (Tübingen: J.C.B. Mohr [Paul Siebeck], 1912) 1, 3, 365. Even if this were the case, at the time of this checkerboard pattern of consolidation, some other principle of unity would have had to function and it would seem from the letters to have been that of the authorized successor to the Pauline role (see note 15). But this implies of the letters more than a strict "church order." Another question raised in connection with this is whether the church structures in the Pastorals represent a later stage of church development (Loisy, *Les Livres,* 204; Wagenmann, 97-100; as well as the supporters of the view that the documents are basically anti-heretic pieces) or are compatible with the time of Paul's life and work (Koelling, 242-48; Weiss, 30-40). As Weiss points out, none of the descriptions of office betrays the highly hierarchical structures emerging in the late second century, and the openness to prophecy as well as the institution of elders is clearly compatible with Paul himself.

[13] Zahn, 22.

[14] Loisy, *Les Livres,* 214.

[15] Timothy replaces Paul in 1 Timothy 4 as Weiss, 6 ff., notes. Titus 2:7-8 offers a similar view of Titus and in the last mentioned letter the use of "we" could be taken to associate the addressee closely with Paul in the work for the churches and the resistance it raises (Zahn, 44-45). One might also see Titus 3:3-8 as an expansion of 1 Tim 1:12-16 to include Titus in the project of being models of conversion for future believers.

[16] Weiss, 30.

anything, the role and example of Paul and the addressees, juxtaposed with the challenge of false teaching, present or future, link the three letters.

C. *Traditional Instruction*

The third interpretation of the letters [17] (1) takes teaching as its point of departure, noting the threat of apostasy and heresy common to all three letters. The letters respond not with a full-blown polemic against the false teaching but by recalling the authority on which the true teaching is founded, i.e. God and Jesus, the bible and the "deposit," and Paul. Community order is a corollary to sound teaching.[18]

(2) The figure of the apostle steps into the limelight, not as the sanctioning authority for community structures, nor as the one to be rescued from heretic mistreatment, but as the divinely appointed teacher and the very type and model of the teaching. Protection from error and regulation of the community follow from Paul's teaching office, an office which is transmitted with its tasks and powers to his associates.[19] The teaching encompasses written and oral tradition on the creed, asceticism, law, and pastoral matters; and the personal conduct of the teacher is a bellwether of the authenticity of his doctrine, as well as of his personal assimilation of it. Consequently, his successors are urged to follow his pattern.

(3) Working with the apostolic model, paraenesis is the letters' intent and the addressees are really church officials of a later age, or the church at large of any period, including Paul's lifetime. If the letters address church officials, rather than delineate their offices,[20] then the imitation of Paul's character and conduct can be fairly close. If, however, the general community is being exhorted, then only certain specifics apply to each segment of it, all against the background of the sanction of Paul and his model of fidelity.

The advantage of this hypothesis is that it steps back from the specific regulations found in 1 Timothy and Titus and considers the addressees and what is asked of them in all three letters. It also tries to account for Paul and the references to himself and to his work. The hypothesis explains Paul's relation to the addressees better than that to the community at large.

More attention to the structure and form of the letters might give particularity to the general depiction of paraenesis and might also relate the blanket designation to the specific catalogues of qualifications, duties, virtues, and vices; to the calls to

---

[17] M. Albertz, *Die Botschaft des Neuen Testaments,* 2 vols. in 4 (Zollikon/Zürich: Evangelischer Verlag, 1952) 1, 2:209-13; H. Schlier, *Die Zeit der Kirche* (Freiburg: Herder, 1956) 131-46; E.F. Scott, *The Pastoral Epistles* (London: Hodder and Stoughton, 1936) xxiv-xxxiv.

[18] Albertz, 211-13 where he cites 1 Tim 1:12; 2 Tim 1:3-5; 3:10-15, and 1 Tim 1:15.

[19] Schlier, 131-33, 137-38.

[20] Scott, xxvii.

remembrance and certitude; to the credal summaries; to the predications of future troubles; and to the anti-heretic declarations. The audience of the letters ought to receive more attention. If it is the church leaders, then what lapse could have provoked such an insistent recall to rectitude? If it is the church in general, then what, if anything, is expected of them beyond an adherence to the shored-up Pauline tradition and its authorized teachers?

Obviously, the sympathy of this present study lies with the third approach to the letters and the attempt here will be to advance the insights already reached. Before proceeding to the analysis of the letters, however, some further remarks are in order on the approach as it has been employed thus far.

II. The Suggestions of von Campenhausen and Dibelius

When attention is paid to the structure and form of the letters, the hopes of a clear, generic determination fade, as the outlines of the manners of expression and of possible purposes in the letters have become blurred and their contents seem to overlap. Does it not seem so inclusive as to be meaningless to say with von Campenhausen that the «*Haustafeln* and polemic against false teachers arise as individual themes, but are bound together by the paraenetic tone of the whole, which the epistolary frame encloses"?[21] In this way von Campenhausen tries to take account of the similarities of parts of the Pastorals to polemic tracts, church order, and other simple, sermonic, admonitory writings, as well as of their own epistolary character.[22] Furthermore, he finds a remarkable parallel in Polycarp's letter to the Philippians, 4-6, where, just as in the Pastorals, community officials are also included among the natural church groupings, like men, women, slaves, as objects of exhortation and regulation.[23]

In another description of the Pastorals, with the help of a parallel in Christian literature, Dibelius calls them regulations for the church, since they deal with matters of church government.[24] Like von Campenhausen, he recognizes a tone

---

[21] H.F. von Campenhausen, "Polykarp von Smyrna und die Pastoralbriefe," *Aus der Frühzeit des Christentums* (Tübingen: J.C.B. Mohr [Paul Siebeck], 1963) 227, where he says this of Polycarp's letter to the Philippians but draws a direct parallel to the Pastorals. Earlier on, 207-8, he says that the Pastorals are not just church orders but are also pastoral writings with material on the care of souls for the spiritual shepherds of the community.

[22] von Campenhausen, "Polykarp," 229. Earlier, he characterizes the letters more narrowly as community rules in *Ecclesiastical Authority*, 122.

[23] von Campenhausen, "Polykarp," 229-30. Here he notes that this model, which attests a development in church tradition, apparently drops out of later Church writing.

[24] M. Dibelius, *A Fresh Approach to the New Testament and Early Christian Literature* (New York: Charles Scribner's Sons, 1936; repr. Westport, CT: Greenwood, 1979) 230-33.

of personal exhortation common to all three letters.[25]   He turns to the *Didache,*
7-10, 14, 15, for similar subject matter in a parallel structure.[26]

As already seen above, the determination of the purpose of the Pastorals has
often proceeded together with hypotheses about their historical situation.   Both
the church orders and household rules in 1 Timothy and Titus are thought to serve
a double function, and this is the view of von Campenhausen and Dibelius alike, as
they compare the letters to contemporary literature with a similar function.   As
instructions of the Apostle to his associates, they give backing to the newly established orthodox teaching in the church, and its official interpreters.[27]   The polemical sections reveal the situation of controversy in which the Pastorals were drafted
as a weapon for orthodox tradition under Paul's name.[28]   The designation of the

---

[25]   Dibelius, *Fresh Approach,* 233, and *Pastoral,* 5-6, where he finds *Haustafeln* (household rules) at the "core" of Titus (i.e. chapter 2). In a less orderly presentation in 1 Timothy,
he finds similar "church order material" as well as "household rules." The absence of a
clear correspondence in the character (the *Didache* is specific and regulatory, the Pastorals
are general and hortatory) and order (only 1 Timothy fits Dibelius' structural comparison
with the *Didache* without slicing up the letter) of the regulations in 1 Timothy and Titus, as
well as the absence of salient elements of the form in 2 Timothy, seriously undercuts Dibelius' characterization of the Pastorals as church orders.

[26]   Dibelius, *Pastoral,* 5-6. The parallel appears contrived in that only parts of 1 Timothy, and nothing from chaps. 1, 4 and most of 6, and only two verses from Titus 1:7-9, are
made to correspond to the church order material in the *Didache.* Moreover, the material itself in the *Didache* is much more formal and specific than that of 1 Timothy. On the other
hand, only the second chapter of Titus and two verses of 1 Timothy are taken as representative of household rules, parallels for which he finds not only in the *Didache* but, as von
Campenhausen did, in Polycarp's letter to the Philippians. P. Vielhauer, *Geschichte der
urchristlichen Literatur. Einleitung in das Neue Testament, die Apokryphen und die apostolischen Väter* (Berlin: Walter de Gruyter, 1975) 235-36, discusses the different parallels used
by Dibelius and von Campenhausen. H. Conzelmann, in his revision of Dibelius' Commentary for the Hermeneia series, includes von Campenhausen's reference to Polycarp on pp. 6
and 7.

[27]   Dibelius, *Pastoral,* 6-7; von Campenhausen, *Ecclesiastical Authority,* 118-19, 169-
70.   [28]   Dibelius, *Pastoral,* 6-7, where he accounts for the material against the false teachers
which he passed over in his structural comparison of the church order material in the Pastorals and the *Didache.*   But he takes no account of the places in the Pastorals where this
material appears. It is not at all grouped into one section as it is at *Didache* 10-13. See also
von Campenhausen, 120, 156-60. In line with his interest in this book, von Campenhausen
insists that the struggle with heresy itself is not the decisive point of Pastorals, but rather the
legal development within the church which the procedures in the Pastorals (e.g. 1 Tim
5:19 ff.) reveal. This stress on the inner development of the church protects him from the
criticism of stressing the anti-heretic nature of the Pastorals despite the fact that the letters
are surprisingly vague on the matter themselves. Dibelius, *Pastoral,* 7, also tries to avoid the
criticism by stressing that the statement of correct teaching draws a line of separation from
heresy. But here again the positive content of the tradition remains only vaguely outlined,
making the line of separation rather like a gossamer.

double function of the rules and orders and the very classification of the material into rules and orders fit the view in these two commentators of the development of the church and the crises which prompted that development. This congruence with the historical hypotheses and the parallels from contemporary Christian literature can lead to overstated conclusions about the form of the Pastorals as a whole and in their component parts. Perhaps, in the end, even from the analysis of the historical situation and parallel literature, one is warranted only to see the Pastorals, as does von Campenhausen, in a Christian tradition of edifying discourse, influenced by popular Hellenistic edification literature and rhetoric, though also characterized by Paul and through him by the Greek Old Testament.[29]

Any analysis of the Pastoral Epistles which proceeds from historical hypotheses risks misinterpreting the letters in the stress on one or other of their component elements. Consequently, another tack is called for in handling these letters, if their character is not to be submerged under interpretative cross-currents. Von Campenhausen and Spicq[30] venture into various streams of contemporary literary parallels for help characterizing the Pastorals. Before following up these suggestions, some important stylistic, structural and formal features of the Pastorals should be noted. Only then can a comparative study proceed on an even keel.

---

[29] von Campenhausen, "Polykarp," 221-22. Again, he is here describing Polycarp's letter to the Philippians but considers the Pastorals in the same light.

[30] Von Campenhausen, "Polykarp," 221-22, where he draws a parallel to "edification literature", 227, where he highlights their paraenetic tone; *Ecclesiastical Authority*, 159-60, where he draws an analogy to the *diadochoi* literature in the philosophical schools, although he does not spell out the details of the comparison. See also A.M. Javierre, "Pistoi Anthropoi (2T 2.2), Episcopado y sucesión apostolica en el Nuevo Testamento," *Analecta Biblica* 17-18 (1969) 2: 109-18. Spicq, *Les Epîtres*, 34-37, where he indicates similarities to the letters of command or instruction; 38-39, where the Pastorals are compared with the protreptic works of advice for various groups; and 39-40, where letter-treatises of rhetors and sophists are suggested for comparison.

CHAPTER II

The Hortatory Character of the Pastoral Epistles

Chapter I has pointed out the inadequacies in the approaches to the Pastoral Epistles as polemical writings for a specific historical situation or as church order documents for a growing church. It has also indicated some promise held out by a study of the letters as paraenetic documents. Before proceeding to a study of the hortatory character of the Pastoral Epistles with particular focus on the use of personal example, it will be useful to attend to the hortatory features of the letters in two ways. First, a general observation of the features will reveal the extent and variety of their use. This will both justify the perspective of the present analysis and will also sketch in the background for the specific hortatory feature of example. Second, a survey of three passages where example is proposed will demonstrate the relation between example and other hortatory features.

In the Pastoral Epistles, admonitions and prescriptions, lists of qualifications and duties, catalogues of virtues and vices, all of these give the epistles their character of decisive, earnest, and even urgent exhortation. These, however, are only the most salient features of the elaborate hortatory technique employed in the letters. The following paragraphs will elucidate the full range of the Pastorals' art of persuasion, which entices the audience readily to adopt the program for life in the church which they propose.

I. Hortatory Characteristics

A. *General Rhetorical Character*

The general rhetorical character of the letters is well-suited to literary exhortation.[1] The loose, unperiodic style[2] is characteristic of hortatory writing of the

---

[1] The categories employed here to describe the rhetorical features of hortatory literature at the time of the Pastorals are suggested by R. Bultmann, *Der Stil der paulinischen Predigt und die Kynisch-stoische Diatribe* (Göttingen: Vandenhoeck & Ruprecht, 1910); W. Trillitzsch, *Senecas Beweisführung* (Berlin: Akademie, 1962); H. Thyen, *Der Stil der jüdisch-hellenistischen Homilie* (Göttingen: Vandenhoeck & Ruprecht, 1955).

[2] M. Dibelius, *A Fresh Approach to the New Testament and Early Christian Literature*

day.[3] The letter form, while it was adopted as a favorite by the earliest Christian writers, was no stranger to the non-Christian writers of exhortation either.[4] The dialogue tone [5] evokes the instructional sessions [6] between teacher and pupil,[7] the public interchange between moralizing preacher and the crowd, and the admoni-

---

(New York: Charles Scribner's Sons, 1936) 217 ff., notes the "accumulation of ethical sayings" in Greek & Jewish exhortation literature and, 230 ff., applies this observation to the Pastorals. See also M. Dibelius and H. Conzelmann, *The Pastoral Epistles*, Hermeneia, trans. R. Buttolph and A. Yarbro (Philadelphia: Fortress, 1972) 5 ff.; C. Spicq, *Saint Paul: Les Epîtres pastorales*, 4 rev. ed., 2 vols. (Paris: Gabalda, 1969) 1: 39 ff.

[3] See H. Peter, *Der Brief in der römischen Literatur: Literargeschichtliche Untersuchungen und Zusammenfassungen* (Leipzig: B.G. Teubner, 1901) 20 ff.; P. Hartlich, "De exhortationum a Graecis Romanisque scriptarum historia et indole," *Leipz. Stud.* 11 (1889) 215 ff., 309, 326; A. Benner and F. Fobes, *The Letters of Alciphron, Aelian, and Philostratus,* LCL (Cambridge: Harvard University, 1962) 5-6; H. Rabe, "Aus Rhetoren-Handschriften," *RhM* n.F. 64 (1962) 290 n. 1; B. Hijmans, *Inlaboratus et facilis: Aspects of Structure in Some Letters of Seneca* (Leiden: E.J. Brill, 1976) 145, 194.

[4] See A. Malherbe, "Hellenistic Moralists and the New Testament," *ANRW,* ed. W. Haase (Berlin: de Gruyter, forthcoming) 2: 26.; K. Thraede, *Grundzüge griechisch-römischer Brieftopik* (Munich: C.H. Beck, 1970) 24-25, 65 ff.; H. Cancik, *Untersuchungen zu Senecas Epistulae morales* (Hildesheim: Georg Olms, 1967) 16, 23 ff., 48 ff.; Peter, 18-19, 225 ff.; R. Coleman, "The Artful Moralist: A Study of Seneca's Epistolary Style," *CQ* n.s. 24 (1974) 276-89; T. Burgess, *Epideictic Literature* (Chicago: University of Chicago, 1902) 186 ff.

[5] See Thraede, 22 ff., 27 ff., 47 ff., 68 ff., 75, 79; Peter, 17 ff., 213, 240; Malherbe, "Hellenistic Moralists"; Rabe, 290 n. 1; Hijmans, 145. The Pastorals exhibit a "dialogue tone" by virtue of their epistolary form ("half a dialogue" according to Demetrius *Eloc.* 223). This dialogue character exhibits itself in the following ways: in the connection between the letter and a previous discussion directly (1 Tim 1:3; Titus 1:5) or by more general reminder (2 Tim 1:13; Titus 3:1); in the use of "I" and "you" (throughout all three letters); in the direct imperatives (throughout all three); in the expectation of a future visit (1 Tim 3:14; 4:13 and cf. 2 Tim 1:4; 4:9) for which the letter serves as an interim substitute (1 Tim 3:15 and cf. Titus 2:15); in the words of personal encouragement (2 Tim 1:7-8; Titus 2:15) and warning (2 Tim 4:15); in the use of "we" (e.g. 1 Tim 1:5, 8; 4:10; 6:7; 2 Tim 1:7; Titus 2:11; 3:3).

[6] For the letter as a surrogate for the teacher's (or correspondent's) actual presence see Thraede, 27, 39 ff., 49 ff., 70-71, 79, 99 ff.; Cancik, 60, 72-73; and 1 Tim 3:14-15; 4:13. See also R.W. Funk, "The Apostolic *Parousia:* Form and Significance," in *Christian History and Interpretation: Studies Presented to John Knox,* eds. W.R. Farmer et al. (Cambridge: Cambridge University, 1967) and Malherbe, "Hellenistic Moralists."

[7] See I. Hadot, *Seneca und die griechisch-römische Tradition der Seelenleitung* (Berlin: de Gruyter, 1969) 165 ff., A.M. Guillemin, *Pline et la vie littéraire de son temps* (Paris: Société d'édition "Les Belles Lettres," 1929) 32; Thraede, 70-71; Cancik, 72,77 ff.; Peter, 225 ff. The teacher-to-student relationship in the Pastorals is evident in the father-child expressions (1 Tim 1:1, 18; 2 Tim 1:2; 2:2; Titus 1:1); in the concern for the youthful addressee to learn proper conduct (1 Tim 3:14 ff., 4:11; 2 Tim 2:22; 4:7; cf. Titus 2:11 ff); in the praise of his learning thus far (2 Tim 3:10 ff).

tions and duties outlined by a superior for his subordinates.[8]   The letters also allow for expressions of friendship and concern, which predispose the audience toward the writer and his message.[9]   References to particular situations and personages in literary epistles allow the audience to assume the unthreatening posture of observer, and yet to find matter applicable to them throughout the exhortation.[10]

The Pastoral Epistles, meant to be read aloud, utilize the very sound of the words (*Klangfiguren*) and phrases to charm the audience, emphasize certain points, and unite or contrast key ideas.   At times the effect can be attributed to the material taken from other sources and incorporated into the letters, or to the natural effect of lists and grammatical relationships.   These aural effects include: anaphora,[11] epiphora,[12] paromoiosis,[13] parallelism of members.[14]   There are other aural

---

[8] For other writings which outline duties and responsibilities of officials see R. Vetschera, *Zur griechischen Paränese* (Smichow/Prague: Rohliček & Sievers, 1911-12) 7, 12-13, 14-15; W. Jaeger, *Paideia: The Ideals of Greek Culture*, trans. G. Highet, 3 vols. (New York: Oxford University, 1939-44) 3:86 ff.; Hadot, 167; Guillemin, 32 ff.; Spicq, 34 ff., and chapters 4 and 5 below.

For lists of duties and responsibilities in the community generally (*Haustafeln*) see H. Campenhausen, *Ecclesiastical Authority and Spiritual Power in the Church of the First Three Centuries*, Trans. J.A. Baker (Stanford: Stanford University, 1969) 116; M. Albert, *Die Botschaft des Neuen Testaments*, 2 vols. in 4 (Zollikon/Zurich; Evangelischer Verlag, 1952) 211-12; Burgess, 228-29; Malherbe, "Hellenistic Moralists," and the bibliography cited; A. Vögtle, *Die Tugend-und Lasterkataloge im Neuen Testament: Exegetisch, religions- und formgeschichtlich untersucht* (Münster i.W.: Aschendorff, 1936); K. Weidinger, *Die Haustafeln: ein Stuck urchristlicher Paränese* (Leipzig: J.C. Hinrichs, 1928); S. Wibbing; *Die Tugend- und Lasterkataloge im Neuen Testament und ihre Traditionsgeschichte unter besonderer Berücksichtigung der Qumran-texte* (Berlin: A. Topelmann, 1959).

The Pastorals contain lists of qualifications and duties for officials and of prescriptions for members of the community. (1 Tim 2:1-15; 3:1-13; 5:3-16; 6:1-2; Titus 1:5-9; 2:2-10). They also offer direct instructions to the addressees on the conduct of their task of community direction (1 Tim 1:3-5, 18-20; 3:14-16; 4:6-5:2; 5:17-25; 6:13-21; 2 Tim 1:6-14; 2:1-26; 3:10-4:5; Titus 2:15; 3:8-11).

[9] The philophronetic character of letter exhortations receives elaboration in Cancik, 50 ff., 61, 71, 75 ff.; Guillemin, 3 ff., 32 ff.; Hadot, 165 ff.; Thraede, 24, 44, 54, 65 ff., 74 ff.; Malherbe, "Hellenistic Moralists". The friendly character of the letters to Timothy and Titus finds expression in the paternal relationship of Paul to his legates (1 Tim 1:18; 2 Tim 1:2; Titus 1:1), the expressions of affection (2 Tim 1:2-3), the desire for a reunion (1 Tim 3:14; 2 Tim 1:4; 4:9, 21; Titus 3:12), the confidence in the addressee (1 Tim 4:6; 2 Tim 1:5; 3:10 ff), the normal epistolary salutations (2 Tim 4:19, 21-22; Titus 3:15), and the full collaboration which the letters outline.

[10] See the general purpose underlying the specific admonitions in the Pastorals as expressed at 1 Tim 3:14.

[11] The alpha-privative words, 1 Tim 1:17 (G adds a third); the *syn*-prefix, 2 Tim 2:11-12; the dative articles, 2 Tim 3:10-11; the prepositions *en* and *pros,* 2 Tim 3:11, 16-17; the dative articles, Titus 2:2.

[12] The dative endings, 1 Tim 1:9-10; the words for prayer, 1 Tim 2:1; the accusative endings, 1 Tim 3:3; the nominative endings, 2 Tim 3:2-5; the dative endings, Titus 2:2.

[13] The list of good works, 1 Tim 5:10; the reduplicated verbs, 2 Tim 4:7.

[14] The christological fragments, 1 Tim 3:16 and 2 Tim 2:11-13. The contrast between

effects which, from the frequency of their occurrence, are more likely the work of the author himself. In this connection note use of repetition,[15] and word play, whether in using the same idea in different grammatical constructions,[16] the same word with several meanings,[17] the same root with different prefixes,[18] the same prefix with different roots,[19] or like-sounding words.[20] The most common device in the persuasive technique of the Pastorals, as the discussion below will establish, and to be included here among the aural effects as well, is antithesis. At times grammatical disjunctives signal the contrast.[21] Otherwise, the antithetical ideas themselves establish the contrast.[22]

Along with these devices in the Pastorals which work through the sound and collocation of the words and phrases, others appear which play upon their sense (*Sinnfiguren*). There is only one rhetorical question in the letters,[23] but metaphorical language abounds. Although personification is rare,[24] there is a wide variety of similes[25] and metaphors.[26]

---

physical and spiritual exercise, 1 Tim 4:8, is different in that the parallelism in expressing the topos seems a creation of the author himself.

[15] *eleēthein* 1 Tim 1:13, 16; *anthrōpos* 1 Tim 2:2, 4, 5; *heis* 1 Tim 2:5; *empesȩ̄* 1 Tim 3:6, 7; *porismos* 1 Tim 5:5, 6; *argai* 1 Tim 5:13; *eparkein* 1 Tim 5:16; *homologia, - ein* 1 Tim 6:12, 13; *ruesthai* 2 Tim 4:17, 18.

[16] *pistin/apistou* 1 Tim 5:8; *planōntes/planōmenoi* 2 Tim 3:13.

[17] *prōtos*, 1 Tim 1:15, 16, for principal in rank and first in time; *paideuthōsin*, 1 Tim 1:20, for chastisement and education; *heuriskein*, 2 Tim 1:17, 18, for physical and spiritual discovery; *desmos/deō* 2 Tim 2:9, for physical and figurative restraint; *katharos*, Titus 1:15, for ritual and moral cleanliness.

[18] *prosechein/parechein* 1 Tim 1:4; *eispherein/ekpherein* 1 Tim 6:7; *eukairōs/akairōs* 2 Tim 4:2.

[19] *perierchomenai/periergoi* 1 Tim 5:13.

[20] *eiden oudeis ... oude idein* 1 Tim 6:16; *paschō ... ouch epaischynomai* 2 Tim 1:12; *lalei kai parakalei* Titus 2:15.

[21] *anomois de* 1 Tim 1:9; *mē en ... all'ho* 1 Tim 2:9-10; *Adam ouk ... hē de gynē* 1 Tim 2:14; *hē gar ... hē de* 1 Tim 4:8; *mē ... alla* 1 Tim 5:1; *hē de ... hē de* 1 Tim 5:5; *tinōn ... tisin de* 1 Tim 5:24; *mēden ... alla* 1 Tim 6:4; *estin de* 1 Tim 6:6; *hoi de ... sy de* 1 Tim 6:9-11; *pheuge; diōke de* 1 Tim 6:11; *ou gar ... alla* 2 Tim 1:7; *mē ... alla* 2 Tim 1:8; *ou kata ... alla* 2 Tim 1:9; *ouk ... monon ... alla kai* and *ha men ... ha de* 2 Tim 2:20; *ou dei ... alla* 2 Tim 2:24; *tēn de dynamin* 2 Tim 3:5; *sy de* 2 Tim 3:10, 14 and 4:5; *ou monon ... alla kai* 2 Tim 4:8; *oudeis ... alla* 2 Tim 4:16; *tois de ergois* Titus 1:16; *sy de* Titus 2:1; *mē ... alla* Titus 2:10.

[22] *thelontes ... mē noountes* 1 Tim 1:7; *manthanetō ... didaskein* 1 Tim 2:11-12; *dakryōn ... charas* 2 Tim 1:4; *katargēsantos ... phōtisantos* 2 Tim 1:10; *pantote manthanonta ... mēdepote eis epignōsin* 2 Tim 3:7.

[23] 1 Tim 3:5.

[24] The law's being fixed, 1 Tim 1:9, is a common idiom and perhaps not consciously figurative. The faith which dwells, 2 Tim 1:5, and the word which cannot be bound, 2 Tim 2:9, as well as grace which teaches, Titus 2:11, come closer to personifications.

[25] The fictive kinship, 1 Tim 5:1-2; the analogous occupations, 2 Tim 2:3-7; Paul's treatment as a prisoner, 2 Tim 2:3; the gangrenous spread of false teaching, 2 Tim 2:17; the stewardship role of the bishop, Titus 1:7.

[26] These appear in adjective form like *hygiainōn* 1 Tim 1:10; 6:3; 2 Tim 1:13; 4:3; Titus

B. *Directly Hortatory Features*

The literary-rhetorical elements singled out so far contribute significantly to the overall persuasive and prescriptive ends of the letters. Directly hortatory features also pervade the letters and these will be treated in the following paragraphs. These range from the technical language of exhortation, words and phrases exuding the hortatory spirit, literary and rhetorical devices normally employed in exhortation, and other grammatical forms and collocations of ideas which comprise the letters' hortatory technique.

First of all, the Pastoral letters speak the language of exhortation from start to finish. Paul is enjoined (*epitagē*)[27] to be an apostle, and himself exhorts and commands (*parakalein, parangellein, parangelia*)[28] Timothy and Titus. The Pauline emissaries are to do the same (*parakalein, parangellein, parangelia, paraklēsis, epitagē, hypotithesthai, paratithesthai, nouthesia*)[29] and local officials also share the responsibility (*parakalein*).[30] In addition to commands and exhortations, the letters are also concerned with reproof, correction, and admonition (*elenchein, elegmos, epanorthōsis, epidiorthoun, nouthesia*).[31]

These expressions from the language of hortatory compositions describe the content and purpose of the letters and the responsibility of their recipients. They find a complement and amplification throughout the letters, as the following examples illustrate. Lists are compiled and direct commands are heaped in quick succession. This appointed duty and corresponding obedience oblige all segments

---

1:9; 2:1; *hygiēs* Titus 2:8; *hygiainōn* Titus 2:2; *enoikōn* 2 Tim 1:14; *katharos* 1 Tim 1:5; 3:9; 2 Tim 1:3; 2:22; *kekaustēriasmenos* 1 Tim 4:2; *nosōn* 1 Tim 6:4; *oikōn* 1 Tim 6:16; *orthotomōn* 2 Tim 2:15; *katargēsas* and *phōtisas* 2 Tim 1:10; *aichmalōtizōn* 2 Tim 3:6; *knēthomenos* 2 Tim 4:3. Metaphorical nouns include: *teknon* 1 Tim 1:18; *strateia* 1 Tim 1:19; *oneidismos* and *pagis* 1 Tim 3:7; *oikos* and *stylos* and *hedraiōma* 1 Tim 3:15; *gymnasia* 1 Tim 4:8; *agōn* 1 Tim 6:12 and 2 Tim 4:7; *themelion* 1 Tim 6:19; *dynastēs, basileus, kyrios* 1 Tim 6:15; *parathēkē* 1 Tim 6:20 and 2 Tim 1:12-14; *gangraina* 2 Tim 2:17; the extended metaphor of the house with varied vessels, 2 Tim 2:20-21; *pagis* 2 Tim 2:26; *analysis* 2 Tim 4:6; *dromos* 2 Tim 4:7; *stephanos* 2 Tim 4:8; *loutron* Titus 3:5. For verbal metaphors see: *nauagein* 1 Tim 1:19; *paideuein* 1 Tim 1:20; *kosmein* 1 Tim 2:9; *empiptein* 1 Tim 3:6; *agōnizesthai* 1 Tim 4:10; *epilambanesthai* 1 Tim 6:12; *phylattein* 1 Tim 6:20 and 2 Tim 1:12, 14; and the words for wandering away from the faith as noted below; *anazōpyrein* 2 Tim 1:6; *katharizein* 2 Tim 2:21; *pheugein* and *diōkein* 2 Tim 2:22; *episōreuein* 2 Tim 4:3 (and see 2 Tim 3:6); *speudein* 2 Tim 4:6; *telein* 2 Tim 4:7; *anatrepein* Titus 1:11; *hygiainein* Titus 1:13.

[27] 1 Tim 1:1 and Titus 1:3.

[28] 1 Tim 1:3; 2:1; 6:13; 1:18.

[29] *parakalein* 1 Tim 5:1; 6:3; 2 Tim 4:2; *parangellein* 1 Tim 1:3; 4:11; 5:7; 6:17; *paraklēsis* 1 Tim 4:13; *parangelia* 1 Tim 1:15; *epitagē* Titus 2:15; *hypotithesthai* 1 Tim 4:6; *paratithesthai* 2 Tim 2:2.

[30] Titus 1:9.

[31] *elenchein* 1 Tim 5:20; 2 Tim 4:2; Titus 1:9, 13; 2:15; *elegmos* 2 Tim 3:16; *epanorthōsis* 2 Tim 3:16; *nouthesia* Titus 3:10; *epidiorthoun* Titus 1:5.

of the community.[32] In addition to *parangellein*, the Pastorals use other ways of expressing commands[33] and they are acutely concerned about criticism, acceptability, and priority.[34]

Other hortatory echoes confirm the basic character of the Pastorals as exhortations. In connection with their concern for reputation and propriety, the letters are filled with references to demonstration, display and witness.[35] Public affirmation of the truth and activity consonant with one's faith claims and teaching fit in with the strong emphasis on instruction in the letters.[36] The Pastorals offer no

---

[32] Paul is designated *apostolos* 1 Tim 1:1; 2:7; 2 Tim 1:1, 11; Titus 1:1; and he sends others (*apesteila* 2 Tim 4:12). Obedient submission is expected from children toward their parents and prospective officials (*en hypotage₁* 1 Tim 3:4; *mē ... anypotakta* Titus 1:6), from women toward men in worship (*en pasē₁ hypotagē₁* 1 Tim 2:11), from women toward their husbands (*hypotassomenas* Titus 2:5), from slaves toward their masters (*hypotassesthai* Titus 2:9), from all toward civil authorities (*hypotassesthai, peitharchein* Titus 3:1). Disobedience characterizes the foolish unbelievers (*anypotaktos* 1 Tim 1:9; Titus 1:10; *apeitheis* Titus 3:3). See nn. 45-47.

[33] *boulesthai* 1 Tim 2:8; 5:15; Titus 3:8; *epitrepein* 1 Tim 2:12; *graphein ... hina eidēₛ* 1 Tim 3:14-15; *paratithenai* 2 Tim 2:2; *diatassein* Titus 1:6; *entolais* Titus 1:14; *nomos* 1 Tim 1:8-9.

[34] *krima* 1 Tim 3:6; 5:12; *prokrimatos* 1 Tim 5:21; *krisis* 1 Tim 5:24; *krinein* 2 Tim 4:1; *kritēs* 2 Tim 4:8; *katēgoria* Titus 1:6; *autokatakritos* Titus 3:11; *loidoria* 1 Tim 5:14; *epitiman* 2 Tim 4:2; *anepilēmptos* 1 Tim 3:2; 5:7; 6:14; *anenklētos* 1 Tim 3:10; Titus 6:7. *anepaischyntos* 2 Tim 2:15; *akatagnōstos* Titus 2:8; *martyria kalē* 1 Tim 3:7; *pistos* 1 Tim 1:12; *episteuthēn* Titus 1:3; *dikaios* 1 Tim 1:9; *exērtismenos* 2 Tim 3:17; *apodektos* 1 Tim 2:3; 5:4; *dokimos* 2 Tim 2:15; *dokimazein* 1 Tim 3:10 *adokimos* 2 Tim 3:8; Titus 1:16; *axios* 1 Tim 1:15; 2:10; 4:9; *apodochē* 1 Tim 1:15; 4:9; *hetoimos* Titus 3:1; *hikanos* 2 Tim 2:2; *ōphelimos* 1 Tim 4:8; 2 Tim 3:16; *anōphelēs* Titus 3:9; *euchrēstos* 2 Tim 4:11; *chrēsimos* 2 Tim 2:14; *artios 2 Tim 3:16; ho prepei* 1 Tim 2:10, *ha prepei* Titus 2:1; *ta mē deonta* 1 Tim 5:14; *aphormē* 1 Tim 5:14; *hieroprepēs* Titus 2:3; *periphronein* Titus 2:15; *kataphronein* 1 Tim 4:12.

[35] *endeiknynai ... tēn ... makrothymian* 1 Tim 1:16; *charis ... phanerōtheis ... dia tēs epiphaneias* 2 Tim 1:10; *tēn epiphaneian autou* 2 Tim 4:1; *kaka enedeixato* 2 Tim 4:14; *zōēs ... hēn ... ephanerōsen* Titus 1:3; *pistin endeiknymenous* Titus 2:10; *epephanē ... hē charis* Titus 2:11; *prosdechomenoi tēn ... epiphaneian* Titus 2:13; *hē chrēstotēs kai hē philanthrōpia epephanē* Titus 3:4; *typos ginou* 1 Tim 1:12; *hē prokopē phanera* 1 Tim 4:15; *hai hamartiai prodēloi* 1 Tim 5:24; *ta erga ... prodēla* 1 Tim 5:25; *hē ... anoia ... ekdēlos* 2 Tim 3:9; *martyrion/martyrein* 1 Tim 2:6; 6:13; 2 Tim 1:8; 1 Tim 5:10; *martyria* Titus 1:13; *diamartyromai* 1 Tim 5:21; 2 Tim 2:14; *martys* 1 Tim 6:12, 2 Tim 2:2; *homologein/homologia* 1 Tim 6:12; Titus 1:6; *homologoumenōs* 1 Tim 3:16; *epangellein theosebeian* 1 Tim 2:10; *ten didaskalian ... kosmein* Titus 2:10; *kērygma* Titus 1:3; *kēryx* 1 Tim 2:7.

[36] In all three letters teaching and exhortation are closely associated. See 1 Tim 4:13, 6:2; 2 Tim 4:2; Titus 2:15, which uses *lalein*, itself associated with teaching in Titus 2:1 and exhortation in Titus 2:6. 2 Tim 4:2 identifies the various hortatory practices as part of the activity of teaching. The use which the theological and christological affirmations in Titus 2 and 3 serve, i.e., as a grounding for the exhortation, also indicates the hortatory thrust to the teaching at least as far as it is expressed in the letters. The same is clear from 1 Tim 4:11 and 6:2 which demands that Timothy *didaskein* and *parakalein* or *parangellein tauta*, i.e., the moral instructions.

new teaching but, rather, urge perseverance in the traditional instruction [37] and practical exercise as a corroboration thereof.[38] A constant in the negative criticism of the letters is the charge that some have strayed from the faith and from truth.[39] And just as true knowledge and faith are proven in works and virtue, so too are ignorance and faithlessness manifested in folly and vice.[40] The letters, however, are not concerned exclusively with knowledge, for the will features prominently as well and thereby furthers the hortatory atmosphere.[41]

An instructional tone pervades the letters. Teaching is an appointed task for Paul (1 Tim 2:7; 2 Tim 1:11) and he regulates its practice, forbidding it to some (women, 1 Tim 2:12; false teachers, Titus 1:11 and 1 Tim 1:3) and expecting it of others as part of their qualifications for office (bishops, 1 Tim 3:2 and Titus 1:9; servant of God, 2 Tim 2:24-25) and its exercise (Timothy, 1 Tim 4:11-13, 16, 6:2; 2 Tim 4:2; Titus 2:1; elders; 1 Tim 5:17; elder women, Titus 2:3; successor officials, 2 Tim 2:2). Indeed the identity of the teacher is important as a corroboration of the doctrine in 2 Tim 2:14.

[37] *epechein* and *epimenein* 1 Tim 4:16; *mē amelein* 1 Tim 4:14; *prosechein* 1 Tim 4:13; *parakolouthein* 1 Tim 4:6; *menein* 1 Tim 2:15, 2 Tim 2:13; 3:14; *phylattein* 1 Tim 5:20; 2 Tim 1:12, 14; 4:7; *tērein* 1 Tim 5:22; 6:14; *antechomenos tou ... pistou logou* Titus 1:9.
This fidelity entails patience in the face of difficulties, e.g. *hypomonē* in 2 Tim 2:10; 3:10; Titus 2:2; and it is reflected in the images for the church, i.e., *stylos kai hedraiōma tēs alētheias* 1 Tim 3:15 and *stereos themelios* 2 Tim 2:19.

[38] See how often the final proof of fidelity rests in *erga* 2 Tim 4:5, 14; Titus 1:16; *erga kala* 1 Tim 5:25; or *erga agatha* 1 Tim 2:10. Thus, *erga kala* or *agatha* are expected of widows, 1 Tim 5:10; of the rich, 1 Tim 6:18; of anyone, 2 Tim 2:21; Titus 2:14; 3:1, 8, 14; of the addressee, 2 Tim 3:17 and Titus 2:7. Thus proper conduct stands as a qualification (*epakolouthein* 1 Tim 5:10 and *parakolouthein ... agōge* 2 Tim 3:10) and as a goal (*pōs ... anastrephesthai* 1 Tim. 2:15; *nomimōs chrētai* 1 Tim 1:8; *anastrophēi* 1 Tim 4:12; *ergatēs anepaischyntos* 2 Tim 2:15; *skeuos ... hētoimasmenon* 2 Tim 2:21). This goal is reached only by a concerted effort (*gymnazein, gymnasia* 1 Tim 4:7-8; *synkakopaschein* 2 Tim 1:8; 2:3; *spoudazein seauton dokimon parastēsai* 2 Tim 2:15; *ekkathairein heauton* 2 Tim 2:21; *anazōpyrein to charisma* 2 Tim 1:6.

[39] *tines astochēsantes exetrapēsan* 1 Tim 1:6; *tines apōsamenoi ... enauagēsan* 1 Tim 1:19; *apostēsontai tines* 1 Tim 4:1; *tēn pistin ērnētai* 1 Tim 5:8; *tēn prōtēn pistin ēthetēsan* 1 Tim 5:12; *apesteremenōn tēs alētheias* 1 Tim 6:5; *tines ... apoplanēthēsan* 1 Tim 6:10; *tines ... ēstochēsan* 1 Tim 6:21 and 2 Tim 2:18; *planōntes ... planōmenoi* 2 Tim 3:14; *apostrepsousin ... ektrapēsontai* 2 Tim 4:4; *anthrōpōn apostrephomenōn tēn alētheian* Titus 1:14; *exestraptai ho toioutos* Titus 3:11; *apestraphēsan me* 2 Tim 1:15. Their misguided persistence is also decried in Titus 1:4, *prosechontes ... mythois*.

[40] 1 Tim 1:9-10, 13; 5:13; 6:3-5; 2 Tim 3:2-5; Titus 1:10, 15-16; 3:3. Titus 1:7-9 relates the contrasting sign value of virtues and vices to the prerequisites expected in the character of a bishop. It also sees these qualities as subsidiary to the hortatory and admonitory task.

[41] At times desire is positive, for salvation is willed by God in 1 Tim 2:4 and by Jesus Christ in 1 Tim 1:15, some community members desire office in 1 Tim 3:1, God wishes Paul's apostolate in 2 Tim 1:1, and Paul longs to see Timothy in 2 Tim 1:4. Often, however, the desire is misguided, as is that of the teachers of the law in 1 Tim 1:7, or unbridled and vicious, as in 1 Tim 6:9, 10; 2 Tim 3:6; Titus 2:12.

C. *Hortatory Forms and Devices*

In addition to the language of exhortation and the emphasis gained by the arrangement of sounds and words, the letters employ several forms and devices to express and confirm the prescriptions and admonitions. Most obvious is the extensive use of verbs in the imperative mood.[42] At times, the verb *dei* expresses the injunction and gives them a "rule book" quality.[43] Obvious, too, are the lists of virtues and vices.[44] These lists often find themselves applied to various segments of the community with a particular notice or other to make them applicable to that group.[45] The qualifications and obligations of office holders are, again, usually virtue lists with some modification for the particular office.[46] And the injunctions to Timothy and Titus themselves cover their modes of conduct as well as the various capacities of their service.[47]

Other hortatory devices may fail to impress the modern reader, but were part of the stock-in-trade of the practitioners of ancient protreptic. Among those employed by the author of the Pastorals, one might mention the vocative or direct address,[48] a device which arrests attention in a dialogue, here subsumed under the letter form. Another is the use of exclamations,[49] which add a note of solemnity

---

[42] Imperatives direct the addressees' activities in 1 Tim 4:7, 11, 12, 13, 14, 15, 16; 5:1, 3, 7, 11, 19, 20, 21, 22, 23; 6:3, 11, 12, 20; 2 Tim 1:6, 8, 13, 14; 2:1, 2, 3, 7, 8, 15, 16, 22; 3:1, 6, 14; 4:2, 5, 9, 11, 13, 15, 19, 21; Titus 2:1, 6, 15; 3:1, 9, 10, 12, 13, 15. They also guide community practices in 1 Tim 2:11; 3:10; 5:4, 9, 16, 17; 6:1, 2; 2 Tim 4:16; Titus 3:14; and, indirectly, the attitudes of hostile individuals in 1 Tim 4:12; Titus 2:14.

[43] It covers the broad area of conduct in the church in 1 Tim 3:15, including regulations for individual offices like that of bishop in 1 Tim 3:2, 7 and Titus 1:7, or of "servant of God" in 2 Tim 2:24. It also declares teaching unacceptable in 1 Tim 5:13 and Titus 1:11.

[44] The virtues of various groups and individuals are listed, e.g. of everyone through the spirit, 2 Tim 1:7; of a purified "vessel," 2 Tim 2:22; of women, 1 Tim 2:9, 15; of everyone as a result of the exhortation, 1 Tim 1:5; of Timothy, 1 Tim 6:11-12; of Paul, 2 Tim 4:6-8. The same is true for lists of vices, e.g. of Paul, 1 Tim 1:13; of the community prior to baptism, Titus 3:3; of the faithless in the end-time, 2 Tim 3:2-5; 4:3-4; of deluded women, 2 Tim 3:7; of false teachers, 1 Tim 1:9-10; 4:1-3; 6:4-5; Titus 1:10. Vices consequent upon false teaching are listed in 1 Tim 6:4-5 and the dire consequences of greed also form a list in 1 Tim 6:9-10.

[45] Regulations for men and women in general appear in 1 Tim 2:1-15; Titus 3:1-2; for women in 1 Tim 3:11; for elder men, women, young men, and slaves in Titus 2:2-6, 9. For widows and for those with widows in their family see 1 Tim 5:5-8, 16; and for the rich see 1 Tim 6:17-19.

[46] For bishops see 1 Tim 3:2-7 and Titus 1:6-7 (also called elders here, unless another hierarchical structure is reflected in the titles); for deacons see 1 Tim 3:8-9, 12; for widows see 1 Tim 5:9-16 and *passim*; for elders see 1 Tim 5:17.

[47] Timothy's role is summed up in 1 Tim 4:11-16, and see 6:11-12; 2 Tim 2:23-25; 4:2, 5; and Titus' role is outlined in Titus 2:7-8.

[48] To Timothy in 1 Tim 1:18; 6:11, 20; 2 Tim 2:1.

[49] There are doxologies, 1 Tim 1:17; 6:15-16; 2 Tim 4:18; a confessional statement, 1

and earnestness to the message. Hyperbole adds attention and importance to the exhortation.[50]   Citations[51] and gnomic sayings[52] (sometimes paradoxical)[53] introduce verification from external authority. From within the addressees the author elicits agreement by recollecting what they already know, what they have heard from him, what their former attitude presumably was, and what is commonly accepted fact or opinion.[54] This device also reaffirms the contact between the teacher and addressees and between both of them and the common tradition they share. The indefinite pronoun offers the author the opportunity to characterize types and speak of situations in a generally applicable way, as well as to refer broadly to proponents and adhrents of false teachings.[55] The author also calls attention to the believers' inner strength for living uprightly,[56] a resource to be called on in following the exhortation of the letters and an encouragement that it can be done.

The use of the indefinite pronoun constitutes an indefinite example, and this is matched by the author's frequent specification of exemplary figures by name. The use of example in the exhortation of the Pastoral Epistles, the special concern of this study, is as pervasive and obvious as the imperatives and lists noted above. The examples are culled from sayings, past history or the contemporary situation, and are both positive and negative.[57] As the discussion below will show, they

---

Tim 3:16; solemn claims to divine witness, 1 Tim 5:21; 2 Tim 4:1; and affirmations of the truth of what is said in 1 Tim 1:15; 3:1; 2 Tim 2:11; Titus 1:13; 3:8.

[50] 1 Tim 1:7, 14; 6:4-5; 2 Tim 1:15; 3:8, 12; 4:16; Titus 1:12, 15; 3:3.

[51] These may be from hymns or confessional statements, 1 Tim 2:5-6, 3:16; 6:7 ff.; 2 Tim 1:9-10; 2:11-13; Titus 3:4-7; from scripture or apostolic witness, 1 Tim 5:18-19; 2 Tim 2:19; 4:14, 17; Titus 2:14; or from secular literature, Titus 1:12.

[52] 1 Tim 1:8; 4:4; 6:7, 10; 2 Tim 2:20; 4:14; Titus 1:15.

[53] 1 Tim 4:7b-8; 5:6; 6:5-6. This device functions like antithesis in presenting a totally other outlook than the one capsulized and opposed.

[54] See 1 Tim 1:3, 8-9; 4:6, 10; 2 Tim 1:3-5, 6, 15, 18; 2:2, 8, 14, 23; 3:10, 13, 14-15; Titus 1:5; 2:12; 3:11. See also 1 Tim 2:15-3:1; 4:1-3 (cf. 2 Tim 3:1-5), 7b-9; and contrast 1 Tim 6:5; Titus 1:16.

[55] *tis* is used in a positive way to refer to the law-abiding person, 1 Tim 1:8; to a person spiritually cleansed, 2 Tim 2:21; and to a candidate for elder, Titus 1:6. Used neutrally it presents a family obligation, 1 Tim 5:8; the prerogatives and obligations of laborers for the church, 2 Tim 2:4-5; and the expectation of suffering, 2 Tim 3:12. More frequently the indefinite pronoun designates teachers who have strayed from the doctrine, 1 Tim 1:6-7, 19 (from the context); 4:1-3; 6:24-25 (from the context); and compare Titus 1:10 (using *polloi*) and Titus 1:14 (using *anthrōpoi*). It also points to the followers of false teaching, 1 Tim 5:15; 6:3-5; 2 Tim 2:19. Finally it calls attention to those fallen into vice, 1 Tim 6:10, or infidelity, 2 Tim 1:15.

[56] Paul claims it for himself, 1 Tim 1:12, 14; and he declares it of Timothy, 1 Tim 4:14; 2 Tim 1:6-8, 14; 4:17; of all the saved, Titus 3:6; and even of those in error and ignorance, 1 Tim 1:12; 2 Tim 3:5.

[57] The scripture saying provides an example of payment for labor in 1 Tim 5:19; the confession of Christ's appearance and justification in 1 Tim 3:16 is the prime example of the

stand in close relationship to the lists of virtues, vices, qualifications, and regulations, as well as to the shorter admonitions in the letters.[58]   In fact, exemplary attitude and action are at times commanded as well as commended in the letter.[59]

D. *Hortatory Techniques*

In order to achieve the full hortatory effect intended, the author is careful to clarify, elaborate, and substantiate the message of the Pastorals.   One technique used is that of corroboration or confirmation, whether of Paul, of his message in the letters, or of the addressee.[60]   Another is that of direct warning before troubles

---

mercy which Paul claims for himself and for all believers in 1 Tim 1:16; the "word" on suffering in 2 Tim 2:11-13 offers a verbal example of the Christian conduct demanded throughout the letter, and the same can be said of the slogan-like sayng in Titus 1:15; the metaphor of the vessels occasions a moral paradigm in 2 Tim 2:20-22; the saying about the Cretans depicts them as beasts and gluttons in Titus 1:12.

The reference to Jesus' witness in 1 Tim 2:6 which J.N.D. Kelly in *The Pastoral Epistles: I Timothy, II Timothy, Titus,* Black's New Testament Commentaries (London: Adam & Charles Black, 1963) 64, sees as the author's comment (but see Dibelius-Conzelmann, 41-42), is both object and example of Paul's kerygma and of the witness the author expects of the community. The tie between the historical paradigm of Jesus' witness and that expected of Timothy is clearer in 1 Tim 6:11-13. Jesus' conquering death in 2 Tim 1:10 and his resurrection in 2 Tim 2:8 provide an example of suffering and reward which Paul himself follows and proposes to his audience in 2 Tim 2:9-12. Other examples from the past range from Paul's oblique allusion to his forebears' faith to the express assumption of a continuity of faith between Timothy, his mother and his grandmother in 2 Tim 1:5. The precedent of the creation of Adam and Eve and of their comparative culpability establishes a ground for current distinctions on the basis of gender in 1 Tim 2:13.   On the negative side, the two legendary figures in 2 Tim 2:8 are paradigms of resistance to authority and to the truth of faith.

From the situation depicted by the letters other examples offer themselves. Paul's claim to toil in hope is an example of the expectation due to the word of God's faithful promise of life in 1 Tim 4:9-10; and he explicitly identifies himself, converted in Christ, as a type of future believers in 1 Tim 1:16. The paradigm of conversion in Christ reappears at Titus 3:10-11 and 2 Tim 4:6-8. He speaks of his fidelity to the task to which he urges Timothy. His own sufferings at 2 Tim 3:11 are a model for the suffering of all Christians. The harmony of teaching the word and living its consequences stands behind the designation of his words to Timothy as a type in 2 Tim 1:13.

Examples of faithlessness and opposition are offered at 1 Tim 1:20; 2 Tim 1:15; 2:17-18; 4:10, 14-16.

[58]   See 198-201, 204-208, 210-11, 213-15.

[59]   See 1 Tim 4:12 and Titus 2:7.

[60]   Paul claims a God-given apostolate in 1 Tim 1:1; 2:7; 2 Tim 1:1, 11; Titus 1:3 and at greater length in 1 Tim 1:11-16. He asserts continuity with traditional faith in 2 Tim 1:3; his gift of grace in 2 Tim 1:9; his conviction based on knowledge in 2 Tim 1:12.

As for message, the formula *pistos ho logos* offers confirmation in 1 Tim 1:15; 3:1; 4:9; 2

and criticism of opponents.[61] Third, the author prefers to support the exhortation and prescriptions with explanations, reasons, purposes, and motivation.[62] Fourth, antithesis found a place above among the devices which work through the

---

Tim 2:11; Titus 3:8, where the injunction is doubly emphasized. Otherwise, the confirmation is made without a formula as in 1 Tim 2:3; 2 Tim 2:7; Titus 1:3.

Finally, the addressee is commended for his fidelity, reminded of his strength, and corroborated in his official position in 1 Tim 1:2, 18; 4:6, 14; 6:12; 2 Tim 1:5-7, 9; Titus 1:4.

[61] 1 Tim 3:13; 2 Tim 3:15; 4:3-4 warn of end-time apostates and their wantonness. 2 Tim 3:12 declares the inevitable suffering of Christians. Titus 1:11 rails at the vices of contemporary false teachers, while 2 Tim 4:15 warns Timothy of the evil deeds of the coppersmith.

[62] The author elaborates on the rules for women, 1 Tim 2:13-14; the rejection of food laws, 1 Tim 4:4; the superiority of spiritual exercise, 1 Tim 4:8; the payment of teachers, 1 Tim 5:18; the preference for older widows, 1 Tim 2:11-13; 2 Tim 2:3-6, the single-minded dedication to service, 2 Tim 2:16-18; Onesiphorus' special claim to God's mercy, 2 Tim 3:9; the reason why some do not advance; the various uses of scripture, 2 Tim 3:16; the recommended change in Timothy's diet, 1 Tim 5:23; the summons to Timothy, 2 Tim 4:10; his suffering without shame, 2 Tim 1:12.

Though expressed as explanations, some reasons actually work to motivate a course of action. The reasons offered for avoiding speculative disputes in 2 Tim 2:16-17, 23; Titus 3:8-9, also assert the advantages of good works. The call for the deacons' good service in 1 Tim 3:13 also looks to the resulting reputation and boldness of speech. The command assiduously to discharge one's office has salvation for its motivating reason in 1 Tim 4:16. The service demanded of slaves for their Christian masters finds its basis in the bond of faith in 1 Tim 6:2. The spiritual profit from religion substantiates the call for an attitude of contentment in 1 Tim 6:6-8. The reminders of his forebears' faith and of God's spirit of power are expected to spur Timothy to revivify his charism in 2 Tim 1:6. An even greater stimulus is Paul's virtual conclusion of his apostolic labors in 2 Tim 4:6-8. The appearance of God's grace and its teaching stand behind the exhortation to a just and pious life, just as the redeeming and cleansing death of Christ implies for his people a zeal for good works in Titus 2:11-14.

Clear expressions of purpose leave no doubt as to the intent of certain actions, prescriptions and exhortations. Among the community prescriptions, 1 Tim 1:5 announces the general purpose of the letter's exhortation to be love, specified in heart, conscience and faith; 1 Tim 3:14-15 aims at knowledge of proper conduct. A peaceful life is the purpose at 1 Tim 2:1-2; an equitable share of the welfare burden at 1 Tim 5:16; protection of God's name and teaching at 1 Tim 6:1; Titus 2:3-5, 10. Qualities are to facilitate exhortation and reproof at Titus 1:7-9; good reputation is to forestall reproach at 1 Tim 3:7; and experience should insure balance at 1 Tim 3:6. As for the duties entrusted to Timothy and Titus, blamelessness is the aim at 1 Tim 5:7; a deterrent example of punishment at 1 Tim 5:20; a change of heart at 2 Tim 2:25-26; forestalling opponents' criticism at Titus 2:7-8; preparation for good work at 2 Tim 3:16-17; and, from the analogy there, pleasing God at 2 Tim 2:3-4.

Paul's intentions are explicit: instruction of apostates at 1 Tim 1:20, salvation for the elect at 2 Tim 2:10. The Lord's purposes are equally clear: at 1 Tim 1:16, it is a demonstration of the Lord's forebearance for all; at 2 Tim 4:17, the completion of Paul's kerygmatic work; and at Titus 3:7, justification.

arrangement and effect of words and phrases. On a broader scale, however, the Pastorals rely on contrasting ideas, conduct, moral qualities, and personalities to set the proper image in focus. With remarkable consistency in all three letters, the contrasting forces assume personal expression in the characters of Paul, his addressees, community members, unorthodox teachers, and followers of false teaching.[63]

E. *Concluding Observations*

From the study above, contrast and personal example emerge as principal hortatory features of the Pastorals. The attention to the use of contrast in the letters alerts the reader to the fact that the tension of opposites provides what loose, overall structure there is in the letters and also much of the structure in their smaller units. The analysis also finds the device of personal example closely allied with this structural technique, just as it serves the other hortatory techniques mentioned above. Explicit confirmation of the special importance of personal example can be found in the Pastorals' concern with the paradigmatic, whether commending it, demanding it, or warning away from it.

---

[63] The contrast of virtues and vices in a delineation of personal character types causes no surprise as the setting for the lists of qualifications and duties in 1 Tim 3:2-11; Titus 1:6-9. Nor should one be surprised at the effective technique in a community exhortation of casting the bad to be avoided and the good to be pursued in adjectives describing the personal character and in verbs denoting the actions of the people exhorted, as in 1 Tim 2:9-10; 5:5-6, 9-15, 17-20, 24-25; 6:2; 2 Tim 2:4-5; Titus 2:3. Such a message and its application is unmistakably lucid. Effective, too, is the testimony by a principal figure in the community to a personal odyssey from vice to virtue, as in 1 Tim 1:13-16. This recollection of prior guilt may even implicate the audience and thereby increase their care for the contrasting condition of virtue they now enjoy, as in Titus 3:1-8, and compare 2 Tim 2:13, 20-24.

Similarly, the Pastorals like to establish the locus of contrast among false teachers and their adherents. The effects here are a heightened appreciation of the orthodoxy and benefit of Paul and his message; an allegiance to and respect for his appointed emissaries and their successors; and, from the feeling instilled in the audience of superior godliness and discrimination of the good and true, a readiness to receive the exhortation. This technique of contrast pervades all three letters and ranges from simple to complex expressions.

Most directly, as in 1 Tim 1:18-20; 4:12; 2 Tim 2:14-19, 23-24; 3:1-17; Titus 3:8-11, the opponents contrast with Timothy and Titus, or, as in 1 Tim 1:3-9, with the orthodox faithful, at times with an admixture of instructional material. Elsewhere, a variety of opposing figures enter the lists, e.g., false teachers, Timothy, Paul and perhaps the community in 1 Tim 4:1-10; false teachers, Timothy, the greedy rich. Paul (and the community) in 1 Tim 6:2-20; Paul, named betrayers, Onesiphorus, and Timothy in 2 Tim 1:12-2:3; Timothy, future apostates, Paul in 2 Tim 4:1-8; Timothy, named companions of Paul, Alexander, those who abandoned Paul, the Lord in 2 Tim 4:9-17; the ideal bishop, insubordinate teachers, Titus in Titus 1:6-2:1.

II. Structure of the Hortatory Features in Three Paradigmatic Passages

The hortatory devices and techniques noted in the Pastoral Epistles are not used at random. They appear within a structure of development which this study will show to be common in the hortatory literature of the period. The passages in which this reaches expression will now fall under scrutiny. This investigation is expected to bring out the special place of personal example in the hortatory method of the Pastorals, and also to catch the other hortatory devices of the Pastoral Epistles in their interplay at three different points in the letters.[64] The similarities among the passages in their structure and in the devices used will sufficiently demonstrate the letters' common hortatory method.

A. *Paul the Example of Christ's Mercy and Patience, 1 Tim 1:3-20*

This passage, which announces the example of Paul, yields the following arrangement: 3-4, a statement of the charge in the negative against heretics, *hina parangeilē₁s tisin mē heterodidaskalein mēde prosechein mythois.* This is explained through its consequences, given in antithetical form (*mallon ... ē*). The positive explanation at 5 is followed by the negative example of the heretics, *tines astochēsantes exetrapēsan.* As the passage continues to develop the statement, it makes a further explanation in antithetical form, 8-10, a positive first, *oidamen ... dikaiō₁ nomos ou keitai,* then negative, *anomois de ... didaskalia₁ antikeitai.* At 11 gospel authority is appealed to.

12-17 establishes Paul as the positive example of Christ's mercy and patience, confirming his claim to the possession of the gospel at 11. The general description of his situation at 12 is filled out with an inner antithesis (13-14, *proteron ... alla ēleēthēn ... hyperpleonasen de*). This is proven by the authoritative saying in gnomic form at 15, *pistos ho logos,* and the reason for the example is then explained, *hina en emoi ... endeixētai ... pros hypotypōsin.*

The section concludes with a restatement of the prescription in positive form at 18-19a, *parangelian hina strateuē₁,* and a second reference to the contrasting example of the heretics at 19b-20, *tines ... Hymenaios kai Alexandros.*

Two hortatory features in this passage merit attention. Clearly, antithesis is the principal hortatory technique in this section and determines the statement of the charge and the proposal of the examples. It even plays a role in the positive example of Paul himself. With antithesis, example also plays a significant role in the exhortation here. The converted Paul is the expressly designated example of the working of Christ's merciful patience. To this, the false teachers present a shadow image of persistent and faithless impiety.

---

[64] This observation of three passages seeks to understand the relationship among the specific hortatory devices and features used therein. It presupposes the general hortatory character and directly hortatory features as established for the letters overall.

B. *The Example of Paul's Saving Words, 2 Tim 1:3-18*

In 2 Tim 1:3-18, the following arrangement of the devices of exhortation can be detected. A philophronetic (*epipothōn se idein*) remembrance and encomium of Timothy and his faith (*mneian, memnēmenos, hypomnēsin*) at 3-5 lays the ground for the statement of the exhortation to follow. The examples of his mother and grandmother corroborate the praise.

The statement of the exhortation comes at 6, *anamimnēskō se anazōpyrein*, followed by an explanatory substantiation of it at 7 in antithetical form (*ou ... alla*). At 8 a more specific restatement of the exhortation appears in both negative (*mē ... epaischynthē̦s ... mēde*) and positive terms (*alla syn-kakopathēson*). 9-10 explain the exhortation by elaborating the *martyrion tou kyriou hēmōn* and the *euangelion*. If traditional material, this is also an appeal to authority.

The delineation of the example begins at 11-12 with the personal testimony of Paul to his situation and attitude. Then at 13 comes the explicit reference to example, *hypotypōsin eche hygiainontōn logōn*. The example, while consisting of sound words, originates with Paul (*hōn par'emou ēkousas*) and will be shown to blend with his personal characteristics. The imperatives at 13-14 (*eche, phylaxon*) further specify the exhortation by referring to the exemplary teaching.

The negative example of faithlessness, with some of the apostates named, at 15 depicts a contrasting reaction to Paul and his teaching. This is, in turn, balanced by a positive, named example of unashamed faithfulness at 16-18. The next chapter repeats (*endynamou, synkakopathēson*) and furthers (*parathou, mnēmoneue, hypomimnē̦ske*) the exhortation to Timothy.

Notice, once again, the interplay of antithesis and example in this section. The faith of Timothy and his forebears at the start meets the faithlessness of the apostates at the conclusion. The abandonment of Paul by the latter contrasts with Onesiphorus' zealous services. The exhortation also finds expression in negative and positive terms. All the people referred to here are named and they exemplify opposite reactions to Paul and his teaching. Even the action of Jesus is an appearance and epiphany of God's favor (*phanerōtheisa, epiphaneia*). This last fact, Paul's attention to his own attitude and actions and the reaction they provoke, and the Pauline source of the example-teaching, all give a personal coloring to what seems to be a didactic example.

C. *The Example of Paul's Life, 2 Tim 3:1 – 4:8*

The section starts at 1 with the negative example of evil people, specified at 2-5a with a vice list and including an exhortation at 5b to avoid them (*apotrepou*). The negative example is further described at 6-9 with a characterization of their tactics, 6-7, an allusion to the traditional personages *Iannēs* and *Iambres*, 8, and a prediction of the inevitable unmasking of the evil people, 9.

The contrasting positive example at 10 encompasses all aspects of Paul's life, 10-11, which Paul commends Timothy for following (*sy de parēkolouthēsas*), especially the sufferings. In this Timothy is contrasted (*sy de*) with the *gynaikaria*, 6, who followed the false teachers. The sufferings are explained by the general application to all the pious at 12 and the contrast to the fate of the wicked, 13.

Timothy then receives the statement of the exhortation at 14a which outlines actions in contrast (*sy de*) to those of the deceived deceivers of 13. The hortatory statement is justified on the basis of his instruction, 14b, and his long-term scriptural knowledge, 15. The declaration-proof of the use and effectiveness of scripture, 16-17, explains this reliance on scripture. A final exhortation specifies the good works to be done at 4:1-2. This is bolstered by the two examples: apostate audiences and their chosen teachers, 3-4; Paul's life of completed service, 6-8. These antithetical examples envelope a restatement of the exhortation, 5.

The juxtaposition of negative and positive examples at the start, 3:1-11, and end 4:3-8, of the section is one aspect of the use of antithesis here. To this one might add the descriptions of initial success and ultimate failure of the opponents, 3:9; of the weak women studying a lot but learning little, 3:7 (*pantote ... kai mēdepote*); the distress of the pious and the progress of the wicked, ultimately to the worse, 3:13; the ignorance of the women and Timothy's learning, 3:14 (*sy de*); the rejection of good teaching and choice of bad, 4:3 (*ouk ... alla*); the turn from truth to fiction, 3:4 (*apo men ... epi de*). As for the example itself, the attention expressly called to the example of Paul at 3:10 (*parēkolouthēsas*) alerts the reader to the reappearance of this example at 4:6 and its negative counterparts at 3:1 and 4:3.

D. *Concluding Observations*

These passages and others in the Pastorals will be discussed at length below.[65] The remarks made here should be enough to indicate the application of the hortatory features noted and the preponderance of two of them, antithesis and example, in the exhortation of the Pastorals. Hortatory literature from a variety of sources in the Greco-Roman world will come under close scrutiny in this study. The discovery in these works of hortatory features and structural relationships[66] similar to those of the Pastorals will help to situate the latter in their context as well as to characterize the type of literature which the Pastorals represent. Particular attention to the Classical theory on example and its use will provide the framework within which to view the employment of that device by the Pastoral letters.[67] The

---

[65] See 198-216.

[66] The complex of hortatory features found in these passages will reappear in the authors analyzed below and will be shown to reflect the rhetorical handbooks' theoretical discussion of and exercises in the development of the chria or gnome.

[67] A study of example in the literature of the Jewish milieu is important for a complete understanding of the device in the Pastoral Epistles. The scope of this study, however, does

advantages of this view of the letters are several. First, it avoids treating in isolation any one element to the neglect of the others. Second, it clears a common ground between the personally hortatory 2 Timothy and the officially regulatory 1 Timothy and Titus. Third, it takes into account the principal stylistic features of the letters. Fourth, it provides a clue to dealing with similar material outside the three passages, e.g., the commands, personages, and affirmations in 1 Tim 4:1-16; 6:11-17; 2 Tim 2:14-20; Titus 3:1-14; 2:15-3:11. Finally, the "church order" material also finds a place in this scheme of things.

---

not permit such an examination within these pages. For the Hellenized depiction of biblical heroes see L. Feldman, "Josephus' Portrait of Saul," *HUCA* 53 (1982) 45-99; "Abraham the Greek Philosopher in Josephus," *TAPA* 99 (1968) 145-56; and C. Holladay, *"Theios Aner" in Hellenistic-Judaism; A Critique of the Use of This Category in New Testament Christology,* SBL Dissertation Series 40 (Missoula; Scholars, 1977).

CHAPTER III

Example in Rhetorical Theory, Education, and Literature

The survey of the hortatory technique of the Pastoral Epistles has yielded evidence of a wide-ranging and rhetorically sophisticated method of exhortation. It also noted that personal example claims a special place in that technique. A look at the rhetorical theory on example [1] is in order now, as a help in evaluating the findings from the Pastorals themselves.

I. Early Rhetorical Theory on Example

Example is a type of comparison and early rhetorical discussions did treat *eikōn, parabolē,* and *homoiōsis.* But consideration of *paradeigma* as such, in a technical sense, began with Anaximenes' *Rhetorica ad Alexandrum* and Aristotle's *Rhetoric,* the latter constituting a continuing influence through subsequent Greek and Latin rhetors. This survey of the rhetorical treatments of *paradeigma* will limit itself largely to the exhortative and dissuasive use of the proof, or *pistis* as it is called in the treatises.

A. *Anaximenes'* Rhetorica ad Alexandrum

In Anaximenes' definition of *paradeigmata* as *praxeis homoiai gegenēmenai kai enantiai tais nyn hyph'hēmōn legomenais* 8 (1429a.21) [3] two notions interest this study. First, he introduces the notion of negative examples, which he explains in 8

---

[1] This overview of the rhetorical theory is largely a summary of the 1975, University of California at Berkeley dissertation by Bennet J. Price entitled "Paradeigma and Exemplum in Ancient Rhetorical Theory." See also A. Holmberg, *Studien zur Terminologie und Technik der rhetorischen Beweisführung bei lateinischen Schriftstellern* (Uppsala: Almqvist & Wiksell, 1913).

[2] H. Rackham, trans., *Aristotle. Problems and Rhetorica ad Alexandrum,* LCL (London; W. Heinemann, 1936); M. Fuhrmann, ed., *Ars rhetorica quae vulgo fertur Aristotelis ad Alexandrum* (Leipzig: B.G. Teubner, 1966).

[3] Examples are "actions that have occurred previously and are similar to, or the opposite of, those which we are now discussing" (LCL).

(1429a.29-31) and 14 (1431a.26-27), i.e., ways of acting counter to the one proposed and errors committed by people in the past, both of which are to be avoided now. Second, while he speaks only of examples from the past, he allows recent examples, *ta nyn ginomena,* in 8 (1430a.7-9) and *paradeigmata ... engytata tois akouousi chronō₁* in 32 (1439a.1-5). In the last mentioned passage, Anaximenes also declares that examples must be *gnōrimōtata,* well-known to the listeners, for them to have any impact. By and large, however, Anaximenes' concern is with examples in forensic or legislative speeches and so most of his remarks have little direct bearing on hortatory discourses. This is largely the case with all the rhetorical theorists summarized in this section.

One category of "inventive" proof discussed by Anaximenes will be seen to have a relationship with the protreptic method of the Pastorals. Anaximenes declares that *paradeigma* is different from *krisis,* Previous Judgment, as a type of proof. Actually, however, the judgment on a similar situation in the past functions like a *paradeigma* for present action and attitude. The difference is that Previous Judgment, *to kekrimenon* or *krisis,* is a procedure or method of argument, while *to paradeigma* is a kind of proof (1[1422a.23-271]) and 32 [1439a.13-17]).

B. *Aristotle's* Ars rhetorica [4]

Aristotle ranges more widely into rhetorical theory than the practice-oriented Anaximenes. He considers *paradeigma* at 1.2.19(1357b) to be a form of induction, *paradeigma ... estin epagōgē kai peri poia epagōgē.* But at 2.20.2(1939a) he speaks of the two types of *paradeigmata:* the historical and the fabricated. Into the ranks of the historical examples Aristotle admits only real, previous events and their named protagonists. He does not, as Anaximenes, allow entrance to descriptions of habits, customs and mores of peoples and states. Among the fabricated *paradeigmata,* Aristotle lists *parabolē* and *logoi.* The former is an analogy different from historical examples in its use of real-life circumstances in the every-day world of types of people, rather than the past deeds of specific individuals. Furthermore, it can be expressed hypothetically, e.g. *homoion gar hōsper an ei tis* (2.20.4[1393b]). The latter are fables, and his recommendation of these is surprising in view of his lack of enthusiasm for myth or reports of poets.

In general, forensic and deliberative speeches preoccupy this theoretician of rhetoric when he recommends enthymemes for the first and *paradeigmata* for the second types of oratory. The inductive and deductive functions of examples in the arguments of a speech are a complicated issue in Aristotle, and fortunately not germane to this study. A paradigm, however, can also function by analogy and move from particular to particular without expressing a universal, as a syllogism would.

---

[4] J.H. Freese, trans., *Aristotle. Ars rhetorica,* LCL (London: W. Heinemann, 1927); R. Kassel, ed., *Aristotelis ars rhetorica* (Berlin/New York: de Gruyter, 1976).

This characteristic suits example for hortatory speeches, as will appear from their function below. Finally, addressing the advantages of using examples in *Problems* 18.3(916b.26-36),[5] Aristotle lauds the easy intelligibility and quick comprehension gained through their illustration of particulars, without losing the audience, as enthymemes might, in a demonstration of the whole. He also credits examples with stirring greater belief, standing as they do as corroborating witnesses to what is being proven.[6]

C. *Transition Period*

Of the two centuries between Aristotle and Cornificius' (?) *Rhetorica ad Herennium* and Cicero's *De inventione*, little evidence remains from the developing theory on *paradeigmata*. More is known of the *exempla*-collections, which sprang up at this time, especially in the Roman world with its emphasis on exemplary figures. One of these, *Facta et dicta memorabilia*, a nine-(or ten-) book collection by Valerius Maximus,[7] is clearly a rhetorical source book, and its examples are organized under, among other headings, virtues and vices.

D. Rhetorica ad Herennium [8]

The *Rhetorica ad Herennium*, discussing the invention of arguments in the part of a speech called *confirmatio*, Proof, lays out a five point plan for the perfect argument: Proposition, Reason, Proof of the Reason, Embellishment, and Resume (*propositio, ratio, confirmatio, exornatio, conplexio*). Embellishment, *exornatio*, is achieved through "comparisons, examples, amplifications, previous judgments, and the other means which serve to expand and enrich the argument" (LCL) ("... exornatio constat ex similibus et exemplis et amplificationibus et rebus iudicatis et ceteris rebus quae pertinent ad exaugendam et conlocupletandam argumentationem," 2.29.46). Price observes two things: one, although these five methods aim at embellishment of an established proof, they in fact also strengthen that proof; second, four of the five, all except *amplificatio*, can be considered analogical arguments.

The *Rhetorica ad Herennium* treats *exemplum* as a Figure of Thought, *sententiarum exornatio* (4.13.18), both in the service of *expolitio*, Elaboration or Refine-

---

[5] W.S. Hett, trans., *Aristotle. Problems*, LCL, 2 vols. (London: W. Heinemann, 1936).

[6] *ē hoti tōi te manthanein chairousi kai tōi tachy; raion de dia tōn paradeigmatōn kai tōn logōn manthanousin ... eti hois an martyrōisi pleious, mallon pisteuomen, ta de paradeigmata kai hoi logoi martyriais eoikasin; hai de dia tōn martyrōn raidioi pisteis.*

[7] Valerius Maximus, *Factorum et dictorum memorabilium libri novem*, K. Kempf, ed. (Leipzig: B.G. Teubner, 1888).

[8] H. Caplan, trans. *Cicero. Ad C. Herennium libri IV; De ratione dicendi*, LCL (Cambridge: Harvard University, 1954).

ment, and as a figure in its own right. Thus, two of the methods available for ela-borating a theme are *simile,* Comparison, and *exemplum* (4.43.56). As here, *simile* or *similitudo* are often mentioned with *exemplum* in this treatise, but also by Cicero and Quintilian. The latter actually translates *parabolē* as *similitudo* and *para-deigma* as *exemplum*. This relates to Aristotle's arrangement of *parabolē* as one type of rhetorical induction, *paradeigma*. Hence, in discussing *exemplum* as a fig-ure in its own right, some attention must also be given to *similitudo*.

Turning then to the second method of *expolitio* noted above, a long discussion of *similitudo* (4.45.59-48.61) precedes the treatment in *Rhetorica ad Herennium* of *exemplum* and contains this definition: [9]

> Similitudo est oratio traducens ad rem quampiam aliquid ex re dispari simile. Ea sumitur aut ornandi causa aut probandi aut apertius dicendi aut ante oculos ponendi. Et quomodo quattuor de causis sumitur, item quattuor modis dicitur: per contrarium, per negationem, per conlationem, per brevitatem. Ad unam quamque sumendae cau-sam similitudinis adcommodabimus singulos modos pronuntiandi.   (4.45.59)

Following the discussion of *similitudo* comes that of *exemplum*.[10] *"Exem-plum est alicuius facti aut dicti praeteriti cum certi auctoris nomine propositio.   Id sumitur isdem de causis quibus similitudo"* (4.49.62). *Exemplum* is the same as *similitudo* in purpose: ornament, proof, clarification, or demonstration. It differs through the distinction between a general juxtaposition of similarities in different things (*similitudo*) and the proposition of some past deed or word of a particular, named agent (*exemplum*). Two elements of the definition which are new with the *Rhetorica ad Herennium* (compare the preface to Valerius Maximus' collection) are the inclusion of *dicta* along with *facta* as a source of *exempla,* and the explicit requirement of a specific, named agent for the reference from the past.

Worthy of note, too, are the four modes of expressing comparisons and, as Price presumes, examples, i.e., *per contrarium, per negationem, per conlationem, per brevitatem*.

E. *Cicero's* De inventione [11]

Cicero, in *De inventione,* also locates *exemplum* in the *confirmatio* of a speech, where it, along with *imago* and *collatio,* is a member of *comparabile,* itself, in turn,

---

[9] "Comparison is a manner of speech that carries over an element of likeness from one thing to a different thing. This is used to embellish or prove or clarify or vivify. Further-more, corresponding to these four aims, it has four forms of presentation: contrast, nega-tion, detailed parallel, abridged comparison. To each single aim in the use of comparison we shall adapt the corresponding form of presentation." (LCL).

[10] "Exemplification is the citing of something done or said in the past, along with the de-finite naming of the doer or author. It is used with the same motives as a comparison." (LCL).

[11] H.M. Hubbell, trans., *Cicero. De inventione, de optimo genere oratorum, topica,* LCL (Cambridge: Harvard University, 1949).

one of the four types of Argument from Probability. He defines example as, "quod rem auctoritate aut casu alicuius hominis aut negoti confirmat aut infirmat" (1.30.49).[12] Price finds *Rhetorica ad Herennium*'s *facta et dicta* in the *homo aut negotium,* and its example's specificity in *alicuius hominis aut negoti.* But Cicero does not insist on a past example and seems here to regard example only in its function within a proof, only one of four goals of example in *Rhetorica ad Herennium.* In this regard, Price notes that *confirmat et infirmat* are equal to the standard terms *protropē/apotropē* or *hortari/dehortari.*

In *Top.* 10.41-45, Cicero treats *exemplum* as a genus or type of argument provided by the Topic of Similarity or Comparison, *locus similitudinis.*[13]   It has two species: *facta* and *ficta exempla.   Facta exempla,* here, means legal precedents as well as historical examples.   *Ficta exempla* are more than fables and a look at *Auct. Her.* 4.53.66 is helpful in clarifying what they are.   Here the author discusses *conformatio,* Personification, *prosōpopoiia* and finds that it consists in "representing an absent person as present, or in making a mute thing or one lacking in form articulate and attributing to it a definite form and a language or a certain behavior appropriate to its character." (LCL)   These are often exemplary and compare past and present.   Cicero echoes this by collocating personifications together with *similitudo* and *exemplum,* more or less loosely, as in *Or.* 40.137 and 138, *De or.* 3.53.204-205, and especially 2.40.168-69.[14]   Moreover, his description of *ficta exempla* in *Top.* 10.45 reflects the illustrations for personification given by the *Rhetorica ad Herennium.*

As noted above, *De inventione* mentions only the function of example in rational proof, and the same is true of *Topica.* Elsewhere, however, the "ethical-pathetical" powers of *exemplum* receive their due.   As effective *loci* of Amplification (*Part. or.* 55), *exemplum* and *similitudo* share the task of stirring the audience's spirits.[15]   They also make believable (*facit fidem*) according to *Part. or.* 40, and

---

[12] "Example is a type of comparison which strengthens or weakens a case by (the?) authority?/precedent? or experience of a certain person or event." (Price, 104).

[13] Price refines this observation on 118 where he finds Cicero's usage in this and other works to be imprecise as to whether *factum exemplum* is a Figure of Thought, a member of the Topic of Similarity, a topic in and of itself, or a constituent of *comparabile,* to be used in the Argument from Probability. The cloudy relationship between historical and legal example only compounds the difficulty.

[14] "168 Ex similitudine autem: 'si ferae partus suos diligunt, qua nos in liberos nostros indulgentia esse debemus?' 169 At ex dissimilitudine: 'si barbarorum est in diem vivere, nostra consilia sempiternum tempus spectare debent.' Atque utroque in genere et similitudinis et dissimilitudinis exempla sunt ex aliorum factis aut dictis aut eventis, et fictae narrationes saepe ponendae." E.W. Sutton, trans., *Cicero. De oratore,* LCL, compl. and intr. H. Rackham, vol. 1 (Cambridge: Harvard University, 1942); H.M. Hubbell, trans., *Cicero. Orator,* LCL (London: W. Heinemann, 1939).

[15] H. Rackham, trans., *Cicero. De oratore III, de fato, paradoxa stoicorum, de partitione oratoria,* LCL (Cambridge: Harvard University, 1942). See also Price, 267 n. 30; *De or.* 3.27.104-5; *Auct. Her. 2.30.47.*

are particularly stirring (*maxime movent*) Figures of Thought in *De or.* 3.53.205. The persuasive power of historical examples receives particular attention in *Or.* 34.120, where Cicero finds that their use both gains the credibility of the speaker and delights the audience.[16] Nonetheless, Cicero's main concern is with judicial speeches and their requirements weight his treatment of *exemplum*. Furthermore, a complete picture of Cicero's thought on *exemplum* is hard to garner since his remarks are spread through various works and over a time span of forty years.

F. *Quintilian's* Institutio oratoria [17]

Whatever systematization Cicero lacked in his discussion of *exemplum*, Quintilian makes up for in his *Inst.* 5.11. Despite the confusion which Price detects in Quintilian's understanding of his predecessors, particularly on the distinction between *exemplum* as artificial proof and as historical example, his definition reflects much of what has been seen in the discussion above. Indeed Quintilian sees no difference except a terminological one between the Greek system's *paradeigma* with its subdivisions *paradeigma* and *parabolē*, Cicero's *inductio* divided into *exemplum* and *collatio,* and his own *exemplum* with subdivisions *exemplum* and *similitudo*. Thus he says: [18]

> 1 Tertium genus, ex iis quae extrinsecus adducuntur in causam, Graeci vocant *paradeigma,* quo nomine et generaliter usi sunt in omni similium adpositione et specialiter in iis quae rerum gestarum auctoritate nituntur. Nostri fere similitudinem vocare maluerunt quod ab illis parabole dicitur, hoc alterum exemplum, quamquam et hoc simile est, illud exemplum. 2 Nos, quo facilius propositum explicemus, utrumque *paradeigma* esse credamus et ipsi appellemus exemplum. Nec vereor ne videar repugnare Ciceroni, quamquam conlationem separat ab exemplo. Nam idem

---

[16] "Commemoratio autem antiquitatis exemplorumque prolatio summa cum delectatione et auctoritatem orationi affert et fidem."

[17] H.E. Butler, *The Institutio Oratoria of Quintilian,* LCL, 4 vols. (London: W. Hinemann, 1920); L. Radermacher, ed., *M. Fabi Quintiliani institutionis oratorae libri XII,* rev. V. Buchheit (Leipzig: B.G. Teubner, 1965).

[18] "(1) The third kind of proof, of those proofs which are brought into the matter under discussion and are not intrinsic to it, the Greeks call *paradeigma*. They have used this word both broadly/generally for every comparison of like with like and narrowly/specifically for those comparisons which rely on the authority of history. Roman writers generally have preferred to used the word *similitudo* for what the Greeks call *parabolē,* although the historical example involves similarity, while the *similitudo* is like an *exemplum*. (2) I, to make the matter simpler, would consider both [historical example, and *similitudo*] species of the genus *paradeigma* and call them *exemplum*. And, although Cicero separates *collatio* from *exemplum,* I don't think he and I disagree; for he divides all argumentation into *inductio* and *ratiocinatio,* just as most Greeks divided it into *paradeigmata* and *epicheirēmata* and called *paradeigma rētorikē epagōgē*." (Price, 132-133).

omnem argumentationem dividit in duas partes, inductionem et ratiocinationem, ut plerique Graecorum in *paradeigmata* et *epicheirēmata,* dixeruntque *paradeigma rētorikēn epagōgēn.   (5.11.1-2)*

Whatever the relation between *exemplum* as genus and as species, it is the latter that is of interest to this study. Quintilian finds historical examples to be like testimony or legal precedent, but even more forceful, *potentior,* because they are above suspicion of bias and prejudice.[19] He adds an important new element to the definition of historical example: "id est rei gestae aut ut gestae utilis ad persuadendum id quod intenderis commemoratio" (5.11.6). The *ut gestae* opens the way to including poetic fictions, fables, and other narratives under historical example. The examples need not be from the distant past for, along with old examples, he makes room for recent ones and even those which are known from daily activity.[20]

Quintilian is unique in his classification at 5.11.5-16 of example into five types, i.e., similar, dissimilar, contrary, from greater to lesser, and from lesser to greater. Although combinations of these are to be found in his predecessors, Quintilian is the first to list the last two. At 5.11.10 he recommends them for hortatory discourses. He admits the use of *exempla* not just for Proof (*probandi causa*) but for Ornamentation (*ornatus*) too. *Amplificatio,* Amplification, is a kind of *ornatus* and one of four methods to achieve it is by *comparatio,* Comparison, of which *exemplum* is one type.

The witness value of *exempla* and the increase of *auctoritas,* Authority, for their user was noted in Cicero's treatment, and Quintilian shares his view. In 5.11.36-44 he distinguishes *iudicia aut iudicationes, kriseis,* from *exempla.* The former are *testimonia,* Warrants, which bolster Authority and they can be expressed as opinions, teachings, traditions, and poetic pronouncements from the past. They can also stem from the beliefs of nations, *dicta* of notable people, proverbial expressions in common use, divine signs, and even the sayings or deeds of the adversary or judge (in legal speeches). Although Quintilian tries not to confuse these with *exempla,* his programmatic statement at 5.9.1 mentions only three types of artificial proof and here, at 5.11.36-44, he continues his treatment of the third type, *exemplum.* Moreover, at 5.11.43-44, he joins *exempla* directly with these

---

[19] "[Exempla]...aut testimoniorum aut etiam iudicatorum optinent locum," 12.4.2, and "[exempla potentiora sunt] quod ea sola criminibus odii et gratia vacant," 10.1.34. They also give the orator authority normally enjoyed only by old men as Quintilian says, "Sciat ergo [orator] quam plurima [exempla]: unde etiam senibus auctoritas maior est, quod plura nosse et vidisse creduntur, quod Homerus frequentissime testatur," 12.4.2 and see 3.8.66 and 12.2.29-30.

[20] "In primis vero abundare debet orator exemplorum copia cum veterum tum etiam novorum, adeo ut non ea modo quae conscripta sunt historiis aut sermonibus velut per manus tradita quaeque cotidie aguntur debeat nosse," 12.4.1 and see 5.11.38. As Price notes, 153, this opens the door to the *mos est ut* type of example from common custom.

warrant-statements and *auctoritas*.[21] His discussion of *proverbia* and *exempla* reveals both a link between them and the qualities which make them persuasive. First of all, Proverbs, which treat of beasts, are akin to Fable, which in turn is a kind of *exemplum*. Furthermore, *proverbiae* and *exempla* are like *testimonia* and are considered true by virtue of their very antiquity.[22] They are particularly persuasive because they seem to come from unprejudiced minds, not fabricated for the particular argument in question by the author himself.[23]

With this summary of Quintilian's instruction on *exempla* and their use, the survey of the rhetorical theoreticians is completed. While some of their definitions and principles of usage are applicable to protreptic works, forensic and deliberative oratory was the focus of attention in these treatises. Tracing the line between the rhetorical theory noted above, with its deliberative and forensic emphasis, and the protreptic use of example by spiritual guides and pedagogues of morality is the next task.

II. The Place of Example in Rhetorical Education [24]

A. *Greco-Roman Pedagogical Principles*

Isocrates [25] notes the key place example occupies within rhetorical education in his *Adv. soph.* 16-18, where he says: *kai dein ton men mathētēn ... ta men eidē ta*

---

[21] Price also calls attention to the similar phraseology of the introductions to the third section at 5.11.1, "Tertium genus, ex iis quae extrinsecus adducuntur in causam, Graeci vocant *paradeigma*," and to the sub-section on *auctoritas* at 5.11.36, "Adhibentur extrinsecus in causam et auctoritas." See Price, 204-8, for the views of Quintilian's predecessors on the relation between *testimonia* and *exempla*.

[22] "Ne haec quidam vulgo dicta et recepta persuasione populari sine usu fuerint. Testimonia sunt enim quodam modo," 5.11.37; and "Neque enim durassent haec in aeternum nisi vera omnibus viderentur," 5.11.41. Moreover Quintilian says of historical examples, 12.4.1-2, "Aut testimoniorum aut etiam iudicatorum optinent locum," and poetic fictions, "vetustatis fide tuta sunt."

[23] 5.11.37 goes on to say" ... vel potentiora etiam quod non causis accommodata sunt, sed liberis odio et gratia mentibus idea tantum dicta factaque quia aut honestissima aut verissima videbantur." For his views on Examples see 10.1.34, "Hoc [exempla] potentiora, quod ea sola criminibus odii et gratia vacant," and for Quintillian on Poetic Fictions see 12.4.2, "... ab hominibus magnis praeceptorum loco ficta creduntur."

[24] For further discussion on Greco-Roman education and the place of example in it see E. Pflugmacher, *Locorum communium specimen* (Greifswald: Hans Adler, 1909); D.L. Clark, *Rhetoric in Greco-Roman Education* (New York/London: Columbia University, 1957); H. Kornhardt, *Exemplum: eine bedeutungsgeschichtliche Studie* (Göttingen. Robert Noske, 1936); A. Lumpe, "Exemplum," *RAC* 6:1229-57; J. Martin, *Antike Rhetorik: Technik und Methode* (Munich: C.H. Beck, 1974).

[25] G. Norlin, trans., *Isocrates*, LCL, 3 vols. (London: W. Heinemann, 1928); E. Drerup, ed., *Isocratis opera* (Leipzig: Dieterich [Theodor Weicher], 1906).

tōn logōn mathein ... ton de didaskalon ... toiouton auton paradeigma paraskein hōste tous ektypōthentas kai mimēsasthai dynamenous. Thus, the teacher of rhetoric does more than instruct his pupils in rhetorical theory, including the use of example. In his own speeches he is an example of the theory put to practice. And the same understanding of the role of the teacher of rhetoric finds expression centuries later in Quintilian, who says, *Inst.* 2.2.8: [26]

> Licet enim satis exemplorum ad imitandum ex lectione suppeditet, tamen viva illa, ut dicitur, vox alit plenius, praecipueque praeceptoris quem discipuli, si modo recte sunt instituti, et amant et verentur. Vix autem dici potest quanto libentius imitemur eos quibus favemur.

The *Auct. Her.* 4.6.9 explain this by exploiting the analogy to cloth samples, which the word example also denotes. Just as cloth merchants are to give samples from the cloth they are selling and not from some other material, so the teacher must give a sample of his own art, which he expects the pupils will pay to learn. Cicero's discussion in *De or.* 2.2.88ff. underlines the fact that this imitation has proceeded through the history of oratory with pupil imitating teacher and himself being imitated by his pupils.

As Quintilian indicates in *Inst.* 2.1-8, the teacher-student relationship also has a decidedly non-academic cast. The character of the teacher is critically important, 2.1; his own purity is to preserve the young pupils from corruption and his seriousness the bolder ones from license, 2.3; he must display self-control himself and control the habits of his pupils, 2.4; he is to act *in loco parentis* and with a parental attitude; his classroom method springs from his own virtue and includes moral admonition as well as methods proper to professional instruction, 2.5-7; his model will be more readily imitated if he gains his pupils' fear and affection, 2.8. [27] Obviously, in the classroom the rhetor handled more than the theory and technique of rhetoric; and his work of moral admonition found exemplification in the life-style which he displayed, just as his speech-making mirrored the lessons in rhetoric.

---

[26] "For however many models for imitation he may give them from the authors they are reading, it will still be found that fuller nourishment is provided by the living voice, as we call it, more especially when it proceeds from the teacher himself, who, if his pupils are rightly instructed, should be the object of their affection and respect. And it is scarcely possible to say how much more readily we imitate those whom we like." (LCL).

[27] On teachers affecting the pupils' morals see also *Inst.* 1.2.4-5. According to *Ep.* 8.32.2, Pliny formed the habits of Junius Avitus as if he were his teacher, standing in the relationship of love and respect which Quintilian here outlines. (B. Radice, trans., *C. Plinius Caecilii Secundus. Epistulae, panegyricus,* LCL, 2 vols. [Cambridge: Harvard University, 1969]; R.A.B. Mynors, ed., *C. Plinii Caecilii Secundi epistularum libri decem* [Oxford: Clarendon. 1963]).

The description of the teacher as surrogate parent echoes Pliny's letter to Titius Aristo, 8.14, where he asks the authority on senatorial procedure for some advice on his own conduct in that body and thereby revives what he claims to be an ancient custom of instruction by word and example by one's father or, in his stead, some distinguished elder: [28]

> (4) Erat autem antiquitus institutum ut a maioribus natu non auribus modo, verum etiam oculis disceremus quae facienda mox ipsi ac per vices quasdam tradenda minoribus haberemus. ... (6) Suus cuique parens pro magistro, aut cui parens non erat, maximus quisque et vetustissimus pro parente ... Omnem denique senatorium morem, quod fidicissimum praecipiendi genus, exemplis docebantur.

This education by example (*non auribus modo, verum etiam oculis*) looks to various individuals for models; but the parent's role is crucial in proposing them when urging that some vice be avoided or that some course be chosen.[29] The parents might propose someone from the family's ancestors as example,[30] or might, like a rhetoric teacher in more institutionalized and technical education, be examples themselves.[31]

---

[28] "But in the olden time it was an established rule that Romans should learn from their elders, not only by precept, but by example, the principles on which they themselves should one day act, and which they should in their turn transmit to the younger generation ... The father of each youth served as his instructor, or, if he had none, some person of years and dignity supplied the place of the father ... Thus they were taught by that surest method of instruction, example, the whole conduct of a senator." (LCL).

[29] Compare Horace *S.* 1.4.103-29, especially 105-7 (H.R. Fairclough, trans., *Horace. Satires, Epistles, and Ars poetica*, LCL, 2 vols. [London: W. Heinemann, 1926]).

[30] Seneca *Con.* 10.2.16, "Solebas mihi, pater, insignium virorum exempla narrare, quaedam etiam domestica. Aiebas: avum fortem virum habuisti, vide ut sis fortior" (M. Winterbottom, trans., *The Elder Seneca. Declamations*, LCL, 2 vols. [Cambridge: Harvard University, 1974]). See also Pliny *Ep.* 5.8.4-5, and Seneca *Clem.* 1.9.1 (J.W. Basore, trans., *Lucius Annaeus Seneca. Moral Essays*, LCL, 3 vols. [London: W. Heinemann, 1928]).

[31] Seneca *Con.* 10.2.16, "O quantam ego cupiditatem gloriae in patre meo vidi, quam iuvenilem. Contendere me vetabat imperio, iubebat exemplo." See also Cicero *Off.* 1.78 (W. Miller, trans., *Marcus Tullius Cicero. De officiis*, LCL [London: W. Heinemann, 1913]). Pliny, *Ep.* 8.13.1-2, calls the father *optimum et conjunctissimum exemplar*.

Sometimes the father's example inculcates vice rather than virtue, a charge levelled by Cicero against Verres in *Verr.* 2.5.137 (L.H.G. Greenwood, trans., *Cicero: The Verrine Orations*, LCL, 2 vols. [London: W. Heinemann, 1928[); Juvenal, *S.* 14.30.27, criticizes *exempla domestica* which lead youths into evil ways (G.G. Ramsay, trans., *Juvenal and Persius*, LCL [London: W. Heinemann, 1918]); Plutarch, *Ed. lib.* 14A-B, recognizes both possibilities (F.C. Babbitt, trans., *Plutarch's Moralia*, LCL, 15 vols. [London: W. Heinemann, 1926]).

B. *Summary and Concluding Observations*

These recommendations of example all share a pedagogical setting and they look to example for the similar function of clarifying and encapsulating the point of the lesson. This pedagogical use of example introduces the device into yet another setting, the classroom, besides the law court, the legislature, and the memorial site. But before the multiplicity of categories and the overlap in their practical application blur into confusion, let the following attempt at reestablishing the lines of difference in category and usage reorient the reader through the detail and to the direction of this study.

First of all, though the theoretical treatises do not mention the use of example as a pedagogical tool, the references above do. First to be noted under this perspective, then, is the fact that in addition to teaching the theory on the usefulness of examples, and offering examples of the theory in practice, the good rhetor himself is an example of the art that he teaches. This is but an institutionalized form of apprenticeship in order to learn the mores of an occupation or public function. Second, that art is both the art of speaking appropriately to the situation and the art of living uprightly. And the same can be said of the mores, i.e., that they include both professional competence and qualities of character. Third, the teacher in the school is considered an extension of, or at least analogous to, the parent in the home. And both teacher and parent, expected to be good examples themselves, also find particularly compelling models in the *domestica exempla,* the pupil's predecessors in civic or familial virtue. Finally, instruction in this broader view sees ethics as inextricably bound up with technical competence and, consequently, moral exhortation and admonition as intrinsic to professional preparation.

Second, example in this usage is not primarily proof or a device in service of a proof but rather demonstration. It finds a source in the past and the present, in proverbs and sayings, in opinions and prior judgments, in commonly acknowledged customs and habitual actions, or in specific individuals and events.

Third, it expresses the best way, to be followed, or the worst, to be avoided. Moreover, it gives a precedent which shows the desired course can be followed or ought not be followed. In its character as protreptic and apotreptic device, example serves various types of discourse, of which deliberative oratory is but one.[32]

Fourth, whatever its source, the example cogently attests the desirability or advantage of a recommended action, attitude, or association, or the harm in those disapproved of. Similarly, it might bolster the authority of the exhorter-admonitor or even offer vindication from undeserved criticism. As such, these attestations serve a forensic function but are not at all restricted to the court room.

---

[32] K. Alewell, *Über das rhetorische PARADEIGMA: Verwendung in der römischen Literatur der Kaiserzeit* (Leipzig: A. Hoffmann, 1913) 27, summarizes the protreptic and apotreptic function of examples from the definitions and descriptions of the device in theoretical treatments from Aristotle to the progymnasmata.

Let this specification of the nature of examples under consideration suffice as this study resumes the main lines of its discussion, i.e., example as a hortatory device. The type of example with which this study is concerned clearly demonstrates what a speech is getting at, but not just for the sake of better comprehension.[33] Action, which imitates or avoids that of the given examples,[34] and virtue[35] are the ends envisaged for their use. The nature of this exhortation to action has been widely discussed with respect to the nuances implied in the words used to describe it. This discussion is also closely bound up with a consideration of the oral and literary forms which have exhortation as their aim. A survey of the hortatory forms and the types of exhortation will now be made.

III. Forms of Hortatory Literature Which Use Example

A. *Diversity of the Forms*

The discussion above established that the hortatory and admonitory uses of example are no strangers to the rhetor's subject matter and instructional method. Their roots, however, reach deeply into the soil of Greek custom and institutions. That such uses of examples were a keystone of customary, domestic education received attention above. Under a more formal view, ethical exhortation and admonition found their place in the various institutions of epideictic oratory, be they epinikia for victors, encomia for leaders and states, or epitaphia for deceased relatives and people of note.[36] And so, for example, Lysias could call to memory *tous palaious kindynous tōn progonōn* for others, *paideuontas d'en tois tōn tethneōtōn ergois tous zōntas*.[37] A similar ethical concern and moralistic or edificatory purpose found themselves a natural home in works with a biographical character.[38] Biographical sketches, like those used by Socrates in *Gorgias* 471A-D and 515C ff., offered concrete illustrations for an ethical point.[39]

---

[33] Cicero *Rep.* 2.6.6 (C.W. Keyes, *Marcus Tullius Cicero. De re publica, de legibus;* LCL [London: W. Heinemann, 1928]) and Quintilian *Inst.* 12.2.2.

[34] Cf. Seneca *Con.* 9.2.27, "Omnia authem genera corruptarum quoque sententiarum de industria pono, quia facilius et quid imitandum et quid vitandum sit docemur exemplo." See also *Ep.* 6.5 (R.M. Gummere, *Lucius Annaeus Seneca. Ad Lucilium epistulae morales,* LCL, 3 vols. [London: W. Heinemann, 1917]).

[35] Quintilian *Inst.* 12.2.30, "An fortitudinem, iustitiam, fidem, continentiam, frugalitatem, contemptum doloris ac mortis melius alii docebunt quam Fabricii, Curii, Reguli, Decii, Mucii, aliique innumerabiles?

[36] F. Dornseiff, "Literarische Verwendungen des Beispiels," *Bibliothek Warburg* 4 (1924-25) 219-20.

[37] *Or. fun.* 3 (W.R.M. Lamb, trans., *Lysias,* LCL, [London: W. Heinemann, 1930]).

[38] D.R. Stuart, *Epochs of Greek and Roman Biography* (Berkeley: University of California, 1928) 121.

[39] Stuart, 124. He declares biography to be the continuation and completion of the prose encomium.

Other genre also exploited the protreptic and apotreptic potentialities of example. This function in the discourses reflecting popular, moralizing philosophy was alluded to above,[40] and will receive further consideration in the sections which follow.

For another class of literature, a historian like Livy could characterize his whole work in these terms:[41]

> Hoc illud est praecipue in cognitione rerum salubra ac frugiferum, omnis te exempli documenta in inlustri posita monumento intueri; inde tibi tuaeque rei publicae quod imitere capias, inde foedum inceptu, foedum exitu, quod vites. (1. Proem. 10)

In a lighter and more personal vein, the poet Propertius, 3.11.5-8, alludes to the suffering which teaches fear in a sailor, a soldier and a lover like himself, as sobering examples for other lovers:[42]

> venturam melius praesagit navita mortem, vulneribus didicit miles habere metum.
> ista ego praeterita jactavi verba juventa: tu nunc exemplo disce timere meo.

Like this, but with consummate seriousness, is the attitude of spiritual guides like Seneca, who realize progress in their lives and, as living examples, look to share their gains with others both through personal association and through epistolary exchange. So Seneca says in *Ep.* 6.3-5:[43]

> Concipere animo non potes, quantum momenti adferre mihi singulos dies videam. "Mitte," inquis, "et nobis ista, quae tam efficacia expertus es." Ego vero omnia in te cupio transfundere, et in hoc aliquid gaudeo discere, ut doceam ... Plus tamen tibi et viva vox et convictus quam oratio proderit. In rem praesentem venias oportet, primum, quia homines amplius oculis quam auribus credunt; deinde, quia longum iter est per praecepta, breve et efficax per exempla.

---

[40] See 11 and n. 32.

[41] "What chiefly makes the study of history wholesome and profitable is this, that you behold the lessons of every kind of experience set forth as on a conspicuous monument; from these you may choose for yourself and for your own state what to imitate, from these mark for avoidance what is shameful in the conception and shameful in the result." (B.O. Foster, trans., *Livy,* LCL, vol. 1 [London: W. Heinemann, 1919]).

[42] " 'Tis the mariner best foretells his coming doom, 'Tis wounds that teach the soldier fear. I once spake boasts like thine in my past youth: Now let my example teach thee to be afraid." (H.E. Butler, trans., *Propertius,* LCL [London: W. Heinemann, 1912]).

[43] "You cannot conceive what distinct progress I notice that each day brings to me. And when you say: 'Give me also a share in these gifts which you have found so helpful,' I reply that I am anxious to heap all these privileges upon you, and that I am glad to learn in order that I may teach ... Of course, however, the living voice and the intimacy of a common life will help you more than the written word. You must go to the scene of action, first, because men put more faith in their eyes than in their ears, and second, because the way is long if one follows precepts, but short and helpful, if one follows patterns." (LCL).

Cutting across a number of these specific genres is the broader classification of edification literature. The techniques and practice of this type of composition were the concern of the schools in the Hellenistic period. This together with the scholastic environment alluded to in the discussion on the theory and practice of the use of example recommend a further look at Hellenistic edification literature. In addition to the light this will shed on the scholastic context of exhortation, this analysis will also clarify the nuanced character of exhortation.

B. *Edification Literature and the Development of Literary Exhortation*

In his analysis of epideictic literature, Burgess makes three observations which are helpful for this study: (1) the epideictic style and material were prominent in the progymnasmata, which, in turn, continued and extended them;[44] (2) the increased use of rhetoric by popular philosophers brought the epideictic elements together with and in service of moralizing paraenesis,[45] just as earlier a protreptic and symbouleutic purpose was legitimated for epideictic speeches;[46] (3) epideictic activity moved into prose forms, whether of the dialogic diatribe or of the half-dialogue or epistle.[47] It cannot be denied, then, that the protreptic cast of edification literature extends to both oratory and other prose. Nor is it inappropriate to consider the Pastoral Epistles within this frame of reference, at least from the aspect of their commands, exhortations, warnings, stylistic tropes, and exemplary figures of reproach and praise. This offers a possible formal context within which to evaluate similarities in structure and detail between the Pastorals and recognized epideictic-edification literature.

Burgess' conclusions about the mixture of protreptic elements with epideictic form confirm, with some corrections, those of an earlier analysis of Greco-Roman hortatory literature done by Paulus Hartlich.[48] The latter attempted to distinguish the *protropē* in epideictic from the suggestion, *symboulē,* in judicial or deliber-

---

[44] T. Burgess, *Epideictic Literature* (Chicago: University of Chicago, 1902) 118 n. 4.

[45] Burgess, 222-29. Thus apophthegms and idealized portraits served the symbouleutic and protreptic ends of the wandering preachers and popular philosophers.

[46] Burgess, 229 and 245, where he discusses Gorgias and Isocrates. This is particularly the case where the praise of qualities or character in general is accompanied by the suggestion that the audience do likewise.

[47] Burgess, 186-87, 234-44.

[48] P. Hartlich, "De exhortationum a Graecis Romanisque scriptarum historia et indole," *Leipz. Stud.* 11 (1889) 207-336. He cites Quintilian *Inst.* 3.8.28 to demonstrate the presence of a protreptic element in both epideictic and deliberative oratory. In another school classification, by Demetrius of Phalerum, deliberative and judicial forms of speech were divisions of epideictic oratory. Another classification added the encomiastic form to the other two divisions of epideictic. In any case, protreptic, epideictic and symbouleutic are not easily isolated as independent rhetorical categories (cf. Quintilian *Inst.* 3.4.14), although the artificial environment of school rhetoric led to attempts at such classification and division. This theorizing was done within a largely scholastic context and at a time when judicial and legislative speeches lost the practical role they enjoyed in the Roman Republic and the Greek city-states.

ative set-pieces, i.e., *suasoriae* and *controversiae*. He identified *protropē,* exhortation or persuasion to a commonly agreed upon good, with *paraklēsis;* and he saw *symboulē,* proposal by precept of a debatable good, as *parainesis.*[49]   But Burgess rightly calls this distinction of *protreptikos logos* or exhortation from *parainesis* by virtue of the use of precept in the latter as too cut and dry.[50]   Nonetheless, it is helpful to observe with Hartlich that a *protreptikos logos* is a speech "by which someone is urged to virtue by the praise of ancestors which is brought forth."[51]

In the *protreptikos logos* as described by Philo of Larissa, Hartlich notes two parts: the *endeiktikē* and the *apelenktikē.*[52]   And while the protreptic here shows the advantages of philosophy, it is philosophy in the popular sense of a virtuous way of life which leads to happiness.[53]   The refutation of adversaries and critics includes both exposure of the inadequacy of their advice and a warning to dissociate from those who fail to follow their own suggestions.[54]

Reproachful and laudatory demonstration play yet another role in protreptic works.   The reproof hits not only at the false teachers but also at the addressees, in order to make clear the actions and attitudes which militate against what is useful for them.[55]   At the same time, the feasibility and advantages of philosophy or of the virtuous life find tangible proof in the exemplary lives of its practitioners.[56]

---

[49] Hartlich, 328-29.

[50] Burgess, 299 ff., where he refers to authors among whom the distinction does hold, to others where the words are interchangeable, and to some where the meanings are loose and indefinite, although they tend to allow the predominance of precept for paraenesis. Libanius' *epistolimaioi charaktēres* 15.5 (in V. Weichert, ed., *Demetrii* et *Libanii qui feruntur TYPOI EPISTOLIKOI ET EPISTOLIMAIOI CHARAKTERES* [Leipzig: B.G. Teubner, 1910]), mentions the purpose of a paraenetic letter to be protreptic and apotreptic. He distinguishes it from a symbouleutic letter not on the basis of precept but in terms of the irrefutable nature of a paraenetic exhortation as opposed to the debate expected in a symbouleutic context. This would place paraenetic and protreptic, as here described, close together.

[51] Hartlich, 329, where he refers to Isocrates *Evag.* 76-77, who calls this technique *paraklēsis,* and to Dionysius of Halicarnassus *Rh.* 6.4 and 7 (H. Usener and L. Radermacher, eds., *Dionysii Halicarnasei quae extant,* 6 vols. [Leipzig: B.G. Teubner, 1904-29]).

[52] Hartlich, 300-303.

[53] Hartlich, 303-4, also cites Eudorus from Stobaeus *Flor.* 2. 48.42 (K. Wachsmuth and O. Hense, eds., *Joannis Stobaei anthologium,* 5 vols. [Berlin: Weidmann, 1894-1919]) to the same effect. Here, however, he sees two types of proptreptic: one which, as part of contemplative philosophy, demonstrates virtues and vices individually and in general; and another which is applied to moral philosophy and deals in action and is bound up with a preceptive element. The relation of exhortation to precept has been referred to above.

[54] For the protreptic and apotreptic aspect see Diogenes Laertius 7.84 (R.D. Hicks, trans., *Diogenes Laertius. Lives of Eminent Philosophers,* LCL, 2 vols. [London: W. Heinemann, 1925]); Seneca *Ep.* 89.14; Epictetus *Diss.* 3.23 and 3.16.7 (W.A. Oldfather, trans., *Epictetus. The Discourses As Reported by Arrian,* LCL [London: W. Heinemann, 1926]); the fragments of Seneca 17, 18, 21; and the discussion in Hartlich, 304 ff.

[55] Hartlich, 309, refers to Epictetus *Diss.* 3.33; 2.2.12, where the point of the protrepsis is to lead one to a perception of the battle in which we are all involved.

[56] Hartlich, *passim,* and see the discussion on example above, 33-37.

The discussion thus far has centered on the characteristics of protreptic pieces, with attention to their epideictic features. Moreover, the neat and thereby enticing distinction between works called protreptic or paraenetic by their use of exhortation or of precept is sharper in modern theory than in ancient usage. And so, when von Campenhausen refers to the "paraenetic tone" of the Pastorals, could he not just as easily have called the tone "protreptic"? Or is there something distinct in paraenetic which lies outside the area which overlaps with protreptic?

The study of Greek paranesis by Rudolf Vetschera, while it accepts the distinction on the basis of precept,[57] goes on to note that a paraenesis is broader in content than a protreptic work. The difference, therefore, is more than formal. *Protrepsis,* in both rhetoric and philosophy, hopes to lead the addressee to obtain a certain knowledge and the *aretē* included in it. *Parainesis,* on the contrary, covers many areas of life, e.g., culture, friends, enemies, good fortune, all of them under the aspect of their usefulness for obtaining a happy and a virtuous life.[58] Thus, while Vetschera sees *hypothēkai hōs chrē zēn* as a distinguishing feature of *parainesis* over against *protrepsis,* the breadth of the areas covered by *parainesis* is also a distinctive element.

He makes two other observations on paraenesis which are helpful for this study. First, the Greeks developed two types of paraenesis: one directed toward the community with rules for the conduct of life in common situations; another directed toward the ruler with precepts covering his rule and relations with his subjects.[59] Second, not much new material surfaces in paraenesis. Traditional material and language is the common fare.[60]

Taking up a suggestion of Spicq's, this survey of hortatory works now turns to the treatises of rhetors and sophists. More than the noted commentator's authority recommends this move. The surveys of epideictic, protreptic and paraenetic works referred to above span the length of Greek cultural history from Hesiod to the Byzantine period, and only a part of the evidence comes from the early Christian period. Hence, a closer scrutiny of the literary remains of that period, and of the trea-

---

[57] R. Vetschera, *Zur griechischen Paränese* (Smichow/Prague: Rohliček & Sievers, 1911-12) 7. He defines paraenesis as "literary work which by its structure and aim delineates a collection of precepts which relate unexceptionally to the practical conduct of life, indeed to promote it, as far as it can, and to lead it to virtue."

[58] Vetschera, 4-6. His evidence for Classical *parainesis* is drawn largely from Seneca *Eps.* 89 and 95 and Isocrates' first three discourses. Syrianus' commentary on Hermogenes (Syrianus, *Commentarium in librum PERI STASEON* in H. Rabe, ed., *Syriani in Hermogenem commentaria,* 2 vols. [Leipzig: B.G. Teubner, 1892-93] 2:190) supports his conclusions with respect to the range of subject matter and its "ethical" direction. The tradition thus spans a long period. The relation with *protropē* is expressed somewhat differently from the ways noted above. *symboulē* appears as a category broader than and inclusive of *protropē,* and there is no explicit mention of precepts. In fact, the concluding examples indicate that the difference lies in the content and not in the form.

[59] Vetschera, 7-8.

[60] Vetschera, 9, where he refers to Isocrates *Ad Nic.* 49-50.

tises which affected literary production at that time is in order. Which, if any, of the above-mentioned features of hortatory works fit the canons and practice of rhetorical productions of the post-Classical age?

C. *Rhetorical Exercise Handbooks*

Two related types of rhetorical exercise in the handbooks reflect the purpose and method of hortatory works singled out above. They are (1) the development of what a person did or said, for the purpose of edification, the *chreia*, and (2) a summary saying, in a statement of general application, dissuading from something or persuading toward something, or showing what is the nature of each, the *gnōmē*.[61] The function of the *chreia* is to urge young people to what is to be chosen and what is not.[62] In addition to the protreptic-apotreptic function, the development of the *chreia* and *gnōmē* employs examples and demonstration by comparison, criticizes contrary stances, and can include precept in its exhortation.[63]

Two more aspects of the development of these exercises must be borne in mind. First, it is explicitly said of the *gnōmē* and its development that they are part of a larger exposition, to which they add knowledge and assurance. By analogy, the same can be said for the kindred exercise of *chreia*.[64] Second, in the development scheme, the *martyria palaiōn* is called upon to support the proposition, the proposition itself is restated, and the rationale behind it is given.[65]

Since the hortatory epistle already emerged in the survey of the forms of hortatory discourse, the link between these rhetorical handbooks and the epistolary genre must be clarified. Two of the figures of exposition are explicitly linked with the letter form in the handbooks: *prosopopoeia*[66] and *ethopoeia*.[67] More generally, the

---

[61] Clark, 186-88.

[62] See Nicolaus *Prog.* 3:458-59 (L. von Spengel, ed., *Rhetores Graeci*, 3 vols. [Leipzig: B.G. Teubner, 1853]).

[63] Nicolaus, 3:462 (Spengel); Aphthonius *Prog.* 2:22 (Spengel). The development of the *gnōmē* follows that of the *chreia*, the difference between the two being located in the presence (in the *chreia*) or the absence (in the *gnōmē*) of a character responsible for the statement being developed. See the discussion of this distinction in Nicolaus, 3:463-64 (Spengel); Theon *Prog.* 2:96-97 (Spengel); Aphthonius 2:25-26 (Spengel); and the Hermogenes *Prog.* 2:5-7 (Spengel). The *apomnēmoneuma* is a fuller elaboration of whas the *chreia* introduces only briefly, as Nicolaus 3:464 (Spengel) notes. For an outline of the hortatory devices suggested in the exercise for the development of the chria see below 98 and the discussion on 97-98. For the devices and the pattern of development in the Pastorals see 198-208; in Seneca see 99; in Plutarch see 76; in the Socratics see 138-43.

[64] Nicolaus 3:464 (Spengel).

[65] Nicolaus 3:462 (Spengel) and Aphthonius 2:22 (Spengel).

[66] Theon 2:115 (Spengel) notes that the epistolary form along with the panegyric and protreptic are appropriate for this exercise.

[67] Nicolaus 3:490 (Spengel) finds it an important exercise for epistolary style where the character of the sender and the addressees must be taken into account.

letter has been characterized as half a dialogue, and therefore can be expected to employ the same *genus dicendi* as appears in the dialogue.[68]

This simple solution, however, dilutes the density of the issue. Some rhetorically accomplished writers of epistles destined for the public eye held that the letter should be free of rhetorical elaboration; but this view was neither unanimously held nor rigidly adhered to.[69] Quite clearly, in the letters which aim at a wide audience, the relation between rhetorical theory and its use in letter writing is met on a level above that of the simple distinction between public and private letters. But the extant epistolary handbooks, which collect and explain letter types, including hortatory and prescriptive letters, seem to have been meant neither for the private letter writer nor for the literateurs of the day but rather for professional letter writers. And it is reasonable to postulate a link between the letter writers and rhetorical theory through the teachers who passed on the distinction and methods among the various letter forms.[70] Unfortunately, little remains of the manuals which initiated students into various forms and styles of letters.

While the information from the handbooks is thin, a look at some of the surviving public letters provide useful data about the use of rhetorical figures in this sort of letter. The type of letter which suggests itself as a starting point is that of

---

[68] Demetrius *Eloc.* 223; and see Weichert's introduction to his edition of Demetrius and Libanius, xii, where he refers to Synesius *Ep.* 138, p. 724 (Hercher) and Philostratus *VA* 4.25.

[69] While Seneca in *Ep.* 75 presumes that a letter should be as spontaneous and free from artifice as a heart-to-heart conversation, Demetrius, 224, allows a degree of elaboration and Weichert notes on xv that after Demetrius a good deal of art found its way into the letter, with the sanction of the rhetors.

[70] H. Rabe, "Aus Rhetoren-Handschriften," *RhM* n.F. 64 (1909) 289, finds that the rhetors concentrated on what would affect larger circles. So, the private letter intended for one addressee would receive little attention, while one aimed at a larger circle would be reinforced by the full rhetorical armament, just like an artful speech. But the latter was not the ordinary end of exercising students for what they would need in letter writing. Just how much exercise in letter writing took place in the grammar and rhetorical schools is unclear and, as noted above, the progymnasmata give scant and, by and large, oblique evidence, with style more of a concern in them than form. Rabe, 289-90 and A.J. Malherbe, "Ancient Epistolary Theorists," *Ohio Journal of Religious Studies* 5 (1977) 12-15, both suspect that grammatical handbooks were not used in the actual teaching of letter writing for the ordinary needs of the grammar school pupil. The basic instruction in letter writing already taken for granted in these handbooks would presumably have been mastered "early in secondary education," Malherbe, 12-13. The handbooks would more likely have been used to train professional letter writers, who were to become familiar with both the official and rhetorical styles, most likely under the schooling of rhetors (Malherbe, 14 with particular reference to Philostratus *De ep.* 12.257.29-258.28 [Kayser]). The literary creations, like those of Cicero, the younger Pliny and Seneca, are also at the extreme end of the class of public letters which seek a wide audience for their message, be it moral exhortation, official prescriptions, or what have you.

precept or command. The reason for this is the likelihood of resonance here with the Pastorals, especially in their characterization of their message as *parangelia*.[71] This analysis is undertaken in chapter V.

C. *Concluding Observations*

The analysis in this chapter has disclosed the details of the theoretical treatments of the device of example and its practical applications. Its use in a school setting revealed both its technical and ethical aspects. The appeal to example for hortatory purposes was to have a long tradition in Greco-Roman literature. The focus on the characteristics of paraenetic works, in league with the elaboration of the categories from example theory, lays the groundwork for the analysis of literary parallels to the Pastorals with which the next chapters are concerned.

The survey of rhetorical handbooks served two purposes. First, it provided a link between the letter form and both the paraenetic enterprise and the device of example as one of its tools. Second, it introduced the patterns of the developed *chreia* (chria) and *gnōmē* (gnome) which employ example in a cluster of other devices for hortatory ends. This pattern and cluster, already found in the first chapter's analysis of the hortatory character of the Pastoral, will reappear in the parallel literature examined below.

The study will now take up three paraenetic discourses of Isocrates to see how example functions in them. The theoretical survey of this chapter will thus find its practical counterpart. Mereover, the particulars of form and content will prove useful in the re-examination of the Pastoral Epistles in the final chapter.

---

[71] 1 Tim 1:3, 5. *LSJ* 1306 and Stephanus' *Thesaurus* 221-24 refer the word to various types of precept or admonition, primarily of the military sort, but civil and royal as well.

CHAPTER IV

The Use of Example in the Kingship Literature of Isocrates, Plutarch and Dio Chrysostom

I. Example in Isocrates' Discourses

Isocrates' discourses represent a significant turning point in the development of the paraenetic tradition in that they represent the earliest attempts to express in prose what was previously contained in poetic works like those of Hesiod, the Greek epigrammists, and Iambic writers like Phoenix of Colophon.[1] The resemblances noted between the first three Isocratean discourses and the Pastorals will establish and clarify the latter's paraenetic nature and will help the evaluation of specific technical devices summoned in support of the exhortation.[2]

A. *The Discourse* Nicocles

1. Character and Genre

The discourse *Nicocles* stands apart from the discourses *Ad Demonicum* and *Ad Nicoclem* in structure and style. J. Frey[3] calls attention to the unique inclu-

---

[1] R. Vetschera, *Zur griechischen Paränese* (Smichow/Prague: Rohliček & Sievers, 1911-12) 12-13; and see W. Schmid and O. Stählin, *Geschichte der griechischen Literatur* (Munich: C.H. Beck [Oskar Beck], 1912) 1:572-77, where Isocrates' influence through the Hellenic period and in the later Atticist revival is documented. Moreover, Schmid-Stählin also points out that the pseudonymous discourse *Ad Demonicum,* along with the Isocratean discourses *Ad Nicoclem* and, less so, *Niclocles,* marked the first attempt to transfer the old poetic *hypothēkai* in elegiac form into a prose collection of sayings. P. Wendland, "Die Rede an Demonikos," *Anaximenes von Lampsakos: Studien zur ältesten Geschichte der Rhetorik* (Berlin: Weidmann, 1905) 82-83, makes the same observation. He summarizes, 90 ff., the arguments for the pseudonymity of the discourse *Ad Demonicum.*

[2] G. Norlin and L. van Hook, trans., *Isocrates,* LCL, 3 vols. (London: W. Heinemann, 1928-45); E. Drerup, *Isocratis Opera* (Leipzig: Dieterich [Theodor Weicher]; 1906. For a description of commonly used devices in Greco-Roman exhortation see chapter 2 and J. Geffcken, *Kynika und Verwandtes* (Heidelberg: Carl Winters, 1909) 1-44; G.A. Gerhard, *Phoinix von Kolophon* (Leipzig/Berlin: B.G. Teubner, 1909) 12 ff.; and A. Dihle, *Die Goldene Regel: Eine Einführung in die Geschichte der antiken und frühchristlichen Vulgärethik* (Göttingen: Vandenhoeck & Ruprecht, 1962) 90-91.

[3] J. Frey, *Studien zur dritten Rede des Isokrates* (Freiburg i.d.S.: Paulus, 1946) 79 and

sion in the *Nicocles* of a *bebaiōsis*-section (10-47) between the introduction (1-9) and the paraenetic section (48-62). The purpose of this section is to confirm the superiority of the monarchical form of government and the legitimacy of Nicocles' own ruling position. At the same time, this will give authoritative backing to his prescriptions. Clear subdivisions mark this and the other parts of the discourse: that is another stylistic features largely lacking in the other two discourses. The conclusion is also more concise than it is in the other discourses.[4] But the significance of the discourse for this study lies not in its differences from its companion discourses but in the use of example in an exhortation to officials on the proper conduct of their office which it shares with the other discourses. The fact that Isocrates writes this discourse in the name of Nicocles, king of the Cyprians, will also be shown to be appropriate to this study of the Pastorals.

As to the form of the work, it seems to be a "political brochure" by Isocrates on political questions.[5] As such, the paraenetic section and a good part of the *bebaiōsis* are free of any specific ties to the reign of Nicocles. In fact, in 46-47 the thought moves from Nicocles' commendation of his own proven virtue, to the recommendation of virtue generally, when it is based on conviction as well as on natural inclination, to the introduction to the prescriptive section, whereby the exercise of this virtue in the political arena is called for. The prescriptions are thereby set in a context which ostensibly aims at obedience to the Cyprian king but actually has to do with conduct in general, or at least with the virtues of good citizenship.[6]

Most striking to the reader of the *Nicocles* in the *gnomic* character of the paraenetic statements. While most of the individual commands can be combined

---

82-85. The *bebaiōsis*-section was a standard division in the rhetorical theory of the handbooks and *progymnasmata*. Cf. Anaximenes *technē rētorikē* 2.85.5; 2.74.11 (L. von Spengel, ed., *Rhetores Graeci*, 3 vols. [Leipzig: B.G. Teubner, 1853]).

[4] Frey, 79-80, 85.

[5] Frey, 88-90. S. Cecchi, *La Paideia ateniese dalle orazioni di Isocrate* (Turin: Loescher, 1961) 50, speaks to the same effect when he asserts that it is a "paedagogical instrument" directed to one person but destined for the eyes of everyone. R.C. Jebb, *The Attic Orators from Anthiphon to Isaeus*, 2 vols. (London: Macmillan & Co., 1893) 2:78, puts *Nicocles* in the category of hortatory letters or essays, though later, 80 and 86, he refers to it as a hortatory discourse. At *Nic.* 11, Isocrates has Nicocles refer to his effort to *dialechthēnai pros hymas*, which would make the speech, *logos*, a dialogue or conversation.

[6] In defending the enterprise of philosophic study, 1-10, i.e., the cultivation of a reverent and virtuous life through discourse, he claims as an overall objective *hopōs an hōs meta pleistōn agathōn ton bion diagōmen*, 2. Even when he narrows down the objective of this discourse, he proposes to show *ha dei poiein tous archomenous*, 11, as a complement to Isocrates' treatment on *hōs chrē tyrannein* in *Ad Nicoclem*. Moreover, despite the fact that Nicocles here is made to defer to Isocrates for instructions to the ruler, the *bebaiōsis*-section actually handles both the theoretical question of the best form of government and the practical one of how a king rules and his subjects obey.

under topical headings,[7] there is no structural order in the section as a whole.[8] And even where particular precepts form a topical unit, each one stands as a statement independent of the others, with its own justification, explanation or conditions. There is no effort to construct an argument with several related statements.

2. Hortatory Features

The hortatory devices employed in the discourse to promote good citizenship are more complex than what might have been indicated by its characterization above as a gnomic paraenesis. The work of exhortation is undertaken throughout the discourse and is not restricted to the paraenetic section proper. Evidence of this is the widespread use of the language of moral instruction and exhortation.[9] Intelligent conviction as a supplement to the natural inclination toward virtue can alone claim to be a sure basis for the virtuous life, 46-47, and this explains the strong hortatory and pedagogical emphasis in the discourse.

Beyond the gnomic imperatives and hortatory vocabulary, other features attract the attention of the audience. First, *chrē*[10] and *dei*[11] supplement the imperatives in the second plural and third singular. Second, whatever form they take, the prescriptions are either protreptic or apotreptic. Often both types of com-

---

[7] Attention to duty, 48-49; riches, 50; secrecy, 51-54; preservation and security, 55-56; children, 57-58; faith and conscience, 58-59; royal will and golden rule, 60-62.

[8] Frey, 75.

[9] *parainein* 10,57; *protrepein* 12,43,57; *parakalein* 12,43; *symbouleuein* 12, 13, 47; *pros-/diatattein* 7, 13, 47, 51, 56; *nomothetein* 7; *exelenchein* 7, 53; *katagorein* 2, 41, 61; *katagignōskein* 13; *dia/memphesthai* 1, 11; *loidorein* 4; *psegein* 1, 4; *enkōmiazein* 7; *dokimazein* 7, 44; *mnēmoneuein* 12; *hypo/epi/en/proepi/proapo/deiknynai* 12, 13, 39, 57, 61; *dēloun* 6, 11, 36; *didaskein* 19, 57; *dialegesthai* 11; *paideuein* 7, 9, 57; *manthanein* 57; *philosophein* 1, 9; *zēloun* 59; *mimeisthai* 61.

Other words exude the hortatory atmosphere, such as *epithymein, epithymia* 34, 39, 55; *aretē* 2, 19, 30, 39, 43, 47, 57; *epitēdeuein, epitēdeuma* 2, 10, 43, 54; *examartanein* 2, 3, 9, 40, 45, 53, 54; *askein, agōnizesthai* 8; *phainesthai* 31, 36, 45; *ōphelein, sympherein* 4, 10, 15, 30, 50, 59; (and see W. Steidle, "Redekunst und Bildung bei Isokrates," *Hermes* 8 [1952] 268); *peithein* 6, 8, 11, 13, 57; *pistē, pistos* 8, 57, 58, 64; *prepein* 10 (and see H. Wersdörfer, *Die PHILOSOPHIA des Isokrates im Spiegel ihrer Terminologie* [Leipzig: Otto Harrassowitz, 1940] 18 ff.); *prosēkon* 11, 30; *axiousthai* 14, 29; *axia* 14, 29; *katagignōskein* 45; *epainein* 1, 43, 46, 61; *martys* 46; *oligōrein, kataphronein, spoudazein* 48; *ethizein* 57; *eudokimein* 43; *doxa* 44, 50; *timē* 44, 49; *ergon* 44, 61; *prattein, praxis* 45, 48, 52, 57, 61, 64; *sōphrosynē* 36, 47 and *passim*.

Frey, discussing similar motifs in *Ad Nicoclem*, finds them to be customary in the old rhetorical works, as is substantiated by Aristotle's *Rh.* 1.5.

[10] 11, 26, 32, 36, 41, 52.

[11] 4, 6, 10, 13, 15, 17, 34, 45, 48, 50, 51.

mand balance each other in the same sentence.[12] Third, there is an ironic exclamation of astonishment at 3, *thaumazō,* over the opponents' views. Fourth, Isocrates summons acknowledgment based on his audience's prior knowledge at 28 (*tis gar ouk eiden*) and at 29 (*pantas an homologēsai*),[13] and on their past witness at 46 (*hymeis d'autoi moi martyres este*). He also asserts the goodness they already possess at 55, and he encourages the audience on the basis of their capability to accomplish all that he wants from them at 64. Fifth, a peristasis catalogue of sorts provides the basis for the resume of Nicocles' accomplishments through *dikaiosynē* in 31 ff. Sixth, the *reductio ad absurdum* at the start of 3, the paradoxical remarks on wealth at 50, the reversal in the command to emulate the highly favored at 60, and the hyperbole at 58 on the *athliōtatous* and *dystychestatous* (and see 5, 9), all partake of the arresting quality of hortatory discourse.

Among those features considered above under the rubric of hortatory techniques, Isocrates uses corroboration of the teaching on the best form of government in his appeal to the tradition about the gods and to common opinion at 26. Moreover, according to 47, the whole expository part of the discourse is a confirmation of the authority behind the particular prescriptions. His own position' of honor is confirmed both by his ancestors and by his own virtues at 29-30. Second, he warns of dire consequences resulting from disobedience (48, 52, 53, 55, 57, and 58). Third, his reasons for the commands and the goal toward which they aim complete the prescriptions (48, 49, 50, 51, 52, 53, 54, 55, 56, 58, 59, 60). The function of the explicit reason or purpose is frequently assumed by a participial phrase, often one expressing a presumption of the audience's awareness of the ramifications of the command (e.g. 48, 50, 52, 57). The purpose of the whole discourse is laid out at 11, i.e., a clear statement of policy to forestall claims of ignorance and to justify criticism for transgressions. Fourth, contrast plays a role in the argument for the very *raison d'être* of this type of discourse, both in the elaboration of its merits at 5-6 and in the face-off between the detractors and Isocrates himself at 10 (*Egō de*). It also functions in the sections where Nicocles uses the failings of other rulers to commend himself for his just rule, 31 ff., and for his moderation, 37 ff.[14] The place of contrast in the sections ancillary to the exhortation is thus secure, but the technique is at work in almost every prescription in the paraenetic section as well. There it functions with the gnomic units to bring out the two faces of a command, its rationale, or its consequences. Antithesis also makes the presentation of the examples in this discourse particularly compelling.

---

[12] E.g., *mē katasiōpate ... all'exelenchete* 53; *diaphylattein* 40, 55, 62; *dia/emmenein* 43, 47, 56, 62; *mē phthoneite ... all'hamillasthe* 60.

[13] In addition to these instances, the appeal to the audience's knowledge is a common feature in the paraenetic section proper, e.g. 48, 50, 52, 55, 62.

[14] The use of contrast appears in the discussions on governmental systems, 14-16, and objectives, 17-21; on citizens 22-23; on war and peace, 24-25.

3. Example in General

Since the device of example warrants special consideration as the central concern of this study, its use in the *Nicocles* will now be examined in detail.[15] The device furnishes proof in the exposition of monarchy as the best form of government at 23-26. Here Isocrates uses many types of examples: those from the past and present, named individuals, entire city-states and empires, the gods, historical incidents, and observations of typical circumstances and actions.

Another function of example appears in the figure of typical critics of philosophical education described at the start of the discourse, 1-9. Isocrates designates them not by name but by the indefinite pronoun *tines* and depicts their activity as *blasphēmein*, like those *examartanontes* against the gods. From the declared contrast at 10 ff., it is clear that they serve as straw-men to set off Nicocles' perception of the benefits of educational discourse. The refutation of their unreasonable views is at the same time a confirmation of the work of the discourse which follows, a recognition of Nicocles' wisdom, and a stimulus to the audience to obey.[16] Actually, a double contrast is at work here. Those who typically err (*examartanontōn*) in action and use eloquence for deceptive (*en tois logois exapatōntōn*) and unjust (*mē dikaiōs chrōmenōn autois*) ends, 2, deserve the criticism even of the undiscriminating opponents of eloquence and serve to place Isocrates' use of rhetoric in an even better light.[17] Yet another use to which

---

[15] See A. Burk, *Die Pädagogik des Isokrates als Grundlegung des humanistischen Bildungsideals im Vergleich mit den zeitgenössischen und den modernen Theorien dargestellt* (Würzburg: E. Drerup, 1923) 105-7, and O. Schneider, *Isocrates. Ausgewählte Reden* (Leipzig: B.G. Teubner, 1874) 1:8, for comment on Isocrates' use of example. See also K.T. Jost, *Das Beispiel und Vorbild der Vorfahren bei den attischen Rednern und Geschichtschreibern bis Demosthenes* (Paderborn: F. Schöningh, 1936) 119-60.

[16] Frey, 82-83, is skeptical that particular literary writers stand behind the *tines*. In this regard, he contrasts this paraenesis to the more clearly polemic works, e.g. *Helen, Busiris*. He goes on to speculate about a possible political intent veiled behind the indefinite pronoun, i.e., a semitic opposition group on Cyprus. Neither suggestion is compelling enough to make the reader see more here than a hortatory device.

Actually the contrast with certain unnamed people (*tines*) who have reprehensible aims and faulty methods is a standard feature in the other two discourses to be surveyed below and, indeed, in moral philosophers in general.

Similar criticism of his critics appears at Isocrates' *Ep.* 9.15 where some (*tines*) who have no learning (*paideia*) undertake instruction (*paideuein*). They make a pretense to intellectual interest (*prospoioumenoi philosophein*) but get lost in pettiness (*epi mikrois*) and envy (*phthonountes*) counsellors on important matters. They criticize (*psegein*) Isocrates' methods but imitate (*mimeisthai*) them nonetheless and are rightly condemned for cowardice (*anandria*) and meanness of spirit (*mikropsychia*), for weakness (*astheneia*) and laziness (*ra₁thumia*).

[17] Steidle, 259, refers to Isocrates' discourse *Adversus Sophistas* where his polemical confrontation with his rival sophists by contrasting his skill with their failings serves as publicity

example is put in this discourse emerges from the observation at 37 that the multitude apes their king's practices and from the implication in Nicocles' remark at 35 that his conduct sets a standard for others. Thus, the discourse exploits Nicocles' example to provide backing and content for some of its prescriptions. Here the example sets a standard or prototype to be imitated.

4. Isocrates' Views on the Use of Example to Urge Imitation

Before taking up the example of Nicocles and its function in the exhortation, it will be helpful to see what Isocrates says about the use of example as a pattern for imitation. *Evag.* 73 ff. offers a resume of the salient features of Isocrates' understanding of the use of exemplary figures. First of all, example serves explicitly hortatory ends (*paraklēsis, protrepein* 76; *parakeleuein* 79; *paroxynein* 80) by presenting a character sketch (*logoi* 74; *athroisas tas aretas ...tōi logōi kosmēsas* 76) of the standard of attitude and conduct (*eikōn tōn praxeōn kai tās dianoias* 73; *hoi tropoi, hē dianoia* 75) which should be imitated (*mimeisthai* 75; *hina zēlountes ... tōn autōn ... epitēdeumatōn epithymōsin* 77). While the example demonstrates the type of character and actions to be pursued, the addressee is urged in the end to unsurpassed excellence in relation to his contemporaries (*hopōs kai legein kai prattein mēdenos hētton dynēsei tōn Hellēnōn* 77 and cf. 81), worthy of his father's example and his other ancestors (*hopōs axios esei kai tou patros kai tōn allōn progonōn* 80) but becoming the person he himself should (*tacheōs genēsei toioutos hoion se prosēkei* 81).[18]

Second, Isocrates prefers exemplars who are close to the family rather than strangers (*ouk allotriois paradeigmasi chrōmenos all'oikeiois* 77).

Third, that which shows the exemplar's spirit e.g., *erga* and *gnōmē* 74) is prized by honorable and enlightened people (*kaloi k'agathoi, eu phronountes* 74) in contrast to those things (like *to kallos* 74 or *lian chairein* 78) which others seek.

Fourth, a contrast also distinguishes the reaction to the example. Slothful inaction (*hoi raithymein hairoumenoi* 75) and inattention (*elleipein* 80) are juxtaposed with the contemplation and study (*theōrein* and *syndiatribein* 76), careful attention (*prosechein ton noun* 77), philosophical labor (*philosophein kai ponein* 78), eager striving (*oregesthai* 80), desire (*epithymein* 80), careful attention (*epimeleisthai* 80), exercise (*askein* 80), and perseverance (*emmenein* 81) which are urged.

---

for his own work and as a means to attract students. This rivalry surfaces here in the *Nicocles* and at *Ad Nic.* 51, but for a hortatory purpose.

[18] Even when imitation looks to contemporary models, it is their culture or philosophical study, including moral exercise, which ought to be replicated, with adjustments in specific activities according to each one's situation, 78. In *Philip* 113-14, Isocrates actually states that he does not expect imitation of all the model's exploits, but rather of the qualities of his spirit, like philanthropy, good will, and, generally, intentions. See also *Panath.* 227-28.

Fifth, the striving expected in this labor of imitation finds expression in the language of athletic contests (*gymnikoi agōnes* and *hoi dromeis* 79).

Sixth, in this connection the exhortation centers on striving and advancement and not settling into final victory or defeat (*hoi peri tēs nikēs hamillōmenoi* 79; *philosophein kai ponein epicheirein* 78; *hōsper en tōi paronti kai ton loipon chronon epimeleisthai kai tēn psychēn askein* 80; *an ... emmenēs ... tacheōs genēsei* 81).

Seventh, the teacher's criticism, then, is not condemnatory or empty abuse (*mē nomize me katagignōskein, hōs nyn ameleis* 78) but a spur to greater achievement (*pollakis soi diakeleuomai peri tōn autōn* 78) with a recognition of what has already been achieved.

Eighth, the objects of the exhortation are a young ruler and his successors (76-77, 81).

Ninth, the older and experienced (*hysterizō gar tēs akmēs tēs emautou* 73) teacher characterizes himself as a friend (*emon men oun ergon kai tōn allōn philōn* 80), but Isocrates does not present himself as a model here, as he does in *Ep.* 8.10.[19] In his teaching function he provides the example to be followed as well as correlative counsel (*symbouleuein* 77) and admonition (*diakeleuomai* 78), some of which come to expression in this section (e.g. *soi de prosēkei; hōs hapasi men prosēkei ... malista d'hymin; chrē de* 80).

Tenth, the addressee can himself expect to become a model of virtue as a result of his striving and to make others abandon excessive pleasures and desire and pursue the same path of instruction (*pollous tōn basileōn poiēseis zēlōsantas tēn sēn paideusin toutōn tōn diatribōn epithymein, aphemenous eph' hois nyn lian chairousin* 78). With this overview of Isocrates' ideas on the use of example for an exhortation in virtue, the use of that device in *Nicocles* and the other Isocratean discourses associated in theme will be better appreciated.

5. The Example of Nicocles

At 37-38 Nicocles explains the double aim of his virtuous conduct: forestalling criticism, *hama men emauton hōs porrōtatō poiēsai tōn toioutōn hypopsiōn;*[20] and setting an example, *hama de paradeigma katastēsai ton tropon ton emautou tois allois politais.* The second aim is nuanced by the contrast to the unreasonable rulers who demand *tous men allous kosmiōs zēn* while they show themselves *mē sōphronesterous tōn archomenōn.* The ruler is not just a natural example for his subjects (*hoti philei to plēthos en toutois tois epitēdeumasi ton bion diagein, en hois*

---

[19] For the teacher Isocrates as model in a rhetorical setting, see *Adv. sophist.* 17-18 and *Panath.* 16-17.

[20] Steidle, 270, elaborates on why Isocrates lays importance on reputation before fellow citizens as well as on the relation between conduct and theory and between inner conviction and traditional content in speech making.

an tous archontas tous autōn horōsi diatribontas); he must show that his practices corroborate his prescriptions, as Nicocles aims to do.[21]

In addition to this explicit reference to the example deliberately established by his own virtue, Nicocles, at 27-47, speaks of his actions in language which denotes their demonstrative nature, e.g., *katidoite* 31; *dēlōsai, phanēsomai* 35; *phanēsomai* 36; *horōsi* 37; *epideixai* 39; *phanēsomai, emauton pareschon, heuroimen* 45; *all'hōs ouk an pisteutheis ek tōn legomenōn; hymeis d'autoi moi martyres este pantōn tōn eirēmenōn* 46. In the same vein, he insists that his virtue be tested as to its operation, and that in circumstances which most militate against it, 44-45. The demonstration he engages in the discourse sets Nicocles apart not only from the common crowd but even from those who claim to be virtuous in most respects, 39-40.

Just as in the last-mentioned paragraphs of the discourse, Nicocles' example becomes more striking throughout the section in contrast to unnamed negative examples. At 31-32 his principled (*oude ... diephtharēn*) actions in adversity (*hosiōs kai kalōs epemelēthēn hōste mēden elleipein*) contrast with those of other rulers (*heteroi*) who act out of self-interest and against their nature. His *praotēs* contrasts at 32-33 with repressive measures; and his appeasement (*katepraüna*) won over the hostile Cypriots and the Persian king, 33-34. His restraint contrasts with others' (*heteroi*) grasping manupulation of their power (*tōn allotriōn epithymein; pleonektein zētousin* 34-35). Unlike the many (*polloi*) rulers who fell because of their wantonness (hybris), Nicocles fled (*ephygon*) the very occasion of offense, 36. While those (*ekeinoi*) kings who are just are accorded some license in personal pleasures (*hēdonai*), Nicocles kept above even the suspicion of such personal indulgence, 37. In contrast both to rulers whose own virtue falls below the level they demand from their subjects (*mē sōphronesteroi tōn archomenōn*) and to those of the public who are almost perfectly self-controlled (*enkrateis*) and who pride themselves on virtue (*hoi ep'aretēi mega phronountes*), except for certain passions (*epithymiai*), Nicocles shows his control (*karterein* 38-39). He cherishes fidelity in marriage and opposes those who are dishonest in this relationship, thereby provoking palace factions and squabbles, 40-41.

These examples, positive and negative, are not brought forth simply to flesh out an encomium of Nicocles, although his demonstrated virtue is indeed worthy of the highest praise (*epainos* 43 and cf. 46) and wins him good repute (*doxa* 44 and cf. 29-30).[22] Rather, they are hortatory. This is clear in his explanation at 37-38 where setting an example is one of the aims of the discourse. The exhortation by example looks in two directions: explicitly toward the subjects who imitate their king and implicitly toward the kings themselves (*epeita kai prosēkein hēgēsamēn tosoutōi tous basileis beltious einai tōn idiōtōn hosōi per kai tas timas meizous autōn*

---

[21] Burk, 150, quotes *Evag.* 44 in his discussion on pedagogical technique and the relation of teacher to student, authority and frankness, 148 ff.

[22] He urges the pursuit of a good name (*chrēstoi dokein* 50) on his addressee and declares popular good will to be a valuable bequest to the rulers' children, 57-58.

echousi). The latter coincides with the contrast frequently drawn to the "other rulers" who act badly. This suggests that Nicocles is not just justifying his claims to the throne, as he asserts, but is also setting an example for other rulers as well.

Another statement which educes a hortatory application from the example concludes 35, where Nicocles challenges other virtuous people to match his standard of conduct (*kaitoi chrē tous mega phronountas epi dikaiosynēi kai prospoioumenous chrēmatōn einai kreittous toiautas hyperbolas echein eipein peri autōn*). Here again, he is not speaking to everyone but to a certain elite among the citizenry.

At 46-47 Nicocles similarly moves from his own example to all those who deserve praise for their acquisition of virtue by reason (*logismos*) and principle (*gnōmē*). These remain firm in that state (*en tautēi tēi taxei diamenousin*) despite life's vicissitudes. Thus, others are to replicate Nicocles' experience, wherein he decided on (*hypelabon* 43; *dianoētheis proeilomēn* 44), achieved (*ēskēsa tēn sōphrosynēn ktl.* 64), and held on to virtue in all circumstances (*en pasi tois kairois* 45).

The establishment of the example receives assistance from the list of virtues and vices. At 43-44 Nicocles selects from among the list of recognized virtues and turns from those which even the base possess (i.e., *andria, deinotēs*) to those acquired only by the good and noble (*dikaiosynē, sōphrosynē, enkrateia*).

6. The Example of Nicocles and the Prescriptions

Prescriptions also work together with Nicocles' example to express the hortatory message. At 47 Nicocles reiterates the intention of the discourse, declared first at 11, to make clear what he counsels and commands his subjects to do. While the addressees thus remain anonymous and seem to include all the subjects (*tous archomenous*), there are indications that he has a more restricted group in mind. And this also account for the commands he lays down and their relation to the royal model.

Although he declares it his intention to teach *ha dei poiein tous archomenous,* his audience does not seem to be the public at large, for they have appointed tasks, 48 and 56; some even oversee (*epistatountes*) royal affairs, 49; they have the ability to acquire wealth and reputation, 49-50; they are heads of households, 51; they engage in public life, 52; perhaps as councillors (*bouleusesthe*),[23] 51; their concerted power can pose a threat to the king and to the polity, 54-55; their example helps educate the next generation in submission to and exercise of authority, 57; they enjoy royal privileges, 57; they have the ability to rise in service and honor, 60; they rule others, 62. In short, the *Nicocles* addresses the class of officials and exhorts them to faithful and virtuous service. The king's example makes sense here as a paradigm for subordinate officials of the true exercise of authority, over against the negative examples. While these are not just young officials, they are to educate their children and

---

[23] Burk, 91, treats the civic nature of the virtue *euboulia*.

accustom them (*ethizein*) to the instruction (*paideusis*) in the discourse. And so, the young are ultimately the object of the teaching.

Since Nicocles' addressees are people who can expect to hold office, he prescribes attitudes and conduct which correspond to the way he exercises his own power. The prescriptions have to do with the virtues attendant on the exercise of official functions rather than with the specific duties themselves. Moreover, Nicocles practices what he prescribes and thereby presents a living model of his teaching, 37. He mentions both obedience to prescriptions (*diaphylattontes tous nomous*) and abiding by his example (*emmenontes tois ēthesi*) as among the aspects of regard required for his royal authority, 56.

The correspondence between example and prescription is visible throughout the discourse. With the call at 48 to the diligent and just (*epimelōs kai dikaiōs*) execution of assigned tasks compare 31 (*dikaiosynē* and see 31-35 generally and also 62-63; and *epimeleia*) and 32 (*epimeleisthai*); with the caution against taking others' property at 49 compare his own action at 32 and 34; with the stress on aiming for virtuous reputation at 50 (*hoi megistas ep'aretē$_i$ doxas echontes*) compare 29-30 (*hē autē doxa*) and 44 (*epi tais doxais*); with the call to temperate (*sōphronesteron*) decisions at 51 compare 36-47 on his *sōphrosynē;* with the caution not to invite slander (*diaballein*) by underhanded actions or suspicion (*hypopsia*) by questionable conduct at 54 compare 37 (*hōs porrōtatō ... tōn ... hypopsiōn*); with the desire to preserve ordered relationships in the family and in the public domain at 55 compare 40-41; with the insistence on a stable code of conduct at 56 (*emmenontes*) compare 44-45; with the concern for children at 57 compare 42. When Nicocles insists that his audience emulate (*zēloun*) the virtuous at 59, vie with (*hamillasthai; peirasthai ... exisousthai*) those honored for their service at 60, and imitate (*mimeisthai*) good people at 62, he expects no more of them than what he himself claims to have accomplished (see 39, *emellon ... dioisein* and 43-44, *proechein*). He calls on the audience to show their good will in deeds (*erga*) rather than in words (*logoi*) at 61, recalling 46 where he alludes to the lacks of persuasiveness of his words (*ta legomena*) in contrast to the deeds he just went through in the demonstration at 31-45. He caution the audience not to do what they condemn in others, 61, and the antithetical examples show that he himself never did what he finds inadequate in others. According to the assertion at 37, the example rests not just in Nicocles' striving in the way expected of his subjects, but also in the preeminent virtuous character (*ho tropos ho emautou*) which he has attained, with particular focus on its justice and temperance (see 43-47). To this exhortation by example, he adds the prescriptive section, 48 ff., which corresponds to it.

His negative examples also find an echo in the prescriptions which detail the attitudes and conduct to be avoided (compare 32 and 34 with 49 on taking others' property and 50 on seeking riches; 40 with 54 on provoking factions; 38 and 61 on not practicing what you prescribe). The antithetical expression of both the examples and the prescriptions underline the complementarity of both features in the exhortation. Just as the discourse proposes norms about what to do and what to avoid, it provides examples of the acceptable and unacceptable conduct and character.

At 57 he demands that his addressees also set an example.[24] This is to accompany their precepts as they exhort young people (*protrepein*) according to Nicocles' insistence. Obviously, he offers an example of this method of instruction by his own teaching through precept and example in the discourse itself.

7. The Aim of the Exhortation to Virtue

The discourse looks to the cultivation and exercise of virtue (*askein* and *epitēdeuein* 2; *emmenein tois epitēdeumasin toutois* 43; *askein* 44; *speudein ... chrēstoi dokein* 50) rather than the satisfied possession of virtue. One facet of this active orientation is the conviction that virtue is more profitable than vice (*mē tēn kakian oiesthe dynasthai men pleiō tēs aretēs ōphelein* 59 and cf. 4) and that benefit accrues both to the one who possesses virtue and, by his relations, to the life of men generally (*ou gar monon hēmas to kath'hautas ōphelousin, alla ... polla ton bion ton tōn anthrōpōn* 30). And so, Nicocles urges his addressees to be useful to others (*chrēstoi* 50 and cf. 51) as he himself was (*eu pepoiēkōs* 35). Likewise, he condemns vice and the misuse of noble powers as the cause of evil (*kakōn aitia* 30 and cf. 3-4).

One aspect of the wrongdoing and deception is the misguided pursuit of riches, 33-34, despite claims to the contrary, 35. Riches are a neutral resource, to be used at the proper time and with virtue, 50. Another misguided belief of the wrongdoers is that their misdeeds can be kept secret, although Nicocles is sure that they will suffer the evil they inflict while the innocent will be duly rewarded, 51-53.

While Nicocles sets out to outline his policy to insure proper obedience, 11 and 14, evil people do wrong themselves and deceive others (*tois logois exapatōntes* 2). By his own statement at 10, Nicocles prefers discourses which give directions on private and official conduct (*hoi peri tōn epitēdeumatōn kai tōn politeiōn parainountes*) and which teach the mutual responsibilities of rulers and subjects (*hosoi didaskousi tous te dynasteuontas hōs dei ... kai tous idiōtas hōs chrē ktl.*). Though a monarch himself, he takes on the teaching role, claiming to be a friend as well, 54 (and cf. 58 on royal *eunoia* as a bequest for his subordinates' children and the ruinous consequences for those *apistoi* to their friends). He teaches his subjects their duties (*ha dei poiein tous archomenous* 11). As teacher, his own example has been shown to feature prominently in the instruction. One aspect of the example not mentioned above is that it keeps the instructor's presence before the mind of the addressee (*ean kai to sōma mē parēi, tēn dianoian tēn emēn oiesthō tois gignomenois parestanai* 51) by making his principles and conduct a part of their moral deliberations 52. This fidelity to the monarch-teacher-friend who trusts them is part of the good conscience that leads to a happy life, 58-59.

---

[24] Other people besides Nicocles already set examples to be imitated, see 59, 60, 62.

The discourse *Nicocles* is just one of a trilogy of related discourses. While it professes to outline what the monarch expects from the subjects, the other two outline the duties of the ruler. All three actually speak to the official class generally and exhort them to virtues appropriate to their office. The *Nicocles'* relation to the other two will now be explored.

B. *The Discourses* Ad Nicoclem *and* Ad Demonicum *as Related to the* Nicocles

1. Epistolary Character

The three discourses have features which relate them in varying degrees to the letter. The *Nicocles* is a political brochure but its author professes to converse with (*dialegesthai*) the addressees. *Ad Nicoclem,* according to Cecchi, is an open letter, a type of manual describing the good prince.[25] Isocrates himself, *Ad Nic.* 2 and 54, calls the work the *dōrea* of a friend, better than the usual royal gift for its usefulness and appropriateness.[26] As an instruction in the general principles of royal conduct, 6-8, it is a hortatory work in prose comparable in intent and in response stirred among the common audience to similar works of poets, 42-43. In scope, however, it is more limited than general poetic paraeneses, 3. The elements of this self-description, i.e., a gift, from a friend, useful, hortatory and corrective, all combine with an overall pedagogical purpose and tone (11-14, 51, and *passim*) to confirm Cecchi's and Burk's observations about *Ad Nicoclem* and to locate the discourse at the start of a long tradition of epistolary instructions to young (implied at 13) officials. While not in the letter form, neither does the discourse *Ad Nicoclem* imply the presence of Isocrates at court. On the contrary, his own association of the works with other writings in poetry and prose, 7 and 48, even with those of antiquity 43, and his characterization of the general aim of the works presume for the discourse a broad circulation over successive generations, and thus place the work on the same level as a literary epistle.

---

[25] Cecchi, 50. Burk, 54, echoes the second description and calls it the first example of a *Fürstenspiegel*. He also sees it as a unique collection of advice to the absolute ruler covering the entire life-conduct and in the tone of a father to his son or of a tutor to his pupil. Vetschera underlines the fact that it presents more than the ideal picture of the king, for it also includes pescriptions for behavior with regard to the king himself and his subjects, with an influence continuing into the Byzantine-era schools, 13. Jebb, 83, refers to it as a discourse, a speech, and a letter, although on 78 the classification is a hortatory letter or essay.

[26] For the letter as a gift see Demetrius *Eloc.* 224 (W.R. Roberts, trans., *Demetrius on Style*, LCL [London: W. Heinemann, 1932]); K. Thraede, *Grundzüge griechisch-römischer Brieftopik*, Zetemata 48 (Munich: C.H. Beck, 1970) 30; H. Koskenniemi, *Studien zur Idee und Phraseologie des griechischen Briefes bis 400 n. Chr.*, Annales Academiae Scientiarum Fennicae, Ser. B, 102.2 (Helsinki: Finnischen Akademie der Wissenschaften, 1956) 35. For its philophronetic character see H. Rabe, "Aus Rhetoren-Handschriften," *RhM* n.F. 64 (1909) 290 n. 1; A.M. Guillemin, *Pline et la vie littéraire de son temps* (Paris: Société d'édition "Les Belles Lettres," 1929) 57. For the letter as a hortatory tool see Isocrates *Eps.* 1.2; 3.14 and *Philip* 17. See also above 38, 42 and Chapter V below.

The discourse *Ad Demonicum* is sent as a gift (*apestalka soi tonde ton logon dōron* 2)[27] and thus Jebb regards it as a letter of advice and a treatise on morality.[28] Moreover, the pseudonymous author surrounds that notion with expressions of friendship, 1-2, a not uncommon epistolary convention.

Isocrates himself, who sends advice and exhortation by letters in the formal sense (see *Eps.* 1.2. and 3.4),[29] also justifies sending an exhortation in a written discourse (*mellō soi logon pempein ouk epideixin poiēsomenon oud' enkōmiasomenon ... alla peirasomenon se protrepein epi praxeis, Philip* 17; and cf. *ho pempsas to biblion* 21; *pemphthēnai soi ton logon touton* 23). He recognizes the difference in persuasiveness between discourses which are spoken and those which must be read by the recipient in the author's absence and thus lacking the contribution of the physical presence of the speaker and the intensity of the occasion, *Philip* 25-27. This discourse, however, is a new type of epideictic work (*ho nyn epideiknymenos* 27), not like the ornate set-pieces of the sophists but written in a simple way (*haplōs* 28)[30] giving attention to the facts alone. Thus, Isocrates asks that Philip hear what he has to say (24 and cf. *dialechthēnai soi proeilomēn* 14) and receive it with *logismos* and *philosophia* 29. Given what was said above about the development of epideictic discourses toward the hortatory letter,[31] and the attention here to the sending of the discourse, its substitution for personal presence, its claim to be a conversation, its simple style, its hortatory aim, and even the allusions to friendship as an aim, 5, and also as the context for its reception 24, there is sufficient reason to regard the discourse to Philip and the three discourses under scrutiny in this section, all of which exhibit these features, as epistolary to some extent.

2. Hortatory Features

The hortatory language in *Nicocles* appears in both *Ad Nicoclem*[32] and *Ad*

---

[27] P. Hartlich, *De exhortationum a Graecis Romanisque scriptarum historia et indole* (Leipzig: S. Hirzel, 1889) 213, calls attention to the difference between this missive by a rhetor and the philosophical essays like Aristotle's *Ethics* and Cicero's *De officiis*.

[28] Jebb, 80-82. The friendly cast given the work from the outset, 1, its classification as a gift, 2, and its professed pedagogical intent, 3, also confirm its place among instructional letters, see n. 26.

[29] A. Lesky, *A History of Greek Literature*, trans. J. Willis and C. de Heer (New York: Thomas Y. Crowell, 1966) 587, summarizes the scholarly opinion on the authenticity of these letters.

[30] The simple, unadorned style is called for in the letter, which pretends to reproduce the normal speech of a conversation. Thus, too, Isocrates calls attention to what he says and not to flourishes of style. See above 10-12 and below 86, 95.

[31] On the development of epideictic see below 39-42.

[32] *parainein* 45, 54; *apo/protrepein* 8, 42; *parakalein* 14; *symbouleuein, symboulos* 6, 38, 42, 49, 52, 53; *prostattein, prostagma* 14, 17, 34; *ataktōs* 31; *nomothetein, nomos* 7, 8, 18; *elenchos* 52; *krinein, kritēs, krisis* 3, 18, 50; *loidorein* 47; *nouthetein, anouthetētos* 4, 42, 49; *mnēmoneuein* 35; *kata/deiknynai* 20, 30, 35, 49; *didaskein* 46; *dialegesthai* 46;

Demonicum[33] and so do the hortatory devices[34] and techniques.[35] The commands are gnomic in form and without an overall structural plan, just like the commands in the *Nicocles.*[36]

---

paideuein, paideusis 2, 4, 8, 12, 51; *mathētēs* 13; *philosophia* 51; *zēloun* 25, 38; *mimeisthai* 17, 38; *paradeigma* 34, 49.

Other hortatory vocabulary in the discourse includes *epithymein* 25, 49; *hēdonē* 45, 50; *aretē* 8, 11, 12, 21; *askein* 14; *gymnazein, gymnasia* 35, 51; *agōn* 48; *agōnistēs* 13; *epitēdeuein, epitēdeuma* 6, 17, 32, 36, 45; *prattein, pragma, praxis, ergon* 9, 26, 33, 35, 37, 38, 45, 46, 50, 52; *syn/hamartanein, hamartēma, hamartia* 3, 28, 33, 43; *phainesthai, phaneros* 10, 22, 51; *ōphelein, ōphelimos* 8, 12, 18, 45, 53; *sympherein* 18, 45; *prepein* 2, 18, 34; *an/axios* 32, 37, 54; *epitithenai* 3; *hypothēkē* 3, 43; *gnōmē* 44; *epiplēttein* 3; *enochos* 47; *atimazein* 14; *epitiman* 28; *parrēsia* 3; *timē* 11; *doxa* 29, 32, 38; *epainein* 28, 36, 42; *apo/dokimazein, dokimasia* 27, 50, 52; *eudokimein* 36; *a/pistos* 28, 41; *spoudazein, spoudaios* 30, 44, 50; *alētheia* 22, 46; *anoia* 43; *zētein* 17; *emmenein* 38; *epimeleia* 12, 15, 31; *sōphrosynē* 31; *metriotēs* 33.

[33] The language is self-consciously hortatory in the theoretical discussion of *paraklēsis, parainesis* and *protrepsis* 3-5. Language of the same sort fills the whole discourse; e.g., *parakalein* 6, 45; *nomos* 9, 11, 13, 16, 36; *parangelma* 44; *psogon* 7, 33, 43; *nouthetein* 45; *apo/dokimazein* 25, 49; *hypomimnēskein* 30; *didaskein* 19; *paideuein, paideia* 2, 3, 33, 45, 52; *kata/manthanein* 8, 18, 51; *philosophein, philosophia* 3, 4; *zēloun, zēlōtēs* 11, 36, 39; *mimesthai, mimētēs* 2, 11, 36.

Other hortatory terms include: *epithymein* 3; *hēdonē* 6, 16, 21; *aretē* 5, 7, 8, 9, 12, 45, 46, 48, 50; *askein* 4, 12, 14, 21, 40; *gymnazein, gymnasia* 9, 14, 21; *synagōnizesthai, antagōnistēs* 2, 3; *epitēdeuma* 12; *prattein, praxis, ergon* 5, 8, 11, 17, 37, 45, 46, 47; *hamartanein* 21, 45, 48; *phainesthai, phaneros* 17, 22, 34; *ōphelein* 4, 6, 29, 38; *sympherein* 40; *peithein* 16, 36; *tērein* 22; *prepein* 2, 15; *kosmos* 15; *anaxios* 49; *hypotithenai* 12; *gnōmē* 1; *epiplēttein* 31, 48; *epitiman* 17; *timan* 1, 13; *parrēsiazein* 34; *diabolē* 17; *aischynesthai, aischynē* 15, 16, 34; *aischros* 11, 15, 16, 18, 19, 21, 23, 25, 26, 43; *dokein, doxa, eudoxia, adoxia, endoxos* 2, 4, 8, 15, 16, 17, 37, 38, 41, 43, 44, 49; *epainos* 7, 33, 37; *eudokimein* 12, 17, 36; *pisteuein, apistein, pistos* 22, 29; *spoudazein, spoudaios* 1, 4, 10, 11, 27, 29, 39, 43, 48; *alētheia* 17; *emmeneien* 13, 51; *epimeleisthai, amelein, epimeleia, meletē* 6, 18, 36, 40, 48, 52; *hypomenein* 7, 9, 19, 21; *diaphylattein* 18; *proairesis* 9, 10; *syneidēsis* 10, 16; *enkrateia* 21, 37, 52; *metriōs* 27; *paradeigma, deigma* 9, 11, 51; *tekmērion, sēmeion* 2, 13; *sōtēria* 43; *anankē* 10; *sōphrosynē, dikaiosynē* 15.

See Hartlich, 221-22.

[34] In *Ad Demonicum: chrē* and *dei* complement direct imperatives, 3, 11, 22, 44; protreptic and apotreptic advice at 5 and in the prescriptions; direct address, 1; appeals to common opinion, 51; presumption of the recipient's positive attitude, 3, 45; inner power of virtue, 7; accessibility of blessing, 49; hyperbole, 42, 29, 38; comparisons (see K. Emminger, "Ps-Isocrates *pros Dēmonikon* [1]," *Jahrbücher fur Philologie und Pädagogik* suppl. B, 27 [1902] 413-14) 9, 11, 12, 18, 19, 25, 27, 29, 32, 44, 45, 52; lists, 6, 7, 15, 21, 31; examples. Examples are varied: the addressee's father, 9-12; historical figure of Theseus and the mythical hero Hercules, 8 (see E. Mikkola, *Isokrates: Seine Anschauungen im Lichte seiner Schriften* [Helsinki: Finnischen Akademie der Wissenschaften, 1954] 221); the mythical Hercules and Tantalus at 50; the gods, 50; historical precedent, 34; living rulers, 36; general types and customary attitudes and actions, 1, 27, 45; parable, 52.

3. The Character of the Discourses

While *Ad Nicoclem* has been descibed above as an open letter, with instructions to the young king on how to conduct himself so as to rule well, 1-2, there are indications that Isocrates aims at a broader audience and has a more generally

---

In *Ad Nicoclem: chrē* and *dei* throughout the introduction, 1-8, the discussion on kingship, 9-14, in the conclusion, 40-54; imperatives, throughout 15-39, both protreptic and apotreptic, direct address, 1; common opinion, 9; agreement of experts, 51; presumed knowledge of the addressee, 16, 31; addressee's possession of power and its effective use, 26; peristasis catalogue, 5-6; hyperbole, 6, 11; paradox, 21; irony, 48-49; comparison to athletics at 11, to food at 45, to medicine at 53; examples. Example wears many guises: model poetic counsellors, 43, 48; the tragedians as a specific class of writers, 48; the general public, 36; habitual popular preference, 44, 50; customary gift-givers, 1; human nature, 45-47 (though not every individual, 47); indefinite, hypothetical instance, 44; historical figure, 35; Isocrates himself, 2, 54; the addressee, 36-37.

[35] In *Ad Demonicum:* the discourse confirms the author's good will, 2, and his hortatory project, 3; warning, 6, 37, 48; motivation and explanation attached to the prescriptions and at 2 for the discourse, 5 for attaining virtue, at 11 for imitation, at 4-5 distinguishing paraenesis from protrepsis, at 44 for the usefulness of the discourse, at 45 for the choice of teachers, at 52 for wide-ranging study; contrast or antithesis (see Emminger, 405-10) both within particular commands and in the introductory and concluding sections to express the aim of the discourse, 4-5, to distinguish virtue from lesser goods, 6-7, as the structural pattern for Hipponicus' example, 9-10, to set Isocrates off from other rhetoricians, 4-5. As in the other discourses the introduction opens with antithesis between the author and, here, otherwise unspecified base individuals.

In *Ad Nicoclem:* corroboration from traditional exhortation at 40-41 and from the unpopularity of the discourse's admonition at 42-43; warning, 1, 4-5, 54; motivation behind and purpose for individual prescriptions throughout the prescriptive section, for his undertaking the discourse as a whole, 3-8, 50; contrast within the prescriptive units justa posing protreptic and apotreptic commands as well as the positive and negative reasons for them, and in the rest of the discourse opposing gifts and gift-givers, 1-2, educational opportunities and lack thereof, 3-4 and 8, priest and king, 6, writers of unbelievable novelty rather than traditional substance, 40, writers of pleasing fiction and myth rather than constructive criticism, 48-49, those who choose flattering and foolish comparisons rather than serious admonitors, 42-47.

[36] The commands in *Ad Nic.* 12-39 are in a concise and self-contained form, often including the reasons for the command (9, 13, 14, 15, 16, 17, 18, 19, 20, 21, 23, 31, 32, 33, 34) or its purpose (18, 19, 28, 31, 32, 33, 38). Isocrates likens them to the *gnōmai* of the poets. There is no logical structure to their arrangement. Isocrates himself says in his *Antid.* 68-69 that the prescriptions are arranged according to general headings.

Ad Demonicum also identifies its prescriptions as *gnōmai* when it contrasts *tas te tōn spoudaiōn gnōmas kai tas tōn phaulōn dianoias* 1. The author compiles them in a rule book, 5, on right conduct, 12 (I. Hadot, *Seneca und die griechisch-römische Tradition des Seelenleitung* [Berlin: de Gruyter, 1969]) 17-18, and Dihle, 90-91). They stand in enstructured arrangement, at least from the aspect of logical progression. In contrast both to Norlin's attempt to see a logical pattern, however rough, of "three main divisions" of the discourse

applicable message. There is no immediate occasion for the discourse, except, perhaps, the young man's recent accession to the throne.[37] In actual fact, the discourse proposes broad admonitions for rulers (*kath' holōn de tōn epitēdeumatōn, hōn chrē stochazesthai kai peri ha dei diatribein*) in a prose counterpart to the poetic *hypothēkai hōs chrē zēn* for the general public, 3 (and see 48-49). He avoids specific recommendations, for counsellors can handle specific circumstances as they arise, 6, and deals with the *ergon* of kings in its totality, 9. Thus, the prescriptions are helpful both now and in the future, 6 (and 54). Although they are targeted toward tyrants and kings (*tyrannoi* 3 ff.; *monarchiai* 8; *basileis* 31), much in the discourse has general applicability as protrepsis toward a life of virtue (implied also at 42-43). Moreover, Isocrates does not hem himself in with an exclusive preoccupation with monarchy, but suggests that his principles apply to a broad range of ruling officials [38] (*hoi kratountes, hai dynasteiai, hai archai* 8; *hoi archontes* 31; *oligarchiai* and other forms of government at 16).

The discourse *Ad Demonicum* has the practical education of the young man in the life of virtue as its aim, 5, with no specific circumstance occasioning the prescriptions. Here the young man is not a king but someone destined for a position of authority, 37. The *paideia* is expressly philosophical, 3-5 and 12, and much less

---

(see 2-3) and to C. Wefelmeier, *Die Sentenzensammlung der Demonicea* (Athens: John Rossalatos, 1962) 65 ff., and the attempt there to deny any consistent organizing pattern in the derivative precept material, B. Rosenkranz, "Die Struktur der Ps-Isokrateischen Demonicea," *Emerita* 34 (1966) 108-9, sees in the collection of precepts "an artistic creation on the basis of traditional, technical teaching," and not a haphazard and random collection. Hartlich, 213, sees it as a *farrago* presenting the doctrine of living well. Wendland, 83 and ns. 2 and 3 also discusses the enstructured arrangement of the paraenetic section. Hadot, 12-13 and 17-18, repeats Dihle's observation at 90-91 of the arrangement of sayings in *Ad Demonicum* into a compendium of formalized ethic based on common sense and comparable to poetic collections of sayings. She finds the typical *Sentenz* in *Ad Demonicum* to be a model example of the Gorgianic style and gives examples of what she means in n. 44. And regarding the collection of these Gorgianic gnomes she quotes Aristophanes' *Frogs* 1113-14, which says, "They are a learned people; each has a book and learns from it what is right." Here, the fifth-century sophistic practice of compiling book-compendia of rules and observations on the conduct proper to various *technai* feels the edge of the playwright-satirist's blade.

Reasons (13, 15, 16, 17, 18, 19, 20, 22, 23, 24, 25, 26, 27, 29, 30, 31, 32, 33, 34, 35, 36, 37, 38, 39, 40, 41, 42, 43) and purposes (21, 26, 38, 40) are added to complete the stated prescription, and there are a few instances of a participle filling in for either of these, 25. There are as many uses in *Ad Demonicum* of conditional clauses to express the presuppositions or consequences of the sayings as in the other two discourses combined.

  [37] Norlin, *Isocrates* 1:39.

  [38] In his *Antid.* 69 Isocrates says of *Ad Nicoclem* that (1) he thought it would help the monarch's understanding and (2) he found the discourse a quick way by which to disseminate his own principles on the conduct of kings and people in authority (cf. *hōs dei tōn politōn archein* 67).

political than that of *Ad Nicoclem*. Wendland[39] finds it to reflect the average paraenetic type of discourse. A self-styled *symboulia* (at 44), it is a *parainesis* set over against *protreptikoi logoi* at 3-5. Wendland also considers the definition of its intentions at 12, *syntomōs hypothesthai di'hōn an moi dokeis epitēdeumatōn pleiston pros aretēn epidounai kai para tois allois hapasin anthrōpois eudokimēsai*, as typical of a paraenetic work.

At 5 the admonition in the discourse seems to fit a broader audience than its single recipient. The pseudonymous author declares that his advice to Demonicus covers *hōn chrē tous neōterous oregesthai kai tinōn ergōn apechesthai kai poiois tisin anthrōpois homilein kai pōs ton heautōn bion oikonomein* (cf. 19). Furthermore, the prescriptions assume an instruction booklet character, for they are not all applicable at the time of the writing but will remain to be drawn upon as from a treasury, 44. That a broad public is intended for these instructions is also confirmed by the pseudonymity of the discourse.[40] The characteristics of the intended audience

---

[39] Wendland, 83. Isocrates uses several words when prescribing attitudes and/or action, i.e., *protrepein, parainein, parakalein,* and *symbouleuein*. The words all appear in conjunction with one another in different contexts and with little difference in meaning: *protrepein* and *symbouleuein* in *Philip* 18; *protrepein* and *parainein* in *De pace* 145 and *Nic.* 57; *parainein* and *symbouleuein* in *Antid.* 67 ff. and 248, *Panath.* 264, *Eps.* 2.1; 6.14; 9.6; *parakalein* and *symbouleuein* in *Ep.* 1.4, *Antid.* 77; *parakalein* and *protrepein* in *Antid.* 84-85, *Philip* 113-16; *parakalein, protrepein* and *symbouleuein* in *Nic.* 12. The words denote both an urging toward a general attitude, stance, or course of action or more specific advice or commands to specific deeds.

[40] For a survey of the question of the authorship of *Ad Demonicum* and a demonstration of its pseudonymity see Emminger, 373-442. E. Albrecht, "Zu Pseudoisokrates *Pros Dēmonikon,*" *Philol.* 43 (1884) 244-48, tries to establish the dependence of *Ad Demonicum* on *Ad Nicoclem* by a literary comparison and thereby to confirm its pseudonymity. E. Brémond, *Isocrates: Discours,* 3 vols. (Paris: Société de l'édition "Les Belles Lettres," 1928) 1:115-18, bases his conviction of pseudonymity on the context of the instruction as well as the style of the discourse. See Emminger, 428 ff., for a similar contrast. Also see Burk, 56 ff., for the various options of explaining the authorship. Vetschera, 12-13 seems to presume its authenticity, as does Hartlich, 213.

The pseudonymity alerts the reader to more than a wider audience. It also supplies an instance of the appeal to the originator of a tradition to underwrite the teachings of his followers. As it turns out, and as is necessarily the case for the literary subterfuge to be effective, the teachings in *Ad Demonicum* make use of the same vocabulary and forms as, although they diverge in content from, the authentic discourses by Isocrates (for a survey of the differences in content see Brémond, 115-18, and Emminger, 428). It may well not be accidental, however, that the pseudonymous work is more explicit in the distinctions drawn to characterize the work, 3-8, and to relate the example to the prescriptions, 11-12, clarifying what the teacher himself kept implicit. Furthermore, the concluding paragraphs have the teacher wishing that the king's other friends bring gifts like his, which they have not yet done, 54. The follower, on the other hand, suggests sipping the best from many sources (*Ad Dem.* 51-52).

can be deduced from the fact that the discourse addresses a person who is well-placed, i.e., with a considerable inheritance at 2, material prosperity at 13, capable of traveling to a school at 19, with servants at 21, and who is likely to hold a position of authority at 37. The work is thus designed for young officials.

These two discourses, together with the *Nicocles,* prescribe the character and conduct expected of officials. The young are especially targeted for exhortation and the discourses profess to be able to serve as manuals for the duration of their official careers.

4. The Aim of the Exhortation

Both discourses urge diligence (*epimeleia, Ad Nic.* 12; *epimeleisthai, Ad Dem.* 40) in following the instructions (*paideusis, Ad Nic.* 12 and cf. *Ad Dem.* 18) in virtue (*aretē, Ad Nic.* 12) and life's most important concerns (*Ad Dem.* 40 and cf. 51, *tois hyph'hēmōn eirēmenois emmenein*). Exercise is an essential part of this diligent application to the instruction. *Ad Nicoclem* requires spiritual training (*gymnazein* 11; *gymnasia* 13) in kingly character, which surpasses that required of athletes (*askētai* 11) because the prize for the contest (*agōnizesthai* 11) is more precious. By this exercise one becomes a successful competitor with those superior in virtue (*agōnistēs* 13). One trains the understanding (*askein tēn...dianoian* 14) by condemning others' folly (*anoia*). In general, training in actual deeds (*to d'ep'autōn tōn ergōn gymnazesthai* 35) is an essential complement to the direction from theoretical study (*to men gar philosophein tas hodous soi deixei*). *Ad Demonicum* calls for training (*gymnazein* 21) in self-imposed toils and exercise (*askein* 21) in self-control (*enkrateia*) and in sound thinking (*phronēsis* 40).

The stress on exercise highlights the importance of virtues as an object of zeal (*Ad Nic.* 30, *ep'aretē₁ mega phronōn...peri ta megista spoudazōn*) and the discourse as pointing the way (*Ad Dem.* 5) along which the soul can progress to it (*Ad. Dem.* 12, *pros aretēn epidounai* and *Ad Nic.* 12). This implies, on the other hand vigilance to avoid errors (*Ad Nic.* 33, *hamartēma*) in word or action. In this way the addressee can become the person equal to his ruling task (*Ad Nic.* 13).

The qualities and pursuits of such a person are manifold, but some are not only prominent in these discourses but find their way into the Pastorals as well. The pursuit of wealth over virtue and true honor suffers repeated condemnation (*Ad Nic.* 1-2, 32; *Ad Dem.* 9, 21, 27, 37, 38, 39). Likewise condemned is slavery to pleasures (*Ad Dem.* 21, 46; *Ad Nic.* 29 and cf. 32) with a contrasting emphasis on virtuous action and true honor (*Ad Nic.* 29, 36; *Ad Dem.* 39). Fair judgment and the avoidance of controversies (*Ad Nic.* 17, 18, 52), the choice of reputable subordinates (*Ad Nic.* 27; *Ad Dem.* 37), piety according to religious and family tradition (*As Dem.* 13; *Ad Nic.* 20), and attention to friendship (*Ad Dem.* 24 ff.; *Ad Nic.* 20-21, 27-28) are some other marks of the noble spirited ruler.

5. The Hortatory Method

a. *Antithesis*

Along with an aim which the discourses share with each other and with the *Nicocles*[41] they also use the same hortatory method, but with stresses particular to each. In their characterization of good teachers and advisers, both discourses warn against flattery and deceit (*kolakeuontes, exapatōntes, Ad Dem.* 30, *Ad Nic.* 29), as well as participation in[42] misdeeds (*synexamartanein, Ad Nic.* 43; *Ad Dem.* 45) and foolish behavior (*anoia, Ad Nic.* 44-46). On the other hand, good and wise instructors to associate with (*plēsiazein*) are to be sought out, even abroad (*Ad Dem.* 19; *Ad Nic.* 13), for they are precious and hard to find (*Ad Nic.* 53). One of the hallmarks of these good instructors and associates is *parrēsia* based on their good judgment (*eu phronountes, Ad Nic.* 28). They condemn shortcomings (*epitimōntes, Ad Nic.* 28) and give constructive criticism for improvement (*nouthetein, Ad Dem.* 45; *nouthesia, symboulia, Ad Nic.* 42, 49). These exhort people to virtue (*epi tēn aretēn parakalountes, Ad Dem.* 45) and good deeds (*Ad Dem.* 46; *Ad Nic.* 45), and dissuade them from faults (*apotrepein, Ad Nic.* 43). Thus they give the most useful advice (*chrēsimos, Ad Nic.* 42, 46; *Ad Dem.* 7, 51-52; *ōphelimos, ōphelein, Ad Nic.* 48; *Ad Dem.* 4).

Ad Nicocles 46-47 describes the contrasting situation. In the company of companions without understanding (*hoi noun ouk echontes*) people flee the truth (*hai alētheiai tōn pragmatōn*), lose sight of their own interests (*oude ta spheter'autōn isasin*), and engage in mutual and pointless rebuke (*ē loidorountes ē loidoroumenoi*) and in idle day-dreams (*euchomenoi*). Both discourses decry a penchant among people to select counsel and teachers as they do food, i.e., the pleasurable and palatable over the wholesome. In contrast, the discourses deny that the addressees are like this at all (*se de nomizō tòunantion toutōn egnōkenai, Ad Dem.* 45 and cf. 3; *polla tōn legomenōn estin ha kai sy gignōskeis, Ad Nic.* 40 and cf. 50).

This antithesis, which is elaborated in the concluding paragraphs of both discourses, is present in the introductory sections as well. *Ad Nic.* 1-2 contrasts the usual, sumptuous gifts brought to kings and the self-seeking motives behind them to his own serviceable (*chrēsimos*) and fitting (*prepon*) discourse on the pursuits and pitfalls of kings, a discourse which seeks to benefit both the king and the subject people alike, 8. *Ad Dem.* 1-4 contrasts the base (flattering, 30) to good people with respect to their loyalty as friends. He also juxtaposes the writers of standard protreptic

---

[41] See the discussion above, 55-56, 59-62.

[42] Concern for proper associations is aired at *Ad Dem.* 5 and 39, and see also 10, 20, 30, 45. The connection with following the example of the associates is obliquely expressed, at best as in the verb *synexamartanein* at 45. But this is surely the point when one looks at associations in connection with the stress in the discourses on the conduct of the exemplary figures to authenticate and demonstrate the moral precepts.

works on oratorical skill which are laudable but of marginal value and those who compose treatises on the vital part of philosophy, improving moral conduct.

The function of these contrasts is three-fold. First, they focus attention on the speaker as a qualified and truly beneficent instructor. Isocrates makes this clear when he associates himself (*Ad Nic.* 3-4, 7-8) with those authors of prose and poetic works which all agree to be most useful (*Ad Nic.* 42-43) and with the friends who freely give useful gifts like his (*Ad Nic.* 54). Second, they highlight the instructions as most useful. Isocrates identifies his compendium (*Ad Nic.* 41) with the typical compendium of poetic maxims (*Ad Nic.* 44) whose value is recognized in their unpopularity. Finally, they nudge the addressee to rise above the crowd (*Ad Nic.* 50) and be like the few who accept admonition and helpful advice rather than seek to be pleased (*Ad Nic.* 49). The descriptions of teachers and pupils, therefore, present positive and negative examples to guide the audience's own choices and attitudes.

b. *Explicit Example*

While these examples are proposed implicitly, explicit use of example in the discourses indicates that this hortatory device is in the mind of the authors. *Ad Dem.* 34 recommends making the past an example for future deliberations (*bouleuomenos paradeigmata poiou ta parelēlythota tōn mellontōn* and cf. *Ad Nic.* 35). Example is not just an instructional precedent but also a pattern for imitation, as is clear from *Ad Dem.* 36, *mimou ta tōn basileōn ēthē kai diōke ta ekeinōn epitēdeumata*. Similarly, *Ad Nic.* 26 calls for imitation (*zēloun*) of those who best use their ruling power, for imitation (*mimeisthai*) of what is good in other countries, 7, and for imitation (*mimeisthai*) of the deeds of people of enviable repute, 38. Just so, one is not to imitate (*zēloun*) those making unjust gain (*Ad Dem.* 39).

Ad Dem. 9-12 proposes a particularly compelling example in the addressee's father Hipponicus (*oikeion kai kalon ... paradeigma*). The author sketches the example in antithetical strokes, 9-10, and by this indicates to Demonicus how he ought to live (*pros hon dei zēn se hōsper pros paradeigma* 11). Demonicus should therefore consider his father's conduct as law and imitate his virtue (*nomon ... tropon hēgēsamenon, mimētēn de kai zēlōtēn tēs patrǫas aretēs gignomenon* 11). The sketch is admittedly incomplete, 11, but the author fills out the exemplary law of conduct with precepts of his own to lead the addressee to vie with his father's conduct (*ephamillos genēsei tois tou patros epitēdeumasin* 12), progress toward virtue, and win high acclaim (*pros aretēn epidounai kai ... eudokimēsai* 12).[43]

---

[43] *Ad Dem.* 36 also balances precepts (*nomos*) and example of the manner of life (*tropos,* and cf. 51).

c. *Examples and Precepts*

The example is a suggestive sketch [44] and is filled out by complementary precepts for several reasons. The given reason is the limitation of time for a full enumeration of all the exemplar's activities, 11. A second explanation offered is that the sketch outlines Hipponicus' nature as a person committed to virtue. This forms the hortatory background for the precepts which lead to the same virtuous condition but are explicitly suited to the status of the addressee looking ahead to an official career, 12.

A third reason suggests itself from other sections of the discourse. As precepts complement example, the example in turn verifies the precepts by showing that these do in fact lead to a virtuous life. The negative examples likewise show that what the precepts warn against leads to corruption. Hipponicus' example demonstrates both of these in the antithetical descriptions of what he was not like (*ou/oude*) and really was (*alla*). In this connection, the author suggests consulting only those people who manage their own affairs well, 35. The same outlook stands behind the precepts not to do what one blames others for, 17, and not to rule others but be a slave to passions, 21. As deceitful words are reprehensible, so is the good person who neglects virtue, for thus he belies the claims of his whole life, 49. This understanding seems to be behind the author's attempt to make the addressee particularly attentive to censure (*psogos* 43) and accusations (*diabolai* 17), even false ones. He even warns against the inevitably unsuccessful attempt to conceal wrongdoings, for when they are discovered they will show the ruler to be a hypocritical accuser of others. His authority is thereby diminished and his precepts vitiated. Precepts, in this view, rely on the examples, whose reputation gives authority to their commands and whose virtue verifies that the commands effect what they promise.

Fourth, stepping back from the immediate context of the discourse, and focusing on rhetorical technique in the exhortation, one notes that the antithetical examples (e.g., Isocrates and the flatterers) and the antithetical expression of an example (Hipponicus) mirror the protreptic and apotrepic prescriptions which the discourse designs to present, 5. Hipponicus did what Demonicus is admonished to do and he avoided what Demonicus is to avoid; Isocrates and other good people also followed the path to virtue while the base and flattering teachers did not. And so, Demonicus and the entire intended audience of the discourse are to adopt the attitudes and actions which the prescriptions outline and the examples incarnate and are to avoid those prohibited and which the examples either avoided or pursued to their own ruin.[45]

---

[44] Only in *Ad Demonicum* are lists used to fill out the positive ideal, 15. A list of vices to be avoided appears at 21.

[45] A fuller discussion appears in A.J. Malherbe, "Hellenistic Moralists and the New Testament," *ANRW* (W. Haase, ed., Berlin: de Gruyter, forthcoming) II.26.

Ad Nicoclem expresses the same concerns that the ruler correct in himself what he reproves in others, 64, and do what he advises for others, 38. Also like *Ad Demonicum, Ad Nic.* 39 finds a person's own condition to be an index of the substance of his advice to others.

An emphasis in *Ad Nicoclem* that is curiously absent per se in *Ad Demonicum* is that the addressee should be an example (*paradeigma*) for others, e.g., in his *sōphrosynē* 31. He is to leave behind him in remembrance not a statue but an image of this virtue (*eikōn tēs aretēs* 36) and a spiritual memorial (*tēs psychēs ... hē mnēmē* 37).

d. *Traditional Nature of the Exhortation*

While *Ad Dem.* 44 makes a great deal of the precepts in the discourse, is careful to explain that this *parangelma* is for the addressee's present and future life (cf. 3-5), and also suggests at 52 that the audience gather useful knowledge (*ta chrēsima*) from a variety of sources (contrast 44), it is in *Ad Nic.* 40 ff. that Isocrates discusses the traditional nature of the precepts he has collected. Before doing so he draws a contrast at 39 between those concerned with important matters (*hoi peri tōn megistōn legontes*) and those who purport to be wise but end up arguing minutely over trifles (*hoi akribōs peri mikrōn erizontes*) and between those in distress themselves but who promise fortune to others and those who bear up well in good and bad circumstances. His discourse aims at cultivating wisdom of the latter sort. To do that the discourse must avoid seeking the novel (*zētein tas kainotētas*), the unconventional (*paradoxos*), incredible (*apistos*), or the unthinkable (*exō tōn nomizomenōn,* and cf. 48-49 where useful discourses are contrasted to those which are full of attractive fictions, *mythōdestatos*). Rather, the discourse largely contains what is already known to the addressee (cf. *Ad Dem.* 15, *hapasi dokei*), admonitions which have most likely been expressed previously by someone, heard by another, seen practiced by others, or practiced by the audience themselves. The accomplished writer of moral discourses is a collector of scattered ideas who then presents them in the best form. Thus Isocrates claims to have done this at 54 in giving all the counsels he knows (*ha te gignōskō parēneka*), even though he says at the start of the discourse that he is breaking new ground in a neglected field, 8.

An aspect of this use of traditional material is the lack of emphasis by Isocrates on his own example.[46] He recommends that Nicocles consult others if his advice is

---

[46] Isocrates uniformly avoids direct reference to his own practice as the basis of obligation for his precepts. He obliquely commends himself for wisdom and for consistency between his own life and the promised fruits of his teaching in *Ad Nic.* 39, but he makes no claim to distinctiveness in his teaching as arising out of any connection with his life experience, 40. The claim to the role of educator is implied in *Ad Nic.* 8, but only his follower places it on his lips directly at *Ad Dem.* 3 and 12, with oblique self-commendation at 35. But again, any particular weight to his own prescriptions (*Ad Dem.* 44) is counterbalanced by

insufficient (*Ad Nic.* 38) and encourages others to give him discourses like his own. The pseudonymous author of *Ad Demonicum* urges his addressee to sip from all available sources like a bee, 51. The teaching is not new with or exclusive to Isocrates.

As a consequence of the traditional character of the exhortation, emphasis rests on what the addressee already knows (*Ad Nic.* 40 and cf. *Ad Dem.* 18) and which the discourse is simply a compilation or reminder of. This knowledge implies that the addressee is already open to the teaching (*Ad Dem.* 2, 45 and cf. *Ad Nic.* 30) and on the way to becoming the virtuous person he ought to become (*Ad Nic.* 13) and claims to be striving toward (*Ad Dem.* 48).

6. Concluding Observations

This brings to a close the survey of Isocrates' discourses. The use of example; the hortatory technique, especially the antithesis in and interplay between example and precept; the traditional exhortation in these open letters or discourses of instruction have all given substance to the theoretical matters discussed in chapter III. The fact that these are exhortations to young people on the conduct of their official obligations make them particularly pertinent to this study of example in the Pastorals, especially in view of the application of the exhortation to the subjects as well as to the rulers. The content of the exhortation will also prove helpful in understanding the Pastorals. A brief look at "kingship discourses" from the New Testament period will (1) confirm that the tradition which began with Isocrates both in content and form, was very much alive and (2) will further nuance some of the discoveries of the preceding analysis.

II. Example in the Kingship Treatises of Plutarch

As seen in the preceding section, the discourses of Isocrates explicitly (*Ad Demonicum, Ad Nicoclem*) and implicitly (*Nicocles*) seek to instruct the ruling class, from the monarch to subordinate officials, in the character, responsibilities and duties laid on them in consequence of their office. In the Hellenistic period, this pioneering effort of Isocrates developed into the literary form of the "Kingship

---

his declaration of their traditional character (*Ad Nic.* 40-41; *Ad Dem.* 15) and by his recommendation of other teachers (*Ad Nic.* 53; *Ad Dem.* 19,51).

One can deduce that Isocrates considered himself to be an example of his own precepts from his criticism of ignorant preceptors in *Ad Nic.* 53. But this is indirect. More direct evidence, in the letter to the rulers of Mytilene (*Ep.* 8.10), appears when Isocrates encourages his "children" about the worth of imitating his character. The letter to Archidamas (*Ep.* 10.15) also refers to those ignorant teachers who criticize Isocrates' efforts but imitate them nonetheless. In general, however, from the evidence of the Isocratean corpus, he seldom offered his own example and action as a model for others to follow.

Treatise" or *principis speculum*. Attention now turns to several of these to survey briefly their hortatory features and, specifically, their use of example. Thematic content and purpose will also be considered insofar as these illuminate the function of the examples. The Pastorals, long noted as epistolary compendia of precepts for community officials, also rely on example figures to flesh-out the precepts and present their teaching on the Christian life in a vivid way. In both respects, they share a world similar to that of these treatises on kingship. The closer analysis here of content and form will map the frontiers of this common territory.

A. *Plutarch's* Ad principem ineruditum [47]

In the surviving fragment of Plutarch's treatise *Ad principem ineruditum,* the author exhorts his unnamed addressee to follow the path of law and virtue in the execution of his office. Unlike the Isocratean discourses, there are no direct prescriptions here, but there are certain resemblances in content and hortatory features, while other aspects of the treatise reflect the development of the kingship treatise.

1. Hortatory Features

The hortatory features of the discourse are those familiar from the Isocratean discourses: hortatory language;[48] *dei* (781C,D) in gnomic statements of obligation (and see 782C); lists of virtues (781A,C) and vices (782C,E); citations (779D; 780C,D,F; 781C; 782A,C,D); appeals to common knowledge (780C) and to authority (782D); rhetorical questions (780C; 781D); personification (781B); comparisons (779F-780B; 780D; 781B; 781C; 781F; 782D). Among the hortatory techniques employed, the reader finds: corroborative attestation (782C); statement of reasons (779E; 780B; 781C, E; 782B) and of purposes (781C; 782A); warning (782C-E, and see below). Antithesis also plays a part, as the following discussion indicates.

---

[47] H.N. Fowler, trans., *Plutarch's Moralia,* LCL, vol. 10 (Cambridge: Harvard University, 1949); C. Hubert et al., eds., *Plutarchi Moralia* (Leipzig: B.G. Teubner, 1925).

[48] *parakalein* 779D; *parakeleuein* 780D; *tattein* 780B-C; *ataktein* 780B; *nomothetein, nomos* 779D; 780E; *symboulos* 779D; *paramytheisthai* 781A; *oneidizesthai* 779E; *kataphronein* 781D; *kategoria* 782D; *katadikē* 782D; *diabolē* 782F; *exelenchein* 782E; *apodeixis* 782D; *epiphanēs* 782F; *endoxos* 782F; *ana/phainesthai* 781F; 782D,E; *epideiknynai* 782E; *philosophein, philosophia* 779F; 782A,B; *paideuein, apaideutos* 780B,D; 782E; *didaskein* 780B; 781B,D; *apo/mimeisthai* 779F, 780A; 782D; *synarmottein* 780B; *zēloun* 781A; *zēlotypein* 782B; *aphomoioun* 781A; *mimēma* 780F; 781F; *eikōn* 782A; *eidōlon* 780F; 781F; *prepon* 781F; *ōphelein* 780C; *ōpheleia* 781C; *prattein/pragma* 780C; 781B,F; *ergon* 780E; 782C; *poiein* 780C; *epimeleia* 780D; dia/para/phylattein, phylax 779F; 780A,C,D; *hygiainos* 779F; *sōtēria* 780D; *aretē* 780E; 781A; 782B; *sōphrōn/sōphrosynē* 781C; 782A; *epithymia* 782F.

2. The Device of Example

The device of example has been reserved for special consideration because of its prominence in the treatise and its importance in this study generally.

a. *Variety and Function of Examples.*

Examples come from various sources: named historical figures (781C; 781C-D; 782A-B; 782F); general types (779F-780B; 780D; 782E); God (781A; 782A); heavenly bodies (780E-F; 782D-E); typical historical figure (780C).

b. *Antithetical Examples.*

The treatise opens with an example, expressed in an anecdote,[49] antithetical to the effort and expectation of the treatise itself. The negative model, the rich and haughty Cyprians, meets the positive example, another anecdote, of the wise and secure ruler Theopompus. This opening highlights the help and protection which philosophy offers the ruler (779F) and which Plutarch, as *symboulos peri archēs* (779D-E) now proffers to his audience. The example's aim is to instill in the audience a favorable disposition toward the rule of virtue being urged in the treatise.

Examples in antithetical relationship serve the exhortation by spelling out the options throughout the treatise (779F-780B; 780F-781A; 781C-E; 782A-B; 780C-D). Antithesis alone, without examples, is a hortatory features of the treatise as well (780C; 781A-B; 781F; 782B-C).

c. *Other Functions of Examples.*

Primary among their functions stands the characterization of the proper attitude in a general and inclusive way, which the treatise urges for emulation (779D-F; 780D; 781A; 781B-C; 781C-E; 782A-B; 782D-E). The treatise explicitly refers to imitation (misguided 779F; or appropriate 780E; 781A; 782A,D). The king, too, after advancing in virtue becomes a model for his subjects (780B). Second, the example warns the addressee (779F-780B; 781E; 782E-F). Third, the examples also illustrate the statements preceding them (780C; 782C).

d. *Examples Supplemented by Lists.*

In the Isocratean discourses, the prescriptions spell out for the audience the details of the model they were to imitate or avoid. In this treatise of Plutarch, lists serve a similar function, whether of virtues (781A; 781C) or of vices (782C; 780A; 782E).

---

[49] Plutarch frequently expands the examples into full anecdotes, e.g., 779D; 779E; 780C; 781C-E; 782A-B.

e. *Royal Example.*

Plutarch considers the character and work of the ideal king to be the principal example, because the king, as Plutarch declares at 780C-D, through philosophy harbors the law of reason within himself like an inner voice. Moreover, unlike those rulers whose claims to *logos* and *dianoia* are unattainable, 780F, he imitates the divine *aretē* and *philanthrōpia*, receiving in turn *eunomia*, *dikē*, *alētheia* and *praotēs*, 781A; divine *themis* and *dikē*, 781B and a host of attendant virtues: *adiaphthoria*, *aidōs*, *sōphrosynē*, *ōpheleia*, 781C.

Examples, both positive and negative, are not only a part of the exhortation in this treatise, they are the critical features. Plutarch does not balk at giving political direction, 779D. He does not give *nomoi;* rather, he describes *tēn politeian* by describing the qualities and action of the exemplary ruler and contrasts them to those of less ideal officials. With this introduction to the political pedagogy of Plutarch, his longer treatise, *Praecepta gerendae reipublicae*, can be surveyed.

B. *Plutarch's* Praecepta gerendae reipublicae

Unlike the treatise just surveyed, this one offers the young addressee Menemachus directives on the entrance into public life and the proper and effective conduct of public office.[50] Moreover, Plutarch embellishes his *parangelmata* with *paradeigmata poikilōtera*, 798C,[51] which makes the treatise pertinent to this study of the Pastorals.

1. Hortatory Features

The hortatory features of the treatise are generally those seen in the Isocratean discourses and in Plutarch's *Ad principem ineruditum*.[52] The precept is expressed at

---

[50] H.N. Fowler, 156, discusses Menemachus' historicity. He is young: from the nature of the advice given about entering public life (804C; 811A) and from Menemachus' application to the more experienced Plutarch for advice on political life (805F-806F).

T. Renoirte, *Les "Conseils Politiques" de Plutarque, une lettre ouverte aux grecs à l'époque de Trajan* (Louvain: Publications Universitaires, 1951) 65-66, 72-82, 112, claims that the treatise is not restricted to the next magistrate at Sardis. Rather, Plutarch generalized his portrait to fit any city. Similarly, M. Arullani, *Ricerche intorno all'opuscolo Plutarcheo EI PRESBYTEROI POLITEUTEON* (Rome: L'Universale, 1928).

[51] The examples, precepts, and directives can be traced to collections of material of this sort, according to K. Mittelhaus, *De Plutarchi praeceptis gerendae reipublicae* (diss. Berlin, 1911) 1-8, 30-31.

[52] E.g., lists of virtues and vices (802F-803C; 806F-807A; 819E; 820A-C; 824C); direct address (798A); citations, *passim;* presumed predisposition of the addressee (798B-C); appeal to common knowledge (816F); claim to possess virtue (820A); rhetorical questions

times by the imperative,[53] but more often by *chrē* and *dei*,[54] or some other general statement of obligation.[55] The examples are sometimes given in the form of anecdotes.[56] Antitheses run throughout the treatise.[57]

2. The Device of Example

Plutarch singles out examples as the principal hortatory devices of the treatise (798C).

a. *Variety and Function of Examples.*

The examples here are personal: sometimes named figures from history,[58] mythology (811D; 819D); contemporary society (813F; 805D); but also general

---

(800C; 809D; 814D-E; 824E); comparisons (799B; 801C,F; 802E; 804C-F; 812D; 813C; 814E); warning (813E-F); explanation of reasons or purpose, *passim*.

As for the hortatory language of the piece, let these examples suffice: *protrepein* 798B; *parangelma* 798C; 818A; *parakalein* 798F; *symboulos* 819E; 823B; *didaskein* 798B; 818C; 824E; *paideia* 816F; *katamanthanein* 821D; *peithein* 801C; 818C; *hypotithesthai* 798B; *nomos* 813C; *krisis* 798C; *dikastēs* 819E; *loidoria* 810C; *psogos* 800D; 810C; *blasphēmia* 816C; *diaballein, diabolē* 798D; 800D; *kataphronein, kataphronēsis* 800F; 801D; 822D; 825D; *paramytheisthai* 819F; *nouthetein* 818B; *hamartēma* 800B; 818B; *parrēsiazesthai, parrēsia* 802F; 810C; 818B; 822F; *paradeigma* 798B,C; 803B; 814C; 821D; 825D; *diamillein* 817D; *mimeisthai* 800A; 813F; 814A; 823F; *epiphainesthai* 799B; 802E; *doxa* 799C; 805A; 813C; 821C; 822D; *eudokimein* 800F; *endoxos* 806B; *epainein, epainos* 809B; 810C; 811D; *pithanos* 803A; *axioun, axios, axiōs* 798B,C,D; 811B; 818C; *apeirazein* 799B; *prepos* 810C; *sympherein* 805A; 817E; *prosēkein* 798C,E; 800A; 825A; *ōphelein* 814D; 820C; *pistis* 799C; 801C; 805B; 821C; 822F; *pisteuein* 800A; 801B; *a/pistos* 812C; 819E; *prattein, praxis, praktēr* 798B,C,D,E; 799A; 800D,E; 820C; 823C; *ergon* 798B,C,E; *a/epimelein, epimeleia* 800D; 801C; 811B,E; 823F; *phylattein* 803C; *agōnizesthai, agōn* 798B; 804B; 819B; 820D; *exaskein* 800B; *aretē* 806B; 821D; 822D,F; *spoudē* 798C,D; 800C,D; 816D; 819B; *proairesis* 799B; *ēthopoiein, ēthos* 799B,C; 800C,F; 802F; 814B; 823D; *tropos* 800B; 801C; *katakosmein, kosmios* 800B,F; *sōtērion* 800C; *sōphronizein, sōphrōn* 800F; 807A; 814B; 823A; 824A-B; *therapeutikos* 810C; *alētheia* 821D; 823D.

[53] Even with the imperatives, the third person is just as likely to appear as the second person, e.g., 798C; 802E,F.

[54] E.g., 799B; 800A; 803F; 804B; 806B,E; 807D; 811F; 812B; 813C,E; 814C,E; 816A; 818F; 825D.

[55] E.G., the verbal adjectives in *-teos* (798E; 800D; 801C; 813A; 817D; 819F; 822A); the subjunctive (819F); the infinitive (818A,E; 824D) or infinitive phrases (801F; 811B).

[56] E.g., 803E; 804F; 807A-B; 812A; 813A; 818E.

[57] E.g., 798C,E; 800A; 802E,F; 803B-C; 804A,B-C,C, 805A-B,B-D; 806F-807D; 811B-D; 813C-D; 814A-C,E-F; 817F-818A; 821B,C-E,F; 823A-C,D,F; 825D.

[58] 798E-F; 800B-C,D-F; 801F; 802C-D,E; 803A-B,C-E, F-804A; 804B,C,E-805A; 805C-D,E; 806B,C-E,F-807B; 807D-808B; 808C,E-F,F; 809A-B,B-D,D-F; 810A,B-D,F811A; 811A-B,B-E; 812C-D,E,F-813A; 813A-B,D-E,F-814A; 814B-C,C-D; 815D,E-

types,[59] groups or classes (801A-B,D-E; 802C); occupations,[60] nationalities (779C-F; 801B; 817A-B); and Plutarch himself (811B-C; 816D-E). The examples are most often presented outright (*passim*), through citation,[61] or in hypothetical or general statements.[62]

The function of the example varies. The specimen illustrations give: the reason for or range of the prescriptions (798C-D; 799C-800A); corroborative precedents or analogues (800D-F; 801A); proof for statements (803C-E). Prototype examples expect imitation (800B-C; 813F), and are tailored to suit the current situation (814B-C); a more refined ethic (811B-C); or more exigent standards (817D).

Plutarch's observations on the use of examples (814A-C) echo the theoretical treatises above and explain the practice in his own works and the others surveyed in this dissertation. He notes: (1) ancestral figures are a rich source, (2) the examples may be *erga, phronēmata,* or *praxeis,* (3) examples lead to imitation (*mimeisthai* or *exomoiousthai*) by the people and are used by leaders to mould or moderate character (*ēthopoiein, sōphronizein*). Here, too, he refers by contrast to the officials who foolishly (*anoētōs*) promote inopportune examples (*asymmetrous tois parousi kairois*) and to the sophists' schoolrooms where these inappropriate examples which swell the pride and recalcitrance of the crowd (*poiei kai phryattesthai diakenēs tous pollous*) find a compatible home.

b. *Antithetical Examples.*

Particularly prevalent in the treatise are examples set in antithetical relationship, with an example set against either another example[63] or the precept itself.[64] Plutarch refers explicitly to the instructional value of antithetical examples at 821D (*skopei de tēn enantian katamanthanōn diathesin en tois paradeigmasi*). And like the Isocratean discourses, this treatise begins with a negative example (798A-C), in this case philosophers who urge people to study but whose teaching and direction amount to nothing (*kai pros tous protrepomenous tōn philosophōn didaskontas de mēden mēd' hypotithemenous*). This rhetorical ploy seeks to garner higher esteem for Plutarch and his treatise as he responds to Menemachus' earnest request for political instruction with a mixture of precepts and examples (798A-C).

816A; 816A-C,E; 817C,E-818A; 818B-C,C-D,E-819A; 819C; 820B,D-F; 821B-C,E-F; 822C,E; 823C-E; 825B-D.

[59] 798D-E; 800A; 801A; 804D; 805B-C; 811E-812B; 814A,F; 820B,C; 822A; 825E-F.

[60] 799A; 801C-D,F; 802A-B,F; 807B-C; 812C; 813E-F; 815B; 816F; 818D-E; 823F.

[61] 803B; 804C; 808D,F; 812E; 815C.

[62] 804D-E; 805B; 811C; 812E (an imaginary dialogue).

[63] E.g., 798E; 799A; 800A,D-F; 802E; 803B-D; 804A,B; 805B-D; 807D-808B; 812D-813A; 814B-C; 820D-F, 821D-F.

[64] E.g., 801A-C; 811D-812B (except for the brief mention of Scipio); 814A,F; 820C; 825B-D.

c. *Example and Precept.*

At 823F he says that the ruler *ta men alla* (i.e., precepts) *tou Sōlonos apodexetai kai mimēsetai kata dynamin.* What Solon prescribed and himself did sets a composite pattern of leadership which others are to accept and imitate (here with Plutarch's reservations). Thus precepts help fill in the details of the exemplary ideal.

d. *Example and Lists of Virtues and Vices.*

Virtue and vice lists also fill in the lineaments of an example [65] and are a standard feature of the kingship treatise genre.[66] Höistad draws attention to the fact that the lists observed in Dio Chrysostom's orations on kingship are synonymous and even identical.[67] Moreover, the qualities predicated of the ideal king in the latter reflect a general social-ethical commitment and responsibility.[68] Plutarch's works, while they emphasize directives on the details of office-holding and its civic consequences,[69] nonetheless correspond remarkably with Dio's in the content of their vice and virtue catalogues.[70] The same has been noted for the lists in the Pas-

---

[65] 822F-823C; 806F; 819E; 820A (cf. 802F-803C).

[66] R. Höistad, *Cynic Hero and Cynic Kung: Studies in the Cynic Conception of Man* (Lund: Carl Blom, 1948) 161-62, 184-87, 213-15, details the antithetical lists by Dio Chrysostom to describe the ideal king in *Or.* 1.11-14; 3.29-41; 4.7-10. Add to these: *Or.* 1.1-8, which also contains the familiar contrast with the inadequate pedagogue and his methodology (see also 4.33-35; 1.61 and Höistad, 155-165, on the double *paideia,* divine and human); 1.43; 2.26; 2.75-78; 3.4-5; 3.7-11; 4.83. For 62.2-3 see Höistad 188-89 (and H. von Arnim, *Leben und Weise des Dio von Prusa* [Berlin: Weidmann, 1898] for a source analysis) and compare 32.27-28, 37, 90-91 describing the subjects in antithetical lists. See also P. Tzaneteas, "The Symbolic Heracles in Dio Chrysostom's Orations 'On Kingship'," (Diss. Columbia University, 1972) 51-52.

[67] Höistad, 186, 189 (see also *Or.* 1.1-8, 43; 2.26, 75-78; 3.4-5, 7-11; 4.83). He posits a pre-Stoic, Socratic-Cynic source behind *Or.* 3.29-41; 1.12-14; 62.2 ff.; but sees those at the end of *Ors.* 1 and 3 as more Stoic.

[68] Höistad, 188.

[69] E.g., 801C ff., 813C ff., 813E ff., 822A ff.; 804A ff.; 806F ff., 814E ff.; 817C; 818E ff.; 819F ff.

[70] Of course, the lists represent only a capsule form of what Dio Chrysostom describes in his first four orations as a whole. The topic headings of *Or.* 1.11-37 as listed in Tzaneteas, 191, read like a catalogue of virtues themselves, and this is true throughout the orations.

For other studies of lists of royal virtues and vices, see W. Schubart, "Das hellenistische Königsideal nach Inschriften und Papyri," *APF* 12 (1937) 1-26; "Das Königsbild des Hellenismus," *Die Antike* 13 (1937) 272-88; "Das Gesetz und der Kaiser in greichischen Urkunden," *Klio* 13 (1937) 54-69; K. Scott, "Plutarch and the Ruler Cult," *TAPA* 60 (1929) 133-34; J.A. Straub, *Vom Herrscherideal in der Spätantike,* Forschungen zur Kirchen-und

torals.[71] The source for these lists seems to be the moral teaching of the popular philosophers. It should not be forgotten that, while the lists catalogue personal characteristics and social functions, in doing this they depict exemplary types to be pursued or avoided.[72] This is obvious where the qualities of Diogenes, Alexander, or Paul are outlined, but it is the fundamental notion, implicit or expressed, of these treatises and discourses in their hortatory outlook generally.[73]

Geistesgeschichte, 18 (Stuttgart: W. Kohlhammer, 1939) 153-56; E. Goodenough, "The Political Philosophy of Hellenistic Kingship," *YCS* 1 (1928) 59-60, 65-73, 73-74, 86-87; Tzaneteas, 190 ff.; E. Thomas, *Quaestiones Dioneae* (Leipzig: Dr. Seele, 1909) 21-41; Hubert, 2-7, 27-28, 57; L.K. Born, "The Perfect Prince According to the Latin Panegyrists, "*AJPh* 55 (1934) 20-35, see also C. Preaux, "L'image du roi de l'époque hellenistique," in *Images of Man in Ancient and Medieval Thought,* (Fest. G. Verbeke, F. Boissier, ed., Louvain: University of Louvain, 1976); and von Arnim, *Leben und Weise,* as well as his *Ein altgriechisches Königsideal* (Frankfurt: Frankfurt Universitätsreden 4, 1916); P. Riewald, "De Imperatorum romanorum cum certis dis et comparatione et aequatione" (Diss. Halle 20, 7; 1912); and A.D. Nock, "Notes on the Ruler Cult," *JHS* 48 (1928) 21-43.

[71] E. Kamlah, *Die Form der katalogischen Paränese im Neuen Testament,* WUNT 7 (Tübingen: J.C.B. Mohr [Paul Siebeck], 1964) 199 ff., observes both the Pastorals' use of traditional lists and their consequent admonition by way of juxtaposing the correct witnesses and the false teachers. A Vögtle, *Die Tugend- und Lasterkataloge im Neuen Testament: Exegetisch, religions- und formgeschichtlich untersucht* (Münster i.W.: Aschendorff, 1936) 22, 74 ff., agrees with Höistad (see ns. 67, 68 above) on the common moral character of the lists of qualities in the kingship treatises, and he finds a parallel to them in the Pastorals. Even the vices are not exclusive to the official class but are popular disorders as well, on 75-76 he refers to Isocrates' *Ad Nic.* 9-39. On this see also Kamlah, 147, 170-71.

[72] Thomas, 25, notes that Dio Chrysostom's treatises describe rather than prescribe, like other examples of the developed *Principis Speculum* form (e.g., Plutarch's treatises). The virtues of a good king are narrated in such a way, however, as to preclude the need for precepts. This establishes a paradigm for rulers in the future. Kamlah, 146 ff., notes the connection between lists of virtues and the depiction in popular philosophy of the ideal wise man. For him, the *Regentenspiegel* is nothing more than a special case of this. Vice lists depict the negative ideal or model. Both he, 199 ff., and Vögtle, 54 ff., 170 ff., find a similar use of lists in the Pastorals to depict the example of good conduct, e.g. Timothy. See also above 53 on Isocrates and 69-70 on Plutarch.

[73] The picture of the ideal ruler varies with the school moral teaching and its view of the "philosophical" person, according to Schubart, "Das Königsbild," 387-88. Vögtle, 58 ff., notes the changing emphasis in the vice and virtue lists from the Stoic system in school instruction to the less structured teaching of the popular philosophers who aimed at a wider audience.

The lists in Dio Chrysostom's *Or.* 32 and the Pastorals' catalogues of the virtues of the various segments of the community all reflect this development inasmuch as the public virtues and those of the officials are largely the same. Plutarch also associates the philosopher and the statesman in his *Praec. ger. reip.* 798B. Vögtle, 73, refers to the popular philosophical view that only the philosopher can be an apt and worthy ruler. See Kamlah, 146, and Höistad, 195 ff., 200-201, 218.

The interests of this study and limitations of time and space prohibit the full delineation of the model official presented in this treatise. Those characteristics will be indicated, however, which will later be shown to relate to the example in the Pastoral epistles.

e. *The Characteristics of the Model Figure.*

The discussion at 821C merits careful scrutiny because it gathers together many of the principal observations on statecraft which the Pastorals later will be seen to echo. First of all, Plutarch notes the statesman's reputation (*doxa*) as a motive for entering office (821C). This calls for judgment (*krisis*) and reason (*logos*) which it implies (798C and cf. 822F, *aretē* and *phronēma*); and contrasts with (798C-799A) empty opinion (*kenē doxa*), contentiousness (*philoneikia*), or idleness (*praxeōn heterōn aporia*), and impulsiveness (*ptoia*). Distinction is gained by conscientious attention to one's office (*oudemias ... apoleipesthai phrontidos oud'epimeleias* and *ouk amelein* 811A-B). In this regard, concern for the common good (*pronoia peri ta koina*) and wisdom (*phrontis* 817D) rather than money-making (798E) is essential. The true crown (820D) in the "sacred contest" of political life (*agōna politeias agōnizomenoi*) is not money but the goodwill and favorable disposition of the subjects (819E-821A).

Second, true *doxa* engenders a trust (*pistis* 821C) which makes political activity possible and which wins approval for his actions (801A-C). In connection with this, the statesman's *aretē* also backs up his frank boldness (*parrēsia* 822F).

Third, the public good will (*eunoia* is a defense against the envy (*phthonos*) and power (*dynamis*) of slanderous and wicked opponents (821C). Similarly, if the statesman develops his character (*exaskein, katakosmein*), and does not neglect (*amelein*) but rather pays careful attention (*epimeleisthai*) to his own character and life-style (*ēthos* and *bios*), becoming, among other things, *sōphrōn* and *kosmios*, he eradicates the occasions of all blame and accusation (*psogos* and *diabolē* 800B-801A and cf. 806F-807A). This includes even those hidden vices which the public eye eventually discovers. Furthermore, his concern for development of virtue summons forth the proper use of his *parrēsia*, i.e., not hostile to those in error or treating them with anger (*orgē*) and insult (*hybris*), his gentle (*praos*) appeal should aim at moral improvement (*eis to emmeles*) and virtue (*aretē*). This type of criticism does not occasion insult (*hybris*) but is a frankness (*parrēsia*) which, without provoking anger (*thymos*), pricks the conscience (*dēgmon ... empoiōn*) and stirs repentance (*metanoia* 809E-810D and cf. 803B-E and 823A). It is kindly (*eumenēs*) and healing (*therapeutikos*), not at all like improper abusive speech (*loidoria*).

Plutarch places great emphasis on the official's work of conciliation, too. Contentiousness (*philoneikia*) is singled out for censure (811D), as are enmity (*echthros*) and disagreement (*diaphoros* 813A-C) and factional discord (823F-825D), where it is contrasted with reasonableness (*sōphronizein*). The official's response should be firm and decisive but also mild and understanding (without *philoneikia, orgē* or *pathos* 825D-F and cf. 818A-E). A political realist, Plutarch at 824E sees a life of harmony and quiet (*meth' hēsychias kai homonoias katabiōnai*) the one advantage for wise people (*eu phronountes*) in a subject nation like Greece both for the intrinsic value of tranquillity and to avoid provoking interference from external forces (814A-816A; 823F-824D).

3. The Pattern of Devices Resembling That of the Development of the Chria

After these observations on the use of example in the treatise as a whole, and on the content of the ideal figure, a closer scrutiny of the interplay of the hortatory features within a limited section of the treatise will reveal a literary phenomenon which links the technique of the treatise to that of the other works surveyed in this study. The section 817F-818E opens with a reference to the negative example of Jason, in deed and word. Plutarch summarily dismisses this as despotic and proposes a more statesman-like precept (*parangelma*), justifying it with an explanation, itself constructed antithetically. A poetic citation lends authority to his own words and leads into a more elaborate restatement of the precept. He adds comparisons with family life and medicine and a statement of purpose. Then the example of Alexander, constructed in an antithesis, provides a royal attitude more congruent with precept, though open to some criticism for its correctness and worthiness. The opening negative example receives another counter-precept, elaborated by a short list of what to avoid and what measures to take. Examples of the proper policy follow, with supporting reason and a comparison. From this brief outline the reader no doubt can recognize the categories from the rhetorical exercise on the development of the chria.[74]

4. Concluding Observations

The preceding discussion has noted the principal features of the kingship treatises of Plutarch and Dio Chrysostom which will prove helpful for understanding the Pastorals in the analysis below: the exhortation to young officials by means of examples; the hortatory function of the official's own example; the role of the lists of virtues and vices as well as prescriptions in complementing the exemplary figures; the commonplace moral teaching in the lists and in the exhortation generally; the use of antithesis to clarify the lines of the exhortation; the cluster of devices found in the developed chria; further details of both content and form. The Pastorals' use of the letter form as such distinguishes them from these treatises, even though some have an "open letter" character. Nonetheless, the content and for-

---

[74] See above 42-43, nn. 63-65, and the pages noted there. For other aspects of rhetoric in Plutarch, see R. Jeuckens, *Plutarch von Chaeronea und die Rhetorik* (Strassbourg: Karl J. Trübner, 1908).

mal features of the exhortation here and in the Pastorals establish an unmistakable bond between the two groups of writings.   The same can said of Isocrates' discourses, and their epistolary character forges an even stronger bond.

III. Menander's "Directives on the Composition of a Panegyric"

The rhetor Menander's directives on how to compose a panegyric for a king[75] (3:368-77, especially 375-76) give evidence that the practical examples of kingship treatises by Isocrates, Plutarch and Dio Chrysostom find their counterpart in theoretical instructions.   The rhetor is interested in content as well as form and the similarity of the section discussed here to the other works studied above will be obvious.

In his work Menander first discusses the need to select uncontroversial details and then handles the preliminary matters of country-of-origin and family stock. Next he turns to the virtues to be praised.   He lists *andreia, dikaiosynē, sōphrosynē, phronēsis* (the principal virtues in the lists of the kingship treatises as they were in moral instruction generally), outlining their wartime applications and then their peacetime works.

In the discussion of each virtue, he outlines the characteristics of the royal ideal, the exemplary king.   The terms are similar to the descriptions in Plutarch and Dio Chrysostom.   Since the qualities are drawn from the common stock of moral teaching, the ideal king can be a model for common folk as well.   This is explicitly stated in the discussion of *sōphrosynē*. Here he makes the claim that when people see *ton basileōs bion* they take up one similar to his, with *gamoi sōphrones, paides gnēsioi tois patrasin, agōnes theioi, panēgyreis meta tou prosēkontos kosmou kai tēs prepousēs sōphrosynēs* as a consequence.

As part of the panegyric's depiction of the ideal king, Menander also calls for mention of vices as well as virtues.   The characterization thus makes use of antithesis by listing those bad qualities and actions with which the king was not tainted.[76]

IV. Concluding Observations

Menander's directives demonstrate the temporal perdurance of the characteristics of the ideal king and of the manner of describing the royal model from the kingship discourses of Isocrates in the fifth century B.C. to his own work at the end of the third century A.D.   They also indicate that what appeared in practice in the

---

[75] In his *GENETHLION DIAIRESIS TON EPIDEIKTIKON* (Spengel) 3:329-46. See also J. Soffel, *Die Regeln Menanders für die Leichenrede: In ihrer Tradition dargestellt, herausgegeben, übersetzt und kommentiert* (Meisenheim am Glan: Anton Hain, 1974).

[76] See Vögtle, 83-84, for his observations on Menander's instructions.

treatises surveyed here also became established in the theoretical instructions of the rhetorical schools. The appearance of parallels in the Pastorals both to these treatises and to the school instructions indicates the level of culture those letters represent and the traditions they call upon for their own purposes.

The Isocratean discourses and Plutarch's treatises on statecraft have been characterized as open letters but, even so, they remain, like the orations of Dio Chrysostom, literary works which are not strictly epistolary in form. They provided valuable evidence of the practice of literary exhortation and the devices and method employed therein, especially the use of example. Complementing this evidence from literary practice was the theoretical work by Menander. This study now turns to epistolary literature, especially works of exhortation, to see how the hortatory character of the Pastorals might become clearer in their light and to determine what relation there is between example and the epistolary form.

CHAPTER V

Example in Epistolary Exhortation

The paraenetic discourses of Isocrates and the kingship treatises of Plutarch and Dio Chrysostom employ hortatory devices which have already been noted in the Pastoral Epistles and a further rapport among the writings will be indicated in chapter VIII. The Isocratean discourses even betray some epistolary characteristics and Plutarch's treatises appear to be open letters of a sort. However, none of these hortatory works is an epistle in the formal sense. Consequently, epistles properly so called from the non-Christian world of Greece and Rome will now be taken up to see how the Pastorals correspond to their use of examples.

I. Example in Official Letters

This study will first consider some actual letters by officials to communities and subordinate office-holders. While it would be unrealistic to expect all of the characteristics from the literary theory and practice to be echoed in these letters, the appearance of the principal characteristics will demonstrate that the literary theory and practice sometimes serve the needs and expectations of public officials, and are not simply fabrications of the rhetors' imagination or the encomiasts' flattery. Furthermore, the relative scarcity of these characteristics will demonstrate the difference in environments between the official letters and the literary exhortations.

A. *Official Letters from the Hellenistic Period*

The royal correspondence of the Hellenistic period which C. Bradford Welles studied bears out his conclusion that the official letter, as opposed to the literary-philosophical epistle, developed without influence from the rhetorical schools.[1]

---

[1] H. Rabe, "Aus Rhetoren-Handschriften," *RhM* n.F. 64 (1909) 289 ff., discusses the general lack of attention given by the early rhetors to letter writing. Their interest was in literary forms which would affect larger circles. At most, the directions for and exercise in letter writing are sparse in comparison with other forms (see Theon, *Prog.* 2:115 (L. von

Rather, the original form of official letters to individuals was that of the private letter, while the form of those to communities followed the prevailing form of communication between communities.[2] Nonetheless, although the forms seem not to have been prescribed in handboooks, Welles admits that the style in the letters "may at times show the rhetorical training of the royal secretaries."[3]

An edict from a later period[4] manifests more explicit rhetorical influence in its elaborate preamble, which celebrates Galba's auspicious accession to the imperial throne.[5] But in this letter, as in the others noted above, the commands themselves are delivered in a straightforward and unadorned way.

Sometimes, the letters carry prescriptions, *entolai,* which aim at an audience beyond their stated addressees and which were probably circulated among several officials.[6] Moreover, it is wrong automatically to associate *entolē* with "edict."

Spengel, ed., *Rhetores Graeci,* 3 vols. [Leipzig: B.G. Teubner, 1853]) on letter writing as an exercise in prosopopoeia). Even Demetrius *Eloc.* 223 (W.R. Roberts, trans., *Demetrius: On Style,* LCL [London: W. Heinemann, 1932]) which refers to the letter as half a dialogue, does not go on to offer an introduction to letter writing. Where interest is expressed it is usually in the letter as a literary showpiece.

[2] C. Bradford Welles, *Royal Correspondence in the Hellenistic Period: A Study in Greek Epigraphy* (Chicago: Ares, 1974) xlii-xliii.

[3] Welles, xlii. Among the letters to individuals encomiastic features can be noted in *Eps.* 14 and 28. The "more polite" tenor of letters of request, as opposed to outright command sent to cities (e.g., 17, 38, 45, 63) also agrees with rhetorical theory on "figured" speech or covert allusion. F. Schroeter, *De regum hellenisticorum epistulis in lapidibus servatis quaestiones stilisticae* (Leipzig: B.G. Teubner, 1931) 33 ff., makes similar observations.

[4] July 6, 68 A.D., according to G. Chalon, *L'Edit de Tiberius Julius Alexander* (Olten/ Lausanne: Urs Graf, 1964) 43.

[5] Chalon, 79.

[6] The second plural forms indicate a broad audience, i.e., the citizenry of Egypt or of Alexandria, as Chalon proposes on 81. Other letters, even when they carry the name of a single addressee, seem to look to a wider audience as well. Schroeter observes that the use of the third person imperative in *Ep.* 14 to Anaximbrotus might mean that the letter to the chief official of Phrygia was also given to other *stratēgoi. Ep.* 65 likewise was presumably given to the *stratēgoi* of separate *pagi,* for the royal decree in 11.11-35 is pertinent to the whole kingdom, so Schroeter says on 37. The fact of the distribution of the letter among several *strategoi* leaps to one's notice in the opening lines of the *entolai* of Mettius Rufus, as E.P. Wegener concludes on 333-34 of his "The ENTOΛAI of Mettius Rufus (pVindob G INV 25825 V-VI 7)," *Eos* 48 (1956). P. Collomp, "La Lettre à plusieurs destinataires," *Atti del IV Congresso Internazionale di Papirologia — Firenze 1935* (Milan: Società Editrice "Vita e Pensiero," 1936) 199-207, discusses four possible modes under which decretal letters in Egypt might have been circulated among numerous *stratēgoi.* This would involve recopying the letter, indicating each time the appropriate addressees and altering the grammatical person and number. But the fact of multiple addressees or readers is common to them all. Moreover, even when the letter remains in the singular and is addressed to one official, displaying the letter on a stone stele not only assured it a wider audience but also indicates that the wider audience was intended from the start.

Some letters contain *entolai* which might better be characterized as "instructions" than as "edicts."[7]   In addition, these circular *entolai* might actually be "memoranda" about the general obligations of an office, given by a superior to a subordinate official upon the latter's assumption of a new position.[8] The "instructions" and "memoranda" are mentioned here not only because they betray rhetorical influence but also because other features in them associate as well with the Pastorals, and these might help understand how the Pastorals might have been written and intended to be read. That is to say, each of the Pastoral Epistles shares with the "memorandum," e.g. pTebt 703, those elements by which a superior official designates to his subordinate officers some of the instructions pertinent to the execution of their new tasks.[9]

B. *The Memorandum pTebt 703 to a Newly Appointed Official*

The memorandum pTebt 703 for the most part contains specific prescriptions concerning the official supervision of agriculture, transport, revenues, and government monopolies, which the addressee is expected to carry out.   To these are appended directives on the treatment of deserters and the protocol of official correspondence.   The last 23 lines, however, differ in that they propose general

---

[7] See Wegener's discussion of Metzger and Kränzlein on the term *entolē* in reference to the *entolai* of Mettius Rufus, 331-32.

[8] Rostovtzeff's introduction to the Tebtunis Papyrus 703 (A.S. Hunt et al., eds., *The Tebtunis Papyri*, 3, 1 [London: Humphrey Milford, 1933] 68-69) claims that the instructions there from a *diocetes* to a subordinate official upon the latter's assumption of office is in the nature of a memorandum, a vademecum or appointment charter, which summarized the details of a personal interview or which excerpted pertinent sections from a more comprehensive instruction. In any case, the instructions herein are the standard instruction by a *diocetes* on the office of an *oeconomus* and are not specific to a particular *nome* or set of circumstances. For the discussion of its character, see Hunt, 68-71. In a contrasting understanding of *entolai*, U. Wilcken, "Urkunden Referat," *APF* 11 (1935) 148 ff., sees the circulated *entolai* as also referring to "letters of appointment," which carry directions on the management of an office. Rostovtzeff, 69, claims that while these may carry news of an appointment, any definition of the office therein would be only in the most general terms. Wilcken's evidence, however, from BGU VIII, 1768, does convincingly link the term *entolai* with an appointment memorandum. In any case, the debate over the word *entolai* holds interest for this study only to call attention to the nature of the document represented by pTebt 703, as distinct from an edict as such, like those discussed above, and as closer to the "instructions" of Mettius Rufus. The publication of the appointment memoranda likewise reveals another function, paricularly when attention falls, with Wilcken, 149, on pTebt 703. 235 ff. which state that "all cannot do whatever they want."

[9] pTebt 703. 258-61, alludes to the encounter of the official with his superior and the instructions given him then, of which this letter is a reminder (*tauta kai d[i]a tou hypomnēmatos kalōs echein hypelabon g[r]apsai soi*). This might help explain the anomalous situation in the Pastorals where Paul supplies significant directives to Timothy and Titus by letter soon after his interview with them in which he presumably gave his associates their apostolic mandates.

instructions on the behavior of the new official. The general character of the exhortation and some of its features resemble what has already been noted in the kingship treatises and other hortatory works analyzed above.

In the first place, at 257-61 the author refers to his face-to-face meeting with his subordinate and the instructions given him then. This document, then, comes by way of reminder (*d[i]ạ tou hypomnēmatos*) and is a literary surrogate for that personal presence.

Second, at 261-64 there is a short list of three general qualities of outstanding rule and more may have been included in the corrupt lines that follow (264-69). Moreover, antithesis is used at 271-75 to urge the official to unwavering uprightness (*eutakt [ein] kaị ạkamptein*) and to flee corrupt associations which could lead to evil (*mē sym[ple]ḳesthai ... pheugein*).

Third, the conduct and striving of the official is to be publicly noticed. There is a hint at 270-71 of the exemplary nature of the official's activities (*eu memartyrēmenēs tēs kath'hēmas anastrophēs kai agōnias*). The call to be *anenklētos* at 276 is another allusion to the official's public example.[10] This mentioned together with keeping the instructions at the forefront of his attention (*echein ta hypomnēmata dia cheros* 277-78). The memorandum thus endorses keeping the prescriptions as the mode of achieving a good reputation for the official and at the same time promotes adherence to the law on the part of the populace. It was stated earlier in the instruction that observation of the official's scrupulous attention to the law would prompt a similar respect for the law among the public (cf. *ou[thenos e]chont[o]s exousian ho bouletai poiein, a[[la] pạntōn oikonomoumenōn apo tou beltistou* 230-32 and 222-34 generally). There is even a suggestion at 270-71 that the official's conduct and striving find their prototype in the superior official (*kath'hēmas*).[11] The *oeconomus* is reminded that he is the representative of his superior in every respect.

The general nature of the instruction here contrasts sharply with the specific requirements in the rest of the document. This is discernible in the vocabulary: *idịōs, katharōs, apo tou beltistou, ta dikaia, ṭ[aut]ạ gar kai toutois paraplēsia, anastrophē, agōnia eutakt[ein], ạkamptein, phauloi homiliai, hapas syndyasmos ho epi kakia[i] genomenos, anenklētoi*. Thus, in the devices of lists, contrasts and example; in the vocabulary conduct; in the general commands expressed by *dei* and a series of infinitives; and in the promise of a reward for good service (*nomizein meizonōn axiōthēsesthai* 277), these last verses are more of an exhortation than a record of specific duties. As such, they represent the technique both of the kingship treatises and of hortatory works generally.

Considering the memorandum as a whole, the author admits the difficulty of writing on so complex a matter at 235 ff. Nonetheless, what he does write he

---

[10] Public reproach, *kataphronēsis*, cautioned against at 161-63, is attributed there to the official's inept execution of his office.

[11] LSJ "*kata*" B IV, 883.

expects to inform *oeconomus* on how to deal with the variety of situations covered and, from that, to get some idea about how to handle other situations which may arise (*kai peri tōn ek tou paratych[ontos pi] ptontōn homoiōs diasapheite [ho]pōs ek [...] ... e anē ... a chrēmatizēi* 241-44). The memorandum thus recalls to the official the instructions he had already been given and knows and also hopes to stimulate his professional expertise.

Nor are the contents of the memorandum only for the *oeconomus* to know. Wilcken finds that a similar "appointment charter" or memorandum, BGU VII 1768, carried with it the requirement that it be published. Such publication has the effect of getting what is prescribed and suggested to the official out to the broader public, for whom the regulations are ultimately intended.

The publication of these instructions legitimates them before the public concerned and characterizes the subordinate officers as authoritative executors of the higher official's will. This executive function entails a degree of discretionary freedom in handling specific situations which go beyond the letter's standard instructions.[12] In the end, it is the subordinate official's careful overseeing of the activities in the area under his charge, as well as his own uprightness of character which assure him a secure and praiseworthy period in office.[13] An expected consequence of his own exemplary execution of the directives is the public's more scrupulous obedience of those prescriptions. Letters of this sort, then, are outlines of the scope of the office and hortatory reminders for the new officials, as well as communications to the communities of what would be expected of them under the new regime. The exemplary presence in the person of the *oeconomus* gives life to the prescriptions. The exemplary presence of his superior, by way of the written memorandum, gives a personal immediacy to the prescriptions both for the official and for his subjects.

C. *The Instructions of Mettius Rufus (pVind 25824b II)*

Another letter, the so-called instructions of Mettius Rufus,[14] is interesting for its list of qualifications for office and the contrast this offers to the hortatory conclusion of pTebt 703. Although not detailed, the qualifications of wealth, age, education, and previous experience form a sort of questionnaire of a rather practical sort. Only the allusion to *hē tou biou agōgē* resembles the unspecified qualities in pTebt 703.[15] The caveats fit the actual situation of the selection of candidates

---

[12] pTebt 703.235 ff.

[13] pTebt 703 *fin.* and 222-34.

[14] Published by H. Metzger with a translation and brief commentary in "Zur Stellung der liturgischen Beamten Ägyptens in frühchristlicher Zeit," *MH* 2 (1945) 54-62.

[15] If Wegener's interpretation of pVind which links *tēi tou biou agōgē* with *ti proteron (epra-) gmateusanto* is correct, then these two phrases refer to prior "professional" activity.

for office, as do the hints at the particular tasks which the office entails.[16] Unlike the qualifications,[17] the official duties are not detailed in the letter. While antithesis is used to set out the qualifications to look for and those which disqualify a person from consideration, example and any other hortatory features are absent.

D. *Concluding Observations*

In comparison with the literary works on kingship which were treated in chapter IV, these samples of official correspondence present some striking similarities, but differences too. The exhortation to an upright life is totally lacking in the brief pVind 25824b II; and even in pTebt 703, where it does appear, it comes at the end and is separate, therefore, from the long prescriptive section. Moreover, the examples, comparisons, sayings, personal details, antitheses, which are woven together with the prescriptions in the literary exhortations, are absent from these letters in their prescriptive sections. Others aspects of these letters, however, e.g., the letter form itself, the situation of superior writing to a subordinate representative, the circular and/or public character of the letters, the mixture (though rare) of exhortation and official directives, will prove helpful in understanding the Pastoral Epistles. And so, while on the basis of the documents examined the line of development to the Pastorals cannot be said to pass directly through the decretal letters, nonetheless, the Pastorals can be said to reflect the latter in certain ways. The difference lies largely in the rhetorical features of the Pastorals which characterize them as something different from the purely regulatory documents. The study of the hortatory discourses and the kingship treatises above and of the epistolary exhortations to follow in this chapter all show the Pastorals to be more at home in an explicitly rhetorical environment.

II. **Example in Hortatory Letters**

The official letters surveyed above were useful in showing the practice of exhortation and prescription in circular letter form as well as some attempt to use the personal example of the official to make the prescriptions concrete. Both of these suggest the practical application of the principles learned in the handbooks

---

[16] pVind excludes members of the same household, inhabitants of the locale, former colleagues in office who carry obligations to other officials or are linked by some compromising relationships. On the positive side, it requires the ability to write, in order to insure service to the community without excessive individual or community burdens, but one which is impartial and competent.

[17] Although there is some overlapping with the example sections, the "church order" sections breathe the same spirit as this excerpt from the prescriptions of Mettius Rufus. The example sections, on the other hand, are work-sketches of a more idealized sort.

and the schools. The discourses on the duties of young officials and kings proved to be better reflections of the theorical treatises on example. They also clearly echo the concerns of the schools for moral as well as technical education. While these discourses exhibit an epistolary character, the combination of hortatory content and method with epistolary form emerges most clearly in literary epistles, like those of Seneca, from the early Empire. Here the literary form of the letter and the hortatory device of example complement each other fully. But long before Seneca, the hortatory literature of popular, moralizing philosophy in the Hellenistic period included the epistle as a favored form, with example as its preferred device. Hence, attention will be paid to the development of this relationship. The theoretical consideration will then be illuminated by the practice of Seneca's letters.

A. *The Epistle in Philosophical and Ethical Exhortation*

H. Peter [18] finds that early in Greek literary history the letter and the speech shared similar laws of elaboration, only the letter was shorter. Thus, the pupils in the schools learned to express themselves according to various life situations and personalities. In the Empire, with the rhetorical schools gradually becoming cut off from real life and losing the practical aim to convince, both the literary epistle and the speech settled into glorying in their own technique and spirit. The same period, however, saw the full flowering of the teaching letter, which developed from the dialogue in the philosophical schools. In fact, as the dialogue also lost its real-life connection and with the geographical spread of the philosophical schools, the letter became a surrogate for the immediate intercourse between the head of the school and his pupils. These letters exhorted as well as taught and the exhortation was both to philosophy and to a corresponding ethical life.[19]

Letters of admonition, as Peter discovered, assumed several forms, depending on the end intended.[20] Guillemin makes similar observations about the use of epistles in instruction and moral direction, and also finds their specific forms to be

---

[18] H. Peter, *Der Briefe in der römischen Literatur: Literaturgeschichtliche Untersuchungen und Zusammenfassungen; Abh. sachs. Ges. Wiss.* 47 Philol.-hist. Klasse 20 (1903) 14 ff. On letter collections see G. Constable, *Letters and Letter Collections* (Turnhout, Belgium: Brepols, 1976) and J. Carcopino, *Cicero: The Secrets of His Correspondence* I (London: Routledge & Kegan Paul, 1951, repr. Westport., CT: Greenwood, 1969).

[19] Peter, 18-19, 225 ff. and see the comments by Rabe, 290 n.l.

[20] Peter finds these varieties of admonitory letters: *parainesis (praeceptio)*, *logos paramythētikos (consolatio, logos hypothētikos (suasio), logos protreptikos (cohortatio), etymologia (causarum inquisitio)* in Seneca *Ep.* 95.65 (R.M. Gummere, trans., *Lucius Annaeus Seneca. Ad Lucilium epistulae morales*, LCL, 3 vols. [London: W. Heinemann, 1917]; L.D. Reynolds, ed., *Lucius Annaeus Seneca; Ad Lucilium epistulae morales*, 2 vols. [Oxford: Clarendon, 1965]), and Syrianus 4.763 (C. Walz. ed., *Rhetores Graeci*, 9 vols. [Stuttgart/Tübingen: J.G. Cotta, 1835]).

dependent upon the end in view,[21] though she sees three basic forms where Peter distinguishes five.[22]

Guillemin strongly emphasizes the fact that this labor of exhortation is not only not inconsistent with a relationship of friendship but is actually a facet of that relationship.[23] Over against instruction and exhortation in public lectures, one finds in certain authors a preference for the more familiar and quietly persuasive tone of letters between friends.[24] A letter makes the friend present in conversation,[25] wherein he acquits himself of the task of friends to exhort and entreat,[26] advise and correct,[27] offer prescriptions and personal example.[28] Viewed from the other side, a person counts on the opinion and guidance of those of his friends who are more experienced.[29]

---

[21] A.M. Guillemin, *Pline et la vie littéraire de son temps* (Paris: Société d'édition "Les Belles Lettres, 1929) 32. Here the epistle is the medium both for official and public instruction in the household establishments and for that undertaken by friends (cf. Pliny *Eps.* 1.14.1; 4.19.7 (B. Radice, trans., *C. Plinius Caecilius Secundus. Epistulae et panegyricus*, LCL, 2 vols. [Cambridge: Harvard University, 1969]; R.A.B. Mynors, ed., *C. Plinius Caecilius Secundus. Epistularum libri decem* [Oxford: Clarendon, 1963]); Cicero *Fam.* 1.12.12; 2.1.2; 4.17.8 (W.G. Williams, trans., *Marcus Tullius Cicero. The Letters to His Friends*, LCL, 4 vols. [London: W. Heinemann, 1927-29]); *Or.* 4.142 (H.M. Hubbell, trans., *Marcus Tullius Cicero. Brutus, orator*, LCL [London: W. Heinemann, 1935]); Horace *Ep.* 2.1.106 (H.R. Fairclough, trans., *Quintus Hortatius Flaccus. Satires, Epistles and Ars Poetica*, LCL, 2 vols. [London: W. Heinemann, 1926]).

[22] Guillemin, 33-36. A letter of friendly admonition reminds the recipient of already known prescriptions (Cicero *Am.* 25.91 (W.A. Falconer, trans., *Marcus Tullius Cicero. De senectute, de amicitia, de divinatione*, LCL [London: W. Heinemann, 1923]); *De or* 2.24.99; 8.24.1 (H. Rackham, trans., *Marcus Tullius Cicero. De oratore, de fato, paradoxa stoicorum, de partitione oratoria*, LCL, 2 vols. [London: W. Heinemann, 1942]). One of the exhortations urges officials to conduct the offices under their direction (Cicero *Fam.* 2.7.1-2; 10.1.2; 12.24.1; *Q. Fr.* 1.1; Pliny *Ep.* 8.24). Finally, the letter of reproach seeks to criticize with frankness but also to show the path to improvement for the common good (Cicero *Am.* 24.88; *Off.* 1.17.58; 1.37.134 (W. Miller, trans. *Marcus Tullius Cicero. De officiis*, LCL [London: W. Heinemann, 1913]); *N.D.* 1.3.5 (H. Rackham, trans., *Marcus Tullius Cicero. De natura deorum, academica*, LCL [London: W. Heinemann, 1933]); Horace *A.P.* 445-46; *Ep.* 2.1.219-22; Pliny *Ep.* 6.17.3; Nepos *Cat.* 2.4 (P.K. Marshall, ed., *Cornelii Nepotis vitae* [Leipzig: B.G. Teubner, 1977]).

[23] Guillemin, 3ff., also I. Hadot, *Seneca und die griechisch-römische Tradition der Seelenleitung* (Berlin: de Gruyter, 1969) 165 ff.; H. Koskenniemi, *Studien zur Idee und Phraseologie des griechischen Briefes bis 400 n. Chr.*, Annales Academie Scientiarum Fennicae, Ser. B, 102.2 (Helsinki: Finnischen Akademie der Wissenschaften, 1956) 35 ff.

[24] *Seneca Eps.* 38.1; 75.1.

[25] *Seneca Eps.* 16.1-2; 27.1; 40.1; 75.1.

[26] *Cicero Fam.* 5.17.3.

[27] *Cicero Am.* 13.44 and *Off.* 1.17.58. See Hadot, 66.

[28] *Cicero Fam.* 5.13.3-4.

[29] *Cicero Off.* 1.14.147; Pliny *Eps.* 1.14.3-4; 1.12.11-12; 4.17.4-9.

Let these remarks suffice to describe the theory of the letter as a hortatory medium and the situation of the epistolary exchange within a context of friendship. The name of Seneca has already been mentioned in this discussion and now he will come under closer scrutiny as a practitioner of friendly exhortation by means of the letter.

B. Seneca's Epistolary Exhortation

1. Hortatory Features

Hildegard Cancik distinguishes two methods of argumentation in Seneca's letters: the theoretical-doxographical and the paraenetic.[30] The paraenetic method commands the interest of this study because the elements of this method repeat themselves in all of the paraenetic literature herein discussed. In its simplest form, the paraenetic method employs commands, prohibitions, advice, warnings. The method, however, can also marshal a broad array of auxiliary devices like declarations, comparisons, examples, explanations, applications, and concluding adhortations.[31]

Cancik devotes particular attention to Seneca's use of example in his prescriptive arguments.[32] She finds that in Seneca's method precept and example, both positive and negative, complement each other and perform the same function of provoking attention and specifying modes of action (*Eps.* 94.42; 95.65). Moreover, examples, allegories and applications stand in the prescriptive sections of the letters where scientific, philosophic or doxographic statements and arguments stand in the descriptive sections.[33]

2. Self-Description and the Letter Form

A large variety of examples is called upon, but the writer-preceptor himself ranks in the forefront among these.[34] This is due to the letter form itself which from the outset carried philosophical paraenesis tied to autobiographical traces. Thus, along with the tone and context of friendship in the instructional letter as already noted above, there is also the self-presentation of the author. These belong to the letter's essence.[35] Friendship offers the presupposition for the

---

[30] H. Cancik, *Untersuchungen zu Senecas epistulae morales* (Hildesheim: Georg Olms, 1967) 16 ff. See also Hadot, 8-9.

[31] Cancik, 23-24.

[32] He calls for their use in *Eps.* 59.6; 78.21; 83.13; 93.8; 98.13.

[33] Cancik, 25 ff.

[34] Cancik, 48.

[35] Demetrius *Eloc.* 227 *schedon gar eikona hekastos tēs heautou psychēs graphei tēn epistolēn; kai esti men kai ex allou logou pantos idein to ēthos tou graphontos, ex oudenos de houtōs hōs epistolēs.* See also Cancik, 50 ff.

exchange of letters and the intimate self-expression is both proper to the letter form and understandable in a context of friendship.[36] The letter, for all intents and purpose, becomes the personal presence of the friend who advises and instructs. Personal presence achieved through the letter may actually be more effective and "pure" than physical presence.[37]

In the literary epistle, as opposed to the real letter, this "epistolary presence" is not merely fortuitous but constitutes an important part of the letter's total effect. While not a real conversation, the letter mediates a description of a mode of existence and offers testimony to it from the author's own experience. Moreover, the literary addressee, and through him the audience actually aimed at by the literary epistle, is drawn into this self-description of the author without ever speaking, a situation quite different from that of the conversation reports in the Platonic dialogues.[38] The letter enables the literary self-description to unfold, and so the personal witness is an integral part of the letter form. The two are so close that the choice of the letter form and the meaning of his self-description for the author are the same.[39]

In order to understand the meaning of the self-description in a letter, a distinction must be made between two levels on which this personal witness is asserted. The first finds expression in the epistolary commonplaces, mostly at the beginning and end of the letter. These establish the situation of the letter, whether real or fictitious, and create in concrete detail the intimate space shared by the friends. In some authors this level of self-description might involve no more than a varied use of common epistolary formulas of greeting and farewell, expressions of concern and well-wishing, notification about health and personal circumstances. In Seneca's case, however, Cancik finds that these merely set the stage for another level of self-description. This is a more elaborate personal testimony found throughout the letter as a whole.

References to the addressee can also function on these two levels. Thus, Seneca's remarks about Lucilius add another dimension to the author's epistolary presence and also establish the pedagogical situation of teacher and learner. On a

---

[36] Koskenniemi, 35 ff., and Seneca *Eps*. 67.2; 38.1; 11.8,10. Personal contact and even life shared with the teacher (Seneca *Eps*. 75.2; 6.6) are important elements in this type of philosophical-ethical instruction (Hadot, 164).

[37] K. Thraede, *Grundzüge griechisch-römischer Brieftopik* (Munich: C.H. Beck, 1970) 70-71. B.L. Hijmans, *Inlaboratus et Facilis: Aspects of Structure in Some Letters of Seneca* (Leiden: E.J. Brill, 1976) 145-46 and n. 34, argues on the basis of *Ep*. 75 that for Seneca the very style used in the letter says much about the moral situation of the writer. See *Ep*. 114.1. Hadot, 175, finds Lucilius to be colorless and flat in contrast to Seneca's own personality in the letters. This, she says, enables the reader to "feel himself transposed without further ado into his place."

[38] Cancik, 60 ff., and Seneca *Ep*. 6.4.

[39] Cancik, 71-72.

second level, however, the addressee joins the author in becoming personal witness to the complex principles which the letter proposes.[40]

3. Self-Description as Example

Cancik, after considering the function of the personal notices in Seneca's letters, finally concludes that the self-testimony serves as an example. Thus, as already mentioned, they do more than formally set up the epistolary situation. The formulaic notices join the personal revelations and even the apparently gratuitous anecdotes and trivial details [41] to create a strong impression of friendship, which for Seneca is the context for his particular manner of philosophical instruction. More than this, however, Seneca's self-descriptions and personal notices attest the measure of success or failure in his own effort to realize the good, the philosophical ideal. In this Seneca demonstrates the difficulty of the undertaking to which he urges Lucilius. Far from the ideal of the wise man himself, Seneca, himself still learning, nonetheless boldly shows the way to his friend. As a result, authoritative demands and prohibitions stand alongside admissions of weakness and imperfection. Seneca the teacher reflects the tension that comes with knowing that education is always likewise self-education (*Eps.* 26.7; 27.1). He also exhorts Lucilius to achieve and exercise a similar unity of self-education and education, of teaching and learning (*Eps.* 89.23; 115.1). In his self-description, Seneca calls attention to his own mores and establishes a concrete and personal example of the striving toward the ideal which he urges on Lucilius. The example of his own life verifies his teaching (*Ep.* 71.7, where he ascribes his own method to Socrates).[42] The personal example of the teacher in the letter is all the more effective because in a context of friendship it has the weight of authority and the persuasiveness of affection.[43]

Clearly, when Seneca proposes his own example through the letter, he does this for the most part in an implicit way. As explained above, it is precisely the letter form which makes this possible. Seneca, however, also uses personal example explicit and as part of the development of his exhortation and instruction (*Ep.*

---

[40] Cancik, 72 ff., where she discusses *Eps.* 5.7-8; 13.12, 14; 24.

[41] Cancik, 75 ns. 121-24.

[42] Cancik, 75 ff. and Hadot, 175. See Hadot 105 ff. for Seneca's and Epictetus' views on the need for exercise in virtue. Seneca *Eps.* 40.12; 100.11 stresses the need for words and deeds to match. K. Döring, *Exemplum Socratis: Studien zur Sokratesnachwirkung in der kynisch-stoisch Popularphilosophie der frühen Kaiserzeit und im frühen Christentum*, Hermes Einzelschriften, 42 (Wiesbaden: Franz Steiner, 1979) 20 adds *Eps.* 26.2; 52.8; 94.48-49. See also *Vit. beat.* 24.4-5 (J.W. Basore, trans., *Lucius Annaeus Seneca. Moral Essays*, LCL, 3 vols. [London: W. Heinemann, 1928]) and A.C. Andrews, "Did Seneca Practise the Ethics of His Epistles? *CJ* 25 (1929-30) 611-25.

[43] Hadot, 176. In addition to authoritative personality and friend, she would add a third "face" to the spiritual director, that of doctor, 143, 164, 172.

6.3-5).[44] Closer attention must now be paid to personal example, whether explicit or implicit, and Seneca's use of the device.

4. Examples in Seneca's Moral Instruction

a. *Theory and Function of Examples*

While his examples are varied in their sources and categories,[45] Seneca focuses as in *Ep.* 6, on personal example and some elaboration of that distinctive kind of example is in order. Even before that is done, however, the diverse relationships that obtain among examples of any kind, the author using them, the reality they call attention to, the end intended in their use, and the audience to which they are directed deserve some treatment.[46]

This brief summary will recall the theoretical survey of chapter III and will advance it by setting the discussion in a hortatory context. In one employment of the device, example is a sample, one instance of a category, a pattern which what is sought after must fit. The author constructs or fabricates the exemplar. The end envisaged is the discovery and recognition of that person or thing. The audience might be expected to join the search or at least to accommodate their perceptions and evaluations to those of the author.

Much like this usage is that of example as specimen.[47] The difference lies in the fact that the author does not construct the exemplar but finds an actual representative of a series of objects or persons. The end envisaged and the audience's reaction remain the same.

Example as prototype or model constitutes a third category. This one resembles the first two in the nature of example as a real specimen found by the author

---

[44] His examples include those from the past, *Eps.* 29.4; 52.2, 7, and from the present, *Eps.* 52.8; 100.12.

[45] H. Kornhardt, *Exemplum: Eine bedeutungsgeschichtliche Studie* (Göttingen: Robert Noske, 1936) 63, finds that the Latin word *exemplum,* as a technical term, encompasses all the configurations of example in the Greek term *paradeigma* i.e., historical example, moralizing anecdotes, *apophthegmata,* comparisons, similes, metaphors, fables, mottoes.

[46] Kornhardt, 10-61, discusses example under the categories adopted in this study. The first part of her analysis notes the meanings of *exemplum* in Latin literature derived from the basic notion of proof of merchandise or its value. These reflect Greek notions like *eikōn, hypodeigma, tekmērion, sēmeion* (62 and n. 26). In the second part, 49-61, she treats the meanings derived from the notion of prototype or model. The analysis in this paper concentrates on the meanings of Kornhardt's second part, but coordinates the categories there with those of the first part.

[47] Kornhardt mentions variations on the demonstrative *exempla* in the first section, 10-13, where the example of particular traits or activities serve as "proof" of the entire character of conduct. A physical gesture or sign and even a person's own activities or his treatment by others can be a witness indicating something about a person, a group, or a circumstance. The purpose behind using the two aforementioned demonstrative examples varies according to the nature of the speech into which they are incorporated.

or his own idealized construct. It differs from both of the preceding in the following significant ways. Attention centers either on the person or thing which imitates or copies the prototype or on the one who at least strives to fashion itself after the model. Thus, the end in view is the effort to imitate the example.[48] The audience is expected to enter or continue a program of instruction and formation as outlined by the author.[49]

Finally, example serves as an instructional experience, on the basis of a precedent in personal circumstances or historical events. The example directs attention toward an analogous set of circumstances or conditions in the present or future. The example is meant to be learned and to be an aid in formulating future decisions.[50]

b. *Variety of Examples*

With these remarks on the categories of example and the effects expected from their use, the topic of personal example can be resumed to see what the range of possible examples there might be. Historical figures were preferred by the theoreticians of rhetoric surveyed above, but they were open to more recent, even contemporary personal figures. Typical characters were also admitted by some alongside specific persons. While the playwright Terence could have Demea say in *Ad.* 411-12, "Salvos sit! Spero est similis maiorum suom...praeceptorum plenust istorum ille," citing familial examples,[51] the models usually chosen by the public at large are the upper classes. Cicero laments that their licentiousness is only too readily adopted by the whole state.[52] As in battle the leader's example carries more weight than his words or his strict discipline,[53] so in civic matters the monarch's example is decisive for the whole state.[54]

---

[48] When Kornhardt, 13-23, treats examples as proofs, or witnesses not to personality but to virtues and vices, a moral, protreptic purpose is evident. The same is true when, through a process of abstraction, the person serves as a personification of a virtue, 24-26.

[49] Kornhardt, 26-33, treats a parallel usage found in illustrative examples employed to give practical advice in education.

[50] Kornhardt, 34-47, sees the same use served by examples which illustrate and clarify and, in a negative way, by examples of punishment, 35-48.

[51] J. Sargeaunt, trans., *Terence*, LCL, 2 vols. (London: W. Heinemann, 1912).

[52] Cicero *Leg.* 3.14.30-32 (C.W. Keyes, *Marcus Tullius Cicero. De republica, de legibus,* LCL [London: W. Heinemann, 1928]) and 1.39.140.

[53] Livy *Ab urbe cond.* 7.32.12, " 'Facta mea, non dicta vos, milites,' inquit (Valerius), 'sequi volo, nec disciplinam modo sed exemplum etiam a me petere' " (B.O. Foster, trans., *T. Livi ab urbe condita,* LCL, 14 vols. [London: W. Heinemann, 1919]).

[54] Pliny *Pan.* 45.6, "Nam vita principis censura est aeque perpetua ad hanc dirigimur, ad hanc convertimur, nec tam imperio nobis opus est quam exemplo. Quippe infidelis recti magister est metus. Melius homines exemplis docentur, quae in primis hoc in se boni habent, quod adprobent quae precipiunt fieri posse." See also *Res gestae divi Augusti* 2.8.16 and Velleius Paterculus *Hist.* 2.126.4 (F.W. Shipley, trans., *C. Velleius Paterculus. Compen-*

These are the models toward which the crowd looks spontaneously; but when thought and care are applied to the selection of examples, other personal types emerge. In the school the teacher himself is the principal model, as the discussions above pointed out. At home, the parent is, as are the *oikeia paradeigmata,* the *exempla domestica,* the exemplary ancestors in the family. This category also applies to the outstanding figures from the history of the civic community.[55] In both applications, this category stands in a line of development from the funeral *epitaphia* and civic *encomia.* Finally, the pupil himself is urged to become an example too, as a result of the progress he makes. Seneca proclaims in *Ep.* 98.13, "Nos quoque aliquid et ipsi faciamus animose. Simus inter exempla!" [56]

c. *Function and Content of Examples in Seneca*

While the preceding paragraphs establish the range of possible personal examples, this must be completed by a look into the exemplary figure to determine what is offered for imitation and what those called to become models are expected to display. Isocrates declares the superiority of an *eikōn tēs dianoias* over material statues, for they give a view of the interior of the person.[57] *Eikōn* is linked with *paradeigma* through their similar function [58] and later theorists include it as a species of the proof *paradeigma.*[59] *Eikōn* is not just *mimēma,* likeness or copy, its original meaning; but, through its function, it serves as model as well.[60] Still, whether *eikōn* or *paradeigma, imago* or *exemplum,* the question still remains, What is the content of the model? What does it mean to say that it is a likeness of the spirit comparable to a statue in marble? And what is to be imitated?

The answer to these questions rests on the function of the example. When demonstration of virtues or vice is the aim, then the deeds or particular qualities given are witnesses not to the whole personality but to the aspect being considered.[61] Sometimes the same qualities, when offered for imitation, are given in a model fig-

---

dium of Roman History, *Res Gestae Divi Augusti,* LCL [London: W. Heinemann, 1924]); Ovid *Met.* 15.8.34 (F.J. Miller, trans., *Ovid Metamorphoses,* LCL, 2 vols. [London: W. Heinemann, 1928]); Suetonius *Aug.* 34.2 and *Tib.* 34.1 (J.C. Rolfe, trans., *Suetonius. Lives of the Caesars,* LCL, 2 vols. [London: W. Heinemann, 1914]). See also Kornhardt, 73, 32-33 n. 71, and A. Lumpe, "Exemplum," *RAC* (Stuttgart: Anton Hiersemann, 1966) 6:1236.

[55] K. Jost, *Das Beispeil und Vorbild der Vorfahren bei den attischen Rednern und Geschichtschreibern bis Demosthenes* (Paderborn: F. Schöningh, 1936) gives copious instances of the use of illustrious citizens from the past as *domestica exempla.*

[56] See Seneca *Ep.* 6 for the notion of exemplary progress in virtue.

[57] Isocrates *Antid.* 7 and compare *Nic.* 36 and *Evag.* 73. (G. Norlin, trans., *Isocrates,* LCL, 3 vols. [London: W. Heinemann, 1928]). See H. Willms, *EIKON, eine begriffsgeschichtliche Untersuchung zum Platonismus* (Münster i.W.: Aschendorff, 1935) 3.

[58] Willms, 4.

[59] K. Alewell, *Über das rhetorische PARADEIGMA: Theorie, Beispielsammlungen, Verwendung in der römischen Literatur der Kaiserzeit* (Leipzig: A. Hoffman, 1913) 20-23, 60.

[60] Willms, 11-13 and n. 32, and see Isocrates *Antid.* 7, *Nic.* 36, *Evag.* 73-75.

[61] Kornhardt, 13, 20.

ure which seems to include a whole life or an entire personality. But, and this is true even when it is a historical personage, in these instances the model appears in a form idealized and suited to the particular teaching or in a typical way, corresponding to the common characterization of the historical figure or of the type of person referred to.[62] In the case of an educational model toward which the pupil is expected to strive, the prototype includes moral qualities as well as exemplary deeds and incarnates a degree of perfection which the student earnestly desires to attain.[63]

In the matter of an example to be imitated, the program of instruction gives some indication of how the model is supposed to be incorporated. As Pliny sees things in *Ep.* 8.23.2, the teacher is a *formator morum,* which implies a process, presumably organized in one way or another. The program in the rhetorical schools had three aspects, according to the *Auct. Her.* 1.2.3: *ars* or *praeceptio, imitatio,* and *exercitatio.*[64] This triad from rhetorical instruction has already appeared above in the description of Seneca's method of moral instruction. Seneca reflects an effort to form himself after his chosen exemplar in a practical way in *Vit beat.* 24.4-5. In *Ep.* 75.7, he uses medical imagery to describe the work of the spiritual guide who prescribes remedies and urges their practical application. In *Ep.* 6 he assumes the role of teacher (4) who prefers examples to precepts (5) and considers life practice of the rules important (6). He stresses assiduous exercise, and striving as the only way to progress (*Eps.* 16.1; 34.3; 69.6). And he sees his teaching role as one of sharing in the same struggle to progress, and of mutual encouragement with the disciple (*Ep.* 34.1-4).

The preference for example over precept expressed by Seneca in *Ep.* 6.5 reflects a common view. Example and precept enjoyed a long and, as seems likely, natural

---

[62] D.R. Stuart, *Epochs of Greek and Roman Biography* (Berkeley: University of California, 1928) 23-24; I. Bruns, *Das literarische Porträt der Griechen im fünften und vierten Jahrhundert vor Christi Geburt* (Berlin: Wilhelm Hertz, 1896) 158-59, 196-97; Jost, 79, 89; G. Misch, *Geschichte der Autobiographie: Das Altertum,* 2nd ed. (Leipzig: B.G. Teubner, 1931) 249-52, finds just such an idealized quality in Seneca's self-presentation. G. Misener, "Iconistic Portraits," *CPh* 19 (1924) 97-123 traces the use of *eikonismos* for identification in the legal sphere and for stylistic ornament in rhetoric (parallel to the rhetorical technique of *charaktērismos*).

[63] Kornhardt, 56-57. See Hadot, 175-76, for a summary of some of the idealized characteristics of spiritual director.

[64] H. Caplan, trans. *Cicero. Ad C. Herennium libri IV: de ratione dicendi,* LCL (Cambridge: Harvard University, 1954). On 7-8 n. c Caplan gives equivalent concepts to those in this triad as *technē* (also *paideia, epistēmē, mathēsis, scientia, doctrina*), *mimēsis, gymnasia* (also *askēsis, meletē, empeiria, synētheia, declamatio*). He traces the original triad to Protagoras, Plato, and Isocrates. In that form it contained nature (*physis, natura, ingenium, facultas*), theory and practice. An introductory bibliography to imitation in classical rhetoric is also included in the note. See J. Martin, *Antike Rhetorik, Technik und Methode* (Munich: C.H. Beck, 1974) 339, where he cites Cicero *De or.* 2.22.92 for the tripartite scheme of precept, imitation, and exercise.

relationship as complementary hortatory devices.[65] And so, even when some writers express a preference for example, the relationship with precepts is nonetheless maintained.[66] Seneca prefers instruction by example in *Ep.* 6.5 because they occasion more rapid learning, "quia longum iter est per praecepta, breve et efficax per exempla," but also because people trust what they see more than what they hear, "quia homines amplius oculis quam auribus credunt." [67]

The complementary relationship between precept and example is worked out by Seneca in *Ep.* 94. At 21 he declares that precepts help root out error by reminding a person and concentrating his attention on what he has already learned,[68] again by precept, as to what he should do in life ("quid agendum sit in vita" 19). In jarring the mind from passive knowledge to attentive readiness (cf. 25-26), practice (*agere*) must accompany learning (*discere* 47). To proceed successfully toward virtue, therefore, the student must be given a pattern to imitate (*imitari ... proposita* 51-52) and must be shown people who exemplify the point of the lesson, 73-74.

Similarly, at *Ep.* 84.10-11 Seneca says that he would like his *animus* to contain many arts (*artae*), precepts (*praecepta*) and examples of many epochs (*exempla*). He uses the image of the bee to describe the person eager to gather useful instruction from every source [69] but describes its assimilation in terms of the living resemblance of a child to his father not a lifeless picture (*imago*) reproducing an original. The key difference is in the unique stamp (*forma*) impressed on the features drawn from the model ("quae ex quo velut exemplare traxit" 8-9).

As noted above in the evidence from the late Republic and the early Empire, the place of friends in the process of instruction was very important.[70] A friendly

---

[65] Lumpe goes all the way back to Homer *Il.* 5.381-402; 6.128-41; 9.524-605; 19.85-136; 24.601-20; *Od.* 21.293-310. Hadot cites Seneca *Ep.* 95.65-73. where Seneca explains the complementarity between precept and illustrative example, be it a verbal outline or historical realization of the qualities outlined. He says of the device of illustrating by examples, which he calls characterization or ethology: "Haec res eandem vim habet quam praecipere. Nam qui praecipit dicit: 'illa facies, si voles temperans esse.' Qui describit, ait: 'temperans est qui illa facit, qui illis abstinet.' Quaeris, quid intersit? Alter praecepta virtutis dat, alter exemplar. Descriptiones has et ut publicanorum utar verbo iconismos ex usu esse confiteor: proponamus laudanda, invenitur imitator."

[66] See Livy 7.32.12; Velleius Paterculus 2.126.4; Plin *Pan.* 65.6.

[67] This sentiment is traced to Herodotus by Gummere, 26 n. a. See also Pliny *Ep.* 8.14.4.

[68] Since paraenesis used traditional material (see 41 above) paraenetic works regularly refer to the fact that the addressees already know what is being prescribed and need only to be reminded or prodded to attention. See Seneca *Ep.* 94.11,25; Pliny *Ep.* 8.14.1; Dio Chrysostom *Or.* 2.25-26; 13.14-15; 17.1-2. (J.W. Cohoon, trans., *Dio Chrysostom,* LCL, 5 vols. [London: W. Heinemann, 1932]). An associated idea is that the addressees are already applying themselves to the teaching. See Seneca *Eps.* 1.1; 2.1; 13.15; 24.16; 25.4; 47.21; Pliny *Ep.* 8.24.1; Cicero *Fam.* 2.4.2; *Q. Fr.* 1.1.8.

[69] The image of the bee is also used in Isocrates *Ad. Dem.* 51. There, as here, the author argues for an eclectic and traditional moral instruction.

[70] See 86-90 above. Hadot, 165-74, insists that friendship is to be under-

association increases the accessibility of the lesson, especially as it comes across in the hortatory model; [71] it allows for the verification of the teaching in the conduct of the teacher-friend; and it thus promotes the speedy incorporation of the lesson and imitation by the pupil.[72] A surrogate for meeting face-to-face is the conversation carried on by letter,[73] with its typical summons to a meeting with the correspondent.[74] This aspect of Seneca's instruction has already been seen.[75] The persuasive presence of the example as presented by and/or in the person of the teacher-friend extends to any of the pupil's associations. Thus, Seneca echoes the frequent cautions of the moral guide against the harmful example of associations given over to vice, when he says in *Ep.* 104.21: [76]

> Si velis vitiis exui, longe a vitiorum exemplis recedendum est. Avarus, corruptor, saevus, fraudulentus, multum nocituri, si prope a te fuissent, intra te sunt. Ad meliores transi: cum Catonibus vive, cum Laelio, cum Tuberone.

Here Seneca ascribes to the historical examples the vitality of living companions, making their qualities the equivalent of the *res praesens* whose efficaciousness he lauds in *Ep.* 6.5 and to which he "summons" Lucilius.

And so, models of virtue and vice are taken seriously as aids or hindrances in assimilating the teacher-friend's instructions. For those who are learning, their

---

stood in the institutional form in which antiquity experienced it and not in its modern-day version of an affective bond. She also finds the instruction by friends a mode as important as the more formal instruction under "house philosophers" and in public discourses. Seneca *Ep.* 88.1 finds the clamor of prepared disputations good for rousing the audience to the desire to learn, but finds a more familiar context and subdued tone better for allowing the message to sink in. Association with a respected, usually older friend for the purpose of practical advice and moral guidance was practiced and recommended by Pliny *Eps.* 1.14.3-4; 1.12.11-12; 4.17.4-9; by Cicero *Off.* 1.17.59; 1.41.147; *Fam.* 5.13.3-4. Moreover, delivering frank opinions and helpful precepts to friends was urged by Cicero *Am.* 13.44 and practiced by him *Fam.* 6.1.1, 6; 5.17.3; Pliny *Eps.* 1.14.3-4; 8.24.1, 10; Seneca *Ep.* 6.4.

[71] Cicero *Fam.* 5.13.3-4.

[72] Seneca *Eps.* 6.5-6; 75.2.

[73] Seneca *Ep.* 88.1 and cf. 40.1 where Seneca recognizes that through letters Lucilius reveals himself to him. *Ep.* 16.2 speaks of Lucilius' letter as if it made him present (*apud me*) to Seneca. Seneca also refers to his own letters as if they were part of a conversation in *Ep.* 27.1, "De communi tecum malo conloquor et remedia communico," and *Ep.* 75.1, "Qualis sermo meus esset, si una sederemus aut ambularemus, inlaboratus et facilis, talis esse epistulas means volo."

[74] Seneca *Ep.* 6.6.

[75] See 87-88.

[76] "If you would be stripped of your faults, leave far behind you the patterns of the faults. The miser, the swindler, the bully, the cheat, who will do you much harm merely by being near you, are *within* you. Change therefore to better associations: live with the Catos, with Laelius, with Tubero." (LCL).

own practice of the lessons is needed for progress in virtue. Seneca makes this clear when he says in *Ep.* 75.7:[77]

> Quando, quae didiceris, adfiges tibi ita, ut excidere non possint? Quando illa experieris? Non enim ut cetera, memoriae tradidisse satis est, in opere temptanda sunt. Non est beatus, qui scit illa, sed qui facit.

It is clear from this discussion that ethical-philosophical education involves a program and looks to intermediate progress as well as to the goal of final perfection.[78] Seneca sees in progress a crucial concept which determines varying levels of virtue and happiness below that of full perfection.[79] Of course, the uninitiated need someone to precede them on the path and to point the way to perfection by urging this, discouraging that, and matching this protrepsis and apotrepsis with examples.[80] The efforts of the teacher and guide must be matched by the perseverance of the pupil.[81]

In this, Seneca reflects the compromise in Stoic ethics which sharply distinguished the ideal sage from the fool but allowed for another category, *hoi prokoptontes,* between the two. These do not yet perform the perfect actions (*ta katorthōmata*) of the wise man, but still act in a manner appropriate (*ta*

---

[77] "When shall you so plant in your mind that which you have learned, that it cannot escape? When shall you put it all into practice? For it is not sufficient merely to commit these things to memory, like other matters; they must be practically known. He is not happy who only knows them, but he who does them." (LCL).

[78] Further on he describes those on the first level of progress in *Ep.* 75.9. These have learned what they have to do but have not yet tested it in practice. *Vit. beat.* 24. 4-5, declares in self-defense and protest that only after the proposed goal of perfection is reached can the critic decry any discrepancy between words and actions. Hadot, 27, recalls Socrates' declaration in Xenophon's *Mem.* 4.4.9 of his unceasing demonstration in action of the meaning of justice. And he credits this with superior persuasiveness to merely verbal witness. See also Pliny *Ep.* 8.24.1.

[79] The distinction appears in *Vit. beat.* 24.4-5 and Seneca outlines three levels of progress in *Ep.* 75.8-15. Long before Seneca, Isocrates spoke of progress that Nicocles could expect through the study of philosophy in *Evag.* 81. In *Ep.* 6.1-4 Seneca calls attention to the progress he himself has made and in *Ep.* 34.1 he rejoices in that made by Lucilius.

[80] Seneca *Ep.* 94.50-51 speak of guidance in the intermediate stage of imperfection for progress toward perfection. Imitation of proper models plays a part in this. Pliny *Ep.* 8.13.1 says, "Pertinet ad profectum tuum a disertissimo viro discere, quid laudandum quid reprehendendum, simul ita institui, ut verum dicere adsuescas. Vides quem sequi, cuius debeas implere vestigia." Similarly, Livy 1. *proem.* 10 and Seneca *Con.* 9.2.27 (M. Winterbottom, trans., *The Elder Seneca. Declamations,* LCL 2 vols. [Cambridge: Harvard University, 1974]).

[81] Seneca *Eps.* 34.4; 75.15; 16.1 recommends zealous and active perseverance. Cf. Isocrates *Evag.* 81. For an overview of Seneca's pedagogical method see A. Sipple, *Der Staatsmann und der Dichter: Seneca als politischer Erzieher* (Würzburg: Konrad Triltsch, 1938) 15-21.

kathēkonta) to their human character and in accord with nature. These *proko-ptontes* were wise in the popular sense and masters of philosophy. At most, Seneca claims to be *proficiens* and it is as such that he becomes a model for Lucilius.[82]

The preceding discussion has observed the content of example and its relation to teacher and pupil. At this juncture, it would help to step back and take a broader view of the place and function of the complex of hortatory devices in Seneca's writings.

5. The Hortatory Features in Seneca's Writings

Albertini and Oltramare[83] both have long since pointed out the diatribal themes of popular philosophy, as well as the influence of rhetorical exercises in Seneca's writings. Cancik notes the great variety of elements in Seneca's paraenetic argumentation, e.g. commands, prohibitions, advice, and warnings mixed with declarations, conclusions, comparisons, examples, allegorical figures, applications, clarifications, and adhortations.[84]

Building on these insights, Coleman finds help in the categories of rhetorical school practice. He analyzes *Ep.* 28 and finds that Seneca uses two chriae, one from Socrates and another from Ariston, to illustrate his point. Furthermore, Seneca develops the second "with all the resources of Senecan rhetoric and imagery." He notes that the chria had much in common with the thesis of philosophical schools, though it was principally a "familiar exercise of rhetorical education (*Ep.* 33.7 and Quintilian 1.9.3 ff.)." From his analysis he concludes that instances of chriae abound in the letters and that the development of them proceeds along the lines of a literary structure, though not a logical one. The movement is by association of ideas in a carefully controlled progression approaching an idea or group of ideas from a variety of angles. "The technique is not that of a philosopher, developing a systematic argument with a logical beginning, middle and end, but of the preacher, concerned to drive home with all the arts of rhetoric one or two chosen doctrinal propositions."[85]

6. The Chria, the Pattern of Its Development and Its Use

To Coleman's mention of Quintilian *Inst.* 1.9 and rhetorical education in connection with the chria, Colson provides some necessary qualification and explana-

---

[82] For a fuller discussion and bibliography see A.J. Malherbe, "Pseudo-Heraclitus, Epistle 4: The Divinization of the Wise Man," *JAC* 21 (1978) 54 ff.

[83] E. Albertini, *La Composition dans les ouvrages philosophiques de Sénèque* (Paris: Thorin et Fontemoing [E. de Boccard], 1923); A.M. Oltramare, *Les Origines de la diatribe romaine* (Lausanne: Librairie Payot, 1926).

[84] Cancik, 23-24, and throughout her analysis of specific letters.

[85] R. Coleman, "The Artful Moralist: A Study of Seneca's Epistolary Style," *CQ* 24 n.s. (1974) 280 ff.

tion.[86] He quotes the progymnatist Aphthonius' description of the chria as a seven part exercise in the development of a theme: (1) encomium of the author of the chria, saying, theme, (2) paraphrase or restatement of the saying, (3) justification or proof, (4) analogy from nature, (5) historical example (personal), (6) testimony of the ancients, (7) epilogue. He also calls attention to the original philosophical character of the chria, which was only later adopted by educationists. In its primary use the chria was written out or memorized in the school of the *grammatistes* or *literator* (Seneca *Ep.* 33.7). It subsequently passed on to higher schools, though it is not clear whether of the *rhetor* or the *grammaticus,* and there it was worked out according to certain rules of development.

Despite the chria's character as a rhetorical exercise, it was a tool of the philosopher as well. The subjects were mainly philosophical and its use of the poets or the "ancients" as vehicles for illustrating moral principles is also philosophical.[87] Reichel cites a wide variety of authors to the effect that mores are improved by the exercise of chria.[88] Consequently, one is not surprised to find the chria used by Seneca, and with all the facets of its rhetorical development. Colson traces Christian discourses which develop a text back, at least in part, to the chria, finding such discourses as early as Origen. He concludes suggesting "that familiarity with this favorite school exercise did much to recommend this form of discourse to the Christian rhetoricians." [89]

While the last remark will be shown to have its substantiation in the Pastorals below, the interest in this section is focused on Seneca. A close look at *Ep.* 104 will expose the full range of Seneca's hortatory technique, his use of examples of varied types, and the arrangement of his hortatory devices in the pattern of the developed chria.

---

[86] F.H. Colson,"Quintilian I,9 and the 'Chria' in Ancient Education," *CR* 35 (1921) 150. C.S. Baldwin, *Medieval Rhetoric and Poetic (to 1400) Interpreted from Representative Works* (New York: Macmillan, 1928) 26-27 adds some refinements. The justification or proof can be direct or by contrast; the epilogue includes an exhortation to follow what was said or done.

D.L. Clark, *Rhetoric in Greco-Roman Education* (New York: Columbia University, 1957) 186-88 summarizes the schemes in Aphthonius and Hermogenes for the development of the chria, outlining the following elements: encomium, paraphrase, direct proof in general statement, contrast, illustration (by comparison), example, authority, epilogue-exhortation. The development of a gnome is similar and has these elements: direct exposition, proof (paraphrase), contrast, enthymeme, illustration (by comparison), example, authority, hortatory conclusion. Compare the *Auct. Her.* 4.56-58 and the seven trope expolitio of a theme: theme, reason, iteration, contrast, comparison, example, conclusion. See also H. Lausberg, *Handbuch der literarischen Rhetorik: Eine Grundlegung der Literaturwissenschaft* (Munich: Max Hüber, 1960) 536, 540.

[87] Colson, 153.

[88] G. Reichel, *Quaestiones progymnasmaticae* (Leipzig: Robert Noske, 1909) 38.

[89] Colson, 153-54.

7. The Hortatory Features of Seneca's *Ep.* 104

Ep. 104.19-34 offers an instance of example used as one of several hortatory devices in a developed exhortation. Numbered among these examples are imaginative patterns of vice which corrupts from within, 20-21; historical and named examples of virtue, 22,27-44; and indefinite models of proper attitude, 25-26. Other devices employed here include imperatives 20, 21, 34; lists 20, 33; direct address 25; exclamations 26, 28; citations of authority 25, 31; knowledge of addressee 33; declaration of inner strength, 23, 24, 26. And of the hortatory techniques, Seneca uses warning 19; explanation and motivation, 20-21, 22, 24, 26, 34; and contrast, within 20, 24, 26 and between 19-21 and 21 ff. Metaphorical comparisons enter at 20, vices as companions; 22, the safe harbor; 22, the fearless soldier; 23, animal vitality; 24, the monarch; 34, the yoke; 32, the implied comparison with Achilles. Rhetorical questions dot the passage, 19, 20, 26.

8. The Pattern of the Development of the Chria in *Ep.* 104

Besides these hortatory characteristics, the passage also contains within it, statements of fact and attitude, i.e., 19, travel is useless; 19, you carry the causes within you (repeated at 20 and 21); 26, they can/cannot do it (repeated at 33 and 34). There are also statements of proof; i.e., 19, all would have long since gone; 34, liberty cannot be gained for nothing. These statements, reiterations, and direct proofs, together with the hortatory features already singled out, reflect the divisions in the outline for the development of a chria (and gnome).[90] The order is largely the same, too, as the argument moves from the statement in question and declaration on the futility of travel, 19; to the restatements and proofs (enthymemes), 19-20; to commands which crystallize the contrast, 20-22; to the comparisons and their application, 23-26; to more extended (than those in 21-22) examples, 27-33; with citations of authority, 24-25 and 31; and concluding with a final exhortation, 34.

The devices and structures of this passage from Seneca's *Ep.* 104 call forth the following observations. First, the structure follows a pattern suggested in theoretical treatises. Second, nonetheless, the author felt free to vary the order and to introduce a variety of devices not explicitly called for in this scheme. Third, hortatory devices and techniques constitute the greater part of these additions. Fourth, the genre of the entire piece is the letter form.

9. Example in *Ep.* 104

The function of example here is varied. Examples incarnate specific vices and virtues in the contrast section, 20-22. In this use, the examples are types of people

---

[90] See 97-98.

and historical figures. The goal in mind is the adoption of the virtuous life and the examples fill out the command to change associations from harmful to helpful ones. In 27 ff. the examples are proposed as historical precedents to support the teaching about and claim of inner strength to act confidently and successfully. The examples demonstrate that this has already been realized in some people. In the same way, the examples also back up the paraenesis which appears obliquely in the list at 33 and clearly in the commands at 34. Finally, the examples in 20-22 attract attention to a single quality embodied by the type or the historical personage and urged on the addressee. Even when the whole life of the exemplar is surveyed, e.g. Socrates' and Cato's in 27-33, it is under the single aspect of boldness in the face of life's hardships.

C. *Concluding Observations*

This chapter has traced the hortatory features and some of the details of content found in the prose works of exhortation (chapter IV) into Greco-Roman epistolary exhortation literature. It has also found aspects of the school aspect of this mode of instruction, like the teacher-pupil relationship in moral instruction, the pedagogical advantage of example, the complementarity of terminology in rhetorical and moral education, and the devices in the developed chria. The discussion of Seneca's letters provided an insight into the particularly close relationship between the letter form and the effort to exhort by example whereby the letter becomes the vehicle for the teacher's exemplary presence both by explicit reference and implicit characterization in the letter's details. The chapter also discussed theoretical aspects of the hortatory use of example and found their exemplification in the letters of Seneca. Finally, it has disclosed matters of content which will emerge again in the Pastorals and will help to anchor the latter in their hortatory tradition. The study now turns to the Socratic Epistles and the insights of this chapter will be brought into service in the study of those letters.

CHAPTER VI

Example in the Socratic Letters

The principal writings which this study has selected for comparison with the Pastorals are the letters collected under the names of Socrates and the Socratics. The fact the Socratic letters employ the device of example for an exhortation in the epistolary form suits them well for this comparative role, as does their pseudonymity and "community" interest. In fact, the pseudonymity and "community" interest, in addition to being integral features of the letter corpus as a whole, also play a significant role in determining the nature and use of example in this collection of letters. Moreover, the Socratic letters themselves, together with Cynic letters under the names of other philosophers, have only recently been made available in a comprehensive, dual language edition [1] and are as yet unfamiliar to the wider audience of American biblical scholars. For these reasons, some introductory remarks are called for in order to clarify the environment in and for which the letters were created, as well as the relationships that obtain not only among the various seg-

---

[1] A.J. Malherbe, ed. and intr., *The Cynic Epistles: A Study Edition*, SBLSBS, 12 (Missoula: Scholars Press for the SBL, 1977). The citations of the Socratic Epistles below are from this edition. Early editions of letters include: L. Allazzis, ed., *Socratis, Antisthenis, et aliorum Socraticorum epistolae* (Paris: Sebastian Cramoisy, 1637); J.C. Orelli, ed., *Socratis et Socraticorum, Pythagorae et Pythagoreorum quae feruntur epistolae* (Leipzig: Weidmann, 1815); R. Hercher, ed., *Epistolographi Graeci* (Paris: A. Firmin Didot, 1873); L. Köhler, ed., *Die Briefe des Sokrates und der Sokratiker herausgegeben, übersetzt und kommentiert*, Philol. suppl. B 20, 2 (Leipzig: Dieterich, 1938); J. Sykutris, ed., *Die Briefe des Sokrates und der Sokratiker*, Studien zur Geschichte und Kultur des Altertums 18, 2 (Paderborn: F. Schöningh, 1933). Principal studies of the letters include: R. Bentley, *Dissertations upon the Epistles of Phalaris, Themistocles, Socrates, Euripedes, and upon the Fables of Aesop* (London: J.H. for H. Mortlock and J. Hartley, 1699; reprinted with introduction and notes, W. Wagner, ed., Berlin S. Calvary, 1874); W. Capelle, "De Cynicorum epistulis" (Diss. Göttingen, 1896); W. Obens, *Qua aetate Socratis et Socraticorum epistulae, quae dicuntur, scriptae sunt* (Münster i.W.: Aschendorff, 1912); O. Schering, *Symbola ad Socratis et Socraticorum epistulas explicandas* (Greifswald: Hans Adler, 1917); J. Sykutris, "Mitteilungen: Die handschriftliche Überlieferung der Sokratikerbriefe," *Philologische Wochenschrift* 48 (1928) 1284-95; "Sokratikerbriefe," *PW* suppl. B. 5, 981-87; W. Crönert, review of Sykutris' edition, *Gnomon* 12 (1936) 146-52; H. Dörrie, "Sokratiker-Briefe," *Kl. Pauly* 5, 257-58.

ments of the letter corpus but also within those very segments. Against this background, it is hoped that the function of example will stand out more clearly, both in the Socratic letters and in the Pastoral Epistles as well.

I. Thematic and Formal Relationships among the Segments of the Socratic Letter Corpus

A. Ep. 28 and the Formation of the Corpus

Ep. 28, of all the letters in the corpus, has received the most extensive scrutiny. This is due to its unique characteristics, to be noted at length below,[2] and to the concomitant claims to authenticity of authorship distinct from the letters. Indeed, its authorship by Speusippus is convincingly argued by Bickermann-Sykutris.[3] Moreover, the latter take the question of authenticity one step further in their suggestions about the development of the corpus as a whole around the authentic *Ep.* 28. For Bickermann-Sykutris, 79-80, the letter became separated from the other

---

[2] See 103-4.

[3] E. Bickermann and J. Sykutris, "Speusipps Brief an König Philipp," *Berichte über die Verhandlungen der sächsischen Akademie der Wissenschaften,* Phil.-hist. Kl. 80,3 (Leipzig, 1928) 1-86. Orelli, vi, accepted its authenticity as written to Philip by an unnamed critic of Isocrates but rejected, 262, Allazzis' claim that Speusippus authored it. More recently its authenticity has been challenged by J. Bernays, *Phokion und seine neueren Beurteiler* (Berlin: Wilhelm Hertz, 1881) 116 ff.; F. Susemihl, *Geschichte der griechischen Literatur in der Alexandrinerzeit,* 2 vols. (Leipzig, 1892) 1:586 ff.; Obens, 31, Schering, 60 ff.; Köhler, 5 and 117-19. K. Boehnecke, *Domosthenes, Lykurgus, Hyperides und ihr Zeitalter* (Berlin: Georg Reimer, 1864) 442-81, defended its authenticity, as did J. Kleck, *Symbouleutici qui dicitur sermonis historiam criticam per quattuor seacula continuatam* (Paderborn: Ferdinand Schöningh, 1919) 104-5. The latter, in addition to questioning the validity of the objections on historical grounds, finds authenticity likely from the letter's earnest treatment of the opposition between philosopher and rhetorician, in marked contrast to the schooled elaborations of later *epistulae commenticiae* and *suasoriae.* He also argues from the quotation by Athenaeus, *Epit.* 11.506e, of Carystius of Pergamum from the second century B.C. who, in affirming that Speusippus defended Plato from Theopompus in a letter to Philip, seems to cite loosely from *Ep.* 28.12 (292.12 ff.). Bickermann argues on historical grounds and Sykutris from the letter's style, speech and composition to the antiquity of the letter. For them, the citation in Athenaeus conclusively associates the letter with Speusippus. They also, 70-78, contrast the well organized *Ep.* 28 with *Ep.* 33, also attributes to Speusippus. They find the latter a disunified mixture of biographical details, more like the other letters in the second part of the collection than *Ep.* 28. Similarly, the other letters of Speusippus, *Eps.* 30 and 31 also differ in style from *Ep.* 28. The obvious differences in length and content must also be noted as setting *Ep.* 28 off from the rest of the letters. Moreover, Bickermann and Sykutris find, 19, 78, that the criticism in *Ep.* 28 is offered from a practical and not a theoretical standpoint and without a trace of a school-like construction compiled from scattered sources. In this they agree with Kleck.

letters of Speusippus and was preserved in the rhetorical schools both because of its own content [4] and through its associations with Isocrates. [5] For the Atticist editor-author of the Socratic corpus, *Ep.* 28 served as the authentic core of the lost Speusippan corpus, which he set about to restore. [6] To this, i.e., *Eps.* 30-32, the exchange with Xenocrates, and *Ep.* 33, a letter to Dion, he added *Ep.* 34, the letter of Dionysius to Speusippus presumably provoked by the tyrant's reading of *Ep.* 33 and *Ep.* 29, a letter of Plato occasioned by *Ep.* 28.12.

The pseudonymous editor-author did not stop with the correspondence of Speusippus. He knew and used the Platonic letters and also could have known the already existing letters of Socrates. Thus, he expanded the scope of his own works to create a record of the exchange among the second generation Socratics. In doing this, he fabricated a platform from which to express his own concerns.

B. *Distinctiveness of* Ep. *28*

The reader of *Ep.* 28 cannot fail to notice its uniqueness in the Socratic letter corpus. Consider, first, the addressee, Speusippus' attitude toward him and his other interests in the letter. Philip is addressed only here and in the next letter, occasioned by this one. Unlike the often mentioned tyrant Dionysius [7] Philip does not figure prominently in the careers of the followers of Socrates. Then, too, the letter employs mythical and historical details, not uncommon to the corpus generally, but makes them serve rhetorical theory in this criticism of Isocrates' encomium of Philip. As such, the king receives no criticism or suggestions for improved conduct (contrast *Eps.* 29, 33). Finally, the letter does not occasion a reflection on the proper conduct of a philosopher vis-à-vis royalty either (contrast *Eps.* 8-13, 23 and compare *Ep.* 34).

Moreover, three other thematic differences distinguish *Ep.* 28 from the other letters. Its argumentative tone is unrelieved by a balancing letter of response. In this, *Ep.* 28 enjoys only partial kinship with the other letters in the collection, where a letter of reply often uncovers another side of the issue in question (see *Eps.*

---

[4] That is, as a description of a proper encomium of Philip and its treatment of rhetorical principles and their application.

[5] Bickermann-Sykutris, 79, n. 4, suggest that the letter was handed on in Isocratean manuscripts. The expanded collection always stands after the letters of Isocrates in the manuscript tradition, Isocrates' perduring influence in the rhetorical schools has been noted by W. Schmid and O. Stählin, *Geschichte der griechischen Literatur.* I, *Klassische Periode der griechischen Literatur,* 6th ed. (Munich: C.H. Beck [Oscar Beck], 1912) 572-77 and see above 77-78.

[6] *Ep.* 29 is occasioned by *Ep.* 28.12, while *Eps.* 30, 31 and 33 represent the correspondence mentioned by Diogenes Laertius 4.3 (R.D. Hicks, trans., *Diogenes Laertius. Lives of Eminent Philosophers,* 2 vols. [London: W. Heinemann, 1925]), with the details for the letters taken from the Platonic epistles. See Sykutris, *Die Briefe,* 122.

[7] Dionysius is mentioned only in passing at 13(292.27). He is negatively evaluated at 10(290.27) but this is not the letter's point. It is merely an example in its technical critique.

8-9, 10-13, 24-25, 30-32).   Furthermore, Hercules enjoys prominence and unequivocal esteem here (see 2[286.10]; 6[288.11,17]; 7[288.27]; 14[292.4]), while the hero receives scant and ambiguous notice in the rest of the letters of the Socratics (see *Eps*. 9.4[246.25]; 13.1[250.17]).   Despite this prominence, Hercules, one of the principal Cynic exemplars, is treated in a politico-historical mode and not in connection with standard Cynic exhortation.   This highlights a more general phenomenon, the absence of Cynic themes in the letter as viewed against the background of the exhortations in the rest of the letters of the Socratics.   Unlike these, *Ep*. 28 carries through a systematic, rhetorical critique of Isocrates' discourse and letters, with only a secondary interest in exhortation.

From a formal point of view, *Ep*. 28 is the longest of the letters in the collection.   Its criticism and correction of Isocrates' half-hearted encomium of Philip airs rhetorical principles and offers instances of their proper application over against those in Isocrates' discourse.   The other letters use rhetorical techniques in the unfolding of their message, but only rarely allude to them directly and never make them the object of their concern.

C. *Link Between* Ep. *28 and the Rest of the Corpus*

Despite these singular aspects of *Ep*. 28, the letter is nonetheless closely linked in both content and form with the other letters of the corpus, for which it served as the nucleus.   Speusippus, Plato's nephew and his successor as head of the Academy, defends his uncle at pars. 2 and 12.   The same interest in and favorable attitude toward Plato as moral guide and devoted head of the academy is found in *Eps*. 10; 14.9; 15.3; 22.2; 23.2,3; 24; 25; 26; 30; 31; 32.2; 33.3.   And so, in this regard *Ep*. 28 enjoys association with letters even outside the Speusippan corpus proper.

Another link with the rest of the letters is the negative evaluation of Dionysius at 10(290.27), to which one could compare *Eps*. 8(244.6) and 33.4(302.14).[8]

The situation behind the letter, that of the philosopher's connections with the court of Philip, also reflects some of the other letters which countenance such relationships (see *Eps*. 9, 10, 11, 13, 23, 27, 33).   This is one aspect of the moderate Cynicism which the corpus as a whole proposes.   The political involvment surfaces on another level in the letters about Socrates' execution (*Eps*. 14-17) and the advice to Arete on her political and financial situation (*Ep*. 27).

Beyond these thematic relationships, formal characteristics and details also relate *Ep*. 28 to the other letters of the Socratics.   First, *Ep*. 28 is a letter of recommendation, to win Antipater a hearing before Philip for his suit against an unnamed Megarian.   *Eps*. 10, 11, and 23 look to a similar intervention at court on others' behalf, although none is a letter of recommendation as such.

---

[8] The other letters also show themselves to be different from *Ep*. 28 as regards the Sicilian monarch, toward whom a negative attitude prevails, broken only by scattered approving references in *Eps*. 9, 23, and 34.

A clearer link can be found in the area of rhetorical theory and its application. Most obvious in this connection is the justification at *Ep.* 28.5 of the use of the letter form itself, i.e., to set the record straight where a face-to-face meeting is not possible. In general, this principle grounds the creation of the letters of the rest of the corpus. Certain letters, like *Eps.* 14(252.16); 15.1(260.3); 15.2(260.15 ff.); 17.1(262.26-27); 18.2(266.17 ff.), also explicitly identify the letter exchange with similar purposes of information and correction.

In the laudatory accounts about Socrates, *Eps.* 14, 17, and, to a lesser extent, 21 apply the theory in *Ep.* 28.4 on the praise of forefathers (and compare *Ep.* 30 on Plato), while *Eps.* 15.2 and 22 set forth the project to create similar writings. Indeed, the whole letter corpus, variously praising as it does the first generation of the Socratic school, wins a benevolent ear from their successors. Moreover, according to *Ep.* 28.1-2, a proper encomium calls for reference to the benefits conferred by the king, and *Ep.* 25 does no less for Plato.

It is in the area of example that the other letters most conspicuously apply the theory in *Ep.* 28.9-10, which restricts the field of examples to the most excellent and just individuals, family members and well-known persons. *Ep.* 29 meets the requirements perfectly as it directs Philip to attend to his brother's example. Socrates' example is proffered in *Eps.* 15, 19, and 21, while *Ep.* 21 praises the addressee for successfully copying Socrates. Plato's exemplary devotion to the Academy in *Ep.* 30 specifies the general admonition to pay attention to the gods, ancestors and benefactors. *Ep.* 25 praises, and thereby obliquely recommends, Plato's example, while the writer of *Ep.* 32.2 boasts that he has followed it. Aristippus at *Ep.* 27.3 commends his own example to his daughter. Conversely, Aeschines at *Ep.* 23.3 withholds commendation of the bad examples of Plato and Aristippus with their in-house squabbling. The discussion below will deal further with the examples proposed in the letters, and will include the indirect references to examples as an aspect of the use of the hortatory device in the letter collection as a whole.[9]

D. *Links Among the Other Letters of the Corpus*

Turning from a demonstration of the connections between *Ep.* 28 and the letters created in association with it, one notices, with Sykutris,[10] ample indications in those letters themselves of the links among the various segments of the corpus. Sykutris also points to references outside the corpus (mostly in Diogenes Laertius) which speak of letters by the several Socratic authors and thereby lend verisimilitude, if not actually occasion, to the fabrications of the pseudonymous author. He notes, further, the author's considerable use of Plato for his reconstructions.

On the thematic side, these letters all share a Cynic viewpoint.[11] They also take a conciliatory stand amid the traditional antagonisms and divergent view-

---

[9] See 135-53.

[10] See Sykutris, *Die Briefe,* 45-103, for the discussion of each letter and its relationships.

[11] See the discussion below, 114-15, 116-21.

points of the Socratics.[12]   In this respect, the letter collection knows and makes use of the doxographical and anecdotal traditions.[13]   In transposing the anecdotes to an epistolary setting in the collection, however, the pseudonymous author does not have an interest in form alone.   On the contrary, the anecdotes, through their new epistolary cast, are able to suggest a harmony of relationships among the Socratic protagonists of the anecdotes which goes beyond the individual accounts.[14]

E. *The Link Between the Letters of Socrates and Those of the Socratics*

The letters under the name of Socrates, as *Ep.* 28, existed prior to the composition of the other letters in the collection.   Their association with the letters of the

---

[12] Sykutris, "Sokratikerbriefe," 984, and *Die Briefe,* 45-57, 74-77, and 113, discusses this aspect of the letters. In his view, the relations among the members of the Socratic circle are harmonized and they are conceived of as a society where their traditional rivalries are overlooked or softened. For evidence of this see *Eps.* 10 and 11, where Aeschines calls on Aristippus to use his influence at court: *Ep.* 13, where Aristippus speaks positively of Simon; *Ep.* 14, where no rancor is expressed over the absence of Plato, Cleombrotus, Aristippus, and Xenophon from Socrates' final imprisonment and execution; *Ep.* 16, where Aristippus approves of the circle's flight from Athens and offers his help; *Ep.* 18, where Xenophon invites the Socratics to celebrate Artemis, noting Aristippus' and Phaedo's earlier visits to the temple; *Ep.* 22, where Plato's influence is noted and concern with Simmias' and Cebes' discrepant views is voiced; *Ep.* 23, which downplays the friction between Aristippus and Plato as jesting and urges that it cease because of the bad impression it creates; *Ep.* 24, where Plato's withdrawal from society is justified; *Ep.* 25, where Phaedrus lauds his education at a mixture of philosophical schools; *Ep.* 26, where Plato's travels and openness to foreign ideas receives favorable notice and, indeed, encouragement; *Ep.* 27, where Aristippus recalls his close association with Socrates as a paradigm for Arete; *Ep.* 30, where Plato's efforts on behalf of the Academy are commended; *Ep.* 32; where Xenocrates characterizes the separation among Plato's followers as an amicable pursuit of distinct principles. Even Xanthippe's stormy relationship with her husband (Xenophon, *Smp.* 2.10 (O.J. Todd, trans., Xenophon. *Memorabilia, oeconomicus, symposium, apologia,* LCL (London: W. Heinemann, 1923) is overlooked in *Ep.* 21, and she surprisingly has established a type of religio-philosophical community with Socrates' other wife Myrto at *Ep.* 27.3(282.28-37).
     Schering, 31-32, also calls attention to the collection's sympathy toward Aristippus, noting that it is actually Dionysius and not Aristippus who comes under attack for luxurious living, e.g., *Eps.* 8; 9.1, 2, 3; 10; 11; 13; 23; 24; 28.10; 33; 34.
     Clearly, the two focal points of tension among the Socratics are Aristippus and Plato. *Eps.* 8, 9, and 12 reflect the controversy surrounding Aristippus' hedonism, while *Ep.* 15 suggests some skepticism over Plato's use of Socrates.
     [13] E. Mannebach, *Aristippi et Cyrenaicorum fragmenta* (Leiden/Cologne: E.J. Brill, 1961) catalogues the traditions about Aristippus, including the controversial aspects of his life-style and the other Socratics with whom he disagreed. A. Swift Riginos, *Platonica: The Anecdotes Concerning the Life and Writings of Plato* (Leiden: E.J. Brill, 1976) does the same for the traditions about Plato.
     [14] See 121-23.

Socratics is both formal and thematic. And the thematic link is founded on particular subject matter as well as the overall conception of the corpus. The editor of the corpus, who is also the pseudonymous author of a good part of it, has molded and arranged his disparate sources into a collection of harmonious, if not uniform, letters.

With regard to the form of the letters, note the variety of letter types represented in both Socrates' and the Socratics' segments of the corpus: e.g., recommendation *Eps.* 2, 3, 10, (28); apology *Eps.* 1, 6, 9, 12, 13, 15, 16, 24, 32; friendly report *Eps.* 4, (20), 23; political warning, comment, advice *Eps.* 5, 7, 14, 17; testament *Eps.* 6, 27.[15] The letters are also explicitly hortatory pieces,[16] e.g., *Eps.* 1; 6; 15.1(260.4-6) and 2(260.16-18, 20, 21); 18; 21; 27; 29, and this despite the variety of epistolary types.

As for the thematic connections, *Ep.* 8, which opens the second sections in the corpus, echoes *Ep.* 1 in the insistence that the philosopher not journey to the court of a tyrant but rather stay home and pursue virtue. The most pervasive thematic link, however, is provided by Socrates himself, author of the first seven letters and referred to in the second part of the corpus as the principal object of *Eps.* 14, 15, 17, 20, 22 and in the background of *Eps.* 9, 12, 13, 16, 18, 19, 21, 25, 26, 27. Socrates unites the corpus as the central figure of the circle of friends and disciples, who become the letter writers of the second part of the corpus. Throughout, the picture of Socrates is consistent[17] in his adherence to principle over against political compromise,[18] his commitment to philosophical education,[19] his rigorous but, at the same time, temperate life-style.[20] His expectation of the mutual assistance among philosophical associates and friends (*Eps.* 1.2-3; 2; 6.8 ff.) is borne out in the letters of his disciples (*Eps.* 10; 11; 15.2; 16; 19; 21; 22.1; 23; 26.2; 27.3-4; 30.2).

---

[15] The letter types are discussed with greater refinement below, 126-28.

[16] Sykutris, *Die Briefe,* 107-8. On 113-14 and 118-21 Sykutris claims that the letters of the Socratics have a biographical rather than a paraenetic or didactic interest. Even where conceptual matters are brought forth, such as the immortality of the soul in *Ep. 14,* Sykutris asserts them to be purely informational. The discussion in the next section of this paper gives arguments and evidence in favor of the hortatory nature of this part of the letter collection as well, 110-13.

[17] Sykutris, *Die Briefe,* 106, sees the picture of Socrates in *Eps.* 1-7 as that common to late, popular philosophy and influenced by Cynic works as well as by Xenophon.

[18] Cf. *Eps.* 1.6; 5; 7; 14; 15.2; 16; 17.

[19] Cf. *Eps.* 1.2; 4; 6.6; 14.5; 17.2-3; 18.2; 20; 21.3; 25.1.

[20] Cf. *Eps.* 1.2; 11; 6.2; 4; 12; 14.8; 15.1; 16; 19; 22.

II. The Character of the Letters

A. *Rhetorical-Hortatory School Setting*

Like many other secular and religious writers in antiquity,[21] the writers of the letters ascribed them pseudonymously to personages of general repute, in this case Socrates, his disciples, and their associates.[22] What might have occasioned this

---

[21] The practice of pseudonymous writing in antiquity is discussed by E.H. Clift, *Latin Pseudepigraphy: A Study in Literary Attributions* (Baltimore: J.H. Furst, 1945); J.A. Farrer, *Literary Forgeries* (London: Longmans, Green, 1907); A. Gudemann, "Literary Frauds among the Romans," *TAPA* 25 (1894) 140-64 (reprinted in Fest. Drisler, New York: Macmillan, 1894, 52-74); M. Hengel, "Anonymität, Pseudepigraphie und 'literarische Fälschung' in der jüdisch-hellenistischen Literatur," *Pseudepigrapha* I, Fondation Hardt, 18, K. von Fritz, ed. (Geneva: Vandoeuvres, 1971) 229-308; R. Picard, *Artifices et mystifications littéraires* (Montreal: Dussault et Pélédeau, 1945); A. Ronconi, "Introduzione alla letteratura pseudepigrafica," *Studi Classici e Orientali* 5 (1055) 15-17; J. Sint, *Pseudonymität im Altertum: Ihre Formen und ihre Gründe,* Commentationes Oenipontanae, 15 (Innsbruck: Wagner, 1960); M. Smith, "Pseudepigraphy in the Israelite Literary Tradition," *Pseudepigrapha* I, 189-214; W. Speyer, *Bücherfunde in der Glaubenswerbung der Antike mit einem Ausblick auf Mittelalter und Neuzeit,* Hypomnemata, 24 (Göttingen: Vandenhoeck & Ruprecht, 1970); *Die literarische Fälschung im heidnischen und christlichen Altertum: Ein Versuch ihrer Deutung,* Handbuch der Altertumswissenschaft 1, 2 (Munich: C.H. Beck, 1971); "Fälschung, Literarische," *RAC* 7 (1969) 237-77; "Fälschung, pseudepigraphische freie Erfindung und 'echte religiöse Pseudepigraphie,'" *Pseudepigrapha* I, 331-66; E. Stemplinger, *Das Plagiat in der griechischen Literatur* (Leipzig/Berlin: B.G. Teubner, 1912); R. Syme, "Fraud and Imposture," *Pseudepigrapha* I, 1-17; H. von Wilamowitz-Möllendorff, "Unechte Briefe," *Hermes* 33 (1898) 492-98; E. Zeller, "Wie entstehen ungeschichtliche Überlieferungen? *Deutsch Rundschau* 74 (1893) 189-219 (reprinted in *Kleine Schriften II,* O. Leuze, ed., [Berlin: Georg Reimer, 1910] 46-90); K. Ziegler, "Plagiat," *PW* 40 halbB., 1956-97.

[22] Obens, 14 ff., but especially 77-79. He considers all the letters to have been written in an Atticizing period and finds in the letters historical discrepancies with the time of Socrates as well as stylistic and linguistic characteristics to support his view. Consequently he places all the letters in the second century A.D. which makes their alleged authorhip impossible. This later dating of the letters is confirmed, though with nuances, by J. Sykutris, "Sokratikerbriefe," 983, who places the first seven letters, from their style, manner of speech, and Cynicizing content, in the first century A.D. and the others, 985, from their Atticism, biographical interest, and knowledge of the handbooks, in the third century A.D. Sykutris makes the same determination in his *Die Briefe,* 111 and 121-22. *Ep.* 28 is a special case but the findings of Sykutris support Oben's claim to the letters' pseudonymity in general.

The authenticity of the letters has long been disbelieved. R. Bentley successfully challenged the authenticity of the collection, 536 ff. See also Orelli, for similar conclusions at 381 by J. Pearson; at 386-87 by G. Olearius; at 426-28 by C. Meinertz. More recently,

literary subterfuge? At times, pseudonymous literary activity can be attributed to the schoolrooms of the Roman Empire, where a standard exercise had the pupils write in the name and character of figures celebrated in myth, history, or literature.[23] Indeed, the Socratic letters give evidence of a school setting.[24] For one thing, Philosophical opinions are sometimes proposed like a teacher's arguments or propositions.[25] Then, too, the style of the letters betrays rhetorical schooling.[26] Moreover, the letters show an acquaintance with literature appropiate to a rhetor-

---

Köhler, 4-5, follows Obens in his assumption about the pseudonymity of the collection in general.

For comments on the derivation and sources of individual letters see H. Dittmar, *Aischenes von Sphettos: Studien zur Literaturgeschichte der Sokratiker* (Berlin: Weidmann, 1912) 194 ff. on *Ep.* 6 and its connection with Aischenes' dialogue Kallias; Capelle, 9-10, on *Ep.* 12 and its relation to Diogenes' *Ep.* 29; R. Hercher, "Zu den griechischen Epistolographen," *Hermes* 4 (1870) 427-28 on *Eps.* 32-34, and "Zu den griechischen Prosaikern," *Hermes* 6 (1872) 55-56 on *Eps.* 35-36; C. Ritter, *Neue Untersuchungen über Platon* (Munich: C.H. Beck [Oskar Beck], 1910) 382 on *Eps.* 31-34 and 382 ff. on *Eps.* 35-36; W. Crönert, *Kolotes und Menedemos* (Leipzig: Eduard Avenarius, 1906) 86 n. 426 on *Ep.* 29. See also the commentaries on the letters by Sykutris, *Die Briefe,* and Köhler, "Die Briefe," as well as Schering, on the various letters.

[23] See above 42-44 ns. 66-70, Demetrius *Eloc.* 227 (W.R. Roberts, trans., *Demetrius on Style,* LCL (Condon: W. Heinemann, 1932) and Sykutris, *Die Briefe,* 118. See also, H.I. Marrou, *A History of Education in Antiquity,* G. Lamb, trans., from 3rd rev. ed., (New York: New American Library, 1964) 238 ff., 276 ff., 383 ff. and J. Martin, *Antike, Rhetorik: Technik und Methode,* Handburch der Altertumswissenschaft 2, 3 (Munich: C.H. Beck, 1974) 7-8, 291-92, 399.

[24] The setting of a rhetorical school has been suggested by Köhler, "Die Briefe," 4-5 and by Obens, 6. One might note the following allusions in the letters themselves which support these claims to an acquaintance with the activities and exercises of a schoolroom: the philosophical dialogue at 9.4(246.30); 14.5(256.6); 25.2(278.11 ff.); the epideictic presentation at 9.4(246.25); the encomium at 13.1(250.16); 28 *passim;* the speech writer and coach, pupils' presentations, critique of delivery at 14.3(254.13 ff.); the oratorical competition at 14.4(254.18 ff.); the dialogue form at 15.3(260.24 ff.); 23.2(274.22 ff.); the literary memoir at 15.3(260.29); 18.2(266.18); 22.2(272.18-19); poetry at 15.3(260.30-31); publication at 22.1(272.6 ff.); schools 25.2(278.14-15); 30; 31; 32; 33.3(302.8-9).

[25] Schering, 32-34, notices this and alludes to the sophistic precepts in the progymnastic works of Theon, Aphthonius and Nicolaus. Unfortunately he gives no further details. Sykutris, *Die Briefe,* 85, seems to make the same observation in referring to *Ep.* 27 as an elaboration in epistolary form of a number of *hypothēkai* of Aristippus. One might also refer, for example, to the statement on grief at 21.2(270.20-22), on the value of asceticism at 12(250.10-12), or on the prohibition against associating with tyrants at 8(244.2-3) and see the respective letters as expansions of these principles.

[26] Sykutris, *Die Briefe,* 10-11, describes *Eps.* 1-7, with their pleasing paraenetic and their elegant Attic style like that of Xenophon, and 118-21, *Eps.* 8-35, with their variety of devices somewhat ineptly employed but with a rhetorically appropriate *ischnon* style.

ical school.[27]   In addition, the variety of letter forms [28] suggests exercises after set
patterns.   The letters also employ devices, like example, which receive extensive
theoretical treatment in the schools, and in the rhetorical handbooks as well.[29]

B. *Hortatory-Philosophical Interest*

While the letters' affinity to the school environment is thus undeniable, they
seem to be more than merely school exercises.   E. Norden [30] declares that the letters of the later Cynics, i.e., from the early Roman Empire, are not rhetorical

---

[27] Sykutris, *Die Briefe,* 112 ff., calls attention to the biographical interest of the letters of
the Socratics (*Eps.* 8-35) and to the sources they employ, mainly biographical sources. On
116-17 he suggests a handbook of the history of philosophy, similar to but richer than
Diogenes Laertius, or perhaps a philosophical lexicon. The opening paragraph of *Ep.* 33,
according to Sykutris, 92-93, reflects a rhetorical handbook's instructions on letter writing (cf.
Cicero *Fam.* 2.4.1). At *Ep.* 6.10 Socrates makes an analogy between his own situation and the
affection between teacher and pupils. Notice, too, the references to literary works and
practices of public reading and exercises, e.g., the encomium at 13.1; dialogues at 15.3 and
23.2; *memorabilia* at 15.2 and 18.2; speeches at 28.4 and 22.2; letters at 28.13; oratorical
practice at 14.3; questioning at 17.2; publication at 22.1; lectures at 23.2 and 28.1,14; critique
of speeches at 28.1. See also n. 24 above. All of these are appropriate to a school setting.
   [28] See the discussion on 126-28.
   On the more limited subject of the theory and practice of epistolary form, J. Sykutris
finds that the opening of *Ep.* 33 closely parallels Cicero's theoretical remarks in *Fam.* 2.4.1.
The writer of *Ep.* 33 seems to have copied for his letter opening a handbook description of
two types of letters, without regard to the consequent literary awkwardness and factual
impossibility of the finished piece. Other indications of the use of epistolary conventions in
the composition of the Socratic letters are noted by Köhler, 128. She mentions the "all is the
same here" at the conclusion of *Ep.* 33 (and see *Ep.* 4). She also directs attention to the
expectation of a longer discussion on the subject in a face-to-face meeting at the end of *Ep.*
6. Other epistolary conventions include the different salutation formulas and their
appropriateness to the situation of the letter in the discussion at the start of *Ep.* 34. At times,
personal or occasional details establish the epistolary context for a discussion or
exhortation on quite another matter, e.g., the opening of *Ep.* 6 refers to the prior request for
care of two visitors but actually establishes the pretext for the lesson on *aphilochrēmatia* (as
Sykutris observed in *Die Briefe,* 32). *Ep.* 22 uses a proverbial saying and its application to
the author and the addressees to lead into a totally different discussion on the writing of
memorabilia. *Eps.* 14, 15, 17, 24, 27, and 28 also evidence some discontinuity between the
staded occasion of the letter and the subject matter really treated therein. Clearly, the letter
form in these instances is a literary vehicle and is being used in a sophisticated way.
   The device of pseudonymity is recognized at *Ep.* 15.3(260.31-33).
   [29] See the direct references to the theory at *Ep.* 5.2(230.21-22) and *Ep.* 28.10
(290.30-33). See also the discussion below on 135-37 on the use of example in general. See
also the comments on 138-43 about the order of the devices in the letters.
   [30] E. Norden, "Beiträge zur Geschichte der griechischen Philosophie," *Jahrb. f. cl.
Phil.* suppl. B 19 (1893) 393. He sees the Christians as the rivals to the Cynics.

exercises but propaganda pieces. The same seems true of these letters, replete as they are with Cynic doctrine though written under the names of Socrates and his disciples. Schering also sees the propagation of Cynicism as their intent, but within a school context.[31] Quintilian has already been observed above to declare that the teacher should aim at the moral as well as the rhetorical education of his pupils.[32] And so, a Cynic moral code could very well have been the aim of these letters, even granted a school environment for them.

Various facets of the letters themselves show that they are more than rhetorical and have more than a rhetorical interest to purvey. In the first place, they are not the diverse creations of students being exercised in the same classroom. The groups of letters which have been distinguished among the collection originated centuries apart. Moreover, there is a uniformity in the style and concerns among the letter groups which suggests far fewer authors than their pseudonymous ascriptions.[33] Second, above and beyond the uniformity in the different segments of the corpus, there is a larger unity to the whole corpus. This is reflected in the very intention to create a collection of Socratic letters,[34] and in a common Cynic viewpoint which cuts across the letter groups.[35] Third, the other side of this pervasive interest in

---

[31] Schering, 32.

[32] See 34-35.

[33] Allazzis asserts the authenticity of all the letters, and claims numerous authors for them. Orelli, vi-ix, though supporting allegations of their pseudonymity, finds in their varied style indications of a large number of authors. Sykutris, *Die briefe,* 106 ff., settles on four authors. Socratic author I is responsible for Eps. 1-7, as their elegant Attic style, the uniform picture of Socrates, the use of the *Apology,* both of Xenophon and of Plato, the paraenetic intent, and the manner of argumentation indicate (contrast Obens, 17, who sees the hands of two authors at work here). Socratic author II created *Eps. 8-27, 29-34,* all of which share a conciliatory tone, a rhetorically schooled but awkward letter style, biographical interest, common sources in the biographical tradition represented by Xenophon, Plato, other Cynic letters, and Plutarch. Two other authors are responsible for one letter each. Author III, perhaps Speusippus, wrote *Ep.* 28 and author IV, a Pythagorean, wrote *Ep.* 35.

[34] Sykutris, *Die Briefe,* 113.

[35] Obens, 8, stresses the fact that the overall, double exhortation to contentment and upright piety is not just an epistolary *prepon,* because it occasions alterations in the characterizations of the personages in the letters, e.g., making the wealthy and noble Xenophon champion *autarkeia* as a person poor and needy in *Ep.* 19. Schering, 32-34 identifies the common viewpoint as Cynic and he finds examples of it in both parts of the collection: i.e., in the letters of Socrates 1, 5 and 6 as well as those of Antisthenes and Aristippus (sic) 8, 11, 12, 20, 21, 22, 26, 29, 32, and 34. The identification of the letters with Cynic philosophy adds specificity to their interest in philosophy generally, be it in its goal of wisdom or virtue at 23.1 and 27.5; in its inculcation through discussion at 13.1 and 25.1-2; in the locus of study in a school or abroad among the public at 20; and in the preservation of traditions at 18.2 and 21.3 and of institutions at 30-32. See Sykutris, *Die Briefe,* 107, for a similar identification with Cynicism. Further discussion on the viewpoint and purpose of the letters will be found below, 113-26.

Cynic philosophy is a bias against inadequate education by venal sophists.[36] Rhetorical exercise alone would not be sufficient motivation for the collection or even for the individual letters. Fourth, the interplay of paraenesis and exemplary practice in the letters implicates even the anecdotal details and letters of apparently simple formal interest in the hortatory program of the whole corpus.[37] Fifth, in the sources which Sykutris determines for the letters, some are exploited for biographical detail but others serve the philosophical interests of the authors of the letters.[38] Moreover, the use of the letters and certain dialogues of Plato by the

---

[36] See *Eps.* 1.1; 6.10; 14.3-4; 28.9; 34.2. K. Funk, "Untersuchungen über die lucianische Vita Demonactis," *Philol.* suppl. B 10 (1905-7) 590, discusses the traditional Cynic antipathy toward sophistic artistry in both the first and second sophistic periods. See also Norden, 406, n. 1.

[37] Sykutris, *Die Briefe*, 106-7, notes this in *Eps.* 2-4, which show the philosopher concerned for and working for the good of his pupils, his friends and his homeland. This confirms by example the principles laid down in *Eps.* 1 and 6. He stops short at claiming a similar interplay in the letters of the Socratics. The discussion below, 124-26, will attempt to establish the instruction/model interplay in the corpus as a whole.

[38] The authors either take over the philosophical issues from the sources (e.g., the ideal of *phronēsis* in *Ep.* 8 from Plato's *Ep.* 7.326c [R.G. Bury, trans., *Plato. Timaeus, Critias, Cleitophon, Menexenus, epistulae*, LCL (London: W. Heinemann, 1929)], and Cynic asceticism from Diogenes' *Ep.* 32; philosophical chastisement in *Ep.* 12 from Diogenes' *Ep.* 29 [p. 137 in Malherbe's edition] and from another source, Stobaeus, *Flor.* 3:492.1 [Hense] [K. Wachsmuth and O. Hense, eds., *Joannis Stobaei Anthologium*, 5 vols. (Berlin: Weidmann, 1884-1919)], the saying about hunger and thirst; the discussion of death in *Ep.* 14 from Xenophon's *Apologia* and Plato's *Phaedo* [H.N. Fowler, trans., *Plato. Euthydemus, apologia, Crito, Phaedo, Phaedrus*, LCL (London: W. Heinemann, 1914)]; the ruler's moral improvement or harm resulting from his association with a philosopher as adapted from Plutarch's *Quom. adul. ab am.* 67C-E [F.C. Babbitt, trans., *Plutarch's Moralia*, LCL, 15 vols. (London: W. Heinemann, 1926)], in *Ep.* 23; to the purely circumstantial use of Plato's *Ep.* 13. 361a ff. the author adds from Plato's *R* 5.496c ff. [P. Shorey, trans., *Plato. Republic*, LCL, vol. 2 (London: W. Heinemann, 1930-35)] the contrast of the philosopher with the beast-like masses in *Ep.* 24, and see also Plato's *Ep.* 7. 325e and *Phaedo* 89d; various sections of Plato's *Phaedrus* are combined in *Ep.* 25 to describe Phaedrus' love of philosophy and his progress under the direction of his teachers; the account of Plato's cosmological and metaphysical inquiries from Plato's *Timaeus* in *Ep.* 26; *Ep.* 27 takes the lesson about the loss of a garden from Plutarch's *Tranq. an.* 469c [W.C. Helmbold, trans., *Plutarch's Moralia*, LCL, vol. 6 (London: W. Heinemann, 1939)]; *Ep.* 33 uses Plutarch's *Quom. adul. ab am.* 69F and combined Plato's *Ep.* 4.321b and the real letter of Seusippus and the call to Dion to upright rule which befits the teachings of the Academy) or add philosophical concerns to the details adopted from the sources (e.g., *Ep.* 5 adds advice on virtue to the details from Xenophon's *An.* 3.1.4 ff. [C.L. Brownson, trans., *Xenophon. Anabasis*, LCL (London: W. Heinemann, 1922)]; the debate between the hedonistic and ascetic life-styles takes off from details from Diogenes Laertius in *Ep.* 9; the expansion in *Eps.* 10-11 of details is from Plato's *Ep.* 13 and Diogenes Laertius 2.79; the lesson on sufficiency in *Ep.* 19 is added to the notice of celebrating the feast at Xenophon's *An.* 5.3.9; the recommendations to his daughter for a life of philosophic contentment and the praise of her secure possession of it in *Ep.* 27 build on the references to his advice to Arete in Diogenes Laertius 2.72 and the description of his grandson as *mētrodidaktos* in Diogenes Laertius 2.86).

principal authors of the letters of the Socratics [39] suggests a deeper acquaintance with philosophical writings than what would be supplied in lexica and compendia like Diogenes Laertius'. By the same token, the author of the letters of Socrates makes extensive use of Xenophon, a favorite Socratic moralist.[40] Sixth, the paraenetic use of example in all segments of the corpus [41] indicates that the display of rhetorical technique has philosophical implications as well. Seventh, the technical rhetorical criticism and political propaganda in *Ep.* 28 leave the reader with an impression that this letter is unique among the letters of the corpus.[42]

III. The Context and Aim of the Letter Corpus

A. *Hypotheses of Authorship*

1. Platonizing

On the basis of the preceding discussion, the blending of the three major segments of the Socratic letter corpus, i.e., Speusippus' letter to Philip, the seven letters ascribed to Socrates, and the editor's own creations, can be marked successful.[43] Nonetheless, this harmony makes a certain thematic discordance all the more strident. The Cynic character of the letters has long been noted,[44] but the letters also give great importance to Socrates and his followers, reflecting a period and personalities not directly associated with the Cynic school. Furthermore, Plato enjoys particular prominence as author of *Eps.* 24 and 29 and as recipient and/or object of discussion in *Eps.* 10; 14.9; 22.2; 23; 25; 26; 28.12; 30; 32 (see also *Eps.* 31; 33.3 on the Academy).

Sykutris focuses on the Platonic references and the editor-author's familiarity with and use of Platonic works in his other letters. Since this familiarity exceeds what would normally be available in the canon of writings typical in the rhetorical school, he presumes that the editor-author is a Platonizing rhetor or a theoretically schooled Platonist.[45]

As can be expected, the best evidence for a broad knowledge and use of Plato comes in connection with the letters of Plato, Xenocrates and Speusippus. The

---

[39] Sykutris, *Die Briefe,* 111-22.

[40] Sykutris, *Die Briefe,* 108.

[41] See the discussion on example below 135-37 and Sykutris, *Die Briefe,* 107.

[42] Bickermann-Sykutris, 19-20, and see the discussion on the relation of *Ep.* 28 to the rest of the corpus in the following notes. See also 103-4 where the use of rhetorical terminology in *Ep.* 28 and in the other letters of the collection is discussed.

[43] If Speusippus' letter is indeed authentic, then it dates from the fourth century B.C. The seven letters of Socrates, as Sykutris, "Sokratikerbriefe," 483, explains, were written in the first century A.D. The letters of the Socratics date from third century A.D.

[44] See n. 35.

[45] Sykutris, *Die Briefe,* 121, and throughout his book, notes the use of Plato as a source in the Socratic letters.

same "Platonizing" interest is not found in the beginning of the corpus. If anything, the letters there are "Aristippizing." Moreover, Sykutris' suggestion does not explain the fact that the letters are interested in the associations in the Academy but not in Platonism. As a matter of fact, the letters give a Socratic cloak to their Cynic doctrine. Nor does Sykutris' view account for the relatively bad light which is cast on Plato's literary works, despite the favor shown toward the memory of his dedication as a moral guide.

2. Cynicizing

Since the major philosophical figure in the letter collection is Socrates one might ask what is behind the letters' appeal to him. A look at another author of the time will help understand this aspect of the letters. Epictetus *Diss.* 3.22 clarifies his description of the true Cynic with appeal to four models: Hercules, Socrates, Diogenes, and Crates. Of these, the model most often cited by Epictetus is Socrates. In doing this, Epictetus points to the ascetic traces of Socrates' way of life, but without claiming for him a special place in Cynicism as such.[46] He also stresses Socrates' role as teacher of morals, a commonplace in the literature of the Empire.[47]

The Socratic letters, also written in the early Empire, share this commonplace view of Socrates, the teacher of morals, ascribing to him the ascetic traits of Cynicism but without making any further formal connections between him and the Cynic movement. In fact, the Cynic tone of the whole corpus [48] indicates that the corpus has gone a step further in Cynicizing the entire first generation of Socratics.

The letters of Plato and his followers fit this scheme as well. *Ep.* 24 sees his voluntary exile from city-life as an escape from the unreason and beastliness of the crowd; [49] *Ep.* 25 lauds philosophical progress toward a goal; [50] *Ep.* 26.2 practices the communality of goods; [51] *Ep.* 29 depicts the battle for virtue; [52] *Ep.* 30 is

---

[46] M. Billerbeck, *Epiktet von Kynismus* (Leiden: E.J. Brill, 1978) 6-7. K. Döring, *Exemplum Socratis: Studien zur Sokratesnachwirkung in der kynisch-stoischen Popular-philosophie der frühen Kaiserzeit und im frühen Christentum*, Hermes Einzelschriften 42 (Wiesbaden: Franz Steiner, 1979) details the use of Socrates in the period.

[47] Billerbeck, 7, where she calls attention to Dio Chrysostom *Or.* 12(13).16-28 and Plutarch *Lib. ed.* 4D.

[48] Schering, 31-34.

[49] See 156-57 below for a discussion of *aphrosynē* and *thēria* as Cynic themes. G.A. Gerhard, *Phoinix von Kolophon* (Leipzig/Berlin: B.G. Teubner, 1909) 67 ff., discusses the philosopher's distancing himself from the crowd as a Cynic trait. See Swift Riginos, 121 ff., for the traditions about Plato's escape from the city.

[50] See Gerhard, 67 ff., for the Cynic confidence in progress toward perfection. See also Billerbeck, 18.

[51] For the help of friends, see below, 158-59. See also G. Bohnenblust, *Beiträge zum Topos "peri philias"* (Berlin: University of Berlin, 1905) 26 ff.

[52] For the pursuit of virtue, see below, 154-56.

concerned with true fame, an upright life, attention to the gods, ancestors and benefactors, and appropriate conduct;[53] *Ep.* 31 stresses the priority of spiritual over physical concerns;[54] *Ep.* 32 speak of distinction in nobility with the help of god;[55] *Ep.* 33 decries pomposity and self-will and recalls teaching delivered in precepts;[56] *Ep.* 34 voices the Cynic antipathy to sophists and money-making and calls for moderation.[57] In these letters, even where the Academy receives special attention, Platonic philosophy does not.

Clearly, a comprehensive view of the letters reveals a Cynicizing and not a Platonizing character. The attention to Plato is best taken together with that given to Aristippus. The effort at rehabilitating these two traditionally controversial Socratics underlines the overarching project of the letters which is to harmonize the relationships among the Socratics.[58] The editor-author's special knowledge of Plato's works thereby remains a matter of sources and does not imply anything about the purpose of the letters in the collection.

B. *School Context and the Choice of Socrates as Exemplar*

Why does the editor-author of the Socratic letter corpus focus on Socrates and his disciples, as opposed to Diogenes or Crates, for his work with its specifically Cynic character? In the first place, the letters of the Socratic corpus grew around the already existing letters of Speusippus and Socrates, and so the expansion to include the Socratics is a natural development from the sources. Second, Epictetus gives evidence of the prominence of Socrates as an ascetic teacher and exemplar in the early Empire. Third, the milder type of Cynicism promoted in the letters[59] would find a poor spokesman in the abrasive Diogenes. Fourth, in view of the fact that the letters opt for a milder form of Cynicism than that of Diogenes, they wisely root this position in the generation of philosophers back to which the Cynics trace their lineage.[60] Finally, the echoes of a rhetorical

---

[53] For good reputation and *bios* as preferable to *logos* in Cynic pedagogy, see below 131-32, 153-54.

[54] For attention to spiritual development, see below, 158-61.

[55] For the notion of the gods' help, see below, 155.

[56] For the dangers of self-centered ignorance of the common good, see below, 159-60. Also see the comments on the use of precepts, 135.

[57] For the polemic against sophists and money-making, see below, 154-55. Moderation is the characteristic of the approach of the whole corpus to Cynicism.

[58] Allusion to this was made above at 105-6 and the project is discussed below at 121-23.

[59] See 117-21.

[60] See Diogenes Laertius 6.2, 11, 54. V. Emeljanow, "The Letters of Diogenes" (Diss. Stanford, 1968) 75, finds an effort in Ps-Diogenes' *Ep.* 39 to Socraticize the view of death which appears elsewhere in Diogenes' letters as more characteristically Cynic. He judges this to be an attempt to place Cynicism on a higher level and to confirm the tradition that it derives from Socrates' teaching (see 97 and 25). R. Höistad, *Cynic Hero and Cynic King*

school which can be detected in the letters,[61] together with their philosophical
interest, suggest a school environment where both the art of rhetoric and the art of
living were taught. The concern for the Academy also fits the scholastic bias of
the letters. In view of this, it would be better pedagogy to depict, as the letters do,
a group of close associates discussing philosophical issues and exchanging friendly
assistance, while at the same time practically engaged in a variety of rhetorical arts,
such as writing letters, apologies, dialogues, and memoirs and participating in
declamations, public lectures and private exhortations. Because of their
association in the school of Socrates, the first generation Socratics lend themselves
readily for adaptation as models of the rhetorical-philosophical education of the
early Empire. On the other hand, the individual, wandering Cynic preacher and
moral critic would hardly meet the requirements of a school situation.

A school context of the letters, therefore, accounts for the mixture of the
rhetorical and the philosophical in the corpus. It also provided a rationale for the
Cynicizing editor-author's focus on Socrates and his disciples. His particular
interest in the continuation of Plato's Academy fits this scheme as well. Moreover,
the biographical and doxographical traditions and the other sources employed in
the creation of the letters, especially in the second part of the collection,[62] are
proper to the schoolroom and serve the scholastic purpose of the collection. That
purpose will be the subject of the next section of this study.

C. *Purpose or Aim of the Collection*

The purpose of the collection of letters is to propose a mild type of Cynicism
as a way of life for its audience. As part of this program, the letters also address

---

(Lund: Carl Blom, 1948) 8-9, discusses the Socratic roots of Cynicism. K. Döring, 16-17,
credits the recourse to Socrates to (1) the archaizing and classicist tendency of the early
Empire, (2) the mood of political opposition, (3) Socrates' traditional lack of needs, (4) the
traditional flexibility of Socrates' image. See also Ch. Lévêque, "La Vie socratique et la vie
cynique," *Academie des Sciences Morales et Politiques: Séances et Travaux* 127, 27 n.s.
(1887) 199-221, who claims that the Cynics did begin with Socratic principles but pushed
them beyond Socrates' own limits and moderation. See also D. Tarrant, "The Tradition of
Socrates," *G&R* 1 (1931) 151-57, where she finds in the later traditions a tendency to color
the philosopher's moral uprightness with traits drawn from Cynic asceticism as well as to
divinize and add a miraculous coloring to the conception of the *daimonion*. The Socratic
letters share all these tendencies. Contrast the earlier portraits of Socrates as outlined in E.
Edelstein, *Xenophontisches und platonisches Bild des Sokrates* (Heidelberg: Dr. Emil
Ebering, 1933). O. Gigon, *Sokrates, sein Bild in Dichtung und Geschichte* (Bern: A. Francke,
1927) 312-13, notes that it was not unusual in any of the Socratic schools to attribute to
Socrates teachings drawn from other sources. See also G. Süpfle, "Zur Geschichte der
cynischen Sekte, I," *Archiv für die Geschichte der Philosophie* 4 (1891) 414-23.

   [61] See 108-10.

   [62] The biographical interest in the second part of the letter collection is noted but not
well accounted for by Sykutris, *Die Briefe,* 113 ff.

the traditional opposition between this brand of Cynicism and the more rigidly ascetic type. The harmonization that results expands to embrace all the divergent Socratics into a mutually supportive association of philosophic friends. Moreover, since the aim of proposing this way of life is to stir action and not just comprehension, the letters engage in exhortation.

1. Mild Versus Rigorous Cynicism

In advocating the milder form of Cynicism, the letter corpus is a tributary to a long-flowing stream of tradition. The existence and direction of a succession of types in Cynicism, i.e., from mild to strict, strict to mild, or a coexistence of both from the start, has been widely discussed.[63] All agree that the mild or hedonistic strain entered at least as early as Teles and Crates, if not with Antisthenes or Diogenes themselves.[64] The particular interest of this study is in the clash between the two strains in the early Empire, which the Socratic letters also reflect.

The first and sixth epistles of Socrates allude unfavorably to other teachers, and Sykutris[65] sees here a two-pronged attack against contemporary, specialized philosophy in esoteric schoolrooms and against sophistic epideixis.[66] Obens,[67] on the other hand, sees here allusive and open criticism of exaggerated Cynic philosophers who, *Ep.* 1.2(218.17-19), demand money for their teaching and, *Eps.* 9.3(246.22-23) and 13.2(250.31 ff.), make a vain show of their rigor.

---

[63] K. Praechter, *Friedrich Überwegs Grundriss der Geschichte der Philosophie, erster Teil. Die Philosophie des Altertums* (Berlin: E.S. Mittler und Sohn, 1926) 432-35. See Susemihl, 1:32 ff., 41 ff.; G.A. Gerhard, "Zur Legende vom Kyniker Diogenes," *Archiv für Religionswissenschaft* 15 (1912), 39 ff.; and *Phoinix,* 40 ff., 67,170 ff., and *passim;* O. Hense, "Eine Menippea des Varro," *RhM* 61 (1906) 13, n. 1; See R. Höistad, 8-9; P. Tzaneteas, "The Symbolic Heracles in Dio Chrysostom's Orations *On Kingship*" (Diss. Columbia University, 1972) 87-89; A.J. Malherbe, "Pseudo-Heraclitus, Epistle 4. The Divinization of the Wise Man," *JAC* 21 (1978) 47-51; R. Hock, "Simon the Shoemaker as an Ideal Cynic," *GRBS* 17 (1976) 48 ff. Emeljanow, 21-22 and n. 40. See also J.F. Kindstrand, *Bion of Borysthenes* (Stockolm: J.F. Kindstrand/Almqvist and Wiksell Distributors, 1976) 64-76; E. Bevan, "Hellenistic Popular Philosophy," in *The Hellenistic Age,* J.B. Bury, ed., (Cambridge: Cambridge University, 1923) 89-90; K. Jöel, "Die Auffassung der kynischen Sokratik," *Archiv für Philosophie, I: Archiv für Geschichte der Philosophie* 20 n.F. 13 (1907) 152; F. Leo, "Diogenes bei Plautus," in *Ausgewählte kleine Schriften I* (Rome: Edizione di Storia e Letteratura, 1960) 185-90; G. Rudberg, "Zum Diogenes-Typus," *Symbolae Osloensis* 15 (1936) 1-18.

[64] See Diogenes Laertius 6.15 for Antisthenes; 6.75 for Diogenes; Julian *Or.* 6.201c (W.C. Wright, trans., *The Works of the Emperor Julian,* LCL, 3 vols. [London: W. Heinemann, 1913]) and Plutarch *Quom. adul. ab am.* 69C-D for Crates.

[65] Sykutris, *Die Briefe,* 15-16.

[66] For the attack on sophistic rhetoric in Cynic writings, see Norden, 406, n. 1.

[67] Obens, 77-78, also finds a parallel criticism by the second-century sophist Philostratus in his *VS* 1.25.2(227/532).

Dio Chrysostom confirms the Cynic connection in the rebuke of the first letter of Socrates. In his defense of true (Cynic) philosophy in *Or.* 32.8 ff., he closely echoes Socrates in *Ep.* 1. He criticizes those who teach only in private or use lecture halls, those Cynics who use jest and derision and debase philosophy among the masses, those who declaim in remote and empty epideixis, and those who rail at their audience with no positive program for their improvement.[68] Here in Dio, as in the Socratic letters, the criticism explicitly includes the harsh and abusive Cynics and serves the positive purpose of recommending the milder and more effective types of philosophy. The letters of Socrates make use of the standard criticism as they too promote a milder and more effective form of philosophy. This philosophy is Cynicism, and other works of the period similarly attack harsh and abusive Cynicism to promote a milder form.[69]

An interesting aspect of this milder Cynicism, again for its parallel with the letters of Socrates, is Dio's stress on the divine commission behind his work in *Or.* 32.11-12.[70] Billerbeck[71] singles out another aspect., i.e., that of political involvement, which rigid Cynicism declines but milder Cynicism, such as that in the orations of Dio and the Socratic letters (*Eps.* 1, 2, 3, 4, 5, 7, 9, 10, 11, 14, 15, 16, 17, 23, 27, 28, 29, 33, 34), to name just two instances, embraces.

2. Programmatic Presentation of Mild Cynicism

While these parallels verify the presence of the milder strain of Cynicism in the Socratic letters, a view of the letters themselves will now underscore the program-

---

[68] See A.J. Malherbe, "Gentle as a Nurse: The Cynic Background of I Thess ii," *NovT* 12 (1970) 205 ff., for a discussion of this passage in Dio Chrysostom. The typical, rough Cynics in the early Empire are subjected to similar criticism by the second century *Grammaticus* Aulus Gellius in his *NA* 9.2; (J.C. Rolfe, trans., *The Attic Nights of Aulus Gellius,* LCL, vol. 2 [London: W. Heinemann, 1927]; by the reform-minded philosopher and emperor Julian in *Ors.* 6 and 7; and by the keen-eyed satirist Lucian in *Demon.* 19.48 (A.M. Harmon, trans *Lucian,* LCL, 8 vols, [London: W. Heinemann, 1913]). See Döring, 91 ff. for similar observations about Dio Chrysostom *Ors.* 13 and 72.

[69] Malherbe, "Gentle," 210 ff., calls attention to the stress on Cynic gentleness in Musonius Rufus, in Lucian's life of Demonax, and in Philostratus *VS* 1.7(205/487). Billerbeck, 3, makes the same point about Musonius and, 68, finds the same mild Cynicism in Epictetus.

[70] Cf. Socrates *Ep.* 1, *passim.* See also Epictetus *Diss.* 3.22.2, 9 ff., 50 ff., 53 ff. (W.A. Oldfather, trans., *Epictetus. The Discourses as Reported by Arrian. The Manual and Fragments,* LCL, [London: W. Heinemann, 1926]). Billerbeck, 8, stresses the Cynics' religious vocation in Epictetus. Malherbe, "Gentle," 215-26, suggests that this may be a deliberate attempt by Dio and Epictetus to dissociate themselves from Cynics like Oenomaus of Gadara who did away with reverence for the gods. Cf. Billerbeck, 120 and 145 and Julian *Or.* 6.192d where he makes Diogenes a servant of Apollo. J. Bernays, *Lukian und die Kyniker* (Berlin: Wilhelm Hertz, 1879) 102 ff. finds in Epictetus' view of Diogenes at 3.24.64 the traits of milder Cynicism.

[71] Billerbeck, 145.

matic character of its presentation. Of all the figures in the letters, the "hedonist" *Aristippus* stands out as the exemplar and apologist of a mild position in contrast to ascetic extremists. The letters treat Aristippus with sympathy [72] and in doing so push beyond the doxographical traditions already favorable [73] to the Cyrenean philosopher. [74]

The letters of the Socratics open with a strong criticism of Aristippus, but the charges laid against him are thoroughly refuted in the other letters. Thus, in *Ep.* 8, the Cynic Antisthenes criticizes Aristippus for (1) associating with tyrants; (2) banqueting rather than seeking self-sufficiency at home; (3) amassing unnecessary wealth; (4) making powerful friends; (5) having dubious friends among the ignorant masses; (6) clinging to pleasures unfit for the wise man. To (1) Aristippus answers in ironic tones in *Ep.* 9 that rather than fawn upon Dionysius, it is the tyrant that treats him as an important person and recognizes him to be the steward of the Socratic teachings. He counters (6) in noting at *Ep.* 9.2 Antisthenes' Cynic garb and habits as unfit for a free Athenian. In answer to (5) he calls attention to his visitors from throughout the island at *Ep.* 9.3. [75]

Taken alone these two letters might seem to do no more than draw the lines of opposition between the two positions, but the other letters betray a decided bias toward Aristippus' position. In *Eps.* 10 and 11 his influence with Dionysius (charge 4) saves the Locrian youths, while Antisthenes' own contradictory position on wealth (charge 3) is exposed. At *Eps.* 9.4 and 11, Simon reiterates the position of ascetic Cynicism against luxury-loving Socratics in answer to jibes at his

---

[72] Noted by Sykutris, "Sokratikerbriefe," 984, and *Die Briefe,* 50-51, 87, 113. Schering, 31-32, detects the same sympathy toward Aristippus, noting that Dionysius and not Aristippus is criticized as a paradigm of luxuriousness at *Eps.* 8 and 9.1, 2, 3 (and see also *Eps.* 10, 11, 13, 23, 24, 28.10, 33, 34).

[73] For a defense of Aristippus' luxurious life-style see Diogenes Laertius 2.68, 76; of his frequenting a common woman see Athenaeus 13.588c (C.B. Gulick., *Athenaeus. The Deipnosophists,* LCL, vol. 6 [London: W. Heinemann, 1927]), and Diogenes Laertius 2.69, 74; of his varied garb see Diogenes Laertius 2.67, 78 and *Gnom. Vat.* 493 (L. Sternbach, ed., *Gnomologium Vaticanum e codice Vaticano Graeco* 743, Texte und Kommentare; eine altertumswissenschaftliche Reihe, 2 [Berlin: de Gruyter, 1963]); of his taking pay for teaching see *Gnom. Vat.* 24; and for comment that his moderation is comparable to Diogenes' see Maximus of Tyre 1.9 (H. Hobein, ed., *Maximi Tyrii philosophoumena* [Leipzig: B.G. Teubner, 1910]) and *Gnom. Vat.* 26; that he opposed excessive wealth see Diogenes Laertius 2.77; that he suffered little from the loss of a field see Plutarch *Tranq. an.* 469c; and for generally favorable comments see Diogenes Laertius 2.66, 71; Ps-Plutarch *De vita et poesi Hom* 2.150. See Mannebach, *passim,* for other citations of these favorable traditions, as well as for those critical of Aristippus which the Socratic letters employ.

[74] G.C. Field, "Aristippus," *OCD,* 90, says that while Aristippus is sometimes credited with founding the Cyrenaic school, that may rather have been accomplished by his grandson Aristippus.

[75] Contrast Diogenes' *Ep.* 32, where the criticism of Aristippus is very harsh, where the picture of Socrates is Cynic in this most rigorous form, and which has no balancing letter of respose from Aristippus.

wisdom. But his own leaning toward milder Cynicism emerges in his calling his
criticism "jest" [76] in *Ep.* 12 and in Aristippus' praise of his criticism of Prodicus'
encomium of Hercules.[77] Aristippus actually favors Simon's wisdom and teaching over against Antisthenes' extreme Cynicism in *Ep.* 13. There, too, in Simon's
circle can be found the nobles and leaders of the city (see charge 4). The reader of
Ep. 16 is surprised to find Aristippus exonerating both Socrates' immoderation
and his fellow Socratics' fearful flight from Athens, as he throws in an offer of
assistance to them. *Ep.* 18 finds Aristippus on good terms with Xenophon and,
implicitly, with the other Socratics. Even the signs of open enmity between Plato
and Aristippus are played down as jests in *Ep.* 23.3, with Aeschines suggesting a re-
conciliation in order to safeguard their public reputations and the appearance of
the Socratics in general. Aristippus' advice to his daughter in *Ep.* 27 [78] includes
avoiding desires for excessive luxury at 27.2 and finding wealth in philosophy at
27.5 (see change 3); tranquillity in minor as well as in major matters at 27.3 (see
charge 2); instruction of her son in a way of life suited to good men (see charge 6).
He recalls his association with Socrates at 27.3, wherein he also echoes Simon's
circle in *Ep.* 13, and he notes the beneficial result of the example of his life in the
trustworthiness of his freedmen.

The sympathy toward Aristippus' "hedonistic" position [79] reflects the general
inclination in the letters of Socrates and the Socratics toward a milder Cynicism. In
addition to what was said above on the direct criticism of the practices of
exaggerated Cynics, one might note the following evidence of mild Cynicism in the
letters. In *Ep.* 1 Socrates, like Demonax in Lucian's sketch, prefers to remain at
Athens rather than take to the road in typical Cynic fashion.[80] Socrates is
involved in civic affairs at *Ep.* 1.5,[81] follows a divine call at *Ep.* 1.7 ff., and looks to
the divine for examples at *Ep.* 6.4. While he depicts his clothing and life-style in
typical Cynic terms at *Ep.* 6.2(232.17-21), at *Ep.* 1.2 ff. he contrasts himself to the
wandering mendicant philosophers and there, as also at *Ep.* 6.8 ff., he speaks of
having some resources to meet necessities and he expects assistance for himself and
his children from the community of friends.

The letters of the Socratics, in addition to the material concerning Aristippus,
also indicate a bias toward a milder Cynicism in the positive evaluation of death,

---

[76] For a discussion of Cynic harshness see 156.

[77] See Schering, 25. Hercules, proffered as the patron-exemplar of ascetic Cynicism, is
also negatively estimated at *Ep.* 9.4 and contrast the favorable view of Hercules, but in a
non-philosophical context, in *Ep.* 28.

[78] Mannebach, 81, dates this letter before Diogenes Laertius, who, he says, uses it at
2.72. He also sees it unlike the other Socratic letters in its addressee who is not one of the
Socratic disciples.

[79] A similar apology for Aristippus' way of life in contrast to Cynic extremism can be
found in Horace *Ep.* 1.17 13-35 (H.R. Fairclough, Trans., *Quintus Horatius Flaccus. Satires,
Epistles and Ars Poetica,* LCL [London: W. Heinemann, 1926]).

[80] See Lucian, *Demon.* 5.

[81] See below, 159-60.

the afterlife and the immortality of the soul at *Ep.* 14.6-8,[82] as well as in their concern for the body of the deceased at *Ep.* 14.10 (cf. *Ep.* 32). *Ep.* 15.1(260.6) praises Socrates for living *hosiōs* and *eusebōs*. *Ep.* 21.3 lauds Xanthippe's rigorous life but urges her not to go to harmful extremes. Philip is urged to gentleness (*epieikeia*) in *Ep.* 29, while *Ep.* 30.2 corrects *Ep.* 32 [83] on the characteristic virtues of an accomplished man when it substitutes careful attention (*epimeleia*) to one's gods, ancestors and benefactors (supplemented in 3 by the virtues of *bebaiotēs* and *pistis*) for *andria, rōmē* and *tachys*. *Ep.* 33 reflects the jesting tradition of the mild Cynics' *spoudaiogeloion*. Mention has already been made above [84] of the assistance expected among the Socratic friends.

3. Effort to Harmonize Relationships

The strain of mild Cynicism, thus, pervades the whole corpus. A parallel interest of the letters as they propose this milder version of Cynicism is to harmonize the relationships among the first generation Socratics and their schools and to group them under that one philosophical standard. Aristippus, while opposing Antisthenes, is found to praise the wiser and more moderate Simon.[85] *Ep.* 23.3 insists on the insignificance of the rift between Aristippus and Plato,[86] but calls for an end of even that trivial sign of division which tarnishes the friends' public reputation. In the letters dealing with the Academy, general principles are laid down which can apply to any philosophical association. On the one hand, there is no attention paid to specifically Platonic doctrine in the remarks on the Academy. On the other, *Ep.* 32.2-3 characterizes the separation of members of the Academy as a matter of personal preference and constitution. Continuity, however, is maintained despite the change in circumstances in the attempt to

---

[82] Sykutris, *Die Briefe,* 113-14, sees this as "purely informational" in a biographical sense. Why, though, would the author have added at *Ep.* 14.8(258.7) "and perhaps the words were also true"?

[83] Sykutris, *Die Briefe,* 89, sees the order of the letters as 31, 32, 30.

[84] See 107.

[85] See the discussion on 120. R. Hock, 50 ff., differs, for he sees Simon as allied with strict Cynicism and mocked by Aristippus.

[86] Swift Riginos records the anecdotal tradition surrounding Plato and the rivalry between him and the other Socratics which surfaces in the Socratic letters. His rivalry with Aristippus (reflecting the tension between the Academics and the Cyrenaics) has already been observed in *Ep.* 23, which minimizes the differences and changes them from the philosophical opposition of *phronēsis* and *hēdonē* to a personal rift. See Swift Riginos, 101 ff., and A. Mauersberger, "Plato und Aristipp," *Hermes* 61 (1926) 208-30, 304-28. Plato's remark that Aristippus was not present with the other Socratics at Socrates' death was taken by the tradition as a sign of his enmity toward Aristippus. On other issues, his trip to Egypt (Swift Riginos, 61 ff.) is favorably interpreted in *Ep.* 26, as is his voluntary isolation (Swift Riginos, 121-23) in *Ep.* 24. He helps Aeschines in Syracuse rather than ignore him (Swift Riginos, 96 ff.) in *Ep.* 23.

achieve a blameless and virtuous life. Even so, *Ep.* 30 and 31 strongly encourage Xenocrates to assume the Academy's direction. Speusippus stresses the importance of preserving Plato's memory and attending to (*epimeleia*) his gods and predecessors. The Academy enhances one's life (*bios*) and reputation (*doxa*), and Xenocrates' commitment to it would be expression of his gratitude (*charis*) to Plato as well as of his own diligent concern (*epimelēs*), reliability (*bebaiotēs*) and faithfulness (*pistis*), virtues in which the members of the school should excel.

In addition to the relations between Aristippus and Plato, the letters also reflect at *Ep.* 15.3 the literary rivalry between Plato and Xenophon, and this will be discussed further below.[87] But what the letters fail to use from the anecdotal tradition is even more striking. A good deal of the traditional criticism of Plato originates with Diogenes and Antisthenes, but Diogenes does not appear in these letters and Antisthenes rebukes only Aristippus. Swift Riginos suggests that the anecdotes on Plato's luxury and arrogance (*typhos*) were actually circulated by later Cynics. She sees in them and in the counter criticism by Plato of Diogenes the work of Cynics and Platonists who use their founders as spokesmen for hostility in the schools from a later period.[88]

The Socratic letter collection, on the other hand, by selective use of the anecdotal tradition and by its own emphases, attempts to replace this rivalry with a more harmonious picture. In doing so, therefore, the letters push the center of focus back to the stage before divisions among the school set in. And so, even the letters' apparently parochial interest in the Academy reflects a real concern for the philosophic life per se, which the letters as a whole paint in muted Cynic tones. Roughly contemporary, Lucian's *Demon.* 5 describes that mild Cynic as a toned-down Diogenes but having most in common with Socrates. Later (62), Demonax, when asked to state his philosophical preferences, says ecumenically, "They are all admirable, but for my part I revere Socrates, I wonder at Diogenes, and I love Aristippus."

The ecumenical nature of the philosophical enterprise finds concrete expression in the Socratic letters at *Ep.* 25.2, where Phaedrus esteems his education in the Socratic teachings "in every appropriate and holy place" (*en panti harmodiō̦ kai hierō̦ topō̦*), be it the Academy, the Lyceum, or the groves near Ilyssus. Socrates' teachings provide the link here at *Ep.* 25.1(278.7-10) and in the letter as a whole.[89]

Over and above teaching and doctrine the letters, in the very least, bring the Socratics into epistolary dialogue and, even more, stress the harmony of personal

---

[87] See 128-30 below. Swift Riginos, 100, ascribes this literary to Alexandrian commentators.

[88] Swift Riginos, 111-17, 148-49. See also J. Geffcken, "Antiplatonica," *Hermes* 64 (1929) 87-109.

[89] In addition to the teachings contained in Socrates' own *Eps.* 1-7, e.g. 1 and 6, and the reports in *Eps.* 14 and 17, note the allusions to their importance to his followers at *Eps.* 9.1 (Aristippus); 12, 13.1, 18.2 (Simon); 15.2, 18.2; 19 (Xenophon); 15.3 (Plato); 20 (Cebes or Simmias); 21.1 (Xanthippe); 21.3; 22.2 (Aeschines); 25 (Phaedrus); 27.5 (Arete).

relations among them. This harmony, while expressed in terms of friendship, is not purely personal but finds its origin in the Socratic philosophical tradition which associates and, perforce, makes friends of all the personalities in the letters (*Ep.* 6.11 speaks of the "kinship of soul" *to gar en tē̦ psychē̦ syngenes*). Hence Socrates can expect, in virtue of his philosophical instruction (*Ep.* 6.10), support from his friends for himself (*Ep.* 1.2-3), for his children (*Ep.* 6.8-12), and for other philosophical associates (*Ep.* 2), just as he exhibits like concern for his friends (*Eps.* 2.5, 7) and their children (*Ep.* 4).

It should come as no surprise, then, to see this bond of friendship echoed among the Socratics themselves, despite their traditional rivalry (*Eps.* 10, 11, 14.9-10, 15.2, 16, 19, 21, 22.1, 23, 24.3-4, 26.2, 28.1, 30.3, 31, 32.1).[90]

4. Friendship and "Community" Interest

There is more to the association of Socrates than their exhanges of friendly support. First, the letters suggest an actual association of presence, by recalling with approval their philosophical circles in the past (*Eps.* 13.1, 25.2, 27.3, 32.2), by looking forward to their resumption (*Eps.* 16, 17.4, 18, 19), and by looking to the establishment and support of similar circles (*Eps.* 20, 27.3, 30, 31, 33.3).

Second, the Socratics engage in a lively literary exchange of which letters themselves comprise just one part. The vehicle most often mentioned for the handing on (*Ep.* 20 *paradidontes*) and preservation (*Ep.* 21 *mēden katabalē̦s*) of Socrates, traditional teachings rests on an accurate record of what he said and did (*Ep.* 15.2). For Xenophon, such written records also furnish the best apology before his detractors and their composition is required by their common friendship (*Ep.* 15.2). Thus, he (*Ep.* 18.2), his son (*Esp.* 14.1; 15.1), and Aeschines (*Ep.* 22.2 and *Eps.* 14; 17 themselves) engage in writing memorabilia, though with some diffidence (*Eps.* 15.3; 22.2).[91] Despite their apologetic purpose, the memorabilia find their first audience within the Socratic circle. In letter form, they inform and console (*Eps.* 14.1; 15.1; 16; 17.1), while in proper memorabilia form they are circulated for pre-publication comment (*Eps.* 18.2; 22.1). The Platonic dialogue represents a special instance of literary production among the Socratics (*Eps.* 15.3; 22.2).

Can anyone deny, therefore, that the letters depict an association of philosophical friends with a striking, if loose, institutional coloring?[92] The central figure, of course, is Socrates, with a focus on his teaching and virtue. The later doctrinal differences among the derivative Socratic schools (e.g., the Academy and the Cyrenaics) are passed over in favor of the Cynic perspective of the letters. Hence, the institutional concerns for the Academy ultimately serve the

---

[90] See Obens, 11-13, for his catalogue of the references to the theme of friendship.

[91] *Ep.* 33.3 similarly uses the letter for its reminder and admonition, postponing the project of writing a memoir on Speusippus' situation.

[92] They even fulfill the services of a burial society at *Eps.* 14.10 and 32.2.

letters' version of milder Cynicism. When the philosophical differences are set in confrontation (e.g., Cynics and Cyrenaics), it is not without ample indication of a resolution in the position of milder Cynicism.

5. Hortatory Aims of the Letters

The letters, however, are not merely descriptive in terms of milder Cynicism or the association of philosophers. They also exhort their audience to adopt a Cynic course of action.[93] In the letters of Socrates typical themes of Cynic exhortation appear, e.g., the criticism of riches at *Eps.* 1.4-5; 6.2-3, 5, 7; the warning against reckless ignorance at *Ep.* 1.10-12; denunciation of the folly and destructiveness of a life of excess at *Ep.* 6.3,6. Positive exhortation enters at *Ep.* 1.10(224.19-20) where Socrates concludes the description of his own restraint with the observation, *oida de hoti ei kai hoi alloi anthrōpoi homoiōs diekeinto, hēttona an ēn kaka en tōᵢ bioᵢ.* A similar point is suggested at *Ep.* 6.2-3 and made explicit at 6.4, where he singles out the divine contentedness as a prime example for one who wants to be wise and happy. *Ep.* 1.4(200.11-15) suggests that friends assist each other (and compare *Ep.* 6.12), while *Ep.* 1.6(220.28-29) explicitly lays out the path to service saying *prōton men gar oimai, kath'ho dynatai hekastos ōphelein, exetazesthai. Ep.* 5.2 urges the virtues of *karteria* and *aphilochrēmatia.*

The letters of the Socratics are more biographical but this emphasis does not entirely rule out an interest in promoting the Cynic way of life. The criticism of riches in *Eps.* 8 and 12 is accepted, but with moderation, at *Eps.* 13.2; 21; 22.1; 27.2. The exhortation in *Ep.* 20[94] is indirect in that it praises the addressee for being an *apeikonisma Sōkratous* (268.14-15) and calls attention to the work of handing on the Socratic teaching to the Theban youth, *paradidontes autois hous ēkousamen logous para Sōkratous* (268.16-17). Xenophon turns these into explicit exhortation in *Ep.* 15,[95] when he calls the Socratic circle to the virtue of Socrates at 1(260.4-6), *dei mentoi ge hēmas andras agathous ginesthai kàkeinon men epainein hōn ebiōse sōphronōs kai hosiōs kai eusebōs* and to the written recording of his teaching and life at 2(260.16-18, 20-21) *dokei mentoi chrēnai hēmas syngraphein, ha pote eipen anēr kai epraxe* and *hēmōn ... eis hapanta ton bion paratithentōn tēn aretēn tàndros.* The exhortation, therefore, has tradition in mind and that in two senses: one didactic, to preserve the teaching in written records; the other ethical, to preserve the teaching in virtuous action. This suggests a hortatory context and purpose even for the biographical letters of the second part of the collection.[96]

---

[93] The hortatory features of the letter collection are treated on 132-34. Example receives special attention on 135-46.

[94] From a Theban member of the Socratic school, most likely Cebes or Simmias, to Antisthenes, in the view of Schering, 8, and Sykutris, *Die Briefe,* 70.

[95] This letter responds to *Ep.* 14, written by Euclides, according to Sykutris, *Die Briefe,* 58. He, along with Terpsion, another Megarian, is the addressee here.

[96] Thus, even the "purely informational" account of Socrates' teaching on death and

Xenophon himself applies this exhortation in *Eps.* 18 and 19. In addition to the preservation of Socrates' teaching in written memoirs, *apomnēmoneumata* 2(266.18), *Ep.* 18 commends the undivided application of his teachings as well in the example of Simon at 2(266.21 ff.). *Ep.* 19, by Xenophon like *Ep.* 18, makes the paradoxical saying of Socrates on sufficiency a model of the recommended attitude of the friends gathered at the new temple. The study of Socrates' teaching which issues into virtuous action preserves that teaching in life practice.

The same exhortation to recall Socrates' teachings and to follow them and his own practice of them appears in *Ep.* 21, among the admonitions against useless grief in the letter of consolation to Xanthippe. Here Aeschines says at 1(270.9-11), *anamimnēskou gar hōn elege Sōkratēs kai tois ēthesin autou kai tois logois peirō akolouthein,* and at 3(270.26-29), *tharrei oun, ō Xanthippē, kai mēden katabalē̦s tōn Sōkratous kalōn eiduia ... kai epinoei auton hopoia ezēse kai hopoia eteleutēse.* The exhortation to consider well the nature of Socrates' actions expands from Xanthippe to anyone when Aeschines concludes at 3(270.29-31), *egō men gar oimai kai ton thanaton autou mega te kai kalon gegonenai ei dē tis kath'ho chrē skopein skopoiē.*

In the letters not directly concerned with Socrates, exhortation still forms part of their purpose. Plato, in *Ep.* 29, urges Philip to royal beneficence and gentleness but links this to the common struggle for virtue, when he says at (294.21-22) *dei ... meta tōn beltistōn agōnizesthai auton onta hena toutōn.* The philosophical path to virtue and his own progress are both extolled in *Ep.* 25 by Phaedrus and by Xenocrates in *Ep.* 32.2. In *Ep.* 26.2[97] the author's offer of help is a practical application of the philosophical adage *koina ta philōn* (280.20-22). *Ep.* 33.3 recalls the virtuous conduct expected of Dion even now after his assumption of ruling power. In fact, he is now to be an example of the best in Greece. Finally, Aristippus' letter to Arete, *Ep.* 27, contains the following explicit prescriptions at 2(282.19) *mē tou pleionos orignasthai;* at 3(282.26-27) *mē epi mikrois tarattesthai, entha oude epi megalois kalon hē orgē.* One might add to these the general exhortations to philosophical friendship at 3(282.30-37), implied when Aristippus

---

immortality in *Ep.* 14 (Sykutris, *Die Briefe,* 113-14), fulfills the exhortation to preserve his teaching, and this is explicitly commended at *Ep.* 15.2, a letter of response to *Ep.* 14. Moreover, according to *Ep.* 15.2(260.18-19), the presentation of his teaching and virtue is also the best apology and "rehabilitation" of the condemned philosopher. This offers another facet of the condemned philosopher. This offers another facet of the purpose behind the biographical *Ep.* 14. *Eps.* 16 and 17, especially the latter with its account of the events after Socrates' death, likewise exonerate Socrates from his condemnation, even if his views and actions seemed excessive to a more compromising Aristippus or were admittedly eccentric by Athenian standards and appeared contentious to his associates (17.2[264.6-9]).

In addition, see Obens, 8-11, for capsule summaries of the hortatory themes throughout the collection.

[97] Written to Plato by Crito, according to Sykutris, *Die Briefe,* 83, who thereby rejects Schering's suggestion of authorship ascription to Phaedrus.

urges her to esteem and live with Xanthippe and Myrto; to mutual assistance among philosophical friends at 4(284.1-9); to a proper evaluation of the riches of a legacy of philosophy at 5(284.13-20).

6. Concluding Observations

The discussion above has identified the dominant tendency of the letters toward a mild form of Cynicism. The method used by the author to propose this involves a moderation of the exaggerations in Cynicism and a generalized and Cynicized treatment of schools like the Academy and the Cyrenaics. The author's effort at harmonizing the relationships among the Socratics has some quasi-institutional characteristics. Finally, the letters exhort the reader to a life of philosophy in the Cynic mode.

IV. The Literary Activity of the Editor-Author

A. *The Letter Form and Its Varied Types*

A variety of literary forms were available to the editor-author of the letter collection by which to accomplish his aims. In dealing with similar material, Lucian chose the biographical essay for his *Demonax,* Dio Chrysostom the discourse (*Or.* 32) as also Julian (*Ors.* 6 and 7), and Horace the poetic epistle (1.17). The sources employed by the editor-author suggested the additional forms of the dialogue and the memoir. The literary medium selected here, however, is the letter, which also appeared among the sources used (the Platonic letters) and which, in the editor-author's use of it, includes biographical traditions and mimics the memoir form. The letter form was dictated, in part, by the material employed as the nucleus of the letter collection, i.e., the letter of Speusippus and the seven letters of Socrates.

The letter types represented in this nucleus appear in the editor-author's own creations, with others included there besides. As far as the nucleus is concerned, Socratic *Eps.* 2 and 3 are recommendations; 4 is a report to Crito on his son's scholastic progress; 7 is a criticism of the political regime of the Thirty with an apology for Socrates and advice for Chaerophon;[98] 1, 5 and 6 combine the (auto)-biographical perspective with a broad exhortation.[99] Speusippus' *Ep.* 28 uses literary-rhetorical critique for an encomium of Philip, all within the setting of a letter of recommendation.

The diversity of letter types in the expanded collection can best be appreciated in the light of the epistolary categories current in the handbooks of the day. When

---

[98] Sykutris, *Die Briefe,* 42-44.

[99] Sykutris, *Die Briefe,* 107-8, finds here the didactic-paraenetic tendency of popular philosophy, expressing the principles of Cynicism.

the handbook *typoi epistolikoi* of (Ps-)Demetrius[100] is applied to the Socratic collection, the following types in the letter emerge: friendly (*philikos*) *Eps.* 25; 31; commendatory (*systatikos*) *Ep.* 10; blaming (*memptikos*) *Ep.* 11; consoling (*paramythētikos*) *Ep.* 21; censorious (*epitimētikos*) *Ep.* 8; admonishing (*nouthetētikos*) *Ep.* 34; praising (*epainetikos*) *Ep.* 20; advisory (*symbouleutikos*) *Ep.* 29; accounting (*aitiologikos*) *Ep.* 22; accusing (*katēgorikos*) *Ep.* 12; apologetic (*apologētikos*) *Eps.* 13, 16, 24, 32; ironic (*eirōnikos*) *Ep.* 9. Some paraenetic letters, akin to the advisory type but different in tone from any of the specific types discussed by Demetrius, are *Eps.* 15, 30, 33.[101] Also not listed by Demetrius are the invitations *Eps.* 18, 19; the travelogue *Ep.* 26; the testament *Ep.* 27 (and *Ep.* 6); and the anecdotal memorabilia *Eps.* 14, 17, 23.

The letter collection thus betrays a knowledge and use of the varied letter types as listed in the handbooks. Furthermore, the subject matter and situations are suited to the presumed writers and addressees. Malherbe[102] observes that such handbooks reflect the school exercises in which, along with the basis principles of letter-writing, style and characterization were exercised. He cites Quintilian[103] as guarding for the rhetor the prerogative of conducting the instruction in style and characterization. This would set the level of instruction in the latter part of the secondary stage under the *grammaticus* or in the tertiary stage under the rhetor. The Socratic letter collection, which reflects this concern for style and character as well as the diverse principles of letter-writing, thus fits this upper level of educational sophistication. This corresponds to the philosophical interest noted in the letters, which is also appropriate to this higher level of instruction. The presence of both the rhetorical and philosophical interests in the letters is, therefore, not anomalous but appropriate to the school environment where rhetorical principles and a philosophico-moral life-style were being inculcated.

It is clear from his letters that the editor-author has embarked on his work consciously choosing certain literary forms and fully aware of their intended effect. As vehicles for the exposition of Cynic philosophy, the editor-author makes use of Socrates and the Socratic circle. For keeping Socrates in memory, *Ep.* 15 proposes two activities: the acquisition of similar virtues at 1(260.4-5) *dei mentoi ge hēmas andras agathous ginesthai;* and the production of a literary record of his virtue and teaching at 1(260.5-8) *[dei] kåkeinon men epainein hōn ebiōse sōphronōs kai hosiōs kai eusebōs, aitiasthai de kai psegein tēn tychēn kai tous epystantas autōi* and at

---

[100] V. Weichert, ed., *Demetrii et Libanii qui feruntur TYPOI EPISTOLIKOI et EPISTOLIMAIOI CHARAKTERES* (Leipzig: B.G. Teubner, 1910). See A.J. Malherbe, "Ancient Epistolary Theorists," *Ohio Journal of Religious Studies* 5 (1977) 8, for discussion of the date and content of this treatise.

[101] Libanius 15.5 lists a paraenetic type separately. On the opening of *Ep.* 33, the parallel to Cicero *Fam.* 2.4.1 suggests the use of a handbook. The same acquaintance with handbook theory is suggested by the deliberation about various letter openings at the start of *Ep.* 34.

[102] Malherbe, "Epistolary Theorists," 12 ff.

[103] *Inst.* 1.9.6; 2.1.1 ff.; 3.8.49; 9.2.29-30; 11.1.41.

2(260.16-18,20) *dokei mentoi chrēnai hēmas syngraphein, ha pote eipen anēr kai epraxe ... [hēmōn] eis hapanta ton bion paratithentōn tēn aretēn tàndros.* Indeed, literary activity of this sort is a concomitant of their philosophical association at 2(260.21-23) *kai phēmi dē adikēsein tēn koinēn hetairian kai, hōs ekeinos elege, tēn alētheian, ei mē asmenoi grapsaimen.*

B. *The Letter Form in the Literary Program of the Corpus*

The editor-author has shown a preference for the letter form, but his letters themselves situate this preference within a general literary program. The letters of Socrates suggest a context of epistolary exchange. The exchange can take place on various levels, like that of the two letters prior to *Ep.* 1 asking for Socrates' presence at court (*Ep.* 1.1) or the more significant criticism of Socrates' attitude toward money mentioned at *Ep.* 6.1 or the letter of political comment at *Ep.* 7.1. These prior epistolary exchanges establish the context for the letters of response which appear in the Socratic corpus.

Among the other letters in the collection, some also refer to exchanges of letters on a commonplace level (*Eps.* 10; 11; 17; 26.2; 27.1; 33.4; 34.3). Others, however, suggest the handling of philosophical matters in the letter form (*Eps.* 12; 27.5). In this regard, the particular concern of the letters of the Socratics has already been seen to rest with preserving the Socratic teachings and life-practice, and this provided both the subject matter and the literary form proposed in the letters. Thus, *Eps.* 14.1,4; 15.1; 16 refer to the epistolary reports' of Socrates' final days which were already dispatched to Xenophon and Aristippus, both absent from Athens at the time (*Ep.* 14.9,10). *Eps.* 14 and 17 themselves are just such letter reports and at 17.1(262.26-27) Aeschines specifies that he expects his addressee Euthydemus to be gladdened by the news of Socrates' posthumous exoneration.

Despite the start represented by the letters in setting down the record of Socrates' teaching, much remains to be done and *Ep.* 15.2 has already been quoted above in its call to the circle to do just that. There Xenophon names Aeschines as one expected to fulfill the task of writing about Socrates (and see *Ep.* 18.2[266. 17-18]). He has already done that in *Eps.* 14 and 17 but expresses at *Ep.* 22.2(272. 15-22) some diffidence as to his adequacy to the task of describing Socrates' virtue in memoirs.[104]

Xenophon himself is also engaged in composing *apomnēmoneumata* (memoirs, memorabilia of Socrates at *Ep.* 18.2[266.18-21]) of which Aristippus and Phaedo approve despite his own reservations about them. Similar reservations surface at

---

[104] Sykutris, *Die Briefe,* 73, despite the obvious tie between the *memorabilia* and Xenophon, sees Aeschines as the author here on the basis of all the other details of the letter: the author's poverty, his presence at Megara for a lecture of his work (Diogenes Laertius 2.62), his timidity about publishing, the comparison with Plato (Diogenes Laertius 2.62), and the mention of Plato's journey to Syracuse, which certainly sets the scene for the next letter in the collection, a letter from Aeschines.

Ep. 15.3(260.27-31), although the corruption of the text leaves unclear what it is that Xenophon cannot recount in memoir form (*ou dynametha apomnēmoneuein*,a surprising admission for Xenophon). For both Aeschines and Xenophon, the literary task of composing *apomnēmoneumata* is a clear obligation and already underway. And both experience a certain diffidence before the project.

Plato, on the hand, composes with no such difficulty at Ep. 15.3(260.23-26) and his works are acclaimed and influential at Ep. 22.2(272.11-13). Nevertheless, both Xenophon and Aeschines dissociate themselves from his works at Eps. 15.3(260.29-30); 22.2(272.14-15).[105] Interestingly, though Plato was absent from Athens at Socrates' death, no memoir-letter is addressed to him. Moreover, while Plato receives favorable treatment at the end of the corpus, his writings are not at issue there, as they are in these two letters. Clearly, the letters do not hold them to be sufficient records of Socrates' teachings and virtue. Rather, the letters favor memoirs, but even in this they are restrained.

The literary form preferred by the Socratic corpus without reservations is the letter itself. In this the letters take a cue from Ep. 28.5(288.2-5) which sees in the letter form the only means to speak to one far off of important things which would otherwise go unmentioned with the passage of time. The letters, in addition to their frequent references to the literary exchanges among the Socratics, also mention philosophical discussion (*dialegesthai*) such as those held with Socrates at Ep. 14.5(256.6) and 6(256.12); among the Socratics at Ep. 22.1(272.9); and with Simon at Ep. 9.4(246.30). They also allude to such discussions in the references to the philosophical company at Eps. 9.3(246.16); 13.1(250.27); 16(262.15); 17.3(264.13); 17.4(264.34); 20(268.18); 21.1(270.6-7); 23.1(274.5, 9, 12) and 2(274.18); 25.1(278.4, 9) and 2(278.18, 21); 27.3(282.35-26); 30.2(296.21).[106] Xenophon identifies the letter as a surrogate for this living association when at Ep. 18.1(266.4-6), he invites the Socratics to visit his Artemision and, failing that, at least to write (see 2[266.17]). He specifies the level of communication, be it in face-to-face discussion or by letter, by announcing the memoir of Socrates which he himself would send them and which the Socratics there had already favorably received.[107]

On the level of theory and practice, three observations can be made to help interpret the data found in the letters of the Socratics. (1) E. Weber notes that the letter was a medium well suited to transmit the store of Cynic *chriae, memorabilia, apophthegmata,* sentences and similitudes.[108] (2) in a school context the letters,

---

[105] Contrast Speusippus' letter, Ep. 28.3, 12, where Isocrates' denigration of Plato comes under fire.

[106] Contrast the harmful associations decried at Eps. 8(244.4); 9.4(246.31); 11(248.16); 24.1(276.8).

[107] He repeats the summons at Ep. 19, Interestingly, Plato, the creator of works of questionable value, seeks total solitude in Ep. 24, as his successor Xenocrates seems to do in Ep. 32.

[108] E. Weber, "De Dione Chrysostomo cynicorum sectatore," *Leipz. Stud.* 9-10 (1886-87) 180. Weber, 82-84, discusses the difference between *apomnēmoneuma* and *chreia* with reference to Hermogenes *Rh.* 2:6.5 (L. von Spengel, ed., *Rhetores Graeci,* 3 vols. [Leipzig:

written in the persons of the heads of the old schools as elaborations of anecdotes about them found elsewhere in briefer form, bring life to the old legends. As reading material for lessons, they would also serve as propaganda for Cynicism.[109] (3) in ancient epistolary theory the letter is considered half of a face-to-face discussion (*dialegesthai*).[110] As such, it does not describe a dialogue with its various participants but rather is the dialogue and its author is one of the dialogue partners.[111] Moreover, the philophronetic tone of the letter contrasts with the seriousness of an epistolary instruction [112] and suits the letter to the aims of popular philosophy.[113]

The letters of the Socratics reserve a special regard for face-to-face dialogue, but settle for the letter as second best. They also encourage writing memorabilia, closely associating these with the letter, but at the same time they denigrate the more remote literary dialogue.[114] In following this course, the letters find a congenial home in the classroom, as exercises in prosopopoeia and as propaganda for Cynicism. They also accord with the method and aims of popular philosophy and as such are particularly favored by the editor-author of this collection with his sympathies for Cynicism.

B.G. Teubner, 1853]). Nicolaus, *Prog.* 3:464 (Spengel), says the *apomnēmoneuma* is an extended *chreia* (or *gnōmē*). The Cynics, as A. Brancacci, "Le orazione diogeniane di Dione Chrysostomo," in *Scuole socratiche minori e filosofia ellenistica,* G. Giannantoni, ed., (Rome: Società editrice "Il Mulino," 1976) 146 ns. 12-13, notes, introduced the chria into the diatribe and made it central to their educational activity. The remarks of Hermogenes and Nicolaus help explain the Socratic Epistles' stated preference for *apomnēmoneumata* as a natural extension of their Cynic propensity toward *chreiai*. On the *chreia* see also H.R. Hollerbach, *Zur Bedeuting des Wortes "chreia"* (Cologne. priv. publ., 1964); G. Rudberg, "Zu den literarischen Formen der Sokratiker: Eine Skizze," in *DRAGMA* (Fest P. Nilsson, G. Adolf, ed., Lund: Håkan Ohlsson, 1939) 427-28; "Zur Diogenes-Tradition," 35; and compare K. Horna, "Gnome, Gnomendichtung, Gnomologien," *GW* suppl. 6 (1935) 74-90.

[109] Ueberweg, 505. Theon *Prog.* 2:115 (Spengel) mentions exercise in *prosopopoeia* through the letter form.

[110] Observed by Demetrius *Eloc.* 223.

[111] Demetrius *Eloc.* 225, 227.

[112] Demetrius *Eloc.* 231-32.

[113] K. Thraede, *Grundzüge griechisch-römischer Brieftopik* (Munich: C.H. Beck, 1970) 24 and see his discussion of Demetrius on 22-25.

[114] V. Emeljanow, "The Letters of Diogenes" (Diss. Stanford University, 1968) 21, discusses (Ps-) Diogenes' *Ep.* 17. Here, discussing the proper means of demonstrating virtue, Diogenes sanctions the use of letters to preserve the memory of the dead but insists on personal presence and living example for those still alive. Similar sentiments are voiced in the Socratic epistles. See G.C. Fiske, *Lucilius and Horace: A Study in the Classical Theory of Imitation* (Madison: University of Wisconsin, 1920) 176-77, for the progression from dialogue to letter in Aristotle. The remarks on the letter form in this chapter and in Chapter V further the observations of W.G. Doty, *Letters in Primitive Christianity,* New Testament Series (Philadelphia: Fortress, 1973) 1-19.

C. *The Letter Form's Appropriateness to Cynic Pedagogy*

The expressed preference in the Socratic corpus for living dialogue or its partial realization through the letter originates, as has been indicated above, in the aims and methods of Cynicism. Emeljanow's observations on the Cynic epistles of Diogenes illuminate this aspect of those letters and the Socratic letters as well. First, in the letters of Diogenes, the author creates letters around the anecdotes and references found in the doxographical tradition. The action and locale in these letters "impinge to generate a response in Diogenes." In the repartee which ensues, not only is the anecdotal saying recorded but a demonstration of some aspect of Diogenes' character emerges as well.[115]

Second, since the anecdote presents merely the dictum or the action without its rationale, the letters supply the missing interpretation and reason.[116] The anecdote is thus "set within an ethical and pedagogical framework."[117] In fact, "the anecdotes assist in the establishment of a concept which transcends the anecdote itself and the ethical content is as a result much more considerable."[118]

Third, the letters demonstrate a process of action and reaction to the Cynic message, be it favorable or not.[119] The reaction is crucial to the Cynic method. Once the prospective disciple is convinced of the error of his ways as presented in the exposition (*logos*), the instruction according to be teacher's life-example (*bios*) and the concomitant practical askesis by the pupil can begin.[120]

With regard to the Socratic letters, on the third point this fusion of *logos* and *bios* in Cynic teaching helps explain the unfavorable view which the Socratic letters have of literary dialogues which inform but do not engage the audience. A letter allows the reader to enter the dialogue as a participant, to come to the insight or decision desired by the author, or at least to encounter the *bios* of the letter writer under a particular aspect. On the second point, the Socratic letters have been seen to carry a philosophical and ethical content beyond that of the original anecdotes. Finally, to the first point, the Socratic letters are also epistolary expansions of anecdotes and the letters themselves will be shown to constitute part of the hortatory example of the corpus.

As has been seen, the Socratic letters emphasize personal encounter and the use of the letter form is a facet of that emphasis. Remember, too, that when they select other appropriate literary forms, the memoir wins out over the literary dialogue. The disinclination toward the latter has already been explained in terms of the search for a more engaging form. Furthermore, *Ep.* 22.2(272.11 ff.) sets up

---

[115] Emeljanow, 111, on *Ep.* 9. Here it is Diogenes' ready wit and reputation as speaker that are demonstrated.

[116] Emeljanow, 25.

[117] Emeljanow, 21.

[118] Emeljanow, 30, discussing *Eps. 30-50*.

[119] Emeljanow, 31.

[120] Emeljanow, 60 and see 25-26.

a distinction between dialogue and memoir on the basis of subject matter.[121] The dialogues seem to concern themselves with Socrates' *sophia,* while the memoirs concentrate on his *aretē.* This preference for memoir comes from the view of some Cynics that Cynicism is not a philosophy with a teaching content but is a way of life which devotes all attention to ethics and which has its end "life according to virtue."[122] But as a way of life, Cynicism is best studied not in writings but rather in the practice of exemplars of the school.[123] The attention given to personal encounter in the Socratic letters establishes the context for this method of studying the Cynic way of life by examining the practices of its exemplary proponents. These the letters propose and themselves represent.

V. The Hortatory Features of the Letters

The preceding section has laid out the literary principles and philosophical presuppositions which guided the editor-author in the choice of the epistolary form. The letters serve the aim of presenting the Cynic way of life to their readers. As such, they do more than inform and teach. They exhort to the pursuit of virtue along Cynic lines. The observations made here will clarify the hortatory character of the letters by noting the hortatory features in the corpus and by focusing on example as their principal hortatory device.

---

[121] *"kai ouch hoti emoi melei mē diapiptein peri tēs doxēs tēs peri tēn sophian, alla ... phrontisteon, mē en emoi kindyneuthē_i tēn ekeinou aretēn kakōs eiponti."*

[122] Diogenes Laertius 6.103-4. In *Ep.* 18.2(266.22-23) Xenophon commends Simon for devoting himself to Socrates' *logoi,* while others skirt doing philosophy, wanting to understand neither the *logoi* nor their contents. This seems to refer to a study of content, but in *Ep.* 13.1 Aristippus praises Simon for doing philosophy in a circle of disciples. Similar philosophical circles formed around Socrates' *logoi* surface in *Ep.* 20, while *Ep.* 21.1 notes the life practice which should issue from these teachings and *Ep.* 25.2(278.18) specifies virtue as the result of the Socratic "lullabies." Virtue is equated with *philosophia* at *Ep.* 25.2(278.23) and a similar connection between philosophy and the course of life comes up at *Ep.* 27.5(284.13-20). *sophia* itself receives a practical identity with the virtues of *bebaiotēs* and *pistis* at *Ep.* 30.3(296.28-29). *Ep.* 17.1(262.17-23) refers to a "school" debate wherein Socrates commented on the nature of virtue and saw it as a universal human goal. In *Ep.* 23.2 (274.17-18), Aeschines modestly limits the extent of his *sophia* to restraint from harm in philosophical *synousia.* For Plato, *Ep.* 26.3(280.32), teaching implies content, but he is also the writer of dialogues and the philosophical recluse.

The editor-author found in the first part of the corpus an approach similar to this own regarding philosophical association and dialogue at *Eps.* 1.2(218.14-15); 6.9(236.27-30); 12(238.32-35) and the task of the philosophical life as the pursuit of virtue at 1.2(222.13-16); 5.2(230.14-15); 6.2(232.19-21); 6.3(232.27); 6.4(234.13-15); 6.5(234.18-19); 6.6(234.28-33); 6.12(238.30-32).

[123] Julian *Or.* 6.189a-b. Here Julian, like our editor-author, holds that Plato's writings are less effective than Diogenes' deeds in the universal pursuit of self-knowledge.

A. *Hortatory Devices and Techniques*

The devices and techniques in the hortatory literature discussed earlier in this study are employed by the authors of the letters in the Socratic corpus as well. Among the devices one finds prescriptions,[124] citations,[125] rhetorical questions,[126] exclamations,[127] appeal to prior knowledge or attitude,[128] assurance of inner resources and strength,[129] gnomic statements,[130] comparisons,[131] catalogues of sufferings,[132] lists of virtues and vices,[133] examples.[134] The following techniques also serve the letters' exhortation: warnings,[135] explanations of prescriptions or viewpoints,[136] corroboration of a teaching or position,[137] confirmation of a person's suitability for a task,[138] and antithesis.[139] Hortatory language abounds in these letters, too, as the index of Greek words in Malherbe's study edition indicates.

While all the hortatory devices and techniques are related to each other in service of the hortatory goal of the letters, some are particularly associated. One instance is the imaginary dialogue in the diatribal mode at *Ep.* 6.7(236.6-14) where the angry parent uses rhetorical questions and antithesis and himself stands in antithetical relationship to the placid and generous Socrates. For another case,

---

[124] *Eps.* 1.5(220.25), 5(220.28-29), 7(222.9); 5.2(230.15,18); 6.2(232.13-17).

[125] 1.7(222.14-16); 5.2(230.16-17); 6.12(238.14-16).

[126] 1.4(220.11 ff., 15 ff); 6.6(234.33 ff.).

[127] 1.4(220.5 ff.).

[128] 1.1(218.1), 5(220.21 ff.); 2(226.14-15) referring to misunderstanding; 5.2(230. 14-16).

[129] 1.4(220.10-11), 5(220.17-20) exposing inner emptiness; 7.4(242.4 ff.).

[130] 1.6(220.29 ff.); 6.4(236.7-9, 9-11), 9(236.20-33); 7.4(242.17-18).

[131] 1.6(222.6); 6.11(238.15 ff.), 12(238.26 ff.), 24.2(276.14-15).

[132] 1.7(222.7-9), 8(222.27-28); 7.1(240.5 ff); 9.1(244.22 ff.) spoken ironically; 16(262. 10 ff.); 33.2(300.27-28).

[133] 5.2(230.18-19); 6.2-3(232.17-30); 13.2(252.6-9); 15.1(260.6); 30.3(296.28-31); 32.1 (298.22-23); 34.2(304.12 ff.).

[134] Treated separately below, 135-46.

[135] 1.10(224.20 ff.); 6.6(236.2-6).

[136] 1.2(218.20 ff.), 3(218.25 ff.), 5(220.25 ff.), 6(222.4 ff.), 12(224.33 ff.); 2(226.19-20); 3(228.7-11); 5.2(230.19-21); 6.3(232.31 ff.), 4(234.7 ff.), 6(234.27 ff.), 10(238.2 ff., 20 ff.), 12(238.26).

[137] 1.11(224.31 ff.); 3(228.7-11); 14.8(258.7); 15.1(260.8-13) and *passim;* 20(268.17-18); 21.1(276.9 ff).

[138] 1.2(218.12-13), 7(222.7-16), 12(226.11-12); 4(228.17-19); 6.8(236.16-18); 10(248.4); 12(250.3-7); 14.4-5(254.28 ff.); 15.1(260.2-4); 16(262.8-10) and *passim;* 17*passim;* 20(268.12-15); 21.3(270.22-24); 23.1(274.3 ff.); 26.2(280.19-20); 27.5(284.18-20); 30.2(296.20 ff.); 32.1(298.13-16) and *passim;* 34.3(304.22-23).

[139] 1.1(218.3-4), 2(218.15-19), 3(218.23-25), 3(220.2-4), 4(220.9-11, 11-15), 6(220.29 ff.), 6(222.1-4), 6(222.4-7), 8(222.21-25), 9(224.1-6), 10(224.14-16, 17-22), 11(224.26-28); 5.2 (230.15); 6.1(232.5 ff.), 2-4(234.18-22), 5(234.18-22), 6(234.33 ff).

the lists of vices and virtues can establish an antithesis or suggest the contours of an example, as they do in *Ep.* 6. Example and antithesis, however, are found most frequently in association as the discussion below will indicate.

B. *Differences in Exhortation Between Socrates' and the Socratics' Letters*

Before beginning a close analysis of example in this letter collection, some more general observations on the diverse application of the hortatory features should be made. Since the letter collection is really a composite of the letters of several authors and since each letter group has a distinctive subject matter, there are some differences in the manner of exhortation as well. The first seven letters are in the name of Socrates and, as will become clear below, the alleged author holds himself up as the prime example in antithesis to those whom he criticizes. The prior knowledge and attitude to which Socrates refers center around what is known about him, the object of the letter's lesson. The antithetical lists also deal with his qualities and others' vices. Nowhere in the other letters of the collection is this connection between the author, the devices, and the lesson found. Similarly, in the application of hortatory techniques, the autobiographical perspective of *Eps.* 1-8 finds the confirmation directed toward Socrates and his work. When the letter writers in the rest of the corpus commend themselves, as in *Eps.* 20, 32, and 34, they are serving the development of another lesson.

Some of the letters of the Socratics also refer to Socrates but, perforce, do so from a biographical and not an autobiographical perspective. Here, too, other philosophical figures enter the hortatory scene. In *Eps.* 8-13 Aristippus is set off in antithesis to Antisthenes and, to a lesser extent, Simon. All three are paradigmatic representatives of modes of leading a philosophical life, which is specified further in the lists of qualities and vices. The antithesis thus exceeds the bounds of individual letters, just as the ideal is not in any one of the options presented in the lists and exemplars but resides in a compromise among them. When Aristippus is approved for the task in *Ep.* 10 by Aeschines, this is not a blanket commendation of hedonism but a step toward an accommodation regarding his views. These letters, in their juxtaposition of the traditional rivals among the followers of Socrates, use the biographical traditions to propagandize the philosophical compromise of a later period.

Eps. 14-19 and 22, written or addressed to either Xenophon or Aeschines, all concern preservation of Socrates' virtue and teachings in both writing and life-practice, as *Ep.* 15 explicitly urges (and compare *Ep.* 18). And so the biographical memorabilia of *Eps.* 14 and 17 (and the fear of falling short of the task in *Ep.* 22) find a rationale in the exhortation to create just such writings. Likewise, the praise of Socrates' virtue in *Eps.* 16 and 19 points to the ideal to be followed. Biographical sketches play a large part in this segment of the letters, for their written form is a response to the exhortation. These sketches thereby present some of the details of the virtuous life which the letters as a whole promote.

Eps. 23-26 and 30-32 are related to Plato. An antithesis arises between his withdrawal in *Ep.* 24 (complimented in *Ep.* 26 but criticized in *Ep.* 25) and his service to the Academy (*Eps.* 30-32). This, together with the prescriptive conclusion of *Ep.* 23, highlights the "institutional" aspect of the exhortation. Socrates and his teachings largely fade from view here (except for references in *Ep.* 25) as the editor-author makes use of Platonic traditions. The hortatory program of the letter corpus is served nonetheless.

Eps. 21, 27, 29, 33, 34 are directly hortatory with a variety of explicit prescriptions, often linked with Socrates' instructions and example. These are incorporated into distinct letter types. *Ep.* 20, on the other hand, is a summary congratulation and declaration of successes in adopting Socrates' ways and teaching.

Within the encomium of Philip in *Ep.* 28 lies rhetorical criticism on the use of example which has direct bearing both on the exhortation of the letter corpus and on the analysis of this paper. And so, with this overview of the variety in the hortatory aims and methods of the corpus, a more detailed study of the device of example will illuminate a principal features of the letters and the hortatory program of the corpus.

C. *The Use of Example in Theory and Practice*

Ep. 28 refers to Isocrates' rhetorical principles [140] on the use of example. Like the rhetoricians cited above on the same topic, Isocrates is quoted as recommending *oikeia kai gnōrima paradeigmata* at *Ep.* 28.10(290.31).[141] The actual examples used by Isocrates are found by *Ep.* 28.10(290.32-33) to be *allotria, aischista* and *enantiōtata pros ton logon*. Here Speusippus mentions the notoriously unedifying Alcibiades and Dionysius, scoring Isocrates' use of these to the neglect of Amyntas, Philip's own father.

More specifically, the example set by one's father was seen above to be preferred by the rhetoricians. These, by way of substitution, also sanction and describe the teacher's exemplary function in paternal terms.[142] Thus *Ep.* 28 is on firm ground in proposing the example of Philip's father. And it does so by juxtaposing the king's father to the example of Alcibiades, a technique of presentation in antithesis countenanced in the rhetorical handbooks (*Ep.* 28.9-10[290.16-26]).[143]

---

[140] Bickermann-Sykutris, 59, dispute the existence of an Isocratean *Rhetoric*. Consequently, they take the plural *technai* at *Ep.* 28.4(286.22) and 10(290.30) to mean Isocrates' discourses offered as models of his teaching or *technē* in the singular (*Ep.* 28.10[290.321]). For another view, which attempts to reconstruct the *Rhetoric*, see M. Sheehan, "De fide artis rhetoricae Isocrati tributae" (Diss. Bonn, 1901).

[141] See above 27, 32, 35, 36, 50, 72, 92.

[142] See above, 34-35.

[143] See above, 30, 40, 42, 49-50.

The practical content of the example, i.e., the important and noble deeds done by the exemplar as noted at *Ep.* 28.9(290.19), is an emphasis from the rhetorical theory on example.[144] Likewise redolent of the formal discussions of example is the hortatory end which the examples serve at *Ep.* 28.9(290.17), *epi praxeis se dikaias parakalōn,* with the intended effect at *Ep.* 28.10(290.28-30) that the addressee *tous spoudaiotatous mimēsasthai, kai zēlōtēn ... tōn dikaiotatōn genesthai.*[145]

These theoretical statements on the use of example in *Ep.* 28 find practical application in the other letters of the collection. The editor-author found exhortation by example in the letters of Socrates. *Ep.* 5.2(230.21-22) alludes to family example (*oikeia paradeigmata*) of the recommended virtues. *Ep.* 6.4(234.9-11) proclaims imitation to be the way to virtue when it declares that the wise person *heauton apeikazei tō*ᵢ *sophōtatō*ᵢ just as the happy person *exomoiōthē*ᵢ *tō*ᵢ *makariō*ᵢ. *Ep.* 1.10(224.10-20) makes the same point where Socrates urges people to adopt an attitude like his *ei ... homoiōs ... diekeinto.* On the other hand, at *Ep.* 6.4(234.14-15) Socrates finds it foolish to pursue (*metadiōkein*) appearance rather than virtue, a contrast which finds a dramatic and symbolic parallel in *Ep.* 1.9(224.3-5) where those who turn aside to another route with Socrates (*tēn enantian ... synapetraponto*) are saved from the destruction of their comrades at Delium who persist on following the main road. The practical emphasis of this example receives a clear statement by Socrates at *Ep.* 6.6(236.1-2) where he says, *ou logois alla kai ergois dēlōsantas.* The preeminence of Socrates as exemplar is founded on his paternal relationship with his children at *Ep.* 6.6(234.33 ff.) and his disciples at *Ep. 6.10-11.*

In his own composition the editor-author also makes use of the device.[146] *Ep.* 29, suggested by *Ep.* 28.12, applies the theory of *Ep.* 28 and uses the family example of Philip's own brother, as it reminds Philip that he is expected *exisousthai* and *hyperballein* his brother's virtue at *Ep.* 29(294.18-20). It also urges at (294.23-27) him *hamillein* his brother's and his own benefactions. The obvious stress here is on deeds. In *Ep.* 33.3, Speusippus writes to yet another monarch, Dion, and urges him to be an example (*deixeis*) of the striving of the best Greeks for justice.

Ep. 20 styles its unnamed addressee an *apeikonisma ti Sōkratous.* The summons to follows (*akolouthein*) Socrates' words and habits at *Ep.* 21.1 (270.10-11) specifies the manner by which the example is to be incorporated and also gives attention to his deeds as well as his teachings (and compare *Ep.* 21.3[270.27-29]).

Plato's virtue, too, was adopted by Phaedrus in *Ep.* 25 through the latter's own conduct and the direction he received from Plato (*periagōn, periagomenos*). Similarly, at *Ep.* 32.2.(298.26-28), Xenocrates attributes his acquisition of Plato's

---

[144] See above, 29.

[145] See above, 34,36-37,40-41.

[146] See below, 141-46.

virtue to observing (*diatērein*) Plato's character. Thus, Plato is a good model and is even called a father in relation to some of his disciples at *Ep.* 30.2(296.22). Aristippus at *Ep.* 27.2(282.16-17) and Socrates at *Eps.* 15.1(260.4-5); 27.3(282.35-36), like Plato, are also good models whose imitation is urged and praised in the letters. Those, on the other hand, among Socrates' opponents who try to imitate Menoeceus receive criticism at *Ep.* 14.3(254.9-10) for their inappropriate and inept effort.

D. *Variety and Function of Example in the Letters of Socrates*

In the letters of Socrates the example types are varied. They are personal, whether mythical (Bellerophon), historical (Pythagoras, those in the battle at Delium), or contemporary (Socrates, his addressee at *Ep.* 1.11[224.24-26]). And, in addition to the individuals, the examples are also drawn from groups both named (sophists) and unnamed (venal teachers referred to with the indefinite pronoun *tines,* wise cities) and from types of people (friends referred to in the hypothetical form, the greedy, the reckless ignorant).

The examples function largely as prototypes, to urge imitation. Socrates makes this explicit at *Ep.* 1.10(224.19-20) when he says, to emphasize the example of his own restraint, *oida de, hoti ei kai hoi alloi anthrōpoi homoiōs diekeinto, hēttona an ēn kaka en tō_i biō_i.* In this connection, the example of Bellerophon and the reckless ignorant serve the same end but from the negative side, as Socrates again makes clear at *Ep.* 1.11(224.29-31) when he says, *kai ouk an hyp'epithymias tōn meizonōn exartheis epiphanesterōn orechtheiēn symphorōn.* Another aspect of Socrates' example, his virtuous cultivation of friends and their support of him, receives comment at *Ep.* 1.4(220.11-15), *kaitoi pōs ou deinon epi men philō_i dokein einai aischron hēgeisthai kai mēd'an biōnai boulesthai heterois onta prosthema kai allotriōn parasitounta agathōn, tàuto de touto pros ta chrēmata peponthota mē aideisthai;* Once again, those who fall into dishonor through their preoccupation with money stand as the negative side of this. And calling attention to a third element of his example at *Ep.* 1.6(220.28-29), Socrates says, *prōton men gar oimai, kath' ho dynatai hekastos ōphelein, exetazesthai.* Thus, he justifies his refusal to Archelaus in terms of service to his own city. Here the negative example of leaders asleep at the job completes the exhortation. Finally, Socrates' obedience to divine prompting receives verification in the poetic declaration at *Ep.* 1.8(222.19-21), *hoti ta men kata tēn toutōn boulēsin prattomena epi to lō_ion ekbainei, ta de para theon alysitelē hyparchei tois praxesin.* The examples of him and his followers at Delium and that of the wisest Greek cities strengthen the exhortation in his current stance, while the disobedient cities and soldiers do so by way of constrast.

This brief sketch of the varied examples in the letters of Socrates indicates that they are not used in a haphazard way but are closely related with one another and with the message of the letters as a whole. This relationship will now be analyzed to see what its structural characteristics might be.

E. *Antithetical Relationship of Examples and the Structure of the Developed Chria*
   in the Letters of Socrates

1. *Epistle 1*

When viewed from the aspect of structure, the examples in *Ep.* 1 take their
place in order alongside the devices and techniques common in the development of
the chria. Thus, at *Ep.* 1.1(218.7-11) Socrates states his position with the words
*ton outh'holōs kalon nomizonta tous en philosophia¡ pipraskein logous, emoi te kai
sphodra aēthes.*[147] This he restates with a general reference to his character and
divine charge at 2(218.12-13). The contrasting examples of his mode of
philosophizing and that of other philosophers follows at 2(218.14-19) and is
explained in a long digression at 2(218.20) - 3(220.5). Another contrast enters at
this point, whic actually establishes the negative example of people engrossed in
the fruitless concern for money at 4(220.5-11). The concluding exhortation comes
in the form of two rhetorical questions at 4(220.11-17). The section ends with a
final comment on the sorry state of the money-minded people (the negative example) and a restatement of the thesis at 5(220.17-23).

Observing the structure of this section, i.e., thesis and restatement; contrasting
examples; explanation and proof by antithetical hypotheses; negative example; concluding exhortation and restatement, one notes that the examples embody both the
attitude promoted and the one cautioned against. The antithesis is made more vivid
when cast in the persons of Socrates and his contemporary philosophical
"opponents" (generalized in the second contrast to include all money-seekers).

The second statement to be developed appears at 5(220.23-25), *entautha me
polla katechei, kai to megiston, hai tēs patridos chreiai.* this is restated at 5(220.25-
27), and proven in terms of personal ability at 6(220.28-29), civic need at 6(222.1-
4), and divine command at 7(222.7). The first proof is completed by a gnomic
statement on responsibility for levels of achievement at 6(220.29 - 222.1); the
second by a comparison to a provocative gadfly at (222.4-7); the third by the
example of suffering obedience at 7(222.7-12) and a poetic citation at 7(222.13-16)
and reference at 7(222.17) -8(222.21). The examples of Greek cities and the
apophthegm about Socrates and the troops at Delium present contrasting attitudes and their consequences at 8(222.21) -9(224.10). 10(224.12-13) brings the predications to the level of individuals and refers to divine authority.

The structure here is more complex than in the preceding section, i.e., thesis
and restatement; triple proof employing gnomic statement; comparison; positive
example; poetic authority; contrasting example; conclusion. The positive example
in the third proof is soon joined and completed by two pairs of antithetical exam-

---

[147] While a chria is usually given as a quotation and then developed, a letter presents
the words of the author and his own development of the thesis. See F.H. Colson, *M. Fabii
Quintiliani institutionis oratoriae liber I* (Cambridge: Cambridge University, 1924) 119, for
the pattern of development and the variety of sayings and actions developed.

ples which show what to do and what to avoid. Again, the general examples are bolstered by the dramatic event, this time from Socrates' military career.

The third statement enters at 10(224.16-18) with a comparison-proof from navigation, *ego de memathekenai archein ou phemi, me eidos de ouk an dexaimen mallon basileuein e kybernan me epistamenos.* The follows an oblique call to imitation 10(224.19-20). The contrast with reckless people confirms the statement about the common good and fortune at 10(224.19-24). The example of the addressee himself is a corroborative support at 11(224.24-26), which the illustrative comparisons demonstrate at 11(224.26-29). The author's own reluctance to overreach himself is confirmed by the authority of the mythographers and the example of Bellerophon at 11(224.29) -12(226.8). The exhortation directs the addressee to the poets' lesson at 12(226.8-9).

Here examples abound in the structure of the section, i.e., statement and comparison; admonition; negative example; positive example; antithetical analogies; negative example; concluding exhortation with citation of poetic authority and restatement. The two alternative attitudes receive vivid demonstration, including the life experiences of the addressee himself, as well as those of the author.

2. *Epistle* 6

In *Ep.* 6 a similar variety of example types is at work. For examples the letter refers to the deity at 6.4(234.5 ff.); to Socrates himself at 2(232.13-21); 5(234.15-19); 8(236.16-20); 9(236.23); 10(238.4), and to typical groups like the luxurious at 2(232.21 ff.); and typical individuals like the poor person at 5(234.23-24), the misguided rich at 5(234.24 ff.), the angry parent at 7(236.6 ff.), the proven friend at 12(238.26 ff.).

That the examples function principally as prototypes becomes clear from the remark at 4(234.9-15) to the effect that only the happy, i.e., the wise and the virtuous, are suitable objects of imitation. The good this imitation produces is true, as opposed to the appearance of good which wealth suggests. The contrast in this statement echoes the contrast already seen in the examples which precede it and which incarnate the models to follow and to avoid. Socrates makes it clear at 2(232.13 ff.) that the issue is larger than the attitude toward material gain. And so he outlines his entire life-style and then at 4(234.5 ff.) associates it with God's contented and happy simplicity, an attitude which he holds up for imitation. The contrasting luxurious life-style, described at 2(232.21 ff.), falls under condemnation in the summary remark at 4, as well as in its very presentation in 2 and 3, e.g., *aporretois hedonais* (232.25), *chroan diephtherotes* (232.26), *alethinen doxan apololekotes* (232.27).

Acquisition of virtue is also the concern in the next part of the apology, the defense of his bequest to his children, as Socrates clearly states at 6(234.33 ff.). The principle is already laid down at 5(234.18-22) in the antithesis between happiness through right thinking and the deceptive trust in silver and gold. The examples of the poor person who comes to his senses and the permanently deceived rich person give bite to the defense at 6(234.33 -236.1) and to the lesson at 6(236.1-6). Socrates also relates the practical example from the first argument to that of the verbal lesson here (*ou logois monon alla kai ergois dēlōsantas*).

The irritation and exasperation of the parent jealous to safeguard his wealth from squandering heirs at 7 contrasts with Socrates' benign bequest of his own modest but truly valuable resources, friends. With this Socrates again demonstrates the way to true happiness, this time in the bequeathing parent. The bequest itself is no less hortatory, for the proven friend, described at 12(238.26-32), serves the needs of his friend's spirit and *eis aretēs logon, hēs chōris ouden tōn anthrōpinōn oninēsi, pleista symballetai.* This ideal is both a specimen, elaborating the content of the inheritance, and a prototype example, establishing what Socrates expects of friends in return for his good deeds on their behalf at 9(236.30 ff.). The contrast here is to money's inability to better anyone at 12(238.24-26).

The final instance of antithetical examples to be noted here is actually the first to appear in the letter. At 1(232.5 ff.) mention is made of the ridicule by Socrates' addressee and the common public over his poverty. This allusion sets up the straw-man whose shallow prejudice casts a favorable, contrasting light over Socrates' reasoned treatment of the questions raised.

Once again, the formal arrangement of the hortatory features in *Ep.* 6 is that of the development of the chria. The statement of the thesis at 2(232.13-17), *ei peri tēn chrēsin tōn sōmatōn diapherontes phanoumetha mē thaumazein, hoti kai peri ton porismon diestēkamen,* introduces the first answer to the questions at 1(232.7-12) and is an explanation and exhortation as well. The contrast at 2(232.17-25 and 234.1-3) presents two opposing ways of life, the disapproved one receiving further elaboration at 3(232.25-30). The latter leads to a demonstration of the reasons for their insatiable need at 3(232.30 - 234.1). A variation of the appeal to authority stands behind the reference to conflicting opinions among the masses and the most excellent people at 3(234.3-4). The divine example and concluding exhortation to copy the virtuous example comes next at 4(234.5-15).

After the opening statement of the position with its explanation and exhortation, follow the contrasting examples: proof and appeal to authority, both in antithetical form; positive example; and concluding exhortation. The development of the position clearly exploits antithesis heavily and the examples do much to display the alternative life-styles which are the objects of the exhortation.

The next statement to be developed appears at 5(234.18-19), *mian archēn eudaimonias egō nomizō phronein eu,* and is elaborated first by way of the contrasting view of the person who lacks understanding, a negative example at 5(234.19-22). Two antithetical illustrations follow at 5(234.22-28). The explanation proves the impossibility of acquiring virtue under the guidance of flattering and pandering instructors at 6(234.28-33). A rhetorical question proposes the concluding exhortation, wherein the author points to his own example and warns against laziness at 6(234.33 - 236.6). The diatribe section at 7(236.6-14) contrasts with Socrates' willing and generous bequest at 8(236.14-20). The value of the bequest is demonstrated at 8(236.20 -10(238.8) and this flows into the illustrative comparison with family relationships and support at 10(238.8) - 11(238.19). The basic principle is restated at 11(238.19-24) and corroborated by citing a common saying at 12(238.24-26). The concluding remarks underline the help expected from true friends at 12(238.26-32).

The structure here is more elaborate than in the preceding instances, i.e., statement; negative example; antithetical illustrations; proof using negative example; exhortation with positive example; negative example in diatribe form, followed by constrasting positive example; proof in antithetical form; illustrative comparison; restatement; appeal to authority; conclusion. Antithesis dominates the section. Accordingly, Socrates' ideas about instruction in virtue and his own practice, along with his dependence on friends, are set off by contrasting examples of failure in these areas.

3. *Epistle 5*

Ep. 5, addressed to Xenophon, sets the exhortation against the background of the latter's campaign with Cyrus. The letter's brevity limits the number of hortatory features. Examples are not given but the reference at 2(230.21-22) to *oikeia ... paradeigmata* reveals an awareness of the rhetorical theory discussed above as well as the proper application of the theory to the exhortation of the letter. The virtues urged are listed (*karteria, aphilochrēmatia*) and explained; the examples, which would ordinarily incarnate them and thereby present them in another form, are presupposed.[148] The letter as a whole is constructed upon an antithesis between the unnamed critics at home (*tines*), perverse by nature, and Socrates and Xenophon in their commitment to virtuous self-improvement (*andres agathoi genōmetha tōn te allōn* 2[230.15]).

F. *Variety and Function of Example in the Letters of the Socratics*

The letters of the Socratics employ a similar variety of example types.[149] As does Socrates in the first part of the corpus, Aristippus refers to the influence of his own example at *Ep.* 27.2(282.16-17) and proposes himself as an example at 27.3(282.28 ff.). Here he urges Arete to join Xanthippe and Myrto in a community

---

[148] Köhler, 97, takes the phrase *oikeia echeis ta paradeigmata* to mean, "You know the examples yourself, I need not recount them." She understands this in a general sense and not related to any particular example. This also suits a school environment, where examples were learned to fit a variety of topics. See above, 28.

[149] Among the specimen examples note the Spartan youth, *Ep.* 17; Timon, *Ep.* 14; and Polyxenus, *Ep.* 33, for individuals both past and present. There are occupational groups like shepherds, *Ep.* 33 and city businessmen, *Ep.* 11. There are also typical characters like Callipides the forgetful actor, *Ep.* 14, and the tyrant in *Eps.* 8 and 9. Classes of people also function as specimen examples, e.g., reciting school-children, *Ep.* 14, and Cynics, *Ep.* 13.

of friendship at Athens. The expectations of a pleasant life there and the preservation of the philosophical inheritance by educating the younger Aristippus contrast with the base grasping of the Cyrenean officials. He offers as an example his own life with Socrates and underlines to Arete the advantages of the move to Athens. Most often in this section of the letter collection, however, the letters hold up other figures rather than the authors of the letters themselves.

G. *Antithetical Relationship of Examples and the Structure of the Developed Chria in the Letters of the Socratics*

1. *Epistle 21*

After his opening remarks and suggestions, Aeschines makes clear his position to Socrates' grieving widow with the thesis *tōn de pollōn soi dakryōn, ō agathē, halis. Onēsei gar ouden, schedon de ti kai blapsei* at *Ep.* 21.1(270.8-9). Aeschines then recommends the example of Socrates to the widowed Xanthippe at 1(270.9-11) and explains why at 1(270.11-13). A comparison with birds and nestlings follows at 2(270.13-15). This comparison is extended allegorically in the hypothetical example describing the contrasting situation where no one survives to care for Socrates' children at 2(270.15-18). Further injunctions appear at 2(270.18-20). A gnomic saying on grief sums up the point at 2(270.20-22) and the citation of two friends' opinions at 3(270.22-26) leads into a reiteration of the command to consider Socrates' teaching and example at 3(270.26-29), with a final opinion by Aeschines on how to view Socrates' death at 3(270.29-31). As in the two letters of Socrates analyzed above, the elements from the development of the chria serve to provide the content and structure of this letter.

The structural similarities between this letter and those of Socrates above are readily discernible, i.e., statement of position; exhortations and positive example; explanatory proof; comparison and negative example; exhortation; gnomic saying and appeal to authority; concluding exhortation and positive example. What interests this study is the consistent use of personal examples in antithetical relationship to illuminate and specify the choice being urged.

2. *Epistle 29*

Ep. 29, which supplies the evidence for Platonic influence on Philip claimed at *Ep.* 28.12, also represents the editor-author's attempt correctly to employ the device of example, the use of which Speusippus found faulty in Isocrates' discourse. The letter opens with a declaration of the exemplary attitude of Perdiccas, Philip's brother, supported by a brief quotation from Hesiod at (294.13-16). The injunction to proper action on Philip's part and its explanation follows at (294.13-16). A contrast is then drawn between the noble and worst people in their hopes for Philip's following the example at (294.16-21). Injunctions then aim to determine Philip's reactions to each group at (294.21-23) and have him join with the nobles in their struggle (*agōnian*), presumably toward virtue. A secondary example is then brought forth, i.e., Philip's own benefactions, and this too is explained at (294.23-27). A general exhortation ends the letter at (294.27-29). Here, the editor-author varies the order and does not use all the features of the developed chria. Nonetheless, enough of the devices do appear here to suggest the development of the chria as a background for the letter. Moreover, the author makes full use of antithetical examples to strengthen his exhortation, just as the theory in *Ep.* 28.12 suggests.

The use of personal example in the development of the moral instructions in these letters is shown to be extensive throughout the corpus. In those letters with a formal pattern of development, example assumes its requisite role. Particularly striking is the use of these examples in antithesis, as positive and negative demonstrations of the position being urged. This usage was outlined by the progymnatist Aphthonius[150] and here finds its application in full.

The examples studied above were all explicitly referred to and employed in the exhortation of the letters as part of the formal structure of the development of their instructions. But the Socratic letters do not restrict themselves to explicit examples in their exhortation. Implicit examples also work to incarnate preferred attitudes and courses of action. The next section of this study will analyze this important use of example in the letters, a hortatory function which is served by the very pseudonymity of the letters.[151]

H. *Implicit Example in the Letter Corpus*

1. Its Use in the Letters of Socrates

Implicit example refers, first of all, to those aspects of the model figure's life and virtue which the letters delineate but do not single out in the direct call for imitation. Thus, Socrates invites the addressee of *Ep.* 6.2(232.13-17) to consider not just one feature, his attitude toward material gain, but also the rest of his moderate and "philosophical" way of life, as sketched by the letter. All of this, both the words and deeds, establishes the paradigm for his own children at *Ep.* 6.7(236.1-2) and for any wise or happy person, as *Ep.* 6.4(234.9-11) implies. Then, too, even though *Ep.* 1 is addressed to a different correspondent than that in *Ep.* 6, under the fiction of the collection it, too, serves the pseudonymous author's program as it "autobiographically" describes other facets of Socrates' life, specifically his teaching aims and practice in the light of his own self-knowledge.

The second facet of implicit example embraces those letters which accompany *Eps.* 1 and 6 but seem only marginally related to the delineation of the Socratic

---

[150] See above, 42.

[151] See Sykutris, *Die Briefe,* 106 ff.

example. Under the perspective of implicit example, the shorter letters of the Socratic section take on more than formal interest. The letters of recommendation
(*Eps.* 2 and 3), therefore, serve to depict Socrates contributing to the mutual support
which he lauds and expects among philosophical friends. In both letters he alludes
to the care he himself has shown the traveling friend.[152]   *Ep.* 4 finds Socrates the
teacher concerned for his correspondent's school-age son, while in *Eps.* 5 and 7 it is
the adviser and goad of office-holders and prominent figures of the city who writes
political advice to his exiled associate. Socrates accepts his absence without
complaint and looks forward to a restoration of order on his return.

The emphasis on virtue beyond the common level at *Ep.* 5.2(230.14 ff.) underlines the stress in the letters on developing a philosophical attitude that is a cut
above that of the crowd (see also *Eps.* 1.8[222.25-28] and 6.3[234.2-4]). In all seven letters, the philosophical attitude is described in outline form and in only sket-
chy detail. This is not unusual, for as Isocrates is made to mention as he proposes
the example of Demonicus' father [153] such a sketch of his nature is sufficient to
stand as an example for one who considers his ways normative and is becoming an
imitator and emulator (*mimētēs* and *zēlōtēs*) of his father's virtue.

2. Its Use in the Letters of the Socratics

The letters of the Socratics also propose implicit examples as an integral part of
their exhortation. Once again, while the letters propose a program to record Socrates' *bios* and *aretē* at *Ep.* 15.2(260.20-21), only some of the details find expression therein. Details about his last days, then, such as those in *Ep.* 14 (and see *Ep.*
21.3[270.28-29]), assume a significance beyond the simple biographical level, for
they help sketch the philosophical attitude proposed in the corpus. This includes
doing nothing unworthy of oneself or philosophy at 14.5(254.32 ff.); following the
will of god at 14.5(256.4); separation from and disdain of the crowd at 14.5(254.8-
11); calm expectation of death as a release for the immortal soul at 14.6(254.19-20);
and freedom from the demands and pleasures of the body at 14.8(256.34 ff.).[154]

The letters dealing with Plato (*Eps.* 24, 25, 26, 29, 30, 31, 32) allude to the
philosophical life and the philosopher's virtue (*Ep.* 32.2[298.27-28]) in a comparable schematic way.[155]   But these letters present the other aspect of the implicit

---

[152] In this regard the letters conform to that aspect of promulgating a principle by
example wherein the instructor's own life-style or expertise becomes an example for his
pupils. See above, 36.

[153] See above, 64.

[154] There is a continuity in the treatment of Socrates in the letters of Socrates and in
those of the Socratics as noted below 150-51. The letters dealing with Plato have a
comparable schematic treatment of the details of the philosopher's life and virtue.

[155] Cf. in *Ep.* 30.1 his esteem for the Academy, 30.2 his concern for Xenocrates and his
friends, 30.3 some of his virtues and the call to exceed the virtuous mean of the majority of
people. Unspecified allusions to his virtue dot the letters at *Eps.* 25.2(278.17-19);
26.2(280.17-20); 32.2(298.23-24).

example which surfaced already in the letters of Socrates, i.e., they capture the philosopher himself putting the philosophical ideal to work.[156] The implicit example in the letters of the Socratics depends on this latter feature as its principal vehicle.

Among the variety of figures and their sometimes clashing principles, no one person or position fully represents the editor-author's ideal. Rather, the editor-author uses the biographical and doxographical traditions to suggest the outline of his own position. Moreover, since this "position" is really a conduct of life in the Cynic mode rather than a doctrinal system or wisdom,[157] the editor-author lets the Socratics express it in their epistolary activity and not by way of long essays. Consequently, interesting (auto)biographical allusions often serve the larger program of the pseudonymous author who chooses to incorporate them. The appeal to Socrates and to his followers then is not just a ploy to provide authoritative backing for the editor-author's program. Much more than that, it seeks to incarnate the paradigmatic ideal which the editor-author hopes his audience will follow and to trace the traditional roots of the teaching.[158]

Direct carry-overs from the letters of Socrates to those of the Socratics are the urging of aid for Socrates' children in *Ep.* 27.4 and the offering of such aid among the friends generally in *Eps.* 10; 11; 15.2; 16; 21; 22; 23; 24.1; 26.2; 27.4. Add to this the insistence that the philosopher stay put in *Ep.* 8, offering advice to a government leader in *Ep.* 29, and offering the leader's kin in that same letter as examples for him. The counselling against grief and for a proper view of Socrates' death in *Ep.* 21 echoes Socrates' own trust in the joys of the afterlife in *Ep.* 15.

New to these letters of the Socratics is the literary side of the philosophical life which is urged and practiced in them.[159] Unique, too, is their manner of proposing the ideal of moderate Cynicism through the lively debate and interaction among representatives of the traditional extremes of the Socratic tradition in *Eps.* 8-13.[160] Attention has already been paid to the "community structure" which emerges from the associations which the letters recall, arrange for, or urge.[161] In conjunction with this last aspect, the letters exonerate those

---

[156] He withdraws from the crowd in *Ep.* 24; he urges Philip on to greater benefactions and to the struggle for virtue in *Ep.* 29.

[157] See the discussion on the letters' stress on virtuous action rather than the pursuit of wisdom above, 131-32.

[158] Döring, 124-25, sees authority as the motive for the use of Socrates' name and for the letter form. The authoritative support from the use of the names of Socrates and his followers is undeniably exploited by the letters. But authority is only one aspect of the function of the figures from Cynicism's alleged philosophical origins, as the discussion above has tried to indicate.

[159] See the discussion of the literary program of the corpus above, 128-31.

[160] See the consideration of moderate Cynicism in the letters above, 116-21.

[161] See the allusions to the letters' "community interest" above, 123-24.

absent from Socrates' death and the subsequent troubles for his followers at Athens,[162] and they look forward to the reunion of all the exiles at Athens in *Eps.* 16 and 17.[163] This casts the exhortation to moderate Cynicism in the letters under the light of a return to the source and a recommitment achieved by the abolition of rival traditions of the later Socratics.[164] The editor-author accomplishes this through the device of implicit example which the letters in the collection themselves represent. The editor-author, thus, expands on a device already found in the letters of Socrates and indeed, one which is rendered possible by the very pseudonymity of the letter collection.

Since the examples, explicit and implicit, express the teaching of the letters, a careful consideration of their content is in order. Furthermore, by observing their positive and negative content, further insight can be gained into the situation of the letters and the program they devise to respond to it.

VI. The Content of the Example in the Letters

A. *The Positive Example*

Sykutris describes the picture of Socrates in the letters under his name as one influenced by Xenophon and Cynic literature and current in later, popular philosophy. He focuses on Socrates' activity, wide-ranging relationships, concern for his friends, poor life-style, dedication to philosophy, carefulness about his position and esteem, strong ethical principles, fundamental rationalism with a coloring of deistic piety, consciousness of his high mission, strict devotion to the education of youth and to moral preaching, authority in making philosophical pronouncements, attention to occasions to convert people, and concern for his family.[165]

Not surprisingly, similar qualities are attributed to Socrates in the letters of the Socratics.[166] More significant, however, is the fact that the other model figures in those letters also share these same qualities. To use the three letters considered for their form in the preceding section, *Ep.* 27 singles out Aristippus' broad relation-

---

[162] Plato, *Ep.* 14.9; Xenophon, 14.10(258.28-31); and Aristippus by implication from *Ep.* 16. The latter surprisingly approves their unphilosophical flight.

[163] Compare Xenophon's attempt to gather them at Laconia in *Eps.* 18 and 19 and Aristippus' attempt to have Arete join Xanthippe and Myrto in a philosophical association on the distaff side.

[164] A paradigmatic return and recommitment can be found in the call to Xenocrates to assume direction of the Academy in *Eps.* 30-32.

[165] Sykutris, *Die Briefe*, 106-7. I would question only Sykutris' view that Socrates troubles himself little about the future of his family because of his ethical principles. Socrates is quite convinced and convincing in *Ep.* 6 that his family will be as well provided for by his circle of friends as he was. This support is a common stipulation in philosophical testaments. The relation of *Ep.* 6 to this form will be treated more extensively below, 162.

[166] See *Ep.* 14 and below, 150-51.

ships, association with and concern for philosophic friends, high evaluation of philosophy as opposed to riches, disdain of excess wealth, unqualified presentation of ethical principles and advice, dedication to educate the young, dependence on the philosophic life for security and esteem, concern for his family. *Ep.* 29 focuses on the need for Philip to eschew riches, to preserve his esteem and reputation, to associate with like-minded men of virtue, to preserve correct familial ties. Beyond the proposed model of Socrates in *Ep.* 21, there is also the exemplary behavior of Xanthippe and her own ties with the Socratic circle, poverty, dedication to the life of philosophy, and derivation of praise and esteem from virtue and principle.[167] Moreover, in *Ep.* 21 Aeschines functions as an implicit example in his active expression of the relationship among philosophic friends, esteem for poverty in moderation, attention to the Socratic philosophical tradition, discovery of honor and nobility in philosophical integrity, authoritative expression of opinions and principles, concern for Socrates' family.[168]

---

[167] Xanthippe and her relationship with Socrates receive a touch-up and highlighting from the pallet of the Cynicizing editor-author. There are no signs of strain between her and Socrates at *Ep.* 4(228.20), in contrast to Xenophon, *Smp.* 2.10. To be sure, Plato, *Phd* 60a notes her grief at Socrates' impending execution, but *Ep.* 21.1(270.8 ff.) goes further and describes her dangerously prolonged mourning after his death. Moreover, *Ep.* 21.3(270.22-24) also credits her with living the ascetic paradox of finding wealth in self-sufficiency, while cautioning her to look to Socrates' and her friends for assistance. J. Sykutris, *Die Briefe,* 72, notes that the *exomis* which Aeschines provides her with seems to be a specifically Cynic garment. Even the contradictory tradition that Socrates had two wives, Xanthippe and Myrto, finds a remarkable resolution, though scarcely a credible one, in these letters. Aristippus, at *Ep.* 27.3(282.28-37), pictures the two of them in a sort of religious-philosophical community, where friendship and not insolence sets the tone. See J. Humbert, *Socrate et les petits Socratiques* (Paris: Presses Universitaires de France, 1967) 173-4, for a discussion of the tradition about the two wives and its possible roots the Socratics and their personal rivalries. The Socratic letters bear out his theory in part, for the favorable picture appears in *Ep.* 21, attributed to Aeschines, who Humbert says enjoyed Xanthippe's confidence and would give a picture different from the commonly accepted slur from the Peripatetics. The harmonized view of Xanthippe is yet another aspect of the conciliatory program of the corpus as a whole. On Socrates' family see also Schering, 17-19.

[168] Another prominent model figure in the second part of the corpus is Simon. Schering, 19-21, discusses the idealized portrait of Simon (see *Eps.* 12 and 13), as does H. von Wilamowitz-Möllendorff, "Phaidon von Elis," *Hermes* 14 (1879) 187-93, where he sees the Simon of these letters as the type of *aretē* and of *eudaimonia* who needs only cut straps *eis nouthesian anthrōpōn aphronōn* and who does not have to fight beasts as Hercules did. His asceticism is the key to growth in virtue in these Socratic letters. See also Hock, 41-53, for a thorough treatment of the presentation of Simon in these letters in an idealized way and with Cynic features. Like Xanthippe (see n. 167) Simon is invested with the Cynic characteristics which Socrates is given in the first part of the collection. And so, in addition to the proposal of the ideal figures in these letters, some of them are also given Cynic traits in a typically stylized way, which adds specificity to the exhortation to pursue virtue through philosophy.

Inevitably some differences surface between the model of the letters of Socrates and that of the letters of his followers. The letters of the Socratics seem to limit themselves to the circle of friends, whereas Socrates' letters see him moving out from that base to confront and convert a broader public. The letters of the Socratics also attend to the preservation of the Socratic tradition, while Socrates is busy creating it, although even in Socrates' letters there is some concern for passing on the tradition as the discussion below will indicate. The poverty in the second part of the letter collection is more explicitly moderated. The deistic piety largely falls away in these letters. Furthermore, except for *Eps*. 8-13 and 33-34, earnestness and not Socratic irony and paradox characterize the letters of the Socratics.[169] Finally, the literary activity of the models in the letters of the Socratics elevates Socrates' letter writing to a principle.

The facets of the positive example in the letter corpus are varied but consistent. As the observations on structure and form above have shown, the positive example is only one side of the letters' technique of exhortation by means of example. The negative example must also be considered for a full appreciation of the content and context of the letters' exhortation.

B. *The Contrasting Negative Example in the Letters of Socrates and Its Relation to the Positive Model*

Balancing the positive exemplary traits outlined above, which the letter corpus urges upon its audience, there are negative characteristics which have no place in the development of the ideal Cynic personality. For the consideration here, all the letters will be treated and not just those where example functions as an explicit feature in the letter's structure. Why extend the range of consideration? Since the letters rely on both explicit and implicit example, only a comprehensive survey will catch the models proposed for adoption and rejection in their full extent.

As a philosopher-teacher, Socrates conducts public (1.2) and free (1.1-2,5; 6.10) instruction at the behest of God who is both counsellor and protector (1.2,7,12). He does not readily move from Athens (1.1,12). He opposes the erroneous opinion of the majority and chooses the way of better people, often with divine indications (1.8-9; 5.2); 6.3. For his efforts he is hated (1.7) and mocked (6.1).

This picture contrasts (1.1-2) with sophistic retailers of education, esoteric Pythagoreans and traveling teachers-for-hire, identified above as practitioners of extreme Cynicism. Though ignorant, these teachers undertake direction (1.10) and since they disobey the gods they suffer great harm (1.8-9). In the meantime, though, they mock Socrates' way (1.4; 6.2) and by flattery (6.5-6) win superficial acclaim (1.5) and insecure material comfort (6.10).

---

[169] Although irony and paradox are used in both Socrates' *Eps*. 1, 6 and 7 and in the Socratics' *Eps*. 8-13, 33-34, in the latter the devices are used for direct criticism of the correspondent while the former include irony and paradox in a more objective, third person discussion of virtuous and corrupt people.

Viewing this philosophy from its effects on the personal character of Socrates and his associates, one finds the acquisition of virtue (*aretē*) to be its principal objective. This virtue specifies itself in various ways. It consists in contentment with possessing life's necessities (*ta arkounta* 1.2) instead of seeking superfluous things (*ta ... eis periousian*). Even more, needing nothing or, at least, not much is the way to happiness, blessedness and enjoyment (6.3-4). Thus virtue is the true good (6.4). The virtuous Socrates choose the practical if more humble way (1.11). Socrates actually reflects the traditional Cynic (6.2) in preferring to eat the plainest food, to wear the same garment all year, to go discalced, and to enjoy only the fame of being prudent (*sōphrōn*) and just (*dikaios*). With respect to virtue, specified at 5.2 as patient endurance (*karteria*) and contempt of riches (*aphilochrēmatia*), Socrates asks of himself and his correspondent not perfection but a commitment to strive toward it. He also expects the gradual acquisition at 6.5, where virtue is described as *eu phronein*. In poverty one is more likely to come to one's senses (*phronein*) than if he is corrupted by affluence. As a consequence of this sensibleness, Socrates stays within the bounds of what he has learned and knows how to do (*memathēkenai, eidōs, epistamenos* 1.10). Happiness is the end result, but also true honor (*alēthina doxa* 6.3).

Those against whom Socrates rails and the people led astray by them aim at the acquisition of wealth (*hautous dia ta kerdē apodomenoi* and *chrēmatismou epimelountai* 1.4) and they trust in silver and gold (*chrysiō_i de pisteuonta kai argyriō_i* 6.5). They are incapable of living simply (*ap'oligōn* 6.3). Moreover, unlike the Cynics, they pursue luxury (*polyteleia*) in diet, clothing, pleasures, and cosmetic adornment (6.2-3). This pursuit of wealth (6.5) thwarts any movement toward right thinking and, in fact, lacking understanding (*ho de nou men mē meteilēphōs*), they are propelled to action by anger (*orgē* 1.4) and passion for greater things (*hyp'epithymias tōn meizonōn* 1.11). In short, they are uneducated and have little concern for it (*paideias oligōrountes* 1.4). Consequently, they expel all that is good and moderate in themselves (*ti kalon ē sōphronikon* 6.6); have a false notion of what it means to be happy; fail to attain truly human goods or even the hope of them (6.5); act in reckless ignorance (*hē tōn mē epistamenōn tolma* 1.10); and get into trouble (*tarachē*), ending up (1.4-5) being given specious honor for their wealth (*timōntai ... dia ton plouton*) but dishonor (*atimia*) in themselves when judged without the prop of fortune, and unable to buy others' acclamation (*euphēmia*) and approval (*eulogia* 6.3).

Socrates commits himself (1.6) to serve the good (*ōphelein*) of his associates, his family and his country. And so he gives hospitality and help to friends (2, 3, 6) and recommends them to the kindness (*charizein* 2) of others. By his instructions, primarily, he brought his friends present and future benefit (*ōpheleia* 6.9) and (6.1) has shown his children, both natural and spiritual (6.10-11), the way to goodness and life in themselves. A bond of affection (*stergein, epipothein*) grows up between the father-teacher and his children-students (6.10) which is a guarantee of material support for him (1.2-3) and a bequest of the necessities, financial and spiritual, for his natural children (6.8,10-12). He wins (6.8) good (*epieikēs*) friends in the process. In the political community Socrates also (1.5-6) serves obvious needs (*chreiai*) by goading (*epegeirōn hōsper myōps*) officials to attend to their responsibilities and the city's welfare (*ta sympheronta*). He gives advice (3) on how to preserve internal and external tranquillity in the state; (4) on the best course of political studies for a young man; (5 and 7) on reaction to political injustice and suspicion. He himself (7.2) puts principle before political and personal expedience.

The other teachers, on the contrary, (6.3,5) serve their own interests through flattery (*kolakeia, areskeia*) and fine speech (*homilēsai deinoi*), as they pander to the masses with public doles and feasts (*dianomais kai hestiasesi pandēmois*). For them (6.5 ff.) money is the only proper bequest, although this sets parents and children at odds and encourages indolence (6.7). They criticize (1.4) the mutual support of friends but, rather than benefit their own associates, (6.6) the parasitic, (1.4) greedy flatters and hedonists lead their willing captives to a miserable death from sloth (*argia*), destroyed by hunger (*limō_i phtharentes*). In the political realm, venal and self-interested officials (5.1) are jealous of others' good fortune and (7.2) act unjustly, even attempting to implicate others in their injustice. They have no clear notion (7.5) of the common welfare (*exapatēsthai peri to sympheron*) and, like inept physicians, try to cure the political ills with greater doses of the repression which causes them. Socrates suggests the antidote for this otherwise incurable illness of oppressive and cruel despotism, i.e., attention to one's own affairs (*tōn seautou epimeleisthai*) and sensible action (*prassein kata noun*). The Bellerophon myth (1.2) captures some of the salient features of the negative example. Excited by desire beyond his own power (*epethymēsen*) Bellerophon ended up in shame and disgrace, losing even the hope of rising from misfortune and also the very boldness of speech (*parrēsia*) upon which a person's life is set aright.

The lines of contrast in the examples of the letters of Socrates are clear. With some modification, they are taken up in the letters of the Socratics. The discussion here will note both the similarities and alternations and will then set the examples into the philosophical background of the day and the program of the letters.

C. *The Contrasting Negative Example in the Letters of the Socratics and Its Relation to the Positive Model*

The positive and negative models here retain the same general lines but interesting new facets emerge under closer scrutiny. Socrates' public and unflattering instruction is recalled (14.2; 17.2) as well as the instruction in the various schools of the Socratics (30; 32), all with no reference at all to payment exacted from pupils. Socrates' life is pious and holy (15.1). The preservation of the tradition of teaching, life and virtue is new here (12; 15.2); 18; 20; 21.1; 22.1; 30.1-2), as also the defense of philosophizing far from home (13.1). Obedience to God in Socrates' case (14.5,9) becomes a pious allusion to the oracle (15.1) and divine providence (18.1; 24.2; 25.1; 26.2; 30.2; 32.2). There is still the criticism of mass opinion (8; 15.1; 24.1; 26.3; 30.2) and here flight from the distracting crowd becomes a possibility (14.5; 24.1; 32.2). But the crowd also appears positively influenced by the philosopher (9.3) and the flight is mitigated by the proximity of population centers (24.1), as well as by the idea of banding together in philosophical association (14.5,9; 17.4; 18.1; 19; 20; 23.2; 25.1; 27.3; 30.1; 33.3). Even the fearful flight of Socrates' companions is exonerated (16; 17.2). The harsh treatment of Socrates for his views is given due attention (14; 15.1; 16; 17.1) and this is seen to be inflicted on his companions as well (14.1). But, just as Aristippus (9, 11, 13) explains away the criticism of harsher Cynics (8,12), so too persistent rebuke is downplayed as in-house jesting in poor taste (23; cf. 12).

On the negative side, sophists are clearly distinguished from philosophers (34.2). The shame of ignorant and inept "experts" is exposed (14.2-3), as is superficial religiosity (17.1-2) which brings about the disaster for Athens of Socrates' execution (17.2). Flattery (*kolakeia*) is one of the tools of the opposition (14.4) but their success is short-lived (15.1; 17.2,4).

As for the personal qualities of the philosopher and his associates in this part of the letter collection, virtue (*aretē*) characterizes their life (15.2; 25.1; 26.2). Again, virtue is specified in many ways. The claim that it accords only with a rugged life-style (9.2; 12; 13.2), i.e., hunger and thirst, one cloak, bare feet, is rejected. The typically Cynic elements of the Socratean ideal in 1.11 are reduced to their absurd extremes (9.2) and shown to lack consistency (11; 13.2). In fact, Xanthippe is chided for going to extremes and failing to acquire even the necessities for herself and her children (21). Actually, even though the harsh life-style is rejected, these letters present a mediating ideal in showing first, (9.3) that pleasures do not impede virtue (*kai phronein dokōn*) or (13.2) friendship (*egō philos ho ra̦stōnēn kai tēn hēdonēn apodechomenos*); and second, (14.8) that one need not avoid pleasures themselves but only enslavement to them (*mē douloumenos tais tou sōmatos hēdonais*), or (27.2) excessive desire for them (*mē tou pleionos orignasthai*). Even the well-to-do Xenophon (19) proclaims the ideal of contentment with whatever is at hand (*ei mē arkesei hēmin tauta, hēmeis autois arkesomen,* and see 6.7). Poverty, in fact, is countenanced because at least it does not necessarily interfere with philosophy (18.2).

Other aspects under which the virtue in these letters is classified also match those in the first 7 letters. These are (20) patient endurance (*karteria*) and detachment from wealth and fame (*ōn epanō ploutou kai doxēs*); (12; 15.1; 29.1; 34.3) prudence or sensibleness (*sōphrosynē, sōphrōn, sōphronōs, sōphronein*); (14.4-5; 33.3) justice (*dikaia legein, mē adikein, eudikia*); (29; 32.1) gentleness (*epieikeia, epieikēs*); and (27.3) not getting upset (*tarattesthai*). *Ep.* 30.2 adds reliability (*bebaiotēs*), faithfulness (*pistis*), and wisdom (*sophia*). The acquisition of virtue is the object of striving (*agōnizesthai*[29]). Coming to one's senses (9.2; 23.1; 26.2) is the highest expression of virtue (*phronein, phronimos, phronēsis*). Finally, the acquisition and exercise of the qualities result (32.1) in merited repute (*doxa prosēkousa*).

In these letters, the culprits warned against are the rugged Cynics who make a show of poverty but are really engaged in the pursuit of money by their crafts and businesses (11; 13.2) and who even use poverty and labor as an excuse for not engaging in philosophy (18.2). More generally, some people, proven ignorant (17.2) by Socrates, rejected the insight and counterattacked (14.2); a foolish populace (15.1) caused Socrates' execution (*aphrainos*); and ignorance in the private and public spheres (24.1) still seems rampant (*amathainousi de kat'idean pasan aphrosynēs*). People of this sort act (27.3) in anger (*orgē*), (14.1) with unabashed boldness (*miaria tolma, thrasos*), and (32.1) exalt impulse and physical prowess as a virtue (*andria, rōmē, tachys*). These succeed for a time but end up accursed for their rashness (14, 15, 17). A stress peculiar to this section is the litigiousness of the opponents (10, 11, 14, 15, 16, 17).

With respect to those with whom the philosopher works, by his labor to make them virtuous and wise he works good in them (20; 23.1; 30.2) for virtue is a sign of health of soul (26.2) and the virtuous person keeps an eye (32.1) on what is useful (*to chrēsimon*). The assistance and support among philosophical friends receives great stress (10; 11; 13.2; 14.9-10; 15.2; 16; 21.1; 22.1; 23.2; 24.1; 26.2; 27.1; 30.2; 31; 32.1). It is, in fact, (15.2) both proper and necessary (*kalon kai anankaion*); constitutes unsurpassed wealth even for a poor person (22.1); and (21.3) in its correlative dependence on friends, is the true definition of poverty. Support is tendered even to the philosopher's family (21; 27.4) because of the spiritual kinship established through the father-teacher (21.2-3; 30.2) and the affection built up among him and his associates (14.8,10; *pothein* 25.1; 29; *epimeleisthai, charin apodidonai* 30.2-3; *pronoia* 32.1). Philosophy and the friends made through it are thus a most valuable bequest (*klēronomia ploutein plouton* 27.4-5) and are a way to goodness (*tēn … poreiēn tēn synēthē agathois andrasin* 27.5).

In the political arena, truth and justice, not self-interest, in the community are to be served (14.4) and (16) persecution is chosen over betrayal of the city by abandoning a standard of virtue. Public benefactions (*euergesiai*) here are praised (29) and not looked on with suspicion as in the first 7 letters. The philosopher's influence on young public figures also receives praise (13) and he is remarkably more politically clever than the average person (27.1).

On the negative side, while the philosopher's detached attitude toward pleasure and its enjoyment is carefully explained, the fact remains that some are rightly criticized for excessive attachment to pleasure (8); for self-indulgence (*akrasia*) and unruliness (*akosmia* 17.2) and (17.1) for causing evil. In the political arena, venal officials are charged with unjustly defrauding less astute persons (27.1-2). They are evil and litigious (14.2) and criticize good people out of envy (29). To counter them with their own weapons is unworthy (*anaxios*) of philosophy and the character which expresses it and would only lead to a slave's existence (14.5). As before, the way to avoid falling into this negative pattern is by careful attention to philosophical instruction (*logōn epimeletēs tōn Sōkratikōn* 9.1; *mimnēskou gar hōn elege Sōkratēs* 21; *poiēteon epimeleian* 30.2; *epimelēs* 30.3; *tēn prosēkousan epimeleian poiou* 32.1) and (21.2) by following the exemplary teaching and mores *tois ēthesin autou kai tois logois peirō akolouthein* 12.1; *to ekeinou ēthos diatērēsas* 32.2).

Contrasting explicit and implicit examples in the two sections of the letter collection need no more demonstration. What background do the features of these examples fit into and how do they serve the larger purpose of the letter collection? The following discussion will seek to respond to these questions.

VII. The Background and Purpose of the Contrasting Examples

These positive and negative examples designate the way to virtue, and this is a Cynic means to a Cynic end. The Cynic, inclined to be practical in his approach to philosophy rather than speculative, offered a short-cut to virtue, by practice and not by theory. He backed his lessons with the spectacle of the wise man in action.[170] Dio Chrysostom reflects another facet of the uniqueness of Cynic education as contrasted with other approaches. Distinguishing two types of *paideia* (*Or.* 4.24 ff.; 6.21 ff.), the divine and the human, he identifies his own (and that of the Cynics) as the former. It centers on individual ethics and the way to virtue, though it also has social-ethical consequences. The clearest manifestation of divine *paideia* is the Socratic-Cynic way of life exemplified in Hercules.[171] At the same time, he criticizes all who are *tetyphōmenoi* and *anoētoi*, but especially the sophists, who think they know more than others. These possess only human *paideia*, if even that. At its worst, this is a preoccupation with pleasure; at its best, it encompasses the traditional curriculum in the Greek schools, which is good only in relation to the divine *paideia*.[172] Notice in both views of Cynic education the

---

[170] D.R. Dudley, *A History of Cynicism, from Diogenes to the 6th Century AD* (Hildesheim: Georg Olms, 1967) 189. Seneca echoes this use of example at *Ben.* 7.8.3 (J.W. Basore, trans., *Lucius Annaeus Seneca. Moral Essays*, LCL, 3 vols. [London: W. Heinemann, 1928]), where he refers to the Cynic Demetrius as *exemplum* and at *Ep.* 6.5 (R.M. Gummere, trans., *Lucius Annaeus Seneca. Ad Lucilium epistulae morales*, LCL, 3 vols. [London: W. Heinemann, 1917]) where he links the short-cut in moral instruction to the use of examples. See also Lucian *Vit. auct.* 11; *Rhet. praec.* 3; Epictetus *Diss.* 3.22.23-25; Julian *Or.* 6.189A-B; 7.235D; Diogenes Laertius 6.104; 7.121; Diogenes *Eps.* 12; 26; 30; 37.4 ff; 44; Crates *Eps.* 13; 21; (in Malherbe, *Cynic Epistles*) and F. Sayre, *Diogenes of Sinope: A Study of Greek Cynicism* (Baltimore: J.H. Furst, 1938) 13. For the diversity among the Greco-Roman authors' applications of the short-cut image see V. Emeljanow, "A Note on the Cynic Short-Cut to Happiness," *Mnemos.* 4 ser. 18 (1965) 182-84.

[171] Julian *Or.* 6.187C; Lucian *Vit. auct.* 8. See Lucian *Demon.* 1-2 for the rational behind proposing Demonax as a contemporary example for the young along with figures from the past. Lucian *Peregr.* 20 burlesques vainglorious and thoughtless imitation of Hercules.

[172] R. Höistad, 56 ff., 150 ff., 173 ff. Cf. Lucian *Vit. auct.* 8 and Gerhard, *Phoinix*, 121 ff., on the necessity of education for the soul. In Lucian *Dial mort.* 1.1 the Cynic considers theoretical debate as laughable. Cf. Dio Chrysostom *Or.* 4. 37 *planōnemous en tois logois* (J.W. Cohoon, trans., *Dio Chrysostom*, LCL, 5 vols. [London: W. Heinemann, 1913]). Diogenes Laertius 6.103-4 reports that the Cynics dispensed with traditional

application to life and sentiment against theory. Notice, too, the reliance on example as a pedagogical tool.

The Socratic letters surveyed above, in their extensive use of that tool and in their confrontation with other forms of pedagogy, reflect an on-going conflict not only among competing schools but also within Cynicism itself.[173] The discussion above has already alluded to the on-going tensions between strict and hedonistic Cynicism and the effort in the Socratic letter corpus to promote a position of harmony.[174] A careful evaluation of the Cynicism in these letters, while necessary, would exceed the limits of this study. A more modest overview of the Cynic themes in the examples outlined and their relation to the competing forms of Cynicism will have to suffice for now. It is hoped that this will be enough to explain the effort of the letter corpus to promote its brand of Cynicism and also the employment of example as a device toward that end.

The issue of public[175] and free instruction in the Socratic letters seems to have formed part of contemporary objections raised against the abusive Cynics by proponents of a milder form of moral instruction.[176] The later letters alter the view on the philosopher's travel from stability in the first 7 letters to movement. In

---

subjects and concentrated on ethics. Diogenes Laertius 6.68 locates the end of education as *sōphrosynē* for the young, *paramythia* for the old, *ploutos* for the poor, and *kosmos* for the rich. Diogenes Laertius 6.10.105 records Antisthenes' position that virtue can be taught, and this leads Diogenes Laertius to consider Cynicism a philosophy and not just a way of life. Stobaeus *Flor.* 5.4.53 has Bion criticize grammarians for busying themselves with Odysseus' wanderings while remaining heedless of their own straying and for wasting time on valueless pursuits. Diogenes Laertius 6.27 ascribes this criticism to Diogenes. Dudley, 92 n. 3 finds the Cynic way of life to be non-doctrinal, referring to Lucian *Vit. auct.* 11. Cf. Julian *Or.* 6.187D. A.J. Malherbe, however, in "Self-Definition among Epicureans and Cynics," in *Self-Definition in the Graeco-Roman World* (B.F. Meyer, ed., [Philadelphia: Fortress, 1982]) argues that while Cynicism in the Hellenistic period did not require adherence to an organized system of doctrine, its leading figures were not anti-intellectual. The Socratic letters reflect this openness to philosophical discourse and their contribution to progress in virtue, *Eps.* 18.2; 20; 25.

[173] A. Oltramare, *Les Origines de la diatribe romaine* (Lausanne: Librairie Payot, 1926) 43-65, lists the common Cynic themes without making necessary distinctions. F. Sayre, on the other hand, accepts as Cynic only teachings of the strictest sort. Others, however, see Cynicism as a variegated and changing movement, e.g., D.R. Dudley; R. Höistad; H. Joly, *De cynica institutione sub imperatoribus Romanis* (Paris: Ernest Thorin, 1869); Léonce Paquet, *Les Cyniques grecs; Fragments et témoignages* (Ottawa: University of Ottawa, 1975); Gerhard, *Phoinix*. See also R.M. Wenley, "Neo-Cynicism," *Encyclopedia of Religion and Ethics* (J. Hastings, ed., [New York: Charles Scribner's Sons, 1928]) 9:298-300.

[174] See below, 116-23.

[175] Epictetus *Diss.* 3.22.15 ff., like Socrates *Ep.* 1, urges that the Cynic, guarded only by his self-respect (*aidōs*), fearlessly set his exemplary life as a public instruction for all to see.

[176] See above, 117-18 and also Lucian *Fugit.* 17 ff., *Reviv.* 34 ff.; Dio Chrysostom *Or.* 32.10-11; Julian *Ors.* 6 and 7 *passim*. See Sayre, 26, for another interpretation of the criticism.

that, they retain the traditional image of the wandering Cynic.[177] The piety of the philosopher and his response to divine direction, which moves away from the traditional indifference in harsh Cynicism to religion and even resistance to superstition [178] and popular religious practice,[179] coincides with the attitudes of Julian *Or.* 6.199A-B and Dio Chrysostom *Or.* 4.13.[180] Rejection of mass opinion [181] as well as of the crowd's acclaim [182] is fundamental to all Cynics. The deliberate cultivation of *adoxia* by outrageous behavior,[183] however, comes under

---

[177] Diogenes Laertius 6.38. Diogenes disapproves of travel at Diogenes Laertius 6.29 but there travel concerns other ends than philosophy.

[178] H. Rahn, "Die Frömmigkeit der Kyniker," *Paideuma* 7 (1960) 280-92, characterizes the piety in the Cynic movement among some of its proponents. See Diogenes Laertius 4.50; Lucian *Demon.* 27; Plutarch *Quom. adul. poet. aud.* 5.21F. Quite opposed to the picture of Socrates in the Socratic letters, Diogenes is said to have ridiculed belief in oracles at Diogenes Laertius 6.21, 24. Julian, the reformist Cynic, *Or.* 6.191A, reports just the opposite and takes to explain the piety behind the irreverence of Diogenes in the tradition (cf. *Or.* 7 7.204A ff., 212C ff., 238B ff.). Gerhard, *Phoinix,* 79 ff., sees two streams of opinion in the 3rd century B.C., long before the Socratic letters: one, a belief in omnipresence and punishment; another, a polemic against superstition and popular religious practice. Dudley, 127 ff., finds in Demetrius, an otherwise austere Cynic, the complete and unquestioned resignation to the will of God, whereas the traditional Cynic was at most resigned to Fate. This theological difference may be due to Stoic influence and ascribable to Seneca, who presents Demetrius in this way. See further M. Billerbeck, *Der Kyniker Demetrius,* Philosophia Antiqua, 36 (Leiden: Brill. 1979) 39-40; J.F. Kindstrand, "Demetrius the Cynic," *Philol.* 124 (1980) 91-92. Julian *Or.* 7.209B ff., criticizes the irreverence of the, to him, exaggerated Cynics of his day, e.g., Oenomaus and his followers. In the milder form of Cynicism reflected by pHeid 310.67 (Gerhard, *Phoinix,* 83) the *daimōn* appears as overseer, just as in Socrates *Ep.* 1. Sayre discusses the question on 24 and see also H.M. Hornsby, "The Cynicism of Peregrinus Proteus," *Hermathena* 48 (1933) 65-84; K. Holl, "Die schriftstellerische Form des griechischen Heiligenlebens," *Neue Jahrbuch für das klassische Altertum, Geschtichte und deutsche Literatur* 29 (1912) 421; M. Caster, *Lucien et la pensée religieuse de son temps* (Paris: Société d'édition "Les Belles Lettres," 1937) 65-84; D. Babut, "La Religion des philosophes grecs de Talès aux Stoiciens," *Littératures Anciennes* 4 (1974) 139-43; A.J. Malherbe, "Pseudo-Heracles," 45-51, "Self-Definition," n. 73; Rudberg, "Diogenes-Typus," 16-17.

[179] The Socratic letters present a practice on burial opposed to Diogenes' views on the afterlife as expressed in Diogenes *Eps.* 22 and 25, and even to Socrates' own wishes at Socrates *Ep.* 14.10 (and contrast Plato in *Ep.* 30.2). See also Gerhard, *Phoinix,* 82 n. 4 and Teles 17.7; 31.3; 59.6 (O. Hense, ed., *Teletis reliquiae* [Tübingen: J.C.B. Mohr, 1909]); Dio Chrysostom *Or.* 6.42.

[180] See also pHeid 310.37-38 (Gerhard) and cf. Socratic *Ep.* 9.1; Epictetus *Diss.* 3.22.82.

[181] Diogenes Laertius 6.58.64; Crates *Ep.* 16; Diogenes *Ep.* 10.2; Dio Chrysostom *Or.* 65.13.

[182] Epictetus *Diss.* 1.24.6; Crates *Ep.* 8.

[183] Sayre, 17 ff., sees the cultivation of popular contempt as a virtue in strict Cynicism, i.e., the absence of *philotimia* or *philodoxia,* and see Diogenes Laertius 6.93 and Diogenes

criticism in Julian *Or.* 6.196D; 7.225A ff.; Dio Chrysostom *Or.* 32.9 ff.; Epictetus *Diss.* 3.22.80; Lucian *Vit. auct.* 10; *Reviv.* 31 ff.; *Fugit.* 13 ff., as also in the Socratic *Eps.* 9.4(246.26-29); 1.12(226.3-4). Nonetheless, the expectation of public rebuke and chastisement is common to all.[184]

On the negative side, the flattery[185] which is criticized is traditionally opposed to Cynic *parrēsia*.[186] Nonetheless, the pointless abuse of harsh Cynics in the Empire does not escape objection[187] and a moderation is urged.[188] When the Socratic epistles object to the ignorance (*amathia*) of the false teachers, they also echo Julian *Or.* 7.225A-B and Dio Chrysostom *Or.* 32.9 on the contemporary Cynics. On the question of learning, the Cynic tradition is actually mixed, for some, like Crates, were educated, but ignorance of traditional learning was also considered a natural consequence of Cynic indifference.[189] Moreover, even Dio Chrysostom *Or.* 4.29 ff. and Julian *Or.* 6.187 ff. distinghish between knowledge which leads one astray (*periagōn, exapatōn*) and wisdom which leads to virtue.

The place of wisdom and the rational faculties in the acquisition and characterization of virtue, which the Socratic epistles claim, demands careful consideration. Sayre, 6, claims there is no connection between knowledge and virtue in Cynicism and that the earliest Cynics were non- and even anti-intellectual. Höistad basically agrees but makes two helpful observations. Commenting, 166 ff., on Diogenes Laertius 6.10,105 he notes that *aretē* is *epistēmē* in the sense of knowing what to do and what not to do, i.e., how to live rightly. On Diogenes Laertius 6.70-71 he observes, 43, that *anoia* does not refer to Socratic intellectualism but to foolishness or unwillingness to follow the Cynic way to happiness. As said above on the Cynic short-cut to virtue, the way to that happiness is not characterized by intellectual deliberation but by decision, by effective training, by strength. The Cynic way is a way of life which gives emphasis to the will, among the powers of the mind.

Ep. 31. Dudley, 195, sees *aidōs* in dress and speech as later replacing this old Cynic *anaideia* and *anaischyntia.* See also Socratic *Eps.* 14.1(252.21); 17.2(264.11); Epictetus *Diss.* 3.22.15 ff.

[184] Diogenes *Ep.* 20; Diogenes Laertius 6.33, 41, 42, 66; Dio Chrysostom *Or.* 8.15-16 who says that the noble person approaches this and all his hardships without fear; also *Or.* 72.14 ff.; Julian *Or.* 7.207D-E, 214D-E.

[185] Höistad, 215, and Diogenes Laertius 6.4.

[186] Socrates *Ep.* 1.12(226.7); Julian *Or.* 7.207C ff.; Diogenes Laertius 6.69. Cf. Oltramare, 59, theme 66.

[187] Athenaeus *Deip.* 13,573C-74C; Dio Chrysostom *Or.* 32.11; Julian *Or.* 6.201B-C; 7.223D; 236A-B.

[188] Lucian *Demon.* 6-7. Cf. Socrates *Eps.* 6.8(236.14-16); 34.1(304.2) and note how Aristippus clarifies and justifies his ridicule (*Ep.* 13) in answer to Simon's complaint (*Ep.* 21). In milder Cynicism self-criticism is promoted as the first step, Julian *Or.* 6.200B-C; Epictetus 3.22.50 ff.; and see Gerhard, *Phoinix,* 39 ff.

[189] Diogenes Laertius 6.73, 103-4 and Sayre, 20. Lucian *Vit. auct.* 11 satirizes this.

Can one be surprised then that the Socratic epistles stress sensibleness (*phronēsis*) in the teacher who, by his *paideia,* imparts that quality in the pupils?[190] Only with that can they choose the style of life appropriate to the virtuous person. The letters of Socrates, commending poverty and minimal needs,[191] follow a common Cynic teaching.[192] Höistad, 134-35, explains, however, that asceticism as a way to happiness (Socrates *Ep.* 6.4) is a hedonistic twist to Diogenes' ascetism, practiced for its own sake and issuing only in *enkrateia.*[193] The goal of *autarkeia* in these letters reflects a longstanding blend of hedonism with rigorous asceticism for it moves from total indifference to an accommodation to whatever one's circumstances present (Xenophon *Ep.* 19).[194] Thus, both parts of the corpus breathe the spirit of hedonistic Cynicism, with the letters of the Socratics in the second section making this quite explicit.

The hedonistic strain surfaces in the letters of the Socratics with the recommendations on dealing with riches and pleasures, a compromise with harsher Cynicism reached much earlier in the school's history.[195] Unlike the position of strong mistrust and contempt regarding riches (reflected in the letters of Socrates and *Ep.* 8 of Antisthenes),[196] an accommodation to wealth, provided it is dealt with reasonably, links the letters of the Socratics with other writings reflecting a milder Cynicism.[197] And what is true for riches is also true for the attitude toward pleasures which they occasion. Here the Socratic letters reject enslavement to pleasures and desires but are open to their reasonable use.[198]

---

[190] Höistad notes that according to Dio Chrysostom *Or.* 32.27-28 through the divine *paideia* one becomes *epieikēs,* a quality also proclaimed in the Socratic epistles as the quality engendered by Socrates in his friends. See also *Or.* 69.4 and Lucian *Demon.* 4. Julian *Or.* 6.197A-B describes the place of *nous* and *phronēsis* in controlling *orgē* and *epithymia.*

[191] Diogenes *Ep.* 36.4 ff. (150.20 ff.); Epictetus *Diss.* 3.22.45-48.

[192] Diogenes *Eps.* 7, 26; Sayre, 24; Oltramare, 49-52, 56.

[193] Cf. Sayre, 7.

[194] See A.N.M. Rich, "The Cynic Conception of *autarkeia,*" *Mnemos.* 9 (1956) 23-29. Dudley, 66 ff., finds this already in Bion. Sayre, 23, follows von Fritz in denying that Bion was ever a Cynic. See also Diogenes Laertius 6.11.

[195] Gerhard, *Phoinix,* 65 ff., shows that in the moderate position of the Cynic poem in pHeid 310 (actually two poems on similar themes) riches are not opposed to virtue in themselves.

[196] See Oltramare, 47 theme 20 (compare theme 20d with Socrates *Ep.* 1.4-5[200.5-20] and 63 themes 82-83). The love of riches is the cause (Diogenes *Ep.* 50[180.22-231]) or mother-city (Diogenes Laertius 6.50) of all evils. Sayre, 11-12, citing Diogenes Laertius 6.71 and Crates *Ep.* 9, sees the negation of appetites and desires as a condition for attaining *eleutheria* and indeed a pleasure in itself. See also Sayre, 25 and Dittmar, 194-202 on *Ep.* 6.

[197] Dudley, 104-5, notes this rapprochement of Cynicism with *hēdonē* already in the 3rd century B.C. Gerhard, *Phoinix,* 105 ff. and 115 ff., discusses the link between riches and wisdom expressed in pHeid 310.71 ff. In the second poem of pHeid 310 there is a call at 77 for the use of *phronein* because, 83-91, the rich are often incapable of using their resources correctly. Compare Aristippus' letters in the Socratic corpus and those of the wealthy but wise Xenophon.

[198] Gerhard, *Phoinix,* 24 ff., 34. He notes that in the strict position money-

The philosopher's acceptance of support from friends (throughout the Socratic letters) and even non-essential aid from the wealthy (in the letters of Aristippus, Aeschines and Speusippus) is enlightening. Begging is a standard feature of strict Cynicism [199] and is based on the conviction that the wise man is worthy of alms [200] and that friends have all things in common.[201] But the begging Cynic comes under fire from two directions: (1) from those who see him debasing philosophy by making of it a money-making venture; [202] and (2) from those who see it inconsistent that one who despises money should ask for it.[203] The Cynicism of the Socratic letters meets these objections by striking a balance both by softening its attitude toward wealth in general and in depending more decorously on support from an association of friends.

Even this friendship represents part of the letters' compromise position. Sayre, 13, claims from Lucian *Vit. auct.* 10 that the Cynic had no friends because friends limit one's freedom. While this may have been an aspect of latter-day exaggerated Cynicism, Diogenes Laertius 6.105 presents the milder position found in the Socratic letters whereby the Cynic wise man is a friend to those similar to him.[204] The relationship of friendship is based on the usefulness of the teacher to his student-friends. Sayre, 6, declares that in the Cynic way of life there was no intent to make people better, and there seems to have been a misanthropic tenor to the exaggerated Cynicism in the Empire.[205] But, just like the Socratic letters,

---

and-pleasure seekers are called *thēria,* and cf. Plato in Socratic *Ep.* 24.2(276.4-5). Diogenes saw reason and passion as opposed to each other, Diogenes Laertius 6.38. For the milder view see Bion's statement in Stobaeus *flor.* 4:429.15 (Hense); Teles 25.4; 43.1; Diogenes *Ep.* 37; Sayre, 2-3; and Oltramare, 48 theme 23. In a reversal of terms, Julian accuses the excessive Cynics of his day of being *thēria* (*Or.* 6.197B). Earlier, the strict Cynics bore the title proudly, as Gerhard, *Phoinix,* 48 ff., explains. Gerhard, *Phoinix,* 76-77, shows that in hedonistic Cynicism riches and justice were not opposed, as they were in strict Cynicism. The basis of the compromise made by the milder Cynicism comes to expression in Julian *Or.* 6.201D (and cf. 188B, 189A ff., 192A) where he asks that passion be subjected to intelligence.

[199] Diogenes *Ep.* 33.3-4(140.28 ff.) raises the issue of begging and its propriety. The pros and cons are debated by Socrates *Ep.* 1. The strict Cynics were calculatedly improvident, living for the day, Diogenes Laertius 6.38 and Sayre, 22.

[200] Diogenes Laertius 6.62 and also 6.11.72; Diogenes *Ep.* 10; Crates *Eps.* 26, 27; Sayre, 5-6.

[201] Crates *Ep.* 27; Diogenes Laertius 6.37.72; and Socratic (Plato) *Ep.*26.2(280.21-22).

[202] See the discussion above 117-18, and cf. Julian *Or.* 6.197B-C; 7.224B ff. People like this are criticized strongly by Socrates *Ep.* 1 as parasites on others' wealth.

[203] Seneca, *Ben.* 2.27.2.

[204] Höistad, 37.

[205] The misanthropic Cynic position of pLond 115V. 23 ff. (perhaps from the 2nd century A.D.) makes friendship dependent on money and poverty resulting in being despised. The writer declares at 28, "I hate all people who live like this." For the text, see Gerhard, *Phoinix,* 170 ff. The 2nd/3rd century A.D. *grammatikos* Athenaeus *Deip.*

Epictetus 3.22.23-25 presents an essentially philanthropic ideal.[206] One is useful to another when he brings him to his senses *chrēstois logois* and leads him to know *chrēsta* and *sympheronta*.[207] The methods of instruction are sometimes harsh, calling on the traditional Cynic *parrēsia*. But the criticism is not for its own sake but for the improvement of the foolish person.[208]

The Cynic's responsibility is measured not only toward his friends but toward his family and the community at large. *Agamia* is a long-standing Cynic characteristic.[209] Epictetus upholds Cynic celibacy, *Diss.* 3.22.68-69, but for the sake of greater service and not an ideal in itself. He also modifies the stricter Cynicism by recognizing, as do the Socratic letters, a spiritual kinship between teacher and pupils, *Diss.* 3.22.82. The natural family is absorbed into the family of philosophical friends.[210]

As for community obligations, could one expect a Cynic to be active in politics when one finds a doxographic tradition opposed to such involvement?[211] Nonetheless, the political involvement throughout the Socratic letters was already part of the Cynic tradition.[212] Dio, who writes discourses on kingship, the ideal

---

13.573e-74c criticizes the basically useless lives of the exaggerated Cynics. Sayre also records the tradition of doing no work as a virtue, 8 ff. and cf. Diogenes Laertius 6.31.

[206] Dudley, 198 ff. and Höistad, 56, 98. Dudley, 68, ties *philanthrōpia* with Crates. Gerhard, *Phoinix*, 32 ff., sees *ōphelein* as a *terminus technicus* for the relationship of friends in mild Cynicism. Diogenes *Ep.* 29 locates the usefulness in bringing the friend to his senses. Diogenes in Stobaeus *Flor.* 3:36.8-10 (Hense) connects the friend's usefulness with justice. Gerhard, *Phoinix*, 89, says that *nomizesthai chrēstos* is the ideal set before the people. See also Epictetus *Diss.* 3.24.64. Malherbe, "Self-Definition," argues that the goal to be of benefit was not due to a sense of duty but to a real sympathy with human suffering and the unnatural bondage in which men find themselves. The Cynic hopes to free others from the evils to which he himself was once subject. Cf. Julian *Or.* 6.201B-C. See also Rudberg, "Diogenes-Typus," 17-18.

[207] pHeid 310.87-91 and Gerhard, *Phoinix*, 121 ff. See also Diogenes Laertius 6.68 and Socratic (Phaedrus) *Ep.* 25.2 (278.11 ff.).

[208] Diogenes *Eps.* 28.5(122.17-18); 29 and Gerhard, *Phoinix*, 33 n. 3, 35-36. See also Socratic (Simon) *Ep.* 12; Julian *Or.* 6.201C; Lucian *Peregr.* 3; *Demon* 6-7; Oltramare, 59 theme 66. Gerhard, *Phoinix*, 35-36 notes that in moderate Cynicism *elenchein* gives place to *nouthetein*. See Julian *Or.* 7.236A.

[209] Diogenes, *Eps.* 21, 47; Diogenes Laertius 6.29,54; Lucian *Vit. auct.* 9 ff. Sexual promiscuity was another theme common in strict Cynicism, Sayre 28.

[210] The tradition in Maximus of Tyre *Diss.* 3.9 that Diogenes avoided marriage to skirt problems like those the tradition ascribes to Socrates and wife Xanthippe is replaced in the Socratic epistles with a picture of harmony and devotion, *Eps.* 4, 21.

[211] Diogenes Laertius 6.24,29; Crates *Ep.* 5. In Diogenes Laertius 6.69. Diogenes is a citizen of the world. He avoids political entanglements in any one city and his concern transcends political borders, Epictetus *Diss.* 3.24.66. See also Maximus of Tyre *Diss.* 36.5 and Rudberg, "Diogenes-Typus," 11-13.

[212] Dudley, 69, calls Bion the first "court philosopher," 74 ff., gives evidence for Cercidas' prominence in the politics of Megalopolis in the 3rd century B.C.; 127 ff., finds De-

of which he finds embodied in Trajan, could also connect justice with a law of virtue or nature. The latter is a universal principle of natural ethics which is prior to the laws of any particular state.[213] The Socratic letters reflect this stance in Socrates' refusal to engage in the legal but unjust confiscations of the Thirty (*Ep.* 7) as well as in Aristippus' declaration that Socrates' unjust imprisonment could rightly have been breached by any possible means (*Ep.* 16).[214]

Despite this position, or rather because of its principled foundations, moderate Cynicism distances itself from the extreme and destructive reviling and iconoclasm, such as that recorded by Dio Cassius *Hist. Rom.* 66.13,1 and 1a,[215] and claims rather to instruct officials in the proper conduct of their office and to insure that the law of justice be upheld.

And so, using traditional Cynic images like the battle for virtue,[216] the doctor curing a disease,[217] the trainer directing exercise,[218] as well as the other thematic material mentioned above, the milder Cynics try to urge their audiences to attend to themselves and their good. The goal was firmly rooted in the Cynic tradition[219] and justified the continual spiritual askesis which the Cynic

---

metrius associated in the Roman philosophers' agitation against the emperors Nero, Vespasian and Domitian. Epictetus *Diss.* 3.22.72 echoes the interest of the Socratic epistles for the common good. Julian *Or.* 6.201C sees the Cynic as naturally socio-political and coming to the aid of his fellow citizens.

[213] Höistad, 166 ff. He alludes to Diogenes and other Cynics who dissociate the virtue of *dikaios* from *nomimos,* in the sense of observing particular laws of city-states. See also Diogenes Laertius 6.11.

[214] Cf. Crates *Ep.* 5, where philosophy is considered superior to law.

[215] E. Cary, trans., *Dio's Roman History,* LCL, vol. 8 (London: W. Heinemann, 1914). See also Dio Chrysostom *Or.* 34.3; Julian *Or.* 7.209A ff.

[216] Epictetus *Diss.* 3.22.69 and Socrates *Ep.* 5.2(230.18 ff.); Diogenes *Eps.* 27; 34(142.18-19); 46(176.11 ff.).

[217] Diogenes Laertius 6.4,6; Diogenes *Eps.* 27, 28, 29, 49; Socrates *Ep.* 7.5(242.24 ff.); Antisthenes *Ep.* 8(244.13 ff.). A.J. Malherbe, "Medical Imagery in the Pastoral Epistles," in *Texts and Testaments: Critical Essays in Honor of Stuart D. Currie* (W.E. March, ed., San Antonio: Trinity University, 1980) 19-35, finds that the extreme Cynics' antisocial rebukes were compared to excessively harsh and ineffective measures of ignorant physicians by proponents of a milder and more remedial sort of treatment.

[218] Diogenes *Eps.* 37.5(156.25 ff.); 32.4(136.1 ff.); 27(118.14 ff.); 9(102.12-13); Crates *Ep.* 11(62.14); 19(68.25-26).

[219] Diogenes in Stobaeus *Flor.* 2:212.15 (Hense) reflects a self-centeredness which milder Cynicism left behind. See Gerhard, *Phoinix,* 129 ff.; and cf. Julian *Or.* 6.201D where he urges the Cynic-to-be *epimeleisthai* himself first. Diogenes in Diogenes Laertius 6.70 stresses incessant spiritual *gymnasia.* Dio Chrysostom *Or.* 8.28 recalls Hercules' exemplary toil and struggle (*ponein* and *agōnizesthai*). Diogenes *Ep.* 12, to Crates, counsels continued training (*epimenein en tēi askēsei*), resistance and warfare (*antitattesthai* and *polemein*) against pleasure, which leads to shameful deeds (*ta aischra*), and hardship, which distracts from good deeds because of fear (*tōi phobōi*). Crates himself, *Ep.* 12, recognizes that virtue is acquired by practice (*askēton*) and not automatically. See also Tzaneteas, 65 ff.; Höistad, 200.

undertook in order to be sure his soul progressed toward a healthy and ethically earnest condition, wherein true happiness resides.[220] Here, and not in possessions, is the basis of *eudoxia*.[221] Here, and not in a preoccupation with wealth, is the anchor of *philia* and *pistis*, for wealth leads only to treason, injury, murder, flattery, theft, and other such misdeeds.[222] This Cynic teaching counters the charlatan Cynics' "escape doctrine" of blanket tolerance, idleness, change of scenery, and freedom from restraint[223] and replaces this with a program of personal, familial, philophronetic, and civic responsibility.[224] The Socratic letters participate fully in promoting this mild Cynic program and include their rather unique preoccupation with a lively association of philosopher-friends. This is the context in which the examples of conflicting life-styles is set. The exemplary life-styles are the heart of the instruction in this philosophy and they are supplemented by rules and prescription.[225] These serve as the pedagogical and hortatory devices for a philosophy with a focus on practice rather than on theory.

On the whole, the letter corpus presents a model of a philosopher concerned with his own life of virtue in active association with and support of like-minded individuals. This model suits the purpose of the letter coprus which is to promote a mild-Cynic type philosophy in a newly established harmony among the traditions of the Socratic school. It also suits the scholastic environment of education of young people in a common and formalized context, where the school substitutes for the family and the teacher becomes the surrogate father.

At *Ep.* 6.9-11 the friendship between the teacher Socrates and his pupils establishes a kinship relationship of father to children and of the children with each other. The letter itself represents a specific aspect of the familial relationship, i.e., the testament or bequest. This study will now focus on the epistolary testament, both because it represents a special instance of the example proposed in the letter corpus and because it recurs among the Pastoral letters as well.

VIII. The Testamentary Letters

Testamentary letters use a traditional form[226] and W. Crönert, analyzing the Epicurean papyrus 1780, isolates eight characteristics of the testament: (1)

---

[220] Socratic (Phaedrus) *Ep.* 25(278.8 ff.). Gerhard, *Phoinix*, 128-29; pHeid 310.93-95.

[221] Gerhard, *Phoinix*, 89.

[222] Gerhard, *Phoinix*, 45.

[223] Dudley, 147.

[224] Malherbe, "Medical Imagery."

[225] Julian *Or.* 6.198D sees the instructional complementarity between the esteemed *nomoi* of Diogenes and Crates, i.e., their rules and prescriptions, and the example of the way they lived. In *Or.* 7.214B-C he notes that the philosopher's deeds (*erga*) actually come before his words (*logoi*).

[226] See Crönert, 81-87 and n. 426; E. Fr. Bruck, *Totenteil und Seelgerät im griechischen*

bequest, (2) description of the bequest, (3) prohibition of sale, (4) special legacies, (5) freeing of slaves, (6) creditors and debtors, (7) exclusion of those not named, (8) executors. He notices in Socratic *Ep.* 27 some reminiscences of the philosophical testaments. O. Schering[227] elaborates this insight about *Ep.* 27 and finds elements of the form in both major segments of the letter collection as he refers to *Eps.* 1, 28, 29, 30, 31, 33. Sykutris adds an important qualification when he finds the testament form itself in *Ep.* 27 not the end but the means by which to bring together the several *hypothēkai* of Aristippus which the editor-author had at hand.[228]

Ep. 27 employs the following characteristic features of the testament from Crönert's list: the bequest and description as property at 2(282.23-25) and as philosophy at 4(284.11-13); charge not to lose the philosophical inheritance at 5(284.13-17); special legacies in the care for Lamprocles at 4(284.1-4) and for Aristippus at 4(284.9-13); freeing and treatment of slaves at 2(282.12-17) and 4(284.4-9); creditors at 2(282.17-18) and debtors at 2(282.12-17). *Ep.* 6 also contains elements of the philosophical testament: the bequest at 8(236.18-20) and 11(238.22-24); the description of the bequest at 9(236.27-30) and 12(238.26-32); the prohibition against alienation of the inheritance at 8(236.20-23), here expressed as a hypothesis; an accounting of debtors and their debt at 9-10(236.30 - 238.4); the executors at 9(236.27-30) and 10(238.8-12). It should surprise no one to find the use of this traditional form in the Socratic letter collection with its great variety of letter types and its awareness of the lesson in the rhetorical handbooks.

Sykutris has established the hortatory purpose which the testament form is made to serve in *Ep.* 27[229] *Ep.* 6 shares the hortatory impulse of *Ep.* 27 as it does the testament form.[230] The hortatory and Cynic character which strikes the

---

Recht (Munich: C.H. Beck, 1926) 256 ff.; C.G. Bruns, "Die Testamente der griechischen Philosophen," *Kleine Schriften II* (Weimar: Hermann Böhlau, 1882) 192-237; the testament of Epicurus 19.2(166.13 - 167.17) in H.K. Usener, ed., *Epicurea* (Leipzig: B.G. Teubner, 1887); and Diogenes Laertius 3.41-43 for the testament of Plato; 5.11 ff. for Aristotle's; 5.51 ff. for Theophrastus'; 5.61 ff. for Strato's; 5.69 ff. for Lycon's; 10.16 ff. for Epicurus'. See also E. Bignone, *Epicuro: Opere, frammenti, testimonianze sulla sua vita* (Rome: "L'Erma" di Bretschneider, 1964) 145-48.

[227] Schering, 53-60.

[228] Sykutris, *Die Briefe,* 85. He does not specify the *hypothēkai* but the reader of the letter might identify them as follows: (1) at 2(282.17-19) "do not desire too much;" (2) at 3(282.25-27) "do not let minor matters disturb you;" (3) at 5(284.15-17) "rejoice in the riches of philosophy and pass them on;" and perhaps also (4) at 4 "philosophy establishes a kinship relation;" and (5) at 3(282.35-37) "live in friendship and without arrogance."

[229] See n. 228.

[230] The assurance that friends will meet life's necessities at 11(238.19-24) resembles the exhortation not to harbor excessive desires; the caution that friendship must be guarded at 8(236.18-23) echoes the to live in friendship; the new kinship relation through philosophy appears at 11(238.9-19); the criticism of the pursuit of wealth and the contrast between money and virtue, right thinking, education, and friendship at 4(234.13-15); 5(234.18-22);

reader of these testament letters has already been shown to be fundamental to the entire collection.

Aside from the specific hortatory themes advanced in these letters, they add an important dimension to the example promoted by the letter collection. The presumed writers of these letters, in addition to being models of incorporating virtue into their way of life, also become models of the careful handing on of the tradition of virtue taught and lived. In this, the example functions implicity.

IX. Concluding Observations

The Socratic epistles make their contribution to this study of the Pastorals in matters both of form and of content. While the same hortatory features are common to all the writings looked at above, the Socratic epistles employ them unmistakably in the letter form.[231] Moreover, the Socratics are truly a collection with more than one kind of letter, though with a generally hortatory cast throughout. Then, too, the Socratics' conscious use of and reference to devices taught in rhetorical schools and catalogued in rhetorical handbooks breathe the air of the schoolroom as a likely context for their creation and use.

The pseudonymity of the Socratics is a striking literary device and all the pseudonymous authors are enlisted both to authenticate the Cynicizing moral exhortation and to stand as examples, explicit and implicit, of its application. The letter collection in its final form acknowledges and bears a significant responsibility to the philosophical tradition behind it as it works to preserve its integrity and transmit it faithfully.

In their exhortation, the letters employ a pattern of individual hortatory features which recalls that of the developed chria, already seen in the rhetorical handbooks, the Pastorals, Seneca and Plutarch. The device of example is thus situated within a context of hortatory devices with a common aim. Moreover, the letters arrange their examples consistently in antithetical relationships, in their effort to show what is to be done and what avoided. Example is also wedded to the letter form itself in the Socratic letter corpus. As a result, the letters themselves, with their (auto)biographical details and particular concerns, serve as implicit examples along with the figures explicitly singled out for imitation or avoidance.

The study now turns to the Pauline homologoumena to trace Paul's use of example in his exhortations to the churches. This will fill in the horizon against which the Pastorals will be placed in the final chapter.

6(234.33 - 236.1); 8(236.18-23) mirror the claim that philosophy is true wealth and a precious bequest. See above 139-41 for further aspects of the exhortation in *Ep.* 6.

[231] In his treatment of symboleutic literature, Kleck notes a formal progression over the course of time from poetic speeches to letters.

CHAPTER VII

Example in the Letters of Paul

The use of example in the Socratic letter corpus finds a clear reflection in the way the Pastoral Epistles use the same device. But before the implications of this similarity which emerged in the preceding chapters receive full elaboration, a look at the other letters in the Pauline corpus is indispensable. What types of example did Paul use in the homologoumena? For what end? And in what formal structure? Once these questions are answered, the continuity and/or discontinuity between the undisputed Paul and the Paul of the Pastorals, will manifest itself.

The analysis of the use of example by the undisputed Paul will be comparatively short. The focus of this study lies elsewhere and the subject of Paul's use of example merits a study of its own. Here, concentration rests on the principal views of the Pauline usage and on Paul's relation to the rhetorical theory and practice of his day.

W. Michaelis' understanding of Pauline imitation will serve as a starting point. His article in *TDNT*[1] has disseminated his views widely and, as a consequence, those views are usually commented on by recent writers[2] on the

---

[1] W. Michaelis, "*mimeomai*," *TDNT* 4 (1967) 666-73.

[2] Besides Michaelis' article, aspects of imitation and example in the Pauline letters are to be found in the following: H.D. Betz, *Nachfolge und Nachahmung Jesu Christi im Neuen Testament* (Tübingen: J.C.B. Mohr [Paul Siebeck], 1967; J.M. Bover, "Imaginis notio apud B. Paulum," *Bib.* 4 (1923) 174-79; N. Brox, *Die Pastoralbriefe*, Regensburger Neues Testament 7 Bd., 4th ed. (Regensburg: Friedrich Pustet, 1969); H. Conzelmann, *1 Corinthians*, Hermeneia, trans. J.W. Leitch (Philadelphia: Fortress, 1975); W.P. de Boer, *The Imitation of Paul* (Amsterdam/Kampen: J.H. Kok, 1962), M. Dibelius, *From Tradition to Gospel*, trans. B.L. Woolf (New York: Scribner, 1935) 238-39; M. Dibelius and H. Conzelmann, *The Pastoral Epistles*, Hermeneia, trans. P. Buttolph and A. Yarbro (Philadelphia: Fortress, 1972); B. Gerhardsson, *Memory and Manuscript*, Acta Seminarii Neotestamentici Upsaliensis, 22 (Uppsala: Almqvist & Wiksell, 1961) 293-94; L. Goppelt, "*typos*," *TDNT* 8 (1972) 246-59; P. Gutierrez, *La Paternité spirituelle selon Saint Paul* (Paris: Gabalda, 1968); E.K. Lee, "Words Denoting 'Pattern' in the N.T.," *NTS* 8 (1961-62) 166-73; P. Lippert, *Leben als Zeugnis: Die Werbende Kraft christlicher Lebensführung nach dem Kirchenverständnis neutestamentlicher Briefe* (Stuttgart: Katholisches Bibelwerk 1968) 173; W. Lofthouse, "Imitatio Christi," *Exp. Tim.* 65 (1953-54) 339; O. Merk, *Handeln aus Glauben: Die Moti-*

same topic, whatever their own particular bent might be.   Second, as is the case with the articles in *TDNT*, his own makes reference to nonbiblical usage, an enterprise compatible with that of this study.   Third, he is sensitive to a variety of meanings for imitation in the Pauline letters but is unwarranted in his stress on one of them, as this investigation will now demonstrate.

I. Summary and Critique of Michaelis' Observations

A. *His Overall Position*

W. Michaelis discusses six passages from the letters of Paul which refer to imitation.   Here imitation is linked with examples and he sees three modes of imitation:

(1) In 1 Thess 2:14 and possibly 1 Thess 1:6 a simple comparison is noted. The Thessalonians have become imitators of Paul and of the churches in Judea, but this is the result of circumstances and not of conscious imitation; (2) In 2 Thess 3:7, 9 and Phil 3:17 there is "the following of an example," and the example is always Paul.   Here recognition of Paul's authority is implied, so that following the example also includes obedience to commands; (3) In 1 Cor 4:16 obedience predominates to the eclipse of the though of example.   Similarly 1 Thess 1:6 and Eph 5:1 place main stress on the element of obedience.   Christ and God are associated with Paul here as authorities to whom the *mimētēs* is related.   Here Michaelis seems bent on avoiding where possible the notion of imitating or copying a model.   Consequently, unless imitation is the only mode of relating to the model, according to the text, the model is a figure of authority and the imitation he calls for is really obedience of his directives.[3]

---

vierung der paulinischen Ethik (Marburg: N.G. Elwert, 1968) 82-83; H.J. Michel, *Die Abschiedsrede des Paulus an die Kirche Apg 20:17-38* (Munich: Kösel, 1973); L. Nieder, *Die Motive der religiös-Sittlichen Paränese in dem paulinischen Gemeindebriefen* (Munich: K. Zink, 1956) 81; J. Roloff, *Apostolat-Verkundigung-Kirche. Ursprung, Inhalt und Funktion des kirchlichen Apostelamtes nach Paulus, Lukas und den Pastoralbriefen* (Gütersloh: G. Mohn, 1965); A. Schulz, *Nachfolgen und Nachahmen: Verhältnis der N.T.-lichen Jüngerschaft zur urchristlichen Vorbildethik* (Munich: Kösel, 1962); D.M. Stanley, "'Become Imitators of Me': The Pauline Conception of Apostolic Tradition," *Bib.* 40 (1959) 859-77; H. Wendland, *Die Briefe an die Korinther* (Göttingen: Vandenhoeck & Ruprecht, 1968); H. Willms, *EIKON: Eine begriffsgeschichtliche Untersuchung zum Platonismus. I Teil: Philon von Alexandria mit einer Einleitung über Platon und die Zwischenzeit* (Münster i. W: Aschendorff, 1935) 48 ff.

[3] Stanley discusses these passages and allows more play in them to the idea of imitation as copying a model. This largely coincides with the view elaborated here, though the reasons explaining the position differ. Lee, 169; de Boer, 18-21, 68, 72-79, 92-196, 209-11; Gutierrez, 174-87, also agree with the emphasis here on imitation rather than obedience.

The evidence for this interpretation is tenuous. He finds a parallel in the school setting, and cites Xenophon *Mem.* 1.2.3; 1.6.3.[4] In the first reference, however, Xenophon outlines Socrates' virtuous character, clearly states that Socrates never laid down a specific command for his pupils to follow, and finally declares that by making his character manifest (*phaneros*) he led his pupils to attempt to imitate and become such as he was (*toioutous genēsasthai*). Imitation is obvious here; obedience seems explicitly ruled out.

Similarly, the teacher's command is only suggested at *Mem.* 1.6.3 in the word *apodeiknyousin*. In his reply, however, 1.6.4 ff., Socrates describes his style of life and clearly indicates that his pupils would be wise to adopt it, if not in its perfected state, at least in its aspect of relentless concern (*meletan*). The immediately preceding section, *Mem.* 1.5.1-6, indicates the function of example in the teaching of Socrates. His lesson includes numerous negative examples to set in relief the "rule" about the importance of acquiring self-control (1.5.4). Xenophon then remarks (1.5.6) that his own deeds showed forth his own self-control even more clearly than his words. As such he is a model to be imitated and not just an authority to be obeyed. Furthermore, Michaelis' recourse to these two passages and a third one cited from Euripides *Hel.* 940-41 represent a skewed vision of the relationship between teacher and pupil and between parent and child. The evidence presented above[5] found instruction by model and imitation to be promoted in both theory and practice within the family and in the schools, which replicate parental teaching functions. Contrary to Michaelis' view, authority and obedience to precept no doubt were a part of the system, but should not replace or even obscure the method of inculcation by example.[6] It has also been noted above that precept and example stand as complements to each other and not as rivals.[7] Moreover, other texts cited by Michaelis admittedly refer to imitation as a response to the model or example.

The discussion of imitation of God produces pertinent passages only from Philo. Here obedience is indeed likely, for "Philo's ethic is centrally controlled by the demands of the Old Testament."[8] Otherwise, Philo verifies the link between obeying and imitating the model's life-style by the *mimētēs*. Consequently, on the basis of his own evidence (and the same can be said for the evidence alluded to in Goppelt's article on *typos*)[9] Michaelis' interpretation of "imitating the example" in terms of obedience to authority is tendentious.[10] Indeed, it is a usage which does not appear in the rhetorical treatises which treat example.

---

[4] E.C. Marchant, trans., *Xenophon. Memorabilia,* LCL (London: W. Heinemann, 1923).

[5] See Chapter III.

[6] This would account for the presence of both in Philo's *Sac.* 68 (F.H. Colson and G.H. Whitaker, trans., *Philo Judaeus,* LCL, 12 vols. [London: W. Heinemann, 1929]).

[7] E.g. 51, 53-55, 65-66, 73, 94.

[8] Michaelis, 665 n. 10.

[9] *TDNT* 8 (1972) 246-59.

[10] Ns. 31 and 28 of this article betray the basis for his view. The latter notes that true

B. *Michaelis' Views on 1 Corinthians*

In noting the New Testament use of imitation and example, 1 Corinthians receives the most prolonged treatment by Michaelis [11] and so this study will use that letter to demonstrate the Pauline use of example. First, however, Michaelis' position must be scrutinized. The clarity of the meaning of obedience in 1 Cor 4:16 is supposedly demonstrated by 4:17, where Paul's "ways" appear to refer not to the "personal walk of the apostle" but to the "solid core of his *didaskein*" Thus, the teaching has a character of command and to accept it is to obey his directions.

But one might counter, first, the context is paraenetic (*entrepōn, noutheton, parakalō*) as well as didactic. Second, the father and children metaphor is associated with the school instruction in technical and moral matters (cf. *paidagōgous*) where exemplary qualities and not obedience are central. Third, the *hodoi* echo *peripatountes* in Phil 3:17, where personal walk is meant to be imitated. Fourth, Timothy reminds them of these first and foremost by his transmission of the letter itself where they set a model for the community's attitude and behavior, as elaborated below. [12]

Further on at 1 Cor 11:1, Michaelis admits the possibility of a summons to follow Paul's example. His interpretation of 4:16, however, pushes him to see obedience as the point here as well, an interpretation which is confirmed by the admonition at 10:32. Michaelis would allow a linkage between command and example were it not for Paul's addition of the reference to Christ at 11:1, *kathōs kàgō Christou*. The fleeting reference in 11:1 (contrast Rom 15:1-5 and Phil 2:4-5) to Christ as model of imitation and the relation of imitation to salvation in 10:33 convince Michaelis that "obey" is the preferable meaning of "imitate me," just as Paul understands his own ministry as Christ wishes. Christ is mentioned as a corroborative authority in a chain of tradition (cf. 11:23 and 7:40b).

Again, a number of observations shed doubt on the conclusiveness of this view. First, 11:1 comes at the conclusion of a lengthy treatment of food offered to idols, wherein Paul explicity refers to his own attitude and practice. A full explanation of the call to imitation at 11:1 has to take into account the previous three chapters and the function of Paul's example in the exhortation there. [13] Second, the imitation of Christ is related to the imitation of Paul but should not supersede Paul's more extensive references to his own example as determinative for understanding his call to imitation. Third, the chain of tradition and authority noted at 7:40b again caps off a chapter where Paul's own life-style is promoted

---

discipleship is on independent direction of one's life in accord with the principles observed in the exemplar; the former indicates a dismissal of any notion of an imitation of Christ.

[11] Michaelis, 668-69. See de Boer, 167-68, for his arguments against Michaelis' interpretation of 1 Cor 11:1.

[12] See also Brox, 148-54; Gerhardsson, 293-94; Dibelius, *Tradition*, 239.

[13] See 181-82.

(7:6-8) and where command is about secondary matters (7:10 ff.) or in conjunction with the example being urged (7:17 ff.). Fourth, this complementary between model and command finds its clearest explanation in the instructional methods of the schools. Fifth, the exemplary pleasing everyone and not seeking one's own good in 10:33 are not easily passed over in favor of the command in 10:32 for the former are the burden of the exhortation of the letter up to and following this verse. Sixth, Michaelis offers no reason for not including 10:31 in the command. And in any case, the commands look to a general attitude and personal stance which need the specification given them throughout the letter in Paul's and other examples.

Thus, the obedience implied is not just to command in 10:32, as compared with Paul's obedience of Christ's will for his ministry. Rather, Paul calls for an obedience which will result in imitating his active concern for the common good (10:33), which he along with the community exercises with the spirit and mind of Christ (1:4-7, 22-25; 2:1-5, 16; 8:11).[14]

With regard to the categories describing the use of example used in this study, Michaelis finds specimen (fitting his "simple comparison") and prototype (promoting imitation) examples.[15] While examples can also add authority to the argument or exhortation, the notion of obedience advanced by Michaelis finds no precedent in the theoretical works surveyed earlier.

II. Paul's Use of Example in 1 Corinthians

After this overview of Michaelis' position, a closer look at example in 1 Corinthians will clarify the view adopted by this study.

A. The Exhortation Section, 1:10 - 4:21

The exhortation period in the first chapter of 1 Corinthians is unusual for its place at the start of the letter [16] (compare 1 Cor 16:15; Phil 4:2; Rom 12:1; 15:30, 16:17; 1 Thess 4:1, 10 and 5:14). And just as it lays the groundwork for Paul's argumentation in the first four chapters, its appearance, in a different formulation, in 4:16 closes the first part of the letter, which deals with the nature and difficulties of the Corinthian community. But while the exhortation section in 1 Corinthians is more than a polite request, friendly exhortation, or moral paraenesis, it does not treat the community's problems merely as a prelude to Paul's main interest in the body of the letter. Rather, the source of the community's divisiveness in chapters

---

[14] See also A. Dihle, *Die Goldene Regel: Eine Einführung in die Geschichte der antiken und frühchristlichen Vulgärethik* (Göttingen: Vandenhoeck & Ruprecht, 1962) 72-75.

[15] He also notes a typological use of O.T. examples at 10:1 ff. which the rhetoricians might refer to as "instructional precedents."

[16] See C.J. Bjerkelund, *Parakalô: Form, Funktion und Sinn der parakalô-Sätze in den paulinischen Briefen,* Bibliotheca Theologica Norvegica, 1 (Oslo: Universitetsforlaget, 1967) 141 ff.

1-4 is also at the root of the particular problems in 5-15. And the true model of Christian consciousness which Paul adduces to meet the difficulty in 1-4 remains the basis of his advice in the rest of the letter as well.[17]

B. *The Double Problem in the Opening Exhortation*

The first formulation of the exhortation (1:10) notes the community's *schismata* which are to be countered by stressing community of thought (*parakalō ... hina ... ēte ... katērtismenoi en tō$_i$ autō$_i$ noï kai en tē$_i$ autē$_i$ gnōmē$_i$*) and declaration (*to auto legēte pantes*). The second formulation of the exhortation (4:16) asks succinctly that the community take Paul as a model of imitation (*parakalō ... mimētai mou ginesthe*). They are both aimed at the double problem in the Corinthian community (or rather at the two faces of the same problem 3:3). The immediate situation seems to be a misapprehension of the relative merits of the community's teachers, which leads to factions grouped around different favorite personalities (1:12; 3–21). But this manifests a far-reaching failure in the community members' own self-estimation, with its exaggerated pretensions to knowledge (3:18-19) and faulty regard or denigration of others (4:6-7).[18].

In treating these two problems, Paul moves from the symptom to the cause. The first exhortation (1:10) addresses the fact of *schismata* but suggests a solution in terms of the community's growth and unity in knowledge and expression. The second exhortation (4:16) also seems to confront the *schismata* by designating the true model of their teacher and father. But this, too, although unspecified in the opening chapters, will be seen to proceed to the root cause of faulty wisdom and judgment when Paul applies his apostolic example to a variety of community problems. In fact, just as the movement in the first four chapters is from the particular instance of divisions to the underlying condition of erroneous wisdom and judgment, so too, in the letter as a whole, the instance of divisiveness and factions is dealt with in the first four chapters but the principles of the solution undergird the later discussion in 5-15.

C. *The Structure of 1:18 - 4:21*

A brief outline of the four opening chapters will make these generalities concrete. After the initial thanksgiving and exhortation (1:4-17), there follow three paradigmatic sections (1:18 - 2:5; 2:6 - 3:5; 3:6 - 4:5), each containing a

---

[17] Merk, 82-83, sees the exhortation as a protreptic to belief and contrasts the moral paraenesis in Phil 2:2; 4:2; Rom 12:16. For a close analysis of chaps. 1-4 and their place in the letter as a whole see N. Dahl "Paul and the Church at Corinth According to 1 Corinthians 1:10-4:21," *Studies in Paul* (Minneapolis: Augsburg, 1977) 40-61.

[18] Stanley, 871, divides the chapters into 2 sections: 1:18-3:4 on the false idea of Christian wisdom and 3:5-17 on the misconception of the apostolic vocation. See also Merk, 82-83, and Schulz, 310. The latter isolates Christ perfectionism as the community's principal fault.

general statement and one or two applications. A clarification of the meaning and purpose of the figurative language comes next and with it a questioning of the community's self-esteem by direct charge and contrast (4:6-13). Finally, Paul reiterates his exhortation, indicates how it is to be implemented, and challenges the obstinate (4:14-21).

In the first paradigmatic section (1:18 - 2:5), the general statement in the first plural (1:18-25) speaks of the apostolic *kerygma* of the cross and its contrast to the world's wisdom. Paul then, in the second plural, applies this general statement about the apostolic *kerygma* to the community's first call to faith (1:26-31). The same contrasts between foolishness and wisdom, weakness and strength, the world and God, which characterized the apostolic *kerygma,* now find a reflection in the person of the first Corinthian believers. Boasting is proper, but in the Lord only (1:31). Paul then reflects on himself (2:1-5 in the "I" and "you" form) and attributes his initial success not to his eloquence or wisdom (*hyperochēn logou ē sophias* 2:1 and *peithois sophias logois* 2:4), nor to his knowledge (*ou gar ekrina ti eidenai* 2:2), but to the crucified Jesus (2:2), his own weakness, fear and trembling (2:3), and to the demonstration of the spirit and of power (*apodeixei pneumatos kai dynameōs* 2:4). And so, it is on the power of God and not on the wisdom of men that their faith rests (2:5).

In the second paradigmatic section (2:6 - 3:5), the general statement considers *didaskalia* (2:13)[19] rather than *kērygma* (1:21). So Paul speaks of *teleiōsis* (2:6) and not of *klēsis* (1:21), and uses *laloumen* (2:6) rather than *kēryssomen* (1:23). Note the "we" form again. The Christian's spiritual gifts (2:12-13), spiritual discrimination (2:14-15), and heavenly knowledge of the mystery (2:7, 16) stand in contrast to human wisdom (2:13) and the earthly man's ignorance (2:14) and consequent lack of discerning power (2:15). The message is painfully clear in Paul's application (again "I" and "you") when he explains his failure to move beyond the elementary stage of discourse with the infantile (*nēpiois*) and too human (*sarkinois* 3:1; sarkikoi 3:3; *anthrōpoi* 3:4) Corinthians. The divisiveness is a sign of their immaturity (3:3) in Christian understanding.

The third paradigmatic section (3:6 - 4:5) speaks explicitly of the apostolic laborers named in the slogans (1:12). Here Paul does not use the "we" form since he names both himself and Apollos. And while all are equally co-workers with God (3:9) there is a distinction of function according to one's gifts (3:5). Consequently, in God's field (3:9) Paul plants and Apollos waters (3:5) while for God's building (3:9) Paul lays the foundation and someone else builds upon it (3:10). The harmony of the apostles directly contrasts with the factions claiming one or other as their favorite, just as the reservation of judgment for a later time

---

[19] Paul uses teaching language but not the noun *didaskalia* here. For the notion of Pauline teaching in the Pastoral Epistles see J.D. Quinn, "On the Terminology for Faith, Truth, Teaching, and the Spirit in the Pastoral Epistles: A Summary" in P.C. Empie et al., eds., *Teaching Authority and Infallibility in the Church: Lutherans and Catholics in Dialogue VI* (Minneapolis: Augsburg, 1980) 235-236.

(3:13-15) contrasts with the premature (4:5) and unfounded (4:7) judgment being carried out in the community.

The first application (3:16-23) identifies the community (in the "I" and "you" form) with the temple of God and of his spirit. From this follows the specific admonitions against pretensions to worldly wisdom, by contrasting it to the "foolish" wisdom of God (3:18-20), and against boasting (3:21).

A second application (4:1-5) has to do with the community's estimation of the apostolic laborers. Rather than see them as factional heroes, Paul insists that the community see them for what they are, i.e., trustworthy servants of Christ and stewards of God's mysteries (4:12). As before, he then turns to himself alone and speaks of God's judgment to come as the only one that matters (thus he applies to himself the principle enunciated in 2:15).

It would be superfluous to do more than note the fact that the double problem of factionalism and imperfect wisdom and judgment, which were the clear objects of the opening exhortation, are treated throughout these three paradigmatic sections. Moreover, wisdom and judgment are stressed as the source of the community's difficulties. The function of Paul's example in the light of these problems is also more readily grasped, for Paul repeatedly calls attention to his personal situation vis-à-vis the community in light of their wisdom and judgment. By comparison in the first application (2:1-5) and contrast in the next two (3:1-4 and 4:1-5) he calls attention to those aspects of his example which he calls to be imitated in the second exhortation.

Then, too, Paul associates his own model with that of the other apostolic preachers and teachers. He names Apollos in the third paradigmatic section, and the same collaborator could be behind the "we" in the first two sections. In the third of these references Paul most directly contests the community's factions, while the misapplication of wisdom and judgment is the burden of the first two.

At 4:6 Paul explicitly states the reason for his reference to himself and Apollos as examples: i.e., *hina en hēmin mathēte to mē hyper ha gegraptai hina mē heis hyper tou henos physiousthe kata tou heterou.* A teaching lesson is clearly in evidence, but it is closely associated with cultivation of a proper attitude. The same didactic-paraenetic link has already been seen in the comments above on Michaelis' interpretation of 1 Cor 4, 16. Is there reason to apply this explanation of purpose and, more importantly, methodology (teaching by example) to the whole of the first four chapters and not just to the third paradigmatic section (3:6 - 4:5)?

D. *The Relationship of 4:6 to 1:10 - 4:5*

There are indications in 1:10-4:5 that more is involved in the verb *meteschēmatisa* than the exemplary use of the analogy of apostolic laborers, and that the antecedent of *tauta* is more than the analogy immediately preceding it.

In the first place, figurative language is found throughout the four chapters [20] and helps describe the situation of early *kerygma* and unsuccessful *didaskalia* as well as the apostolic cooperation. The other figures like irony, hyperbole, and metaphor can be related to *logos eschēmatismenos* in its strict, rhetorical sense,[21] i.e., an artifice of dissimulation or fiction, of making an oblique reference to a delicate subject, which thereby becomes hidden by "color" or covered by *schēma,* so as not to offend the listeners. Then, too, the model or limit to be learned (*to mē hyper ha gegraptai*) cannot be restricted to the laborers' analogy. Indeed, in each paradigmatic section Paul presents the general picture of apostolic labor and his own situation and he evaluates the community against these. Moreover, the problem of factionalism arising from pride and faulty judgment (*heis hyper tou henos physiousthe kata tou heterou,* 4:6) was seen above to run throughout the first four chapters (1:29-31; 3:21) and does not just appear in the third paradigmatic section. Fourth, Paul and Apollos could very well be the "we" of the first two paradigmatic sections. The opening slogans (1:10) introduce their names. Paul make no pretensions to being the unique kerygmatic teacher (Rom 15:20) and Apollos had an independent ministry to the Jews (Acts 18:24-28). Paul also admits a community of spiritual gifts in 2:12, spelled out in the laborer's analogy. One might then agree with Parry [22] who refers *tauta* to the whole of the preceding argument, going back to the slogans and factions.

But is Parry also correct in assigning the faction apologetic a primary role in the four chapters? The suggestion above was that it is a double problem that Paul faces in these opening chapters. The relatively simple matter of factions would readily be met by the laborers' analogy, which presents the community's teachers

---

[20] E.g. apostrophe (1:10, 26; 2:1; 3:1; 4¡6); anthropomorphism (3:6-7); hyperbole (1:13; 2:2; 3:22; 4:11-13); irony (4:8-9); contrast (1:23-25; 2:1, 5; 3:14-15; 4:10); metaphors, similes, allegories (1:24, 26 ff., 30; 3:2, 5 ff., 16; 4:1, 5).

[21] See J. Ernesti, *"schēmatizein,"* *Lexicon technologiae Graecorum rhetoricae* (Leipzig: Caspar Fritsch, 1795) 341, and D. Schenkeveld, *Studies in Demetrius on Style* (Amsterdam: A.M. Hakkert, 1964) 117. The terms *eschēmatismenē* (*hypothesis*) or "veiled argument, covert allusion" and *schēmatizein logon* or "to compose a speech with veiled meaning" became standard in the rhetorical glossary. Cf. W. Wright, trans., *Philostratus and Eunapius,* LCL (London: W. Heinemann, 1922) 570. The use of this manner of discourse is discussed by Quintilian *Inst.* 9.1.4, 27 (H.E. Butler, trans., *The institutio Oratoria of Quintilian,* LCL, 4 vols. [London: W. Heinemann, 1920]) and Philostratus *VS* 1.21.11(218/514); 25.24(228/532; 2.1.27-28(235/547); 2.17(271/620). For a less technical use of the terminology, compare Quintilian *Inst.* 9.1.14; 8.6.44; 9.2.46, 65. For mention of figures of speech associated with covert allusion see Dionysius of Halicarnassus, *Rh.* 9.323, 1 (H. Usener & L. Radermacher, eds., *Dionysii Halicarnasei quae extant,* 6 vols. [Leipzig: B.G. Teubner, 1904-29] and Quintilian *Inst.* 9.2.44, 65 (irony); *Inst.* 9.2.3 and 8.3.83 (hyperbole); and the passages noted above for a less technical use of the terminology (metaphors, similes, analogies).

[22] R. Parry, *The First Epistle of Paul the Apostle to the Corinthians* (Cambridge: Cambridge University, 1916) 44.

in harmonious service of God and thereby undercuts the elevation of one over another. The statements of wisdom and judgment, which appear in the application sections (3:16-23 and 4:1-5), have more in common with the apostolic preaching of the cross (1:18-25) and with the gifts of wisdom and discernment among the perfect (2:6-16). The analogy addresses itself to these matters only indirectly. And so, it is not just that a figure is applied to Paul and Apollos for the community's instruction on the matter of factions. Rather, Paul and Apollos become figures themselves, to which the community are to look for their own improvement (*hina en hēmin mathēte* 4:6). And the figures are to be found in each of the three paradigmatic sections, with the general statements, about the apostles, offering the community an oblique chastisement or exhortation with regard to the surface problem of factions and its underlying cause of faulty wisdom and judgment.

Here, Paul proceeds not out of fear for his *asphaleia* (for he inevitably makes his charges clear), but out of *euprepeia* and with respect for the dignity of the persons charged with faults.[23] Conscious that they might take it ill if their sins are accused outright, Paul proceeds with their censure and paraenesis to improvement by indirection, at least in part. He praises them in their past goodness (1:26-28) and refers to himself and Apollos as exemplary apostolic laborers in order to incite the wayward to emulation[24] and to a desire of like

---

[23] These are cited by the rhetoricians among the motives for employing covert allusion. See Dionysius of Halicarnassus *Rh.* 9.341 and 8.281; Demetrius *Eloc.* 288 (W.R. Roberts, trans., *Demetrius 'On Style,'* LCL [London: W. Heinemann, 1932] and G.M.A. Grube, *A Greek Critic: Demetrius on Style* [Toronto: University of Toronto, 1961]); Hermogenes 4.13 (H. Rabe, ed., *Hermogenis opera* [Leipzig: B.G. Teubner, 1913]); Quintilian *Inst.* 9.2.65.

[24] Demetrius, 292, and Dionysius, 9. 324 and 327 speak of the paraenetic use of figured speech or covert allusion. The meaning of *to mē hyper ha gegraptai* is much discussed. W. Wallis, "Ein neuer Auslegungsversuch des Stelle 1 Cor 4, 6," *TLZ* 75 (1950) 506-8, summarizes the theories of a scribal gloss, a scriptural reference, or a current saying, and he shows their inadequacies. He suggests putting a comma after *hyper* and reading *mē hyper* as a *Schlagwort* akin to *nihil nimis*. Parry links the phrase with contractual language in papyri. Hence he translates "not to go beyond the terms" as teacher. H. Schlier, "*hypodeigma*," *TDNT* 2 (1964) 32-33, suggests the practice in Hellenistic grammar schools whereby the teachers "write under" or "trace letters for children to write over" (see also LSJ and Plato *Prot.* 326D, *hoi grammatistai tois mēpō deinois graphein tōn paidōn hypograpsantes tēi graphidi* C.W. Lamb, trans., *Plato. Laches, Protagoras, Meno, Euthydemus,* LCL [London: W. Heinemann, 1924]. The same type of exercise seems to lie behind Clement of Alexandria *Strom.* 5.5.49.1 *alla kai tritos hypogrammos pheretai paidikos-marpte sphinx klōps zbychthēdon* although W. Dindorf, ed. *Clementis Alexandrini opera,* 4 vols. (Oxford: Clarendon, 1869) sees this as a grammarian's model for memory or pronunciation exercises, vol. 4, 350.

Seneca refers to the same penmanship practice of imitating a model of the letters in *Ep.* 94.51 (R.M. Gummere, trans., *Lucius Annaeus Seneca. Ad Lucilium epistulae morales,* LCL, 3 vols. [London: W. Heinemann, 1917]). *hypographō* then becomes used for delineating an archetype or rhetorical practice for others to follow, Dionysius *Is.* 628.6 (S. Usher, ed.,

praise (4:5). Thus, it is not *metus* but *pudor* which will prompt a change in their attitude.[25]

If the rhetorical device hits the mark, then the factionalists will re-evaluate their attitude toward the teachers in the light of the image of their harmony in 3:5-15. And they will also re-estimate their own wisdom and judgment in the light of their own initial acceptance of the *kerygma* of the cross (1:26-31) and with respect to the apostolic example both in the *kerygma* (1:18-25) and in the *didaskalia* (2:6-16).

One might object that while the figurative allusion is to the example of Paul and Apollos together, the personal application by Paul to himself intrudes regularly (2:1-5; 3:1-5; 4:3-5) until it supplants that of the joint laborers in 4:14-21 (and that right after the impassioned description of the common apostolic toils in 4:9-13). One also wonders how the paraenetic covert allusion to the common apostolic example *hina en hēmin mathēte* (4:6) can be reconciled with Paul's open censures and exhortations (cf. 2:5; 3:1-4, 18, 21; 4:1, 2, 6-13).

Perhaps a way to a resolution of the difficulties can be found in the dual nature of the community problem as treated in the first four chapters. The problem of factionalism is an outgrowth of the faulty wisdom and judgment in the community. The negation of factionalism rests on a positive growth in wisdom and judgment (1:10; 3:1-4; 3:18; 4:5). The common apostolic model, while applied to wisdom (1:18-25; 2:6-16) and judgment (2:13-15), is more apt for undercutting the factional lionizing of one teacher over another by depicting their harmonious cooperation with the particularized gifts from (3:5-15). The fundamental qualities of wisdom and judgment are taken by Paul as his special responsibility, since he alone laid the foundations of the community's faith (2:1-5; 3:10-11).[26] The intrusion of Paul's example in these first chapters leads to its exclusive application in the rest of the letter, as the fundamental issue of the community's wisdom and judgment is faced in a variety of settings. *Mimēsis* and *metaschēmatisis* merge, and the virtuous example that Paul urges the community to imitate emerges as his

---

Dionysius of Halicarnassus. The Critical Essays, LCL [Cambridge: Harvard University, 1974]). The *paradeigma* is also applied to following laws (the context of the quote from Plato *Prot.* 326A). A king might outline (*hypographōn*) in his own character the moral habits he wishes the state to adopt, Plato *Leg.* 4.711B (R.G. Bury, trans., *Plato. Laws,* LCL, 2 vols. [London: W. Heinemann, 1926]). Clement of Alexandria sees God as the perfect *paidagōgos nēpiōn* for he offers himself as the *hypogrammon* that he wishes us to follow. The advantage of seeing the phrase in 1 Cor 4:6 in terms of a school exercise is that this preserves the rhetorical harmony of the context and provides a parallel in usage as far as character imitation goes. The exact phrase, unfortunately, has yet to be located in a rhetorical handbook.

[25] Quintilian *Inst.* 9.2.76.

[26] Plutarch *Prof. virt.* 85Ff. (F.C. Babbitt, trans., *Plutarch's Moralia,* LCL, 15 vols. [London: W. Heinemann, 1926] offers a striking parallel to the analogy of edification by the virtuous man with a variety of materials upon a golden foundation. He concludes by asserting that such a person speaks clearly and without the need to *metaschēmatizein.*

own. Paul's life and teaching become a metaphor for the community's striving, as they seek to become like their founder and father.

As for Paul's direct criticisms and admonitions, the ironical and critical characterizations of the community (3:1-4 and 4:6-13) depict the shadow image of the apostolic image being promoted. They also contrast with the idealized picture of the community from its early days (1:26-31). As such, they complement the paraenesis by example in these chapters. The declarations of what to do and what to avoid also complement the paraenesis by specifying its parameters.

E. *The Conclusion of the Exhortation and the Positing of the Apostolic Example*

Paul mitigates any harshness in tone in the preceding exhortation by his statement of intent in 4:14 (*ouk entrepōn ... alla ... nouthetōn*) and by his favorable application of the child-father relationship (note *agapēta* and contrast 3:1-4) to the community and to himself. This is not an unusual figure,[27] but Paul invests it with particular significance in view of his relationship to the community.[28] He presents himself not as a co-worker among others with God, but as father of the community. And it is this fatherly concern for their well-being that turns the *entropē* to *nouthesia*.[29] Just as in 1 Cor 11:27 ff. Paul considers the divine afflictions as aimed at the community's correction, so here his paternal admonitions look toward community reform.[30]

What form do these admonitions take? Paul leaves the *tauta* unspecified in 4:14 and the demonstrative pronoun seems to refer most directly to the stinging contrasts and irony of the immediately preceding verses (4:7-13). However, the admonitions referred to in 4:14 seem a concomitant of Paul's special, paternal relationship with the community (4:15) and are associated with the apostole's own example (4:16). The special relationship shines through from the first discussion of Paul's founding *kerygma* to the community (2:1-5) and recurs throughout the

---

[27] E.g. Epictetus *Diss.* 3.22.95 (W.A. Oldfather, trans., *Epictetus. The Discourses as Reported by Arrian, the Manual and Fragments,* LCL [London: W. Heinemann, 1926]) says that the person who is *philos tois theois, hypēretēs* and *metechōn tēs archēs tou Dios* puts himself under the direction of Zeus and of destiny and can speak to his *adelphous* and *tekna,* not as one meddling in other people's affairs but as one who *episkopē ... ta idia.*

[28] Conzelmann, *I Corinthians,* 91, notes that Paul is not speaking metaphorically but in a proper sense. But it seems rather that Paul is obviously using a figure in a highly charged way. Stanley, 860 and *passim,* finds this special relationship with the community to be the basis of Paul's call to imitate him repeatedly throughout his letters (2 Thess 3:7; Gal 4:12; Phil 3:17 and 4:9; Acts 20:35, [2 Tim 3:10]). See also Gutierrez, 178-79.

[29] *entrepein* is also used at 1 Cor 6:5 and 15:34; 2 Thess 3:14; Titus 3:8; where shame is intended. But in 1 Corinthians and 2 Thessalonians, both addressing the community, the end is not the shame but rather a change of heart, much like the *nouthesia* of 1 Cor 4:14. Stanley notes that the use of *tekna* occurs only three times in Paul's letters (here 2 Cor 6:13 and Gal 4:19) in similar contexts of affectionate urging.

[30] Gutierrez, 188-93.

four chapters (1:16-17; 3:1-4; 3:7; 3:10-11). And the Pauline model is established both in conjunction with Apollos (1:18-25; 2:6-16; 3:5-15) and, more particularly, alone (2:1-5; 3:1-4; 4:3-6). The reference to the model or example is not unusual in rhetorical and philosophical instruction, although in the latter case the instructor offers himself as a model comparatively rarely.[31] The function of shame in admonition aimed at improvement, and even the contrast between teacher and pedagogue are also to be found in the philosophical traditions of Paul's time.[32]

Furthermore, a look at the subject matter of the criticism intended for the community's improvement will help to determine the antecedent of *tauta*. In the preceding paragraph the link between the *nouthesia* and the Pauline example was noted. But a look at 4:7-13 and the supposed antecedents of *tauta* there will show that the faults criticized there (unwarranted distinctions in the community 4:7, security and boasting in one's wisdom 4:8, 10, and even the pride of social standing implicit in the terms used in 4:10 when compared with like "sociological" vocabulary in 1:26-28)[33] have been seen to be recurrent in the whole expository section. In form, too, admonition runs throughout the four chapters in direct reference to the Corinthians' less than ideal condition (4:8 ff.; 1:10 ff., 3:1-4; 3:16-17; 4:3) and also in the imperative form (4:16 but already used in 1:31; 3:18; 4:1,5). There is also a more didactic form of admonition by way of recalling principles already transmitted to the community (4:7 and already in 1:26; 3:1-3; 3:16).

The *tauta* can then be taken to refer to the admonitions of the whole hortatory section. These admonitions are varied in form and are all aimed at improvement of the community, with Paul's own example as a global touchstone for community thought and practice. It would be helpful to recall some characteristics in the Greek, particularly the Hellenistic, rhetorical and philosophical tradition of the philosopher and father as exemplar and thereby to highlight Paul's unique application of this common image.

F. *Paul's Use of Example in the Light of Rhetorical and Philosophical Tradition*

Often the philosophers and rhetoricians refer to the example of others (great men in history or literature, or more recent figures noted for excellence in their life or

---

[31] In addition to the discussion on 33-35 above, see also C. Walz, *Rhetores Graeci,* 9 vols. (Stuttgart/Tübingen: J.G. Cotta, 1835) 6, *Anon. Proleg. Rhet.* 34,15, *paradeigma esti progegonos pragmatos parathesis kath'homoiotēta tōn hypokeimenōn pros parainesin protropēs ē apotropēs heneken.*

[32] See the discussion on 40-41 above and Plutarch *Virt. mor.* 452C-D where exhortation and censure accomplish conversion and a sense of shame. See also Quintilian *Inst.* 9.2.76 and Dio Chrysostom *Or.* 72, 9-10 (J.W. Cohoon, trans., *Dio Chrysostom,* LCL, 5 vols. [London: W. Heinemann, 1932]). The latter also compares this method to the pupils' clash with their pedagogues, as also Seneca *Ep.* 11.8.

[33] See G. Theissen, "Soziale Schichtung in der korinthischen Gemeinde," *ZNW* 65 (1974) 232-72. E. Judge, "The Early Christians as a Scholastic Community," in *JRH* 1

art) for their pupils to adopt for their own improvement.[34]   But they offer themselves, too, as paradigms for their pupils.[35] The notion of imitation is linked with fatherhood as well, whether it is God who is conceived of as father,[36] or one's ancestors or natural father,[37] or those who teach noble living.[38] This last category, in which the proposed model combines father and teacher lies behind the Pauline exemplar (4:15 and 17).

The realization of the model in the life of the imitators comes with effort and exercise, whereby they pass from a state of immaturity to perfection and clarity of perception.[39] As seen above, the teacher's example acts in concert with his words, by way of exhortation and shame, as a spur to the listener's ardor and purpose,[40] and it also serves to encourage him in the hope that the end can be attained.[41] Indeed, there is also talk of *synaskēsis* of both teacher and pupil.[42]   Love and

(1960-61) 4 ff., connects the elevated class status of at least part of the Pauline communities with a scholastic interest much like that of other groups gathered around sophists and professional rhetoricians. This would account for Paul's use of rhetorical devices in dealing with their problems and would also establish the grounds for further development in the post-Pauline communities of the Pastoral Epistles.

[34] See the discussion above on 27, 30, 32, 35-36 and also Plutarch *Prof. virt.* 84C; Philo *Cong.* 69-70. For more remote witnesses see Isocrates *Ad. Dem.* 2, 8, 36, 51; *Nic.* 13; *Panath.* 136-37; *Antid.* 205, 208; *Paneg.* 82 (G. Norlin, trans., *Isocrates,* LCL, 3 vols. [London: W. Heinemann, 1928]); and Plato *Prot.* 326A.

[35] See the discussion on 33-35 above on the practice of rhetoricians to exemplify their art and proper moral conduct. See also Dio Chrysostom *Or.* 55.4-5 and 18.21; Epictetus *Diss.* 3.21.1-6; Seneca *Ep.* 94.49; Plutarch *De se ipsum citro inv.* 544D, 15-F *fin;* Ps-Diogenes *Ep.* 15 (108.17) and 18 (110.17) (A.J. Malherbe, ed. and intr., *The Cynic Epistles: A Study Edition.* SBL Sources for Biblical Study, 12 [Missoula: Scholars Press for SBL, 1977]); as well as the older Isocrates *Adv. sophist.* 17-18; Xenophon *Mem.* 1.6.1 (E.C. Marchant, trans., *Xenophon. Memorabilia,* LCL [London: W. Heinemann, 1923]); Plato *Smp.* 209B-C (C.W. Lamb, trans., *Plato. Symposium,* LCL [London: W. Heinemann, 1925]), which single out this quality in a good teacher. Some even approach Paul's bold and direct citation of his own example. Cf. Seneca *Ep.* 6.5; Ps-Diogenes *Ep.* 33 (140.31); 15 (108.14); 38 (160.28); 46 (176.7); and Isocrates *Antid.* 239, 273. Ps-Diogenes also "sends" pedagogues to establish their charges in the life practices they themselves pursue, *Ep.* 29 (124.19 ff.).

[36] See Philo *Sac.* 68 and *Congr.* 177 (which mentions *nouthesia*).

[37] See Philo *Conf.* 63 and also Isocrates *Philip* 113; *Ad Dem.* 9.11.

[38] See Philo *Conf.* 149; Lucretius *Rer. nat.* 3.5; 6.35 (C. Bailey, ed. and trans., *De rerum natura libri sex,* 3 vols. [Oxford: Clarendon, 1947]); and also Isocrates *Ep.* 8.10. Gutierrez, 51, cites Theognis *Elegies* 1.1049 but with some reserve.

[39] See Plutarch *Prof. virt.* 85B which ties example with progress; Philo *Congr.* 19 (start with milky food), 27 (contest imagery), 81 and 135 (maturing in knowledge of virtue and vice and in perception); Ps-Diogenes *Ep.* 30 *passim* and 28 (the beginning of poverty, given by the teacher, must be safeguarded by the pupil).

[40] See also Plutarch *Prof. virt.* 84C and *De se ipsum citra inv.* 544F 16.

[41] See Plutarch *De se ipsum citra inv.* 544E and *Prof. virt.* 84C.

[42] See Ps-Diogenes *Ep.* 9 (102.12). Michaelis, 668 misreads Paul's "imperfection" in Phil 3:12 ff. as an indication that Paul demands obedience rather than imitation. It is preci-

affection for the *diathesis* of those whose deeds are being emulated is a sign of advancement, while the opposite is true when the disciples exhibit *philoneikia* and *phthonos* toward their betters and a chafing at another's *doxa* and *dynamis* with no regard for his *aretē*.[43]   And while the teacher's presence is desirable, a letter is a comparable substitute for a face to face encounter.[44]   Discourses too can present the model for imitation.[45]

These details are echoed in 1 Corinthians.   Growth is a concern for Paul who uses the child's food image (3:2) in criticizing the Corinthians' failure to mature. But his example of perfection in 2:6-16 bolsters his exhortation to this maturity (1:10 *katērtismenoi en tōᵢ autōᵢ noï* and 3:18 *hina genētai sophos;* also 14:20) by indicating that the ideal has been reached by some.   Factionalism is taken as a sign of a lack of progress (3:3-4), while love signals growth (13, 2 and 11).   Paul even alludes to a sort of *synaskēsis* (13:12-13; 9:25-27).   And while he plans to come himself (4:19), he uses the letter to present the model in the meantime.[46]

In the call to imitation, both as to its purpose and to the details of the exhortation, Paul reflects usage found in Hellenistic philosophers and rhetoricians.   But, is there anything distinctive in Paul's usage of himself as model?

G. *Distinctiveness in Paul's Use of Example*

In Rabbinic tradition, if someone teaches the son of another the Torah, it is as if he had begotten him (b. Sanh 19b).[47]   And in 1 Cor 4:15 Paul replaces the Torah with the gospel as the matrix of generation.[48]   So Paul is not just presenting him-

---

sely the struggle that is to be imitated. Stanley, 862, calls attention to the *syn*-compounds in connection with the gradual assimilation to the "image" of Christ. See also A. Reiff, *"Interpretatio, imitatio, aemulatio: Begriff und Vorstellung Literarischer Abhängigkeit bei den Römern"* (Diss. Cologne, 1959) for the Roman idea that imitation by virtuous struggle makes one *con-simile*, not *simile*.

[43] See Plutarch *Prof. virt.* 84E. He goes on to speak of the advanced person's eagerness to take on the characteristics of good men and even not to shrink before exile, imprisonment, penury, prosecution (and compare the catalogue of hardships at 1 Cor 4:13). See A.J. Malherbe, "Hellenistic Moralists and the New Testament," *ANRW*, W. Haase, ed. (Berlin: de Gruyter, forthcoming) II.26, for *peristasis*-catalogues in Hellenistic moralists.

[44] See Ps-Diogenes *Ep.* 3 (94.9) and the discussion of Seneca on 87-90 above. The Socratic epistles have been seen on 128-32 to indicate great reliance on the letter form for their exhortation.

[45] Isocrates *Evag.* 75. But, as shown above on 56-57 the discourses are "sent" and function much like letters.

[46] He also sends Timothy as Ps-Diogenes sends pedagogues to Dionysius in *Ep.* 29 (126.2-35).

[47] I. Epstein, ed., J. Schachter & H. Freedman, trans., *Hebrew-English Edition of the Babylonian Talmud* (London: Soncino, 1960).

[48] Gutierrez, 125, and cf. O. Betz, "Die Geburt der Gemeinde durch den Lehrer," *NTS* 3 (1956-57) 314-26.

self as a paradigm of virtue in a moralistic way but refers to his fatherhood of the community, i.e., to the fact that he alone established among them the pattern of Christian living from the first days of their faith.[49] And life according to this pattern is not just a moral struggle toward virtue, but has to do with the appropriation of salvation and the gifts of the spirit offered the community by Christ (1:18 *hēmin sōzomenois;* 1:30 *hos egenēthē sophia hēmin ... dikaiosynē te kai hagiasmos kai apolytrōsis* 2:7 *sophian en mystēriō*$_i$; 2:12 *ta hypo tou theou charisthenta hēmin;* 2:16 *hēmeis de noun Christou echomen;* 3:16 *naos theou este kai to pneuma tou theou en hymin oikei;* 3:23 *panta hymōn, hymeis de Christou*).[50] The father-child image therefore indicates a real community of nature *en Christō*$_i$ (4:15, 17) between the founding apostle and the community called to grow in resemblance of him.[51] Paul calls for imitation, then, as a consequence (*oun* 4:16) of his fatherhood of the community in Christ.

The fatherly example to be imitated is to be found in *hai hodoi* and in the common teaching of Paul (see also 7:17; 11:16; 14:33, 36), which Timothy will recall for the Corinthians (4:17). But how are two sources of instruction related? It seems *hodos* refers to a person's way of life, and thus 13:1 mentions the *kath'hyperbolēn*, which is the way a loving person acts (see also 3:3). And it is a way which Paul demonstrates (*deiknymi*), recalling like demonstrations of his procedures and convictions in 2:4; 4:9; and 4:19-20. And this demonstration of Paul's way of life becomes explicit in his many precepts (1:10, 31; 3:21; 4:1, 5, 16; 5:9, 12, 13; 6:18, 20; 7 *passim;* 8:9; 10:10, 12; etc.). But the halakic instruction is accompanied by more properly didactic reminders and declarations (1:18 ff. the folly of the kerygma of the cross; 2:12, 16 and 3:21 the spiritual gifts; 3:16 and chaps. 5 and 6; 9:13; 24 the recurrent *ouk oidate* formula recalling teachings the community should be aware of).

Again, precept and instruction delineate the content and conduct of the Christian life.[52] The example of the founding apostle breathes life into this and provides his community with a stimulus and a hope of emulating Paul and thereby attaining the salvation promised in Christ. The doctrine and precepts specify the imitation that Paul desires, as he treats the community's difficulties.[53] Not that

---

[49] de Boer, 145-46, 153.

[50] de Boer, 90 and Lofthouse, 339.

[51] de Boer, 79. It seems that Merk, 86-87, restricts the imitation too much when he associates it with the attitude of the apostle as shown in 4:9-13. While that is the most obvious antecedent of *tauta,* it has been suggested that the whole presentation of wisdom and judgment in chaps. 1-4 is referred to by the demonstrative pronoun. Consequently, the example includes the recurrent self-references to Paul's labors in *kerygma* and *didaskalia,* as well as to the attitude of humility and long-suffering in 4:9-13.

[52] Similarly J. Moffatt, *The First Epistle of Paul to the Corinthians* (London: Hodder & Stoughton, 1951) 146. Cf. Dio Chrysostom *Or.* 55.13.

[53] L. Nieder, 81. n. 41 citing Bonnard. As argued above, Michaelis lays too much stress on the "solid core of Paul's teaching" and obedient acceptance of Paul's *didachē,* 668.

Paul seeks a servile and minute imitation. Rather he wants the community to acquire the deepest and most central attitudes of the Christian life and apply them properly in particular cases.[54] Some examples of this are offered below in the discussion of the use of the Pauline model in the latter part of the letter.

Paul distinguishes between himself and the many pedagogues (4:15) in the community. And he sends Timothy (4:16) to remind the Corinthians of his ways and teachings, until he himself comes. What is the relation of the pedagogue to the master? Where does Apollos fit into the scheme? Does this indicate why Paul stresses his own example over the common apostolic model?

Here and in Gal 3:14 the pedagogue plays a subordinate and assisting role to the teacher, but in no way is it valued negatively.[55] Note how Timothy's role is described. He is not himself the teacher Paul but he stands in the same relationship of affection (*agapētos* 4:17) and filiation (*teknon* 4:17) with him as does the Corinthian community (4:14). Moreover, he is *pistos* (4:17), a quality with which Paul says any steward would like to be credited (4:2). And his work is done *en kyriō̧*, as is Paul's (4:17). The same collaboration in the Lord is noted at 16:10. And there Paul warns that the community not belittle him (16:11).

In 16:12 Apollos is mentioned. He, too, is a co-worker of God together with Paul (3:5-15).[56] But strangely enough there is no indication of warmth between him and Paul. His subordination to Paul is clearly stressed in the laborers' analogy (3:5-15), but the reason for his not coming to Corinth despite Paul's urging is not given. The negative will of God and the infelicitous circumstances alluded to in 16:12 might be connected with lingering factionalism which Apollos' presence might re-ignite, especially while Paul is still absent. Perhaps it was the volatile community situation that also leads Paul to straddle the fence and both counter exaggerated praise of one or other apostolic figure by the paradigms of apostolic collaboration and at the same time stress his own unique position as father and standard of the community's life and belief.[57]

The use Paul makes of his example in instructing the community reveals that he does his own way of life before them for imitation, at least in part. But it is not the general Christian conduct which teaches everywhere (de Boer, 146-47). Rather a balance in interpretation is to be sought between life-style and its specification in precept and doctrine.

[54] Gutierrez, 183. Cf. Isocrates *Nic.* 6 and *Philip* 114.

[55] Cf. Ps-Diogenes *Ep.* 29 (126.3-7 and 128.13) for a favorable view of pedagogues for their severity, see Ps-Diogenes *Ep.* 29 (128.15 ff.); *Ep.* 40 (170.24 ff.); and Seneca *Ep.* 11. Contrast Paul's benign view of the pedagogue with Moffatt's characterization of him as an interloper of low character, 51. For this view, see also Plato *Lysis* 233A-B and *Prot.* 325C.

[56] H. Meyer, *Critical and Exegetical Handbook to the Corinthians,* trans., D. Bannerman (New York; Funk and Wagnalls, 1884) identifies the pedagogues of chap. 4 with the *potizontes* and *epoikodomountes* of chap, 3.

[57] Meyer, 124, and Wendland, 41.

H. *Additional Call to Imitate Christ*

In 11:1 Paul expands the parameters of imitation when he adds to the command *mimētai mou ginesthe* the rider *kàgō Christou*. The Christ element is not absent from 4:14-21 as the horizon of the community's faith and of the apostles' labor (4:15 *paidagōgous ... en Christō_i* and *en ... Christō_i ... egennēsa;* 4:17 *piston en Kyriō_i* and *tas hodous mou tas en Christō_i*).[58]   But Paul in 1 Corinthians seems to envisage an imitation of Christ mediated by imitation of the community's father.[59]

The imitation is specified by verses 31-33. A similar exhortation, only without the association with Christ, is found at 9:19-23. Here Paul's positive identification with Jews and Gentiles offers a clear example of what the command in 10:32; "Give no offense to Jews or to Greeks or to the Church of God," implies. This connection v. 33 verifies, and that verse also points to the same motivation of the general good for Paul's self-effacement (9:22b-23). Here Paul calls this common good salvation.

On the other side of the coin, an insistence on the prerogatives of superior knowledge leads to the destruction of weaker individuals in the community (8:11). This is directly opposed to Christ's death on their behalf and Paul's determination not to do the things which might cause his brother to fall. The reference to Christ is as fleeting here as it is at 11:1 but it seems related paradigmatically to the self-effacement on behalf of others which Paul practices and which he urges on the Corinthians.

This self-effacement on behalf of "weaker" members of the community, which Paul presents here as a paradigm for the attitude of the community, he speaks of at the opening of the letter as his own kerygmatic method (1:26-29 and 2:1-5). The references at 8:10-11 to the ambivalence of knowledge, at 8:11 to Christ's death, at 9:22 and 10:33 to salvation, and at 9:23 to the gospel confirm the link between the principles resolving the food issue in chaps. 8-10 and Paul's description of the presuppositions and aims of his first preaching in Corinth. There is a methodological link in the attention Paul calls to his own example in both sections. The opening chapters also help understand what he might mean by the rider attached to 11:1; i.e., *kathōs kàgō Christou*.

At 2:2 Paul declares that he limited his knowledge to "Jesus Christ and Him crucified," and identified with the "weak" (2:3). In this he became like the weak and foolish of the Corinthian community (1:26-27) and gave this expression in content and form in a kerygma informed not by Greek wisdom but by divine power (2:4-5). That Paul sees his own attitude and action as a pattern for the community is clear from 3:18-19.

---

[58] The Christ element mediated by the apostle's work is also seen in 1:17, 23; 2:1, 16; 3:1; 4:1. For the community's faith see 1:30; 3:1, 11, 23.

[59] Stanley, *passim,* and de Boer, 165, who notes other instances of direct appeal to Christ (Phil 2:5) or to Paul alone with no reference to Christ (Phil 3:17).

Looking in the other direction, Paul contrasts the wisdom of God and worldly wisdom (2:20-21). Paul claims to understand God's gifts and spiritual truths because of his possession of the revealing and teaching spirit (2:10-13). As a consequence of receiving this spirit Paul can comprehend the thoughts of God (2:11) and can declare that he has the "mind of Christ" (2:16). This is not a private possession but Paul imparts this understanding in spiritually informed teaching (2:13). In short, Paul has been schooled in a way of understanding that is like that of the spirit of God and he seeks to establish the same mode of understanding in those reached by his preaching and teaching.

Paul's evangelical commission came from Christ, as did also the mode of its exercise not in eloquent wisdom but in the power of God. The word of the cross contradicts human wisdom (1:18) and its significance is impervious to the "rulers of this age" (2:8). Indeed, the cross is equated with the gospel (1:17) and as such is itself a dramatic proclamation of God's power. Paul's spoken kerygma succeeds and proclaims this gospel of the cross. Paul, thus, does not just have the spiritual understanding, which he calls the mind of Christ, he also exercises a gospel ministry which declares verbally what Christ declared dramatically.

Moreover, Paul has been seen to connect the death of Christ on behalf of the weak brother (8:11) with voluntary self-effacement on behalf of the common good. The model self-effacement appears in Paul's description of his missionary work in Corinth (2:1-5) and comes through in the bold contrasts between Paul and those who boast in the community (4:8-13).

The point of *kathōs kågō Christou* (11:1) becomes clearer. Paul's imitation of Christ relates to these three elements of his attitude and practice: spiritual understanding, preaching the cross, self-effacement for the common good. He goes on to specify the imitation he expects from the Corinthians but in general it includes both the spiritual understanding and self-effacement.

I. *The Apostolic Parousia*

Not satisfied with the positing of his own example by way of the letter and of his faithful emissary and collaborator Timothy, Paul ends the exhortation section with a promise to pay the community a visit (4:19). He takes particular aim at those who are puffed up, and wants to test their power. Here the threatened presence of the model is a direct challenge to those who think that he does not have the nerve to come, or better that their own wisdom would profit nothing from his presence — erroneous opinions which have been confirmed by his sending of the letter and of Timothy alone.[60]

Once again, Paul seems to confront the faulty pretensions to wisdom in the community. For real, divine *dynamis* has nothing to do with human wisdom but undergirds preaching and living (through self-effacement) of *ho logos ... ho tou*

---

[60] Meyer, 127.

staurou, 1:18; and the *kerygma* of *Christos estaurōmenos*, 1:23-24; 2:2-5. This contrast between human and divine wisdom strikes at the heart of the community's problem. And Paul offers his own example not as a threat but as a help for the community to see things for what they are and not take them as they seem to the world.

The reference to God's kingdom in power and not in word (4:20) undercuts the erroneous claim to rule already (4:8). But Paul dissolves whatever polemic there is in these last charges by returning to the affectionate and paternal tone with which he began the concluding section (4:2 and compare 4:14-15).

J. *The Use of the Pauline Example in the Remainder of the Letter*

In the rest of the letter Paul proposes his example as a norm in each of the problems handled, and in that way further specifies the model which he wants the community to adopt as its standard of life. Sometimes Paul refers to a situation in the first person but in a generalized way ("I" = "one"). This usage occurs in the excursus on love 13:1-13, where it is life-style and not doctrine that is at issue in Paul's and any mature person's growth in love. Here, too a *synaskēsis* involves both model and imitator. In 6:12-20 the first-person slogans provoke a model moral reflection which Paul offers as a pattern for the community to appropriate and adapt to particular situations. The same model reflection appears in 8:1-13 and 10:29 ff.

Another type of apostolic example is that where Paul places himself with the community in some shared experience. In 5:3-13 Paul vividly pictures himself in assembly with the community and passes judgement with them (5:4). He cites the motive of a common celebration of the passover feast in purity (5:8), and thereby stirs the community to take action, relying on their union with Christ (5:4, 7). The *synaskēsis* (9:25 ff. and 13:10 ff.) also falls into this category, as does Paul's close association of himself with the common tradition and practice of the churches (11:16, 23) and his citation of the scriptures written for our admonition (10:11).

The last category presents Paul's real personal example. In chap. 9 he reflects on his apostolic prerogatives and fixes on the principle of a voluntary curtailment of them for the good of others (9:19). He proposes the same principle to the community in the question of meat offered to idols in chaps. 8 and 10. On the questions of celibacy (chap. 7) and gifts of the spirit (chap. 14), Paul proposes his own practice as the most desirable (7:7a; 14:18-19) but once again insists only on the community's adoption of the proper attitude which stands behind this model (freedom from care and desire to please the Lord in whatever circumstance, 7:29b-32, and an apostolic attitude of edification and instruction which allows the exercise of all gifts but in proper order, 14:31). The same personal example leading to a proper attitude for the community can be noted in 15:30-32. The meaning of 11:1 has already been discussed above.

In all of these instance a correct self-evaluation and proper exercise of this wisdom in judgment for the benefit of others are the recurrent goals of the model proposed. This carries over the basic difficulty of the community from the initial exhortation, resolves particular stress situations which result from the erroneous wisdom and judgment, and provides the community with precepts, doctrine, and their living exemplification in the action and attitude of the founding father Paul.

From these observations on 1 Corinthians it is clear that Paul refers to his own example in both a direct and an indirect way. Whatever obedience he has in mind in these references, imitation lies within his sights as well. Indeed, the model and the precept work hand in hand in Paul's moral instructions.

Moreover, the model role, while primarily Paul's preserve is not so exclusively. Apollos' association with the apostolic model in chaps. 1-4 has been described above. One might look at 1 Cor 8:9-13 for the deleterious effects of a bad example in the community and its function of contrasting with the Pauline model. The example of the wilderness generation in 1 Cor 10:1-11 (and compare 11:29-30) is an instructional precedent and so is an example which does not call for imitation. Imitation, however, seems to be implied in the attention given to Stephanas, his household and Fortunatus and Achaicus at 16:15-18. In 16:15 Stephanas' household are commended for their service of the community (*hoi hagioi*). The collaboration and toil in 16:16 recall the model apostolic laborers in chap. 3. This practical service and labor for the common good, also characterized as refreshment for Paul and the community in 16:17-18, are just what Paul hopes to instil as a practical attitude in the community at large. The call to recognize (*epiginōskete*) people like this has more than a notional objective here in 16:18. Paul again widens the horizon of the model to be imitated. Furthermore, his call for obedience of Stephanas' household in 16:16 (*hypotassēsthe*) might look forward to the imitation of their attitude and service, in addition to submission as a "voluntary yielding in love." [61]

The preceding discussion of 1 Corinthians has established that the examples there, Paul's as well as others', do indeed seek to stimulate imitation. A brief look at the five other Pauline passages considered by Michaelis will fill out the picture of Paul's use of this device.

III. The Imitation of Paul in the Other Pauline Letters

A. *1 Thess 1:6; 2:14*

Michaelis rightly suggests that 1 Thess 2:14 and even 1 Thess 1:6 represent the use of imitation in a "simple comparison." No deliberate imitation is meant but the troubled condition of the Macedonian community is like the persecuted church

---

[61] *BAG, hypotassō,* 1b. B., 848.

in Judea and also like the suffering Paul and Christ.[62]   In this respect the Thessalonians themselves become an example (*typos*) for other churches in Macedon and Achaea (1:7).

B. *Phil 3:17*

Michaelis accepts the idea in Phil 3:17 of imitation of the example of other members of the community.   He rightly distinguishes Paul from these others (*houtō peripatountes*) but he does so on unclear grounds of vocabulary rather than by noting the obvious priority ascribed to Paul in *kathōs echete typon hēmas.*[63] He goes further astray because of the bias toward connecting imitation with obedience to apostolic authority.   He challenges the notion of imitating the Pauline model by pointing to Paul's own admission of imperfection at 3:11 ff., to which he compares 1 Cor 9:27.   Here Michaelis overlooks two things.   One, the teacher often calls his pupils to *synaskēsis,* to imitate his own striving toward the goal of perfection.[64] Two, the context does indeed speak of Paul's claim to perfection (3:4-6) but goes on to relativize it (3:7-11) in the light of Christ.   Paul tries to become like him in his death (*symmorphizomenos tō_i thanatō_i autou,* 3:10) so as to achieve the resurrection from the dead (presumably like Christ).   This passage reflects the thought on example already noted in 1 Corinthians.   The notion of apostolic command is quite alien to this passage.   The call to *synaskēsis* appears in both letters.   The element of Christ and His cross looms behind the Pauline model.[65]   Paul allows for other models than himself.[66]   The ideal conduct is expressed in the image of walking (Phil 3:17) or way (1 Cor 4:17).

---

[62] Note the reference to *agōn* at 2:1-2.

[63] Even here becoming *mimētai* is a process and, not an instantaneous achievement. Thus, Paul uses the phrase *en pollō_i agōni* (1 Thess 2:2 and compare the training image and the cognate *agōnizomenos* at 1 Cor 9:25-27). See also Betz, 143. The suffering has an immediate referent in the catalogue of sufferings at 1 Cor 4:11-13 and to the contrasts between the Corinthians' lofty self-esteem and the apostle's lowliness at 1 Cor 4:8-10. The suffering of the Thessalonians is also connected with the death of Christ, with a resonance at 1 Cor 1:18-25 and the kerygma of the cross. This Christ is the foundation for Paul's preaching at 1 Cor 3:11 and his ways at 1 Cor 4:17 might threfore include the aspect of his suffering as an apostle. Phil 3:17-18 seems to corroborate the link between the cross, imitation and authentic apostolic preaching. See Stanley, 871, and Schulz, 287.

[64] Note the play on the words *ouch hoti ēdē ... teteleiōmai* 3:12 and *hosoi oun teleioi* 3:15; the emphasis on conduct in *stoichein* 3:16, and *peripatountas* 3:17, and *peripatousin* 3:18; the call to join in a common imitation in *symmimētai* 3:17.

[65] Allusion to the exemplary attitude of Christ was already made at 2:5 while the suffering first appears at 1:29-30 (here the word *agōn* is used).

[66] A contrast between Paul who places no stock in the flesh, and those who do (3:2 ff.) and between those conformed to the image of Christ and the enemies of Christ's cross (2:17 ff.) establish positive and negative examples.

C. *2 Thess 3:7*

Michaelis also accepts imitation of the model for 2 Thess 3:7 and for the *typos* in 3:9. There is no compelling reason to conclude that *mimeisthai* "implies recognition of authority" from the mention of *paradosis* in 3:6. First, the Pauline example in 3:7a is directly connected by way of contrast with the negative example of those living "in idleness and not in accord with the tradition" in 3:6. Thus, the *paradosis* is to be seen as part of the model to be chosen or avoided and not independently. Second, choice of patterns of conduct (*peripatōn*) is the object of the command here (*parangellomen*). Third, Michaelis himself has not indicated clearly how *paradosis* comes to imply recognition of authority (and presumably obedience to it).[67] Fourth, the integrity and unity of the thought of this, as well as the other passages noted, is best served by not allowing the extraneous idea of authority to intrude, or at most to allow authority and obligation to serve as specification of the Pauline model to be imitated.

D. *Eph 5:1; Gal 4:12*

Two more passages can be mentioned. Michaelis discusses the imitation of God mentioned in Eph 5:1. This does not fit the concern of this study which is directed toward the example of Paul and the models in relation to him. Michaelis does not mention Gal 4:12 which does not use the word *mimētēs*. Here Paul wants the Galatians to imitate him, to become like him, in his freedom the law through faith in Christ (3:23-29).[68] When he refers to his having become like them, he seems to suggest the effort of assimilating himself to the attitudes and points of view of his audiences as declared at 1 Cor 9:19-23. The latter has already been shown to be connected with the imitation of Paul's example in 1 Corinthians.

E. *Concluding Observations*

To sum up this section of the discussion, Paul's example serves as both a specimen (for comparison) and a prototype (for imitation) in these letters. The assumption of an interpretation of the imitation along the lines of accepting or following authority is unfounded and unnecessary. Other model figures share the

---

[67] 2Thess 3:14 directly refers to the instruction by way of letters in Paul's *paradosis* which includes both his words and his actions. The letters of the Socratics saw in their preservation of Socratic *paradosis* a service to the continuation of Socrates' virtue among his followers.

[68] This stands in contrast to his attitude at 1:13-14 and that of the false brethren at 2:4-5. Compare 4:8-11 as another statement of freedom. Another contrast appears in the motivation behind the zeal of Paul and other teachers in Galatia (4:17-19). Note the father-child image and the reference to the Christ image, here unspecified, at 4:19.

function of Paul's example. Negative models are also in evidence to present an unacceptable option of attitude and conduct. The use of example is thus consistent with that found in 1 Corinthians. Some observations on form are now in order to bring this treatment of example in the homologoumena to a close.

IV. **The Form of Paul's Exhortations to Imitate His Example**

The discussion above has confirmed that Paul's example does indeed expect a response of following which implies imitation. The focus of the present analysis falls on the form of the example passages, specifically the structural consistency in the use of the example figures and the cluster of devices which surround them (e.g., the use of antithetical examples, the development of the examples with lists and prescriptions, the use of devices familiar to the pattern of the developed chria). The principal question here is whether the Pauline passages reflect the formal patterns already noted in the Pastorals and the Socratic letters.[69] Secondary questions include the use of explicit and implicit examples, and the relation between the Pauline example and that of other members of the community. Related to the formal questions is the issue of the content of the example.

A. *Antithetical Examples*

Paul uses antithesis to contrast himself and his teaching (Gal 1:10 ff.; 4:12 ff., 5:11 ff., 6:14-15; Phil 3:3 ff.) to the people who are disturbing his churches and to their erroneous message. In this usage, however, the opponents are not described as general types of people whose vicious life-style is to be avoided. They are presumed to be known, their tactics are exposed, and they are rejected directly (Gal 1:6 ff.; 4:17; 5:7 ff., 6:12-13; Phil 3:2). Phil 3:18-19 alone casts the negative examples in a stereo-typical mold and here the negative example is set against Paul's explicit call for imitation (Phil 3:16-17). Nonetheless, the context is specific.

In another use of antithesis, Paul opposes his own example to the addressees in the second person (1 Cor 4:6 ff.) (cf. *tines ... en hymin,* 2 Thess 3:6 ff). Once again, these are specific abuses which Paul counters with his own exemplary action and attitude, they are not described as negative models in a generally applicable way. Moreover, the alternating positive/negative pattern in 1 Cor 4 is unique.[70]

There is no contrasting example in 1 Thessalonians. Paul does mention some negative attitudes which he himself did not opt for (1 Thess 2:3-7) but these are not attributed to any exemplary figures, hypothetical or real. Another instance where

---

[69] See 22-24 and 138-46.

[70] When the Socratic letters employ a contrast in the "you" form (e.g., *Eps.* 8-13, 21) the two divergent expressions of cynicism are being opposed instead of the Pauline focus on a single abuse.

Paul provides both poles of the example is Phil 3:5-11, but Paul would not expect anyone to come close to adopting the ultra-Jewish outlook, which he practiced but now rejects. As such the negative example is not a prototype but an illustration.

B. *Lists and Prescriptions to Fill Out the Example*

There is no consistent use of lists of virtues and vices and/or prescriptions together with the examples in order to further specify the examples.[71] The vices denied at 1 Thess 2:3, 5, 7 and the virtues claimed at 2:10 help specify the character traits which Paul sees imitated at 1:5-6 and which he urges at 4:1 ff.[72] The qualities which Paul singles out in himself at Phil 3:4 ff., however, are not part of the example offered for imitation. The prescriptions at Gal 5:1 ff. do not fill out Paul's example, while those at 1 Cor 10:6 ff. do spell out the example. 2 Thessalonians has no lists in association with the example, and has only the simple command against idleness associated with the example of Paul's own practice (2 Thess 3:6 ff.).

C. *Explicit and Implicit Example*

Since the letters respond to specific situations, Paul stresses those aspects of his character which would show the community an example of the attitude or behavior necessary to resolve their difficulties. Thus, Paul makes his example explicit, rather than instruct in an implicit way. This has already been discussed for 1 Corinthians.[73] In his other letters, Paul calls attention to his example for imitation explicity at Gal 4:1 ff.; Phil 3:12 ff.; 2 Thess 3:6 ff. Philippians is unique in that it bolsters the commands to rejoice (2:18; 3:1; 4:4) with the implicit example of Paul's indomitable joy (1:4, 18; 4:10).

Like most of the other instances the example in 1 Thess 1:5 ff. is also explicit, although it does not seem to focus on imitation as its aim. The example of his own uprightness at 1 Thess 2:10 ff., which leads into the exhortation to right conduct at 4:1 ff. is likewise explicitly spelled out.

A further observation can be made concerning the explicitness of Paul's example. Paul elaborates details of his ministry and background in order to bolster his authority as he confronts the issues in his churches. This verification of his own apostolate and character appears at 1 Thess 2:1-7; Gal 4:12 ff.; Phil 3:2 ff.;

---

[71] Lists of virtues and vices are plentiful in Paul's letters but appear largely in sections other than the explicit example passages. But see E. Kamlah, *Die Form der katalogischen Paränese im Neuen Testament*, WUNT 7 (Tübingen: J.C.B. Mohr [Paul Siebeck], 1964) 199.

[72] For a full description of the paraenetic nature of 1 Thessalonians, see A.J. Malherbe, "I Thessalonians as a Paraenetic Letter," (rev. version "Exhortation in First Thessalonians", *NovT* 25 (1983) 238-56.

[73] See above, 168-84.

1 Cor 4:9-13, 18-21; 9:1-3. Thus, he draws attention to himself not just as a model but as an authentic admonitor.

D. *Other Members of the Comunity as Examples*

Paul's example is the pre-eminent one in his letters and others, who share that function, do so in direct and explicit relation to his example. In 1 Corinthians, as noted above, Apollos' example is subordinate to Paul's [74] and Stephanas' is derivative from it.[75] In 1 Thessalonians, whereas Paul begins with the example of the suffering Judean churches at 2:14, he ends up talking about his own at 2:16, echoing 1:7 where he mentions himself and Christ directly. Phil 3:17b directs attention to others in the church, provided they conduct themselves according to Paul's model. Imitation of the latter is the primary objective at 3:17a.

E. *The Pattern of Hortatory Devices*

While 1 Thessalonians and Galatians use a variety of hortatory devices in the example passages,[76] they lack the broad range of these which the hortatory works including the Socratics and the Pastorals analyzed above contain. Philippians 3, on the other hand, does resemble those other works as it elaborates its exhortation with the cluster of devices specified for the development of the chria.[77] The aim of the passage, however, is not purely hortatory. Throughout, Paul engages the false teachers in a polemic and likewise reasserts his own authority.

More consistently hortatory is 1 Corinthians 8:1 - 11:1 (except for 9:1-3) and the range of devices matches the pattern of the developed chria,[78] but the development here is much more diffuse than what has been encountered above. Like 1 Cor 8 ff., 2 Thess 3 is hortatory and also employs the full pattern of devices.[79] It does

---

[74] See above, 180.

[75] See above, 184.

[76] E.g., antithesis, 1 Thess 2:1-7, 9-10; Gal 4:6 ff., 16 ff.; comparison, 1 Thess 2:7-8, 11; Gal 4:1-2; prescription, 1 Thess 2:11-12; Gal 4:12a; 5:1b, appeal to scriptural authority, Gal 4:21 ff.

[77] I.e., negative example 2 ff.; Paul's example, 4b-11; racing metaphor, 12 ff.; statement of the correct attitude, 15a; promise of its proof, 15b; restatement 16; command, 17; contrast, 18-19; gnomic saying and elaboration, 20-21; concluding command, 4:1.

[78] I.e., statement, 8:1 ff.; proof, 4 ff.; restatement, 13; example, 9:1 ff.; comparisons, 7; appeal to authority, 8 ff.; metaphor, 11; restatement and elaboration, 12 ff.; comparisons, 24 ff.; examples of personal application, 27; instructional precedents, 10:1 ff.; commands, 6 ff.; new statement, 14; verification, 15 ff., original statement repeated, 23 ff.; negative example, 25 ff.; counter proof, 27 ff.; restatement of general principle and positive example, 31 ff.; command, 11:1.

[79] I.e., statement, 1-2a; proof, 2b-3; restatement, 4-5; command, 6; example, 7 ff., authority, 10; negative example and concluding commands, 12 ff. Only comparison is not employed from the pattern of the developed chria.

so, however, in a compact development of the argument and it alone of the Pauline letters reflects the writings analyzed above.

F. *Conclusion*

The Pauline homologoumena reflect the hortatory techniques and devices common to comparable writings of their day, some of which have been analyzed above. Example has been shown to be a prominent feature in Paul's hortatory method and he aims at imitation rather than obedience of his authoritative prescriptions. In the next chapter, these letters will be compared with the Pastorals in an effort to determine more closely how the two parts of the Pauline corpus relate with each other and with their literary surroundings, particularly in their use of example. At this point, one cannot fail to notice Paul's concern with the immediate occasion; the predominant position of his own example; and some formal differences in the way he employs example and other hortatory devices.

Chapter VIII

Example in the Pastoral Epistles

In the effort of this study to understand the use of personal example in the Pastoral Epistles, three types of non-Christian writings have come under scrutiny: (1) theoretical treatments on the use of example, (2) instructions to young officials, (3) epistolary exhortations. As the following summary will show, each of these contributes important information on the use of example in exhortation literature. As such, they help to characterize the Pastoral Epistles and to appreciate the hortatory features which those epistles employ.

I. Summary of Results from the Preceding Analyses

A. *Theoretical Treatments*

From the theoretical treatises on examples one expects a variety of examples: from the past or present, named individuals or members of a class or type, historical persons or fictitious and hypothetical figures. In all, the preference rests with well known personages for greater impact. Comparison and contrast are achieved through antithetical examples. Examples are closely associated with metaphors and other analogies and are accompanied by apposite sayings and statements.

In the development of works of exhortation from epideictic speeches to the hortatory discourse and the epistle, the protreptic and apotreptic aims are well served by recourse to examples. The selection of family models and warning against people to avoid make the lesson clear. In more formal school instruction, the teacher's own model can be expected to serve as a standard both for rhetorical accomplishment and moral uprightness, thus replacing the familial examples, particularly that of the father.

More properly paraenetic works are characterized by the use of prescriptions and of traditional hortatory material together with a variety of hortatory features. One such features meriting close attention is the chria (and the closely associated gnome) because of both its popularity in the protreptic and apotreptic exhortations of popular philosophy and its developed form in school exercises. In the latter instance examples, both positive and negative, complement direct exhortation; and these join other hortatory features in a structured hortatory "argument."

While in epistolary theorists and their handbooks evidence for a direct link with the principles from rhetorical theory is slim, the practice in the letters studied above confirms the connection.   Hortatory letters, whether of individual moral counselors or of teachers in a school context, are lineal descendants in a long tradition of exhortation literature.   The Pastoral Epistles, with their heavy complement of hortatory features,[1] stands in this tradition.   These, together with their abundant prescriptions and traditional material to be detailed below, give the Pastorals a paraenetic character.

Thus, the discussion of theoretical works helps situate the Pastorals in their literary tradition and also establishes the principles according to which the Pastorals' use of example can be judged.   The second body of literature, the instructions to young officials, brings the theory into the practical order.

B. *Discourses to Young Officials and Kingship Treatises*

As admonitions to young men on the duties of office, they bear a thematic resemblance to the Pastorals.   In their elaboration of the admonitions, they employ formal features which also appear in the Pastorals.

Considering the formal features, first, one notes from the very outset of the treatises, the juxtaposition to contrasting examples, whether of other teachers, of another type of audience, or of both.   This initial contrast is also picked up later in the treatises.   Second, antithetical examples are used to promote other aspects of the admonition as well.   Third, examples, both positive and negative often illustrate individual prescriptions in the effort to instruct by deeds as well as by words.   Fourth, the examples are sketches rather than detailed descriptions and the authors have recourse to lists of virtues and vices to trace the outlines of the paradigms.   Fifth, while the form of the works is that of the treatise or discourse, epistolary characteristics like friendship, sending the treatise, and surrogate presence through writing also color the form of the treatises.   Sixth, Plutarch's use of examples alone or of examples with prescriptions demonstrates that an author can vary form of his exhortation.   Seventh, a wide range of hortatory devices surrounds the examples in all these works.   Plutarch uses the arrangement of hortatory features outlined in the development of the chria.

As far as concerns thematic material common to the exhortation in these works, first ancestral figures and even the addressee's father are the preferred models, although ruling figures are also mentioned as typical examples.   Second, both deeds and words are referred to in the model figure.   Third, harmful associations with those whose actions betray ignorance and lack of virtue are to be avoided.   Fourth, the addressee is himself to become a model.   Fifth, becoming an exemplar involves a process of persistent exercise and struggle regulated by attention to the prescriptions concerning personal virtue and public duty.   Sixth,

---

[1] See above 10-25.

the qualities of an exemplary ruler are actually suitable for the broader public who look to the ruler instinctively for their norm of conduct. Seventh, the ruler must do what he prescribes and must avoid criticism, be it occasioned by a double standard or by his own ineptitude. Public exposure of such wrongdoings, even when temporarily hidden, is inevitable. Eighth, different from this sort of avoidable criticism is the constructive criticism by which good teachers and friends help their associates and pupils to progress in virtue. This pedagogy is preferable to indulgent flattery, which is ultimately destructive. Ninth, the mindless are contrasted with those who achieve right thinking and instruct others in it. Tenth, the vain allure of riches receives particular criticism, and self-control and contentment are promoted instead. Eleventh, usefulness for the individual and for the common good is a hallmark of the instructions. Twelfth, the instructions do not propose novelties nor do they indulge in quibbling and debates, but rather hand on traditional exhortation. Thirteenth, as such, the writings are not occasional pieces but claim perennial applicability and usefulness as instructions on how to fulfill one's official obligations, on how to conduct one's life and decide what to do and what to avoid. Fourteenth, the youthfulness and relative inexperience of the addressees provides a reasonable setting and pretext for these instructional "handbooks." Fifteenth, Isocrates uses a pseudonymous ascription to give an appropriate setting for his work *Nicocles,* and his follower seems to have ascribed *Ad Demonicum* to Isocrates so as to anchor the traditional exhortation in the teaching of the master.

C. *Epistolary Exhortation*

Epistles formed the third class of literature examined and the official letters underline the difference between specific instruction and more general exhortation. When the latter does make its way into these circular "memoranda," it brings with it the formal and thematic features noted in the "epistolary" discourses. The thoroughgoing epistolary exhortations exploit these features to the full.

Seneca's letters represent the product of the development of the hortatory discourse to the epistle or "half-dialogue" in the more intimate context of the moral guide and his protege. The potential of the epistolary form is fully realized. The commonplaces of epistolary presence and friendship make the instructions palatable, invite the audience to enter the common enterprise of moral improvement, and pose the author's example both explicitly and implicitly. The wide variety of examples and Seneca's inclination toward rulers, notable persons, family members, and teachers agree with the rhetorical theory and with current and prior hortatory practice. The complementarity of precept and example is both noted and practiced. The examples are sketches of apposite qualities of the entire character. Antithetical examples abound. The letter form helps establish implicit examples to supplement the explicit ones. The chria and the exhortation following the structured pattern of its development are part of Seneca's hortatory arsenal.

Among the thematic commonplaces is the call to imitate the examples, and to exercise the virtuous qualities. There is, thus, the stress on progress. A corollary to the imitation of good examples is the warning to avoid bad associations.

The Socratic letters, like Seneca's are hortatory and they also consciously apply rhetorical theory on the hortatory use of example. Unlike Seneca's letters, however, they represent a school effort to preserve and promote authentic teaching in the face of aberrant forms of it. The device of pseudonymity sets before the audience the principal exemplar of the letter collection both explicitly and implicitly. In addition to Socrates, a variety of other personal examples is used and the examples are well known to the addressees from their family, civic and philosophical background. This meets the theoretical requirements for personal example pressed both in the treatises and in the letter corpus itself.

Other formal features of the letters' use of example link them with the theoretical treatises and the practice in the hortatory works. First, antithesis in the juxtaposition of positive and negative examples abound. Second, some letters start off with the criticism of bad teachers and their misguided followers. Third, the examples are sketched and not detailed. Fourth, some use of lists and precepts complementary to the examples is noted. Fifth, a large variety of hortatory devices is used and they are sometimes grouped and arranged according to the pattern of the developed chria.

The letters as a collection present implicit and explicit examples and, as such, are the product of both a deliberate choice of literary form and a commitment to a literary effort. The epistolary form grows out of and serves its particular philosophical school environment in preserving its anecdotal and doxographical traditions while at the same time developing them. As in Seneca's use of the letter, the form gives the audience easy access to and interaction with the teaching and its paradigmatic contours.

From the side of thematic content, first the closeness of the exemplar and friend implicates all the associates in a relationship of spiritual kinship. Second, both deeds and words are deemed important in a full transmission of the tradition. Third, there is a concern for proper associations to insure correct training. Fourth, the followers become exemplars in their turn. Fifth, exercise and attention to the instructions are necessary for the acquisition of virtue. Sixth, a bad reputation with the general public, whether for a ruined character or for petty infighting, is to be avoided. Seventh, constructive criticism is to be prized over harmful flattery as well as over harsh rebuke. Eighth, the false guides are characterized as mindless in contrast to the right thinking people of virtue. Ninth, the snare of the pursuit of riches is exposed, and contentment and self-sufficiency are promoted instead. Tenth, the teaching is fundamentally beneficial. Eleventh, the letter corpus aims to preserve the tradition of Socrates' virtue and teaching. Twelfth, by the device of pseudonymity, the authors recall the origins of the teaching and thereby reaffirm its continuity and legitimacy.

The letters are unlike the kingship discourses and treatises in that they all look to a broad audience for which they use far fewer lists and prescriptions.

Nonetheless, they comprehensively elaborate a manner of life. The Socratic epistles do this in a special way through the examples of the first generation Socratics.

II. Example as the Starting Point for Understanding the Exhortation of the Pastoral Epistles

With these results of the preceding analyses in mind, the Pastorals themselves can now come under direct scrutiny. The passages where personal examples function explicit have been chosen for analysis. First, Paul's example is studied and then those of his addressees and other community members. Next, the implicit use of example is investigated. Finally, the paraenetic character of the letters is considered and a general survey is made of the positive and negative examples which the letters propose.

A. *Karris' Insight into the Contrast of Teachers*

In his study of the paraenetic elements in the Pastoral Epistles,[2] R.A. Karris examines the traditional lists of virtues and vices as well as the *Haustafeln* and *Gemeindeordnungen*. He accepts Dibelius' insight that the lists are to be regarded as commonplaces. Because of their traditional and typical nature, one would be amiss to look for any significance in the specifics of the lists. They are, in this understanding of them, merely paraenetic devices serving their particular contexts and arguments, the point of which is not necessarily to promote these specific virtues or correct those particular vices. Karris verifies this insight in the case of the Pastoral Epistles by a wide-ranging survey of non-Christian and Christian authors from the fifth and fourth centuries B.C. and the first three Christian centuries.[3] In the polemic writings surveyed Karris finds that the lists of virtues and vices used in the discussions of sophists and wandering philosophers appear with remarkable similarity in the Pastoral Epistles and the other Christian writings. This indicates that the lists in the Pastorals are commonplace material. From this survey Karris also finds a plausible context or *Sitz-im-Leben* for these lists in the Pastorals, i.e., a polemic which seeks to "present a code of conduct which enhances sound teaching."[4]

---

[2] R.A. Karris, "The Function and Sitz-im-Leben of the Paraenetic Elements in the Pastoral Epistles" (Diss. Harvard University, 1971). See also his "The Background and Significance of the Polemic of the Pastoral Epistles," *JBL* 92 (1973) 549-64.

[3] Karris, Introduction and 2 ff. for anti-sophist criticism and 24 ff. for criticism of wandering philosophers.

[4] Karris, Introduction and 3.

The *Haustafeln* and *Gemeindeordnungen,* on the other hand, while also traditional, were widely used in Greco-Roman literature as guides to life, concrete codes of conduct, "Handbooks" for the examination of conscience. These ubiquitous admonitions on virtue (cf. Dio Chrysostom *Or.* 69.2) had a social as well as an individual value for, serving the best interests of society, they were the "building blocks of Greco-Roman society." [5] Unlike the lists of virtues and vices, the content of these materials does have significance of its own and they do not merely serve as commonplaces in their respective contexts. In the Pastorals, their function is similar to that of the lists in that they present a norm for behavior which accompanies the objective norm of belief. Thus, they form part of the sound teaching entrusted by Paul to Timothy and Titus.

These insights and discoveries of Karris are helpful and, when blended with what has been noted above in this study, can be pushed further to a fuller understanding of the paraenesis in the Pastoral Epistles. Karris notes that the Pastorals depart from what he finds in the parallels inasmuch as they oppose not good teaching to bad teaching but the good teacher to the bad teacher, good and bad because they follow sound or faulty teaching. Thus, the element of polemic is transformed from a consideration of teaching to that of the teacher.[6] He also observes that the imperative instructions are in antithetical style and that the author departs from the imperatives occasionally in order to motivate them by referring to the opponents, accenting the departures with *gar,* the future indicative, *eidōs,* and at times with *sy de.*[7]

What if one were to start with this observation of the fundamental uniqueness of the Pastorals, i.e., their effort to contrast not teachings but teachers? Doing that one could then use another of Karris' observations to full advantage. On 72, discussing 1 Tim 6:2b-21, he remarks that Phil *Det* 72 and Lucian *Fugit.* 16, which expands the description of the Cynics in Athenaeus *Epit.* 13.611b-d, show how catalogues of vices can be introduced into the descriptions of the philosopher/sophist. If this is true, then in the Pastorals at 1 Tim 6:2b-21 and, indeed, wherever personal description and lists coincide, the lists might well be in the service of the description and not the other way around, as Karris prefers. Moreover, the problem at 1 Tim 1:3-11 of the contextual motivation for the vice list [8] might also find a more satisfying resolution if the list is really part of the description of the false teachers. The same would be true of the lists of virtues and their relationship to the descriptions of the good teachers. Furthermore, where the antithetical-imperative style turns off into descriptions of the opponents, good and bad, the author may not be motivating the imperatives but rather getting to the heart of his exhortation in a description of ideal types, both positive and negative.[9]

---

[5] Karris, 84 ff.
[6] Karris, 51 ff.
[7] Karris, 56 ff.
[8] Karris, 62 and 69.
[9] For this usage in Seneca, see above 92-93.

B. *Formal Consistency Between the Pastorals and the Literary Parallels*

All this, of course, remains to be demonstrated, which is precisely the task of the next section of this study. A good measure of confidence that the direction opted for here is the correct one comes from a consideration of literary form and the end to which it is put. While the parallels in Karris' study are compelling in their content, they stem largely from treatises and discourses over a broad time span. This study, on the other hand, has chosen a letter corpus to which the principal comparison with the Pastoral Epistles is drawn; and all the letters stem from roughly the same time period, i.e., the "second sophistic," or the first three Christian centuries.[10]

In the Socratic letter corpus examples in antithetical relationship proved to be a key device in the exhortation. In fact, the letters themselves serve as implicit examples, embodying as they do the attitudes and actions of the people to whom they are ascribed. The contention of this study is that the same is true of example in the Pastoral Epistles.

C. *Thematic Consistency*

Nor is form the only consideration. The Socratic epistles instruct their audience in a particular life-style, which the examples flesh out and which the letter writer expects the audience to imitate or follow. The attitudes and actions to choose and avoid are not simply confirmatory of the correctness of the teaching; they are the teaching. This study will indicate that the same is true of the Pastoral Epistles. There is an ongoing polemic in which these letters take one side but the letters are hortatory pieces and not polemical writings.[11] The antitheses within and among the letters reflect a polemical background of conflicting modes of conduct and their proponents. As these antitheses function in the Socratic corpus, however, they help to identify and promote a particular way of life. In this usage, the Socratic letters reflect a use of antithesis in non-polemical contexts noted by A.J. Malherbe in other popular philosophical works in the early Empire.[12] The analysis of the Pastoral Epistles which follows here will concentrate on their use of example as a principal feature of their exhortation. The connection between example and other hortatory features like the lists,

---

[10] Seneca, Plutarch and Dio Chrysostom also date from this period. Only Isocrates and pTebt 703 are earlier, but the hortatory principles they employ are largely the same as those of the later authors.

[11] M. Dibelius and H. Greeven, *James,* Hermeneia, trans. M.A. Williams (Philadelphia: Fortress, 1976) 2-11, finds that the letter of James similarly does not give evidence of a specific conflict but rather proposes traditional paraenesis for its audience. See also P. Trummer, *Die Paulustradition der Pastoralbriefe,* BET 8 (Frankfurt am M.: Peter Lang, 1978) 161-72.

[12] A.J. Malherbe, "Gentle As a Nurse; The Cynic Background to I Thess ii,"*NovT* 12 (1970) 214.

prescriptions and, most importantly, antithetical relationships will be detailed.[13] Further resonances between the hortatory technique and content of the Pastorals and those of the other works studied above will be referred to in footnotes.

III. Explicit Example in the Pastoral Epistles

A. *Paul's Example*

1. 1 Timothy 1:3-20 [14]

Paul calls explicit attention to himself as example at 16. He exemplifies Christ's purpose to save sinners (*alla dia touto ēleēthēn, hina en emoi prōtō$_i$ endeixētai Christos Iēsous tēn hapasan makrothymian pros hypotypōsin tōn mellontōn pisteuein ep'autō$_i$ eis zōēn aiōnion*). While *hypotypōsis*[15] is the principal word designating the example, *endeiknymi* shares that function. The *egō* of the example is known to be Paul from the letter's greeting, but the audience of the example is broadly inclusive and only generally specified (*tōn mellontōn pisteuein*). The parameters of the example are filled in at 12-14 and include Paul's present situation of being a Christ-empowered (*endynamōsas, charis*), loving (*meta agapēs*), and faithful (*pistos, meta pisteōs*) servant (*eis diakonian*) in contrast with his impious (*blasphēmos*), inimical (*diōktēs, hybristēs*), ignorant (*agnoōn*), and faithless (*en apistiā$_i$*) past. Here Paul's former situation is presented in a list of vices[16] and in the picture of his current situation virtues play a fundamental role.

---

[13] L.T. Johnson, "II Timothy and the Polemic Against False Teachers: A Re-examination," *Ohio Journal of Religious Studies* 6-7 (1978-79) 1-26, notices this use of antithesis for paraenetic rather than for polemical purposes in various Greek authors and in the Pastorals as well.

[14] For these three passages from the Pastorals refer to the outline and discussion above 22-24.

[15] For discussions of the Greek words for example and model see W.P. de Boer, *The Imitation of Paul: An Exegetical Study* (Amsterdam/Kampen: J.H. Kok, 1962) 1-23; L. Goppelt, *"typos," TDNT* 8 (1972) 246-56; G. Kittel et al., *"eikōn," TDNT* 2 (1964) 381-97; H. Lausberg, *Handbuch der Literarischen Rhetorik: Eine Grundlegung der Literaturwissenschaft* (Munich: Max Huber, 1972) 194, 227 ff.; E.K. Lee, "Words Denoting 'Pattern' in the N.T.," *NTS* 8 (1961-62) 166-73; A. Lumpe, "Exemplum," *RAC* 6:1229-57; A. Reiff, "Interpretatio, imitatio, aemulatio (Diss. inaug. Cologne, 1959); H. Schlier, *hypodeigma," TDNT* 2 (1964) 32-33; A. von Blumenthal, *"TYPOS* und *PARADEIGMA," Hermes* 63 (1928) 391-414; H. Willms, *EIKON: Eine Begriffsgeschichtliche Untersuchung zum Platonismus* (Münster i.W.: Aschendorff, 1935) 48 ff.; K.J.Woolcombe, "Le sens de 'type' chez les Pères," *La Vie Spirituelle* suppl. 16 (1941) 84-100.

[16] In the practice of exhortation by example, lists have been seen to complement the example in Isocrates, 53, 65; Plutarch, 68, 73-75; Menander, 77; the official letters, 82; and the Socratics, 133-34. The lists, like the examples, are anthithetical in Plutarch and Menander. See also E. Kamlah, *Die Form der katalogischen Paränese im Neuen Testament,* WUNT 7 (Tübingen: J.C.B. Mohr [Paul Siebeck], 1964) 199-200.

The example demonstrates that the salvation which the superlative sinner (*prōtos*) Paul received, 15, is available to all who believe (*alla dia touto eleēthēn* 16).[17]

How does the example coordinate with and support the exhortation of this section? The goal or final outcome (*telos* 15) hoped for from the charge is *agapē ek katharas kardias kai syneidēseōs agathēs kai pisteōs anypokritou*. Paul's example includes *agapē* 14, and *pistis* 12, 13, 14, 16 and cf. 11, and a good conscience is surely implied in his being saved from sin, 15. Thus, the example illustrates the state to which the charge points.

The content of the charge, 3-4 is *mē heterodidaskalein mēde prosechein mythois ktl.*, the main fault of which is their promotion of *ekzēteseis mallon ē oikonomian theou tēn en pistei.*[18] The bone of contention is the ethical consequence of the teaching and mystical speculation, i.e., that it leads to wrangling rather than to the divine "training" (*BAG* 562, emphasizing personal growth) or "administration" (Abbott-Smith 313) or "management" (Zerwick-Grosvenor 627, emphasizing official responsibility) in faith. Once again, Paul's example fills out the charge[19] by

---

[17] De Boer, 197 ff., calls Paul's example here a "typical illustration," recommended for others. See also Lee, 171-72 and also J. Roloff, *Apostolat-Verkündigung-Kirche: Ursprung, Inhalt und Funktion des kirchlichen Apostelamtes nach Paulus, Lukas und den Pastoralbriefen* (Gütersloh: Gerd Mohn, 1965) 240, 249.

[18] Some use in the "myths and genealogies" indications of a polemic against Judaism, Gnosticism or some combination of the two: e.g., J. Kittel, "Die *genealogiai* der Pastoralbriefe," *ZNW* 20 (1920-21) 49-69. However, one finds a similar complaint in Rom 1:21 in the general description of the wayward gentiles. F.H. Colson, "'Myths and Genealogies' — A Note in the Polemic of the Pastoral Epistles," *JTS* 19 (1917-18) 265-71, suggests that the phrase has its origins in the grammatical schools and their collections and classifications of legendary and historical allusions and of biographical details. Excessive attention to such research was regarded as senseless and distracting by Quintilian *Inst.* 1.8 (and see the discussion of Isocrates' *Ad Nicoclem* on 66). Thus, the phrase in the Pastorals could well refer to the *quaestiones* in a pagan school context, which would accord with other school-like characteristics in these letters. But, as Colson admits, a Jewish context wherein Hellenistic literary criticism and dialectical skill were pursued would also fit this detail in the Pastorals. The "antitheses of so-called knowledge" (1 Tim 6:20) might then refer to the legal and dialectical disputes and the "physical exercise" (1 Tim 4:8) to the training of the *palaestra* which complemented rhetorical education. He admits, but remains unconvinced of, the possibility of incipient gnosticism behind the letters. Along the same lines as Quintilian *Inst.* 1.8, Plutarch, *Prof. virt.* 80B-C charges that *zēteseis* impede progress in virtue and *Rat. aud.* 37C-39B favors listening to talking and stresses the need to hear solid material rather than to talk foolishly and for the sake of beating another in argument (F.C. Babbitt, trans., *Plutarch's Moralia*, LCL, 15 vols. [London: W. Heinemann, 1926]). Similarly, Seneca *Ep.* 88.35, 37, cautions, against inquiries into nonessential and useless knowledge which only render a person a troublesome, wordy, tactless, and self-satisfied bore (R.M. Gummere, trans., *Lucius Annaeus Seneca. Ad Lucilium epistulae morales*, LCL, 3 vols. [London: W. Heinemann, 1917]).

[19] For the complementarity of example and precept and the function of example to verify that following the precept actually achieves the stated goal or avoids a harmful pitfall

demonstrating the requisite correct teaching and service (*kata to euangelion ... ho episteuthēn egō* 11; *piston me hēgēsato themenos eis diakonian* 12).

Some of the features already noted in the example emerge in the restatement of the charge (18-19a, *pistis* and *agathē syneidēsis*). The addition of *strateuein ... tēn kalēn strateian*[20] reflects the aspect of "training" in *oikonomia* 4. This is not a feature of the example here, but will enter the idealized picture at a later point in the Pastorals.

A negative example also coordinates with the exhortation and outlines[21] the objectionable type of person. The author indicates that he has people in mind and not just disembodied qualities when he uses the word *tines*,[22] 6 and 19, and then goes on to name two of them at 20 as representatives of them all (*hōn estin*). These embody the characteristics which are the opposite of those in the exhortation and in Paul's positive example. At 6 and 19 it is asserted that they have strayed from and rejected[23] (*astochēsantes, apōsamenoi*) those very virtues which the charge looks to as its completion. It is surprising at first to note that instead of these virtues they turn not to the vices which oppose them but *eis mataiologian* 6.[24] But this merely echoes the contrast given in the explanation of the consequences of the charge that *ekzētēseis parechousin mallon ē oikonomian* 4. The primary character-

---

see the discussions above on Isocrates, 45-47, 50, 52, 54-55, 65-66; Plutarch, 69-70; Seneca 87-88, 93-94; official letters, 82; the Socratics, 125, 138, 145.

[20] For the use of the military image for religious and moral struggle see C. Spicq, *Saint Paul: Les Epîtres pastorales,* 2 vols., 4th rev. ed., (Paris: Gabalda, 1969) 1:350; O. Bauernfeind, "*strateuomai,*" *TDNT* 7 (1971) 701-13; "*strateuomai,*" *BAG* 770.

[21] The example consists of particular deeds or qualities and not all the qualities of the exemplar's personality, as shown for Isocrates, 50, 54, 56, 64; Plutarch, 69; Seneca, 92-93, 99-100; and the Socratic letters, 134, 136-37, 144-41.

[22] Fictitious, typical or hypothetical examples, as opposed to named historical figures, have been admitted since Aristotle, 27. See also the discussion on rhetorical education, 38. The indefinite pronoun for this type of example, usually negative, has been seen in use in Isocrates 49. Unnamed proponents of adversary positions appear in Isocrates, 49-50, 52, 63-65; Seneca, 91, 99-100 and the Socratics 137-41.

[23] The Pastorals make abundant use of vocabulary of physical movement to describe the intellectual and moral condition of the faithful (*apotheisthai* 1 Tim 1:19; *apostrepesthai* 2 Tim 3:5; *parakolouthein* 1 Tim 4:6; 2 Tim 3:10; *anastrephesthai* 1 Tim 3:15; *epakolouthein* 1 Tim 5:10; *orthotomein* 2 Tim 2:15; *pheugein* 1 Tim 6:11; 2 Tim 2:22; *diōkein* 1 Tim 6:11; 2 Tim 2:22) and of the faithless (*astochein* 1 Tim 6:21; 2 Tim 2:18; *proserchesthai* 1 Tim 6:3; *empiptein* 1 Tim 3:6, 7, 9; *apoplanan* 1 Tim 6:10; *ektrepein* 1 Tim 6:20; *apostrephein* 2 Tim 1:15; 4:4; Titus 1:14; *enkataleipein* 2 Tim 4:8, 16; *prokoptein* 2 Tim 2:16; 3:9, 13; *agein* 2 Tim 3:6; *planan* 2 Tim 3:13; Titus 3:3; *ekstrephein* Titus 3:11). For similar usage in the Socratics see *Ep.* 39.

[24] For the depiction of the foolish ignorance of the negative example compare what was said of Isocrates, 49, 55, 62-63, 66; Plutarch, 70, 72, 75-76; and the Socratics, 137-40, 148-51. See also F. Zucker, "Verbundenheit von Erkenntnis und Wille im griechischen Sprachbewusstsein beleuchtet durch Erscheinungen aus der Bedeutungsentwicklung von *AGNOIA, AGNOEIN, AGNOEMA,*" in *Studies Presented to D.M. Robinson II* (G.E. Mylonas and D. Raymond, eds., St. Louis: Eden, 1953) 1063-72.

istic of the negative example and that at which the exhortation takes express aim (*mē heterodidaskalein* 3) is their spurious and uninformed teaching (*mē noountes* 7; *hina paideuthōsin* 20). The list of vices, 9-10, spells out the vicious character of one who opposes the sound teaching (*hygiainousa didaskalia* 10) in favor of a brand of his own. Vice and false teaching go together as a commonplace in the criticisms of sophists and wandering philosophers. Beyond the connection between vice and false teaching as a polemic *topos*,[25] they have a close relationship here because the good teaching has direct ethical aims (5).[26] The contrast furthers the letters' exhortation.

The negative example, as one would expect, bears a direct if antithetical relationship to Paul's example. Paul has been brought out of the condition toward which the apostates have turned, e.g., blasphemy (compare *blasphēmos* 13 and *blasphēmein* 20), ignorance (*mē nooutes* 7 and *agnoōn* 13), lack of faith (*en apistia* 13 and *tēn pistin enauagēsan* 19), self-will (*anypotaktois* 9 and *hybristēs* 13), sin (*hōn prōtos eimi egō* 9-10 and 15). Paul's positive example takes the charge that certain people (*tines* 3) should not teach falsely and thereby persist in that estrangement from the path to virtue one step further. It offers not only the alternative life-style but also the assurance that this way of salvation is offered to all sinners who would believe (*hina en emoi prōtō endeixētai* and *pros hypotypōsin tōn mellontōn pisteuein* 16). The false teaching is thus outweighed in its origins (ignorance), content (foolishness and vice), and end (shipwreck). Thus, Paul takes strong measures to teach the wayward to reform, 20,[27] and, in that, models the *makrothymia* in his own action as well as in Christ's action in him.

2. 2 Timothy 1:3-18 [28]

Paul refers Timothy to the type of his sound words at 13, *hypotypōsin eche hygiainontōn logōn* [29] *hōn par'emou ēkousas en pistei kai agapē tē en Christō Iēsou.*

---

[25] Karris, 60-61, characterizes this as an example of the polemic topos of vice and false teaching.

[26] The theoretical recommendation of the use of antithetical example (see, 26-27, 30,32) is applied to the exhortation of what to do and avoid (see 34-35, 40) and put to use in the development of the chria (42 and see the references in n. 63, p. 42), and in Isocrates (48-49, 50, 52-55, 65-66); Plutarch (74-76); Seneca (see 95, 99 and *Eps.* 94.48-50 and 95.13), the official letters (82); and the Socratics (133-34, 137-40, 148-51). See also Kamlah, 199.

[27] Strong censure is part of the method of paraenesis, to make clear the alternatives which are harmful (see 40, 62-64, 70). The aim of criticism is to correct and not to dishearten or abuse. It is contrasted with useless flattery or harsh reviling by Isocrates, 63; Plutarch, 69, and the Socratics, 117-18, 151, 159-60.

[28] See above 23.

[29] *logos* as the "word of God" seems to denote a doctrinal content (1 Tim 4:5; 2 Tim 2:9; Titus 1:3; 2:5) but closer scrutiny detects other meanings. It refers to the qualifications for office (1 Tim 3:1) and to the promotion of spiritual exercise (1 Tim 4:9) and of good

Ostensibly, the *hypotypōsis*[30] is not personal and therefore falls out of the purview of this study. However, several features of the presentation of the *hypotypōsis* indicate a personal aspect to it which make of it a personal example.[31] First of all, Paul reminds his correspondent that they are the sound words which *par'emou ēkousas en pistei kai agapē*$_i$. Their source is Paul.[32] Moreover, in 1 Tim 1:3-5, 10-11, 14, the sound teaching is inextricably linked with virtue toward which it charts the way.[33] Thus, as in 1 Tim 1:2 ff. the teaching is exemplified by Paul, so too here Paul's own virtue, 7, and faith, 12, form the living context to which his teaching points. There is an inner relationship (*di'hēn aitian* 12 between his designated role in 11 as *kēryx kai apostolos kai didaskalos* and in 12 his unashamed suffering (*paschō all'ouk epaischynomai*), his informed faith (*oida gar hō$_i$ pepisteuka*), and confidence of divine protection (*dynatos esti tēn parathēkēn mou phylaxai*). Thus Paul stands in full view as bearer and model of the teaching.[34]

---

works (Titus 3:8), even when its doctrinal implications are expressed in capsule confessions, when the passage itself carries a hortatory message urging constancy (1 Tim 2:11) or the context points to the ethical dimensions in a corresponding personal example (1 Tim 1:15). *logos* is paired with *didaskalia* (1 Tim 5:17) and seems equated with it (1 Tim 4:12). Elsewhere, it is specified by verbs of teaching and exhortation (2 Tim 4:2; Titus 1:9). The latter usage is further expressed by references to Paul's entire ministry (Titus 1:3) and to those of Timothy (2 Tim 2:15 and, obliquely 2:9) and of Titus (Titus 2:8). When *logos* is used in the plural (1 Tim 4:6) the context suggests that it refers to the exhortation of the letter (cf. 1 Tim 6:3; 2 Tim 1:13; 2:15). 2 Tim 2:17 describes the harmful effects of the opponents' *logos*. In effect, then, *logos* assumes the meaning of "charge" or "exhortation," and does not refer to doctrinal teaching only. Similarly, the *logoi* of Socratic *Ep.* 1.1(218.11), designating his philosophy, take on a hortatory tone at *Ep.* 14.8(258.5) where they refer to what a philosopher should be. The *logoi* at *Ep.* 20(268.17) are linked with Socrates' example (see also 18.2[266.23, 25]; 21.1[270.11]). This connection is also made at 28.10(290.33) and here the singular *logos* is used in reference to the hortatory lesson (contrast 28.4, 11, 13, 14 where *logos* means "speech" and 28.8 where the plural means "observations"). Only once, *Ep.* 26.3(280.32), does *logos* mean doctrinal teaching. *Ep.* 22.2(272.12) uses *logoi* for Plato's writing. In general, then, *logos* includes the idea of exhortation or charge in both sets of letters and is not to be taken to refer to doctrine alone. For discussion of the phrase *pistos ho logos* see J.C. Duncan, "*pistos ho logos,*" *ExpTim* 35 (1923-24) 141; F. Rendall, "Faithful to the Word," *Expositor* 53 n.s. (1887) 314-20; J.M. Bover, "Fidelis Sermo," *Bib.* 19 (1938) 74-79.

[30] For the relation between *hypotypōsis* and example see L. Goppelt, 246-56 and n. 15 above. See also de Boer, 197 ff.

[31] See also H. Schlier, *Die Zeit der Kirche: Exegetische Aufsätze und Vorträge* (Freiburg: Herder, 1956) 131.

[32] Paul even calls it *hē parathēkē mou.*

[33] See A.J. Malherbe, "Medical Imagery in the Pastoral Epistles," in *Texts and Testaments: Critical Essays in Honor of Stuart D. Currie,* ed. W.E. March (San Antonio: Trinity University, 1980) 19-35, and Bover, 74-79, for a full discussion of the hortatory implications of "sound teaching."

[34] The teacher is the principal model of his instruction as noted above in rhetorical theory, 33-35, and in the practice of Isocrates, 53-55, 65-66; Plutarch, 69-70; Seneca,

Another aspect of the "personality" of the *hypotypōsis* is evident from the "traditional" material in 9-10.[35] First, this is styled the *martyrion tou Kyriou hēmōn* 8, which itself suggests a declaration backed by the character of the person making it.[36] Furthermore, Timothy is not asked to accept or understand the gospel teaching but to bear ill treatment along with it (*synkakopathēson*). This reflects the reference to Jesus' trial at 1 Tim 6:13 and looks forward to the general statement on inevitable suffering for the pious at 2 Tim 3:12. Second, the life and work of Christ Jesus are described at 10 as an *epiphaneia* in which divine purpose and favor are manifested (*phanerōthēnai*).[37] The content of the teaching, therefore, is the personal manifestation in Christ of the saving plan of God.

87-89, 92, 95-97, and *Ep.* 98.13; official letters, 82; and the Socratics, 115, 138-41, 142-53 (here the founder of the school is looked to as the chief example of the mild cynicism exhorted and is followed in that function by his disciples).

[35] For a discussion of the traditional material in the Pastorals see E. Lohse, *Die Ordination im Spätjudentum und im Neuen Testament* (Göttingen: Vandenhoeck & Ruprecht, 1951) 80 ff. E. Käsemann, "Das Formular einer neutestamentlichen Ordinationsparänese," *Neutestamentliche Studien für Rudolf Bultmann* (Berlin: Alfred Töpelmann, 1954) 261-68, finds in 1 Tim 6:11-16 the paraenetic use of already formulated material which the author passes on to the community leaders, here represented by Timothy.

[36] The genitive *tou Kyriou* is taken as a subjective genitive in BAG 494 (and see 1 Tim 6:13) and *martyrion* is there understood to mean "Christian preaching and the gospel generally." A sepulchral epitaph quoted in MM 390 extends *martyrion* to an "upright life." The Lord's witness is paralleled with Paul's, *mēde eme* 2 Tim 1:8. This parallel stresses the unashamed confession regardless of opposition (e.g., from Pilate at 1 Tim 6:13, or from Paul's judges and captors at 2 Tim 1:8). Timothy is called to a similar confession (1 Tim 6:12; 2 Tim 1:8, and see Lohse, 80). P. Lippert, *Leben als Zeugnis, die werbende Kraft christlichen Lebensfürung nach dem Kirchenverständnis neutestamentlicher Briefe* (Stuttgart: KBW, 1968) 31-38, sees this witnessing as synonymous with the example of the Christian life which the letters propose. See also C.J. Ellicott, *The Pastoral Epistles of St. Paul: With a Critical and Grammatical Commentary and a Revised Translation,* 4th rev. ed. (London: Longmans, Green, 1869) 31. J. Thurén, "Die Struktur der Schlussparänese 1 Tim 6:3-21;" *TZ* 26 (1970) 245, calls the public confession of Jesus in 1 Tim 6:12b-14 the "ground and model" of the baptismal and ordination confessions. For the notion of the witness in the popular philosophical context see A. Delatte, "Le Sage Témoin dans la philosophie stoïco-cynique," *Académie Royale de Belgique. Bulletin de la classe des lettres et des sciences morales et politiques,* 5 sér., 39 (1953) 166-86 and Seneca *Ep.* 20.9.

[37] While *epiphaneia* refers to Christ's future coming at 1 Tim 6:14 and Titus 3:13, here and at 2 Tim 4:1, 8 it denotes his earthly life. The latter is also expressed by the verb *phaneroun* at 1 Tim 3:16 and Titus 1:3 as well as in this passage. This way of speaking appears elsewhere only in 1 John in the N.T. and is appropriate to the Pastorals' exhortation by example and their stress on individual and communal witness. See Ellicott, 127. I. Oberlinner, "Die 'Epiphaneia' des Heilswillens Gottes in Christus Jesus: Zur Grundstruktur der Christologie der Pastoralbriefe," *ZNW* 71 (1980) 192-213 examines the Pastorals' "Epiphany" Christology. For the word itself see E. Pax, *EPIPHANEIA: Ein religionsgeschichtlicher Beitrag zur biblischen Theologie,* Münchener Theologische Studien 1, 10 (Munich: K. Zink, 1955) and D. Lührmann, "Epiphaneia: Zur Bedeutungsgeschichte

From these indications one can reasonably conclude that the example is personal. The example figure is Paul, with Christ in the background, and the example's principal aim is to illustrate unashamed witness to the gospel and tenacity in faith despite consequent suffering. This example receives corroboration in the ancillary examples of unalloyed faith in Lois and Eunice, 5b, and amplification in the list [38] of God-given qualities [39] claimed by Paul for himself and Timothy at 7, i.e., *ou ... pneuma deilias alla dynameōs kai agapēs kai sōphronismou* (and cf. 14, *dia pneumatos hagiou tou enoikountos en hēmin*).

This example is directly related to the exhortation at 6; with the specifications *mē epaischynthē͵s ... alla synkakopathēson* 8, and *hypotypōsin eche ... tēn kalēn parathēkēn phylaxon* 13-14. This double exhortation demands retention and safeguarding of the teaching and unashamed suffering in consequence of this. Paul's example illustrates both aspects of the exhortation, 11-12, and shows that the one aspect of the exhortation, faithful safeguarding, implies and finds its modality in the other aspect,[40] unabashed suffering.

---

eines griechischen Wortes," in *Tradition und Glaube* (Fest. K.G. Kuhn, G. Jeremias et al., eds. Göttingen: Vandenhoeck & Ruprecht, 1971) 185-99.

[38] For the relationship of lists to examples see 53, 69, 73-75, 134.

[39] The common possession of the Spirit is reiterated at 2 Tim 1:14. The *charisma* has been given to Timothy by Paul. 2 Tim 1:6 (but see 1 Tim 4:14). Paul here asserts that Timothy possesses the gift of love and he calls for its exemplary demonstration at 1 Tim 4:12; 6:11; 2 Tim 2:22. He claims it for himself at 1 Tim 1:14 (cf. 2 Tim 1:13) and names it as one of the goals of his exhortation. 1 Tim 1:5 (cf. 1 Tim 2:15; Titus 2:2). The fearless constancy is exercised by Paul in the face of his opponents (2 Tim 2:9-10) and is expected of Timothy as he exercises his ministry (2 Tim 2:15, 24-25) just as he has already shown himself (2 Tim 3:10 ff.). The common gift of wisdom is also mentioned at Titus 2:2 and it, too, is the goal of the continuing exhortation (cf. Titus 2:4, 6; 2 Tim 2:9, 15; 3:2; Titus 1:8; 2:2, 5).

These are just some of the qualities which Timothy and Titus share with their exemplar Paul. Even their ministries parallel each other, which is not surprising for Timothy and Titus are Paul's successors in a full sense. For further discussion see H. Maehlum, "Die Vollmacht des Timotheus nach den Pastoralbriefen" (Diss. Basel: Friedrich Reinhardt, 1969) 52 ff.; N. Brox, *Die Pastoralbriefen* (Regensburg: Friedrich Pustet, 1969) *passim;* and H. Schlier, 132-33. The correspondences include *parakalein* (1 Tim 1:3; 2:1; 4:13; 5:1; 6:2; 2 Tim 4:2; Titus 2:6, 15); *paratithesthai* (1 Tim 1:8; 2 Tim 2:2); *parangellein* (1 Tim 1:8; 6:13; 1:3; 4:12; 5:7; 6:17); *didaskein* (1 Tim 2:7; 4:6, 13, 16; 2 Tim 1:11; 3:10; 1 Tim 6:2; 2 Tim 4:2; Titus 2:1, 7); *kēryssein* (1 Tim 2:7; 2 Tim 1:11; 4:2, 5); *mimnēskein/mnēmoneuein* (2 Tim 1:3-6; 2:8, 14; Titus 3:1); *hypomenein/paschein* (2 Tim 1:12; 2:9-10; 3:11; 1 Tim 6:11; 2 Tim 1:8; 2:3; 3:11; 4:11); *tērein pistin* (2 Tim 4:7; 1 Tim 6:14). A clear distinction is nonetheless maintained, with the addressees always being *tekna* (2 Tim 1:13; 2:2) of Paul. Though they are *diakonoi* with him (1 Tim 1:12; 4:6; 2 Tim 4:5), they are never *apostoloi*. They continue Paul's tradition (1 Tim 4:6; 2 Tim 2:2; Titus 1:5) and preserve what they are given in trust (1 Tim 6:20; 2 Tim 1:13-14) but only Paul calls it his deposit (2 Tim 2:8) or his gospel (2 Tim 1:12). Paul is involved with a universal mission (1 Tim 2:7; 2 Tim 4:17) and not with local churches as are Timothy and Titus.

[40] de Boer, 199-200.

As for the teaching itself as a model, de Boer seems correct when he sees it not as a definite form of belief but an outline of Christian teaching and preaching, an outline or basic pattern. Paul does not call for exact imitation of his teaching but rather to give due regard to this standard of Christian preaching, to regulate one's teaching by it, and to pass it on. As seen elsewhere in the letters, the teaching includes life practice as well and is verified by that practice.

Other facets of the example find expression in what is said and expected of Timothy. The spirit of virtue which Paul claims, 7, is the same as that by which he expects Timothy to be inspired, 14. Paul also reminds Timothy of the *agape* and *pistis* operative in his first acceptance of the teaching, 13, qualities which form part of Paul's own example, 7 and 12. Finally, the prefix to *synkakopatheson*, in connection with 3:12, calls Timothy to a similar experience of trials. In general, Timothy would fulfill the exhortation by following Paul's example.

There are negative examples referred to in this section as well, i.e., 15, *pantes*, like *Phygelos* and *Hermogenes*, who abandoned Paul. These are contrasted to Onesiphorus and his household, who tendered unashamed and persistent service to Paul at Rome and to the church at Ephesus, 16-18. Thus, Onesiphorus fulfills in an exemplary way the exhortation against feeling ashamed[41] at Paul's imprisonment, which all the others fail to do.

The other part of the exhortation, faithful safeguarding of the tradition,[42] is implied here as well, both in the verb *apestraphesan*[43] 15, describing the negative examples' apostasy, and in the end-time (*en ekeine tē hēmera*) consequences of Onesiphorus' *diakonia* 18.

In the expanded exhortation of the next chapter, the features of this section are repeated, e.g., *endynamou* 1; *ha ēkousas par'emou* 2; *synkakopatheson* 3; *dōsei ... synesin* 7; *to euangelion mou* 8; *kakopathō* 9; *hypomenō* 10; 11-13 generally.

3. 2 Timothy 3:1 – 4:8 [44]

The example in this section is Paul and appears in two places. The first is at 3:10-11 and it is signalled by the verb *parēkolouthēsas* 3:10,[45] and by the prediction

---

[41] Shame is addressed here in 2 Timothy with the background of Paul's undeserved imprisonment. Elsewhere, as at 2 Tim 2:15, the disrepute or reproach is occasioned by one's misdeeds or by slanderous opponents (1 Tim 1:13, 20; 3:2, 7; 4:10, 12; 5:7, 14; 6:1, 2, 4, 14; 2 Tim 3:2; Titus 2:5; 3:2). See also E.F. Brown, "Note on 2 Tim ii, 15," *JTS* 24 (1923) 317.

[42] Example, whether of the ancestors in a family, of the heroes or historical leaders in a community or state, or of the customary virtues or paraenetic ideal types, finds its persuasive weight in tradition (on the theory and use of *martyria palaiōn* see the discussion on rhetorical theory, 27, 32-33, 36-37; Isocrates, 50, 64; Plutarch, 69, 71 Seneca, 94, 99; and the Socratics, 105, 135-36. Traditional material and not novelty is the content of paraenetic works like those discussed above (see 41, 66-67, 124-25, 128, 150).

[43] See n. 23 above.

[44] See above 23-24.

[45] G. Kittel, "*akolouthein*," *TDNT* 1 (1964) 215, interprets *parakolouthein* to mean

of a common fate for all pious people 3:12. The second is at 4:6-8a and is signalled by the promise of like reward for all who love Christ's appearance, 3:8b. The first is a sketch in catalogue form of some facets of Paul's character, activity and experience. In the second, Paul looks back over his life-long struggle in the pursuit and service of virtue [46] and faith, and ahead to the crown of justice.[47] Some of the particulars of the example at 3:10 have already been noted above, e.g., *mou tē$_i$ didaskalia$_i$* 1 Tim 1:10; 2 Tim 1:11-12; *tē$_i$ pistei* 1 Tim 1:5, 14, 19; 2 Tim 1:13; *tē$_i$ makrothymia$_i$* 1 Tim 1:16; *tē$_i$ agapē$_i$* 1 Tim 1:5; 2 Tim 1:13; *tē$_i$ hypomonē$_i$* and all of 11 at 2 Tim 1:8; 2:9. The sketch-like nature of this list is seen in the broad and inclusive words which head the list at 3:10: *didaskalia, agōgē, prothesis* and which are followed by a sampling of particulars.[48] The same conjunction of general qualities and the exemplar's particular situation is found at 4:6-7.

"follow a teaching which has been grasped." BAG, 619, takes the verb to mean "follow faithfully, follow as a rule." Brox, 257 ff., however, finds that the "following" actually involves following Paul's exemplary way of life. See also de Boer, 200-201, Ellicott on 1 Tim 4:6 and 2 Tim 3:10; G.H. Whitaker, "2 Timothy III.10," *Expositor* 8 ser. 18 (1919) 342-43; and "Note on 2 Timothy iii. 10," *Expositor* 9 ser. 1 (1924) 456-57. Brox further suggests that in his "following" the pupil becomes the ideal picture of the church official. For classical parallels see Reiff, 9-15, 82-87, 107. See Whitaker, 342-44, for the connotations of educational discipline and teacher-to-student challenge in these verses. Other educational connotations are noted by L.H. Bunn, "2 Timothy ii.23-26," *Ex Tim* 41 (1929-30) 235-37.

[46] Athletic imagery is a common mode of describing the exercise in and pursuit of virtue in the sources examined in this study, e.g., in Isocrates, 50-51, 55, 62; Plutarch, 75; Seneca, 93; and the Socratics, 149 and 160. The teacher also shares in the struggle toward virtue in Seneca, 89-90, and *Vit. Beat.* 24.4-5 (J.W. Basore, *Lucius Annaeus Seneca. Moral Essays,* LCL 3 vols. [London: W. Heinemann, 1928]), and *Eps.* 6.1; 34.2. Cf. Paul's call to share his suffering at 2 Tim 1:8; 2:3 and the suffering and life of Christ 2 Tim 2:11. For a full treatment of the image in the Pastorals see V. Pfitzner, *Paul and the Agon Motif: Traditional Athletic Imagery in the Pauline Literature* (Leiden: E.J. Brill, 1967) 182 ff. and *passim.* See also J.M.T. Barton, "Bonum certamen certavi ... fidem servavi," *Bib.* 40 (1959) 878-944; C. Spicq, "Gymnastique et morale, d'après 1 Tim IV, 7-8," *RB* 54 (1947) 229-42; and A.J. Malherbe, "The Beasts at Ephesus," *JBL* 87 (1968) 74. Cf. K. Deissner, *Paulus und Seneca* (Gütersloh: C. Bertelsman, 1917) 21-24. See also P. Wendland, *Philo und die kynisch-stoische Diatribe,* Beiträge zur Geschichte der griechischen Philosophie und Religion (Fest. H. Diels, P. Wendland et al., eds. [Berlin: Georg Reimer, 1895]) 43-44; H.G. Ingenkamp, *Plutarchs Schriften über die Heilung der Seele* (Göttingen: Vandenhoeck & Ruprecht, 1971) 74-123.

[47] For the crown as reward in Isocrates see 62; in Plutarch, 75; and Pfitzner, 184-85.

[48] Seneca *Ep.* 95.65 ff. discusses the advantage of illustrating particular virtues by examples (a technique he calls "ethology" or "characterization"). This makes the hortatory prescription all the more compelling and induces imitation of the samples (*iconismus*). At 95.72 he suggests both outlining the requisite features of good men and providing personal examples of their embodiment. The select list of virtues made concrete in their attribution to Hipponicus by Isocrates *Ad Dem.* 9 ff. accomplishes the motivation for adopting the practices in the longer prescriptive section which follows. What is done with Paul here in the

The example here reminds Timothy of a general standard of teaching, conduct and attitude. The example corresponds to the first exhortation and its explanation which cover *didaskalia* (*mene en hois emathes kai epistōthēs* 14; *grammata oidas* 15; *pros didaskalian* 16) but also *agōgē* (*pros pan ergon agathon* 17) and virtue (*sophisai eis sōtērian dia pisteōs* 15; *pros elegmon, pros epanorthōsin, pros paideian tēn en dikaiosynē$_i$* 16).[49]

The restatement of the exhortation mentions all these aspects. Even though it orders at 4:2 *kēryxon ton logon, epistēthi* and ties teaching to this heralding of the word, this is a call to preach rather than to teach. Moreover, the rest of the commands stress the concern for conduct (*elenxon, epitimēson, parakaleson en pasē$_i$ makrothymia$_i$ kai didachē$_i$* 4:2).

In the concluding exhortation, the attention to one's official duties (*ergon poiēson, plērophorēson* 5) and the call to sober endurance (*nēphe, kakopathēson*) find their realization in Paul's endurance under trials, 3:10-11, and his self-sacrificing commitment to faith's demands, 4:6-7.[50] Thus, the aim of the exhortation, *hina artios ē$_i$ ho tou theou anthrōpos, pros pan ergon agathon exērtismenos* 3:17, is met in the example provided for adoption.

The negative examples, 3:2-9, 13; 4:3-4, propose the counter-option to be avoided (*toutous apotrepou* 3:5).[51] These people are unnamed, except for *Iannēs* and *Iambrēs,* their antecedents in the Jewish apocrypha. Led astray themselves they do the same to others (*planōntes kai planōmenoi* 3:13 and cf. *anthistantai tē$_i$ alētheia$_i$ ... katephtharmenoi ton noun* 3:8 and *hē anoia autōn* 3:9). This is unlike the informed stability exhorted of Timothy (*mene ... emathes ... epistōthēs ... eidōs ... emathes ... oidas ... sophisai* 3:14-15 and cf. *epistēthi* 4:2). Their faith is questionable (*adokimoi peri tēn pistin* 3:8), whereas the exhortation is explained in terms of a saving faith (*dia pisteōs* 3:15). They pander to their audience's pleasure, 4:3, but Timothy is to exercise pointed but helpful criticism (*pros elegmon, pros epanorthōsin* 3:16 and cf. 4:2).[52] Their activity encourages *hamartia* 3:6 and *epithymia* 3:6; 4:3, while Timothy's is to lead to *sōtēria* 3:15 and *dikaiosynē* 3:16.

Pastorals is accomplished with Timothy and Titus elsewhere, where they also are used to incarnate the virtues of the ideal church leader (e.g., 1 Tim 4:6-16; Titus 2:6-8). The same is true of the named opponents and apostates, who embody the errors and vices enumerated of people of that ilk (1 Tim 1:3-10, 20; 2 Tim 1:15; 2:16-18; 3:1-9; 4:14-16).

[49] The vocabulary (*sophizein, elegmos, epanorthōsis*) when seen in the light of 4:2 suggests the hortatory enterprise called *nouthesia* (see n. 27 and Titus 2:15; 3:10). See 51, 57, 59, 63, 75, 86, 131, 147, 156.

[50] This includes personal striving and official duty (teaching).

[51] See A. Vögtle, *Die Tugend- und Lasterkataloge im Neuen Testament exegetisch, religions- und formgeschichtlich untersucht* (Münster i.W.: Aschendorff, 1936) 28-29, where he sees the opponents' description as typical of the future rather than specifically polemic. At other times, 34-35, he finds the lists, like those at 1 Tim 1:9; 6:4; and Titus 3:3, to be descriptive of the particular difficulty in the community.

[52] See n. 27 and Malherbe, "Medical Imagery," *passim.*

Their latter-day appearance, 3:1, and new teaching 4:3, contrast with the long-standing tradition which Timothy has learned from known teachers (*eidōs para tinōn emathes*), has held all his life (*apo brephous*), and is to maintain, 3:14-15 as he does the work of evangelist, 4:5.

The vice list adds some detail to the sketch of the negative example. The sham piety[53] with which the list concludes, 3:5a, contrasts with the expectation of good work from Timothy *ho tou theou anthrōpos* and also with the general characterization of the faithful as *hoi thelontes eusebōs zēn* 3:12. The word *morphōsis* suggests the unsuccessful attempt by the false teachers to present a proper example.[54]

The negative example also contrasts with that of Paul. This is true generally for matters of teaching, conduct and character, but is summed up explicitly in the outcome of the two approaches. The false teachers *ou prokopsousin epi pleion* 3:9 and *prokopsousin epi to cheiron* 3:13.[55] Paul, on the other hand, expects *ho tēs dikaiosynēs stephanos* 4:8 from the Lord, *ho dikaios kritēs*, as the fruit of his faithful struggles. One cannot fail to notice the contrast between Paul's teaching which Timothy followed, 3:10, and which is linked with other orthodox teachers, 3:14, and the pandering and mythical teaching of the parvenu pedagogues, 4:3-4.

The negative example is further nuanced here with the references to the audience[56] of these objectionable teachers, i.e., silly women trapped in sin and ignorance (3:6-7) and apostates who choose instruction that suits their pleasure (4:3-14). Timothy is told to avoid the first difficulty by keeping to what he has already learned (3:14-15) and the second by maintaining moral sobriety (4:5, *nēphe*).

---

[53] For instances of the commonplace criticism of teachers whose actions belie their claims see 40, 52-53, 63, 65, 72, 138, 140, 141, 151-152.

[54] Here, the bad teachers are not named but they function as examples nonetheless. Isocrates *Ad Dem.* 51 uses *paradeigma* to refer to the unnamed, general characterizations of the virtuous and vicious in 45 ff.

[55] For the theme of progress or advancement see the discussions of Seneca, 95-97, and *Eps.* 11.1; 32.2; 94.50; Isocrates, 51, 62, 76; and the Socratics, 151. See also C. Brokate, *De aliquot Plutarchi libellis* (Göttingen: Robert Noske, 1913) 35.

[56] It has been noted above in the example theory, 27, 30, that the example is effective because it recalls a previous judgment and applies it to the current argument. Similarly in paraenetic literature, traditional material other than new principles is promoted (see 41, 66-67). The prescriptions are meant to be perennially useful (see 56, 59-62). This type of instruction proves superior and is to be sought rather than encouragement and association in one's foolishness (see 63-64, 160). The traditional and non-controversial character of paraenetic works, and thus of the Pastorals, lends support to L. Johnson's observation, 1 ff., that the letters are not meant to re-establish the authority of Paul for this authority is never in question. Rather, the letters appeal to him as the accepted and traditional authority. See also Brox, 69 ff., 76 ff.

B. *The Examples of Timothy and Titus*

In all three section discussed above, the example referred to is Paul. Timothy and Titus are also expected to be models for the community.[57] 1Tim 4:12 states the explicitly and antithetically: *mēdeis sou tēs neotētos kataphroneitō, alla typos ginou tōn pistōn en logō$_i$, en anastrophē$_i$, en agapē$_i$, en pistei, en hagneia$_i$.* Like Paul at 1 Tim 1:16 Timothy is to be a model for others who believe. The list of *en* phrases sets out the range of application of the example. With the last three, importance is given to the virtues of the example.[58] Mention of *anastrophē* lays stress on conduct. This stress and the very virtues listed were seen above in Paul's example in Chapter I.[59] As a result, the importance of *logos* is not only balanced but diminished and made relative to matters of conduct and character.

The entire section affirms this interest which can be called paraenetic. At 4:11, 13, 16a (and cf. 6) *didachē* shares the focus with *parainesis*. The juxtaposition of instruction in virtue and mythical speculation has already been seen.[60] Moreover, Timothy's *prokopē* and its public demonstration, 15, lie behind the exhortation here.[61] An element in the advancement is useful[62] (*ōphelimos*), spiritual exercise (*gymnasia*),[63] which Paul indicates has been his own way at 7b-10.[64] The *eusebeia*[65] acquired from this exercise bears with it the promise of

---

[57] Besides the example of the teacher himself, a variety of other examples is forseen in the example theory 26-30, 32-33, 35, and put into practice, 49, 53, 64, 69, 91-92, 105, 136-37, 41-43, 146-49. This includes the example of the addressee as indicated by Isocrates, 51, 66; Plutarch, 69-70; official letters, 82; Socratics *Eps.* 15.1(260.4 ff.); 20; 21.3(270.22 ff.); 29(294.16 ff.). See A. Vögtle, 54 ff., for further comment on the exemplary role of the church officials in the Pastorals.

[58] *en agapē$_i$, en pistei, en hagneia$_i$.*

[59] The goal of the exhortation is salvation for Timothy and his audience, v. 16.

[60] At v. 7 Timothy is told to avoid foolish myths in favor of good teaching and words of faith.

[61] See n. 55.

[62] Advantage or usefulness for growth in virtue and the acquisition of happiness is noted as a characteristic of this exhortation and example highlights the prospects for success (see 36, 40, 55; 63, 149, and contrast 95-96, 148-51, 156).

[63] See n. 46. For exercise as a part of rhetorical training see *Auct. Her.* 1.2. (H. Caplan, trans., *Cicero. Ad C. Herennium libri IV; de ratione dicendi,* LCL [Cambridge: Harvard University, 1954]). For a survey of exercise in Epictetus' moral education program see B.L. Hijmans, *ASKESIS:Notes on Epictetus' Educational System* (Assen: Van Gorcum and Co., 1959). In the latter, note the role of example to show that the ideal is not out of reach and thereby to encourage the pupil to strive to set his affairs right, 72 ff.

[64] Paul expresses the notion of striving in the homologoumena, e.g., Phil 3:12-16; 1 Cor 9:24-27.

[65] W. Foerster, "*EUSEBEIA* in den Pastoralbriefen," *NTS* 5 (1958-59) 213-18, sees *eusebeia* as a religio-ethical virtue the exercise of which promotes right order (see his article in *TDNT* 7 [1971] 175-78, 181-84. See also Pfitzner, 177. Spicq, *Epîtres,* 482 ff., considers it in a more religious sense).

present and future life, which parallels the aim of the specific prescriptions and the establishment of the example, i.e., *touto gar poiōn kai seauton sōseis kai tous akouontas sou* 16b.

The various prescriptions specify what the exemplary Timothy is to do in his role of service for the community, 6. But particular emphasis falls on the care Timothy is to take of himself (*mē amelei* 14; *meleta, isthi* 15; *epeche, epimene* 16; and *gymnaze* 7), for his own salvation, 16. This emphasis invites two observations. First, it is common to hortatory literature of this sort.[66] Second, it meets the circumstance of the letter, where Paul is commissioning his young associate to carry on his works[67] and wants to be sure that his youthfulness[68] is no obstacle (*mēdeis sou tēs neotētos kataphroneitō* 12). His youthfulness is also superseded by the *charisma* endowed on him by the presbyterate, 14.

The positive example of Timothy finds its negative counterpart in the anonymous (*tines* 1), latter-day, apostate teachers, shown by Karris to be largely a commonplace portrait.[69] They follows *tois pneumasin planois* and *didaskaliais daimoniōn* 1, while Timothy follows *tois logois tēs pisteōs kai tēs kalēs didaskalias* 6. Their obtuse consciences and physical asceticism, 2-3, contrasts with the exercise in *eusebeia* urged on Timothy at 7b-10.

In the prescriptions and descriptions in the last chapter the letter again uses antithesis to reemphasize the acquisition of the good qualities in Timothy's exam-

---

[66] See A. Dihle, "Posidonius' System of Moral Philosophy," *JHS* 93 (1973) 53-54, 57. Precepts were seen above to complement the examples (53-55, 65-66, 68, 70, 72-73, 93-94, 100, 135, 140-46, 166-67, 179, 181, 184, 187-88). Care for one's virtuous state and attention to oneself is also a commonplace in the hortatory literature surveyed, e.g., for Isocrates see 50, 54, 62, 75, 82, Plutarch, 134; official letters, 147; Seneca *Eps.* 4.1; 16.1; 34.3; 69.6; Socratics, 150, 152.

[67] In addition to the parallels between Paul and his associates and addressees drawn in n. 39, one notes the explicit delegation at 1 Tim 4:13. The exemplary role which Paul plays is likewise exercised by Timothy and Titus (1 Tim 4:12; Titus 2:7) and they are responsible for choosing successive generations of teachers and officials (1 Tim 5:9; 2 Tim 2:2; Titus 1:5).

[68] The literature surveyed above is directed toward a youthful audience. This sets the context for the admonitions to avoid criticism, especially for self-indulgence, errors of judgment and choice of friends. (See the discussions on Isocrates, 51, 54, 61-62, 65, and Seneca *Eps.* 1.5; 4.2; 11.1. For the same theme in the Pastorals, see also 2 Tim 2:22 and Titus 2:7-8 (falling as it does in the admonition to young men, and see 2:15). There is no need to identify the "youthful passions" in 2 Tim 2:22 with the excesses of the heretical opposition, as does W. Metzger, "Die neoterikà épithumiae in 2 Tim 2,22," *TZ* 33 (1977) 129-36.

[69] The censure of deceitfulness in proponents of other teachings is typical as Karris, *Function* 57, asserts and material surveyed above verifies (for Isocrates, 49, 52-53, 63; Socratics, 139-40, 148-50, 152, 156). See also 2 Tim 3:13 and Titus 3:3 (cf. also 1 Tim 2:14). For Further discussion of the trope in classical literature see P. Wendland, "Betrogene Betrüger," *RhM* 49 (1894) 309-10.

ple and the rejection of the detrimental aspects of the false teachers and their teaching. The negative example, indefinite and hypothetical (*ei tis*), is someone whose teaching is heterodox, unsound and impious, 6:3; who is ignorant, querrulous and venal, 6:4-5; and who wandered from the faith under false claims to knowledge, 6:21. On the contrary, (*sy de* 6:11) Timothy is to flee this and pursue a variety of virtues; to fight the fight of faith, 6:12; to keep himself blameless, 6:14; and to safeguard the traditional teaching, 6:20.

Titus' example is also called for, at Titus 2:7-8. The rubric *typos kalōn ergōñ*, the noun *semnotēs*, and the aim of avoiding adverse criticism, all indicate that Titus' general attitude and actions (*peri panta*) are essential to the example, which also includes *didaskalia* and *logos hygiēs*.[70]

The antithetical example precedes Titus' (1:10-16), as has often been the case above.[71] These people are unnamed (*polloí*), specified as Jewish (*hoi ek tēs peritomēs*),[72] and sketched out in commonplace vices which reflect those seen in the negative examples above, i.e., *anypotaktoi, mataiologoi, phrenapatai* 10; money-seeking teachers who upset households, 11; *pseustai, kaka thēria, gasteres argai* 12; given to *mythois* and *entolais* of human devising, perverters of the truth, 14; *apistoi*, unclean in mind (*nous*) and conscience (*syneidēsis*), 15; falsely claiming to know (*eidenai*) God, *bdelyktoi, apeitheis*, unfit for any good deeds, 16.

The exemplary mode of dealing with them is varied. One approach calls for sharp rebuke in hopes of eventual reform (*elenche ... hina hygiainōsin* 13 and cf. 11 and 3:10-11).[73] Another depends on keeping oneself above reproach (2:8). Both are expressed at 2:15 (and cf. 3:10-11). In connection with the second, Titus is also to avoid any connection with speculations and controversies which are *anōpheleis* and *mataioi* 3:9.[74]

The aim of the examples, both positive and negative, finds expression at 2:11 ff. This too appears antithetically, fitting the two types of examples. The instruction first calls for denying *asebeian kai tas kosmikas epithymias* and then living *sōphronōs kai dikaiōs kai eusebōs*. In the latter condition one would live, as Christ made possible, *apo pasēs anomias, zēlōtēs kalōn ergōn*. The emphasis on attitude and action needs no more mention.

---

[70] See n. 29.

[71] Like Timothy, Titus presents the negative figure first. This technique has already been noted in Isocrates, 49, 51, 63-64; Plutarch, 69, 72; and the Socratic *Eps.* 1.1; 5.1; 6.1.

[72] Trummer, 165, finds little biographically reliable or significant in the Jewish coloring of the opponents' description in the Pastorals. G. Rudberg, "Die Diogenes-Tradition und das Neue Testament," *ConNT* 2 (1936) 41, finds *nomikoi* to be a stock derogatory adjective in the Diogenes traditions.

[73] See also 1 Tim 5:20; 2 Tim 2:24-26; 3:16; 4:2 (see 1 Tim 1:20) and n. 27.

[74] The prescription to avoid harmful company reinforces the commands to steer clear of vice and this commonplace use of negative example has been seen in rhetorical theory, 40; Isocrates, 113; official letters, 63; Seneca, 95, 100, *Eps.* 7.2; 32.3; 104.20-21; Socratics, 152 and *Eps.* 8, 9, 11. See also 1 Tim 4:7; 6:20; 2 Tim 2:16; 3:5; 4:15; and Vögtle, 34-35.

C. *The Example of the Community*

The letter to Titus connects the conduct of various members of the community with the way the Christian message is received. The example of the teaching in action demonstrates its acceptability in theory. So, young women are to be schooled in domestic virtues *hina mē ho logos tou theou blasphēmētai* 2:5.[75] The blasphemy here might simply be a reference to the women's own unworthy behavior, but 2:8 clearly identifies the opponents as the source of negative remarks. The totality, *peri panta,* of Titus' exemplary conduct has the aim *hina ho ex enantias entrapēᵢ mēden echōn legein peri hēmōn phaulon* (cf. 2:15).[76] In the same section 2:9-10, the conduct of slaves also has a positive function with regard to the teaching, i.e., *hina tēn didaskalian tēn tou sōtēros hēmōn theou kosmōsin en pasin.* The epistle to Titus thus relates the virtous actions of the community members with the example of Titus himself, 2:7,[77] and they all exercise the same function of verifying the teaching to those outside the community.

As he is for the other qualities, Paul is the example of blamelessness which his young representatives and the community adopt. Though he is imprisoned, it is only as if he were a wrongdoer (*hōs kakourgos* 2 Tim 2:9). He remains unashamed, 2 Tim 1:12, however, and the word of God suffers no setback (*alla ho logos tou theou ou dedetai* 2 Tim 2:9). The latter is precisely the aim of setting an example of conduct which is above reproach.

1 Timothy also links the virtue of blamelessness[78] with the example of Timothy and is concerned with the exemplary role of the community as well. The command that Timothy *tērēsai ... tēn entolēn aspilon anepilēmpton* 1 Tim 6:14, comes at the conclusion of the summary description of the contrasting examples of the money-hungry false teachers, 3-10, and Timothy, 11-12 (cf. 2 Tim 2:15).[79] As for widows, domestic virtues are again urged *mēdemian aphormēn didonai tōᵢ antikeimenōᵢ loidorias charin* 1 Tim 5:14 (cf. 5:7, 12). Slaves are called to service *hina mē to onoma tou theou kai hē didaskalia blasphēmētai* 1 Tim 6:1. The

---

[75] In "Lois and Eunice: Women in the Pastorals, a Functional Approach," an as yet unpublished study on the mixed role of women in the Pastorals, J. Bassler of Georgetown University finds evidence that the letters are attempting to forestall external criticism of excessive liberality perceived in the Christian community.

[76] The insistence on being above criticism and reproach is commonplace and is linked with the need for the teacher to be an example of his own teaching, as seen in rhetorical theory, 33-35, 40; Isocrates, 49-55; Plutarch, 69-70; official letters, 82; Socratics, 136, 157.

[77] The mention of the pedagogical epiphany of grace at 2:11 ff. adds to the stress on teaching by example in this section. Just as Jesus gave himself to redeem and cleanse his people 2:14, so too, the audience are called to self-denial and piety, 2:12.

[78] See n. 76.

[79] Brown, 317, understands the worker as someone "not to be ashamed of" rather than "not to be ashamed."

blamelessness which is urged on Timothy at 1 Tim 6:14 appears as a qualification for the bishop, 1 Tim 3:2, along with the necessity of having *martyrian kalēn ... apo tōn exōthen, hina mē eis oneidismon empesē* 3:7 (cf. Titus 1:6-8). The expectation is the same for deacons, 1 Tim 3:10.

In addition to removing the grounds for rebuke by setting a good example, an upright and blameless life also serves a positive function. From good service, the deacons *bathmon heautois kalon peripoiountai kai pollēn parrēsian en pistei* 1 Tim 3:13. The bishop's blameless conduct, character and teaching are prerequisites *hina dynatos ē kai parakalein en tē didaskalia tē hygiainousē kai tous antilegontas elenchein* Titus 1:9.[80] The example of one's own life and adherence to what is taught gives authenticity to the positive teaching and criticism of others' failings.[81]

The community, in close association with Timothy and Titus, play a role in verifying or contradicting the teaching by their examples. This role passes to them from Paul, the prime exemplar in the letters. Up to this point, however, this analysis of the Pastorals has concentrated on explicit references to example. Attention turns now to the implicit example in the letters.

IV. Implicit Example in the Letters

2 Tim 3:10-11 refers to Paul's life in a comprehensive way and thereby suggests that Paul's example includes more than the details of character, conduct or teaching listed by the letters when they explicitly outline the example. Paul also reveals himself through what he says and does in other places in his letters. It is proper, then, to look an other details in the letters to appreciate the full range of the example device in the Pastorals. While he hands down prescriptions (1 Tim 1:3, 18; 2:1; 6:13) he also obeys the divine command to become an apostle[82] (1

---

[80] As observed in n. 76, one's own example influences the acceptability of his teaching. This is particularly true with regard to the exemplar's blamelessness as a foundation for his *parrēsia* or constructive criticism of wrongdoing and deficiencies. Self-criticism, therefore, is an important step toward becoming blameless. These themes have been noted in Isocrates, 52-52, 54, 63, 65-66; Plutarch, 69, 75-76; official letters, 82; Seneca, 89; Socratics, 139, 150, 158-59. See also n. 27 and above 54, 56-58, 72, 86, 103, 105, 131, 151-52, 156. See also E. Peterson, "Zur Bedeutungsgeschichte von *parrēsia*," in *Zur Theorie des Christentums* (Fest. Reinhold-Seeberg, W. Koepp, ed., [Leipzig: A. Deichert (D. Werner Scholl), 1929]) 283-97.

[81] For further discussion see Lippert, 17-60. Karris dismisses him too easily. Blamelessness in the Pastorals is not formal and meaningless. As noted above ns. 76 and 80, it relates to the function of example and substantiates *parrēsia* and *nouthesia*. In the lists where this quality is cited it is either first or last and is sometimes the only quality mentioned.

[82] The source and end of Paul's ministry is God. His obligation to the church and its ultimate salvation is a basic distinguishing element between the Pastorals and the purely philosophical/paraenetic works surveyed above.

Tim 1:1; Titus 1:3; 2 Tim 1:1; 2 Tim 1:9). He is *apostolos,* but also *kēryx* and *didaskalos* (1 Tim 2:7; 2 Tim 1:11; 4:17; Titus 1:3), entrusted with the *euangelion* (1 Tim 1:11; 2 Tim 2:8). He is an affectionate friend of his addressees [83] (2 Tim 1:4; 4:9, 19-21; Titus 3:15) and asks for their presence and support (2 Tim 1:18; 4:9, 11, 13; Titus 3:12), just as he asks the same for others (Titus 3:13). Even more than a friend, he enjoys spiritual kinship as a father of his addressees [84] (1 Tim 1:2, 18; 2 Tim 1:2; 2:1; Titus 1:4). He travels (1 Tim 1:3; 2 Tim 3:11; Titus (1:5) and uses the letter as a surrogate for his personal presence [85] (1 Tim 3:14-15) in order to inform his chosen representatives (1 Tim 1:3; Titus 1:5) of his mind.[86]

Into this use of the letter form example fits perfectly. The references to his own situation by the author provides authoritative backing for the commands.[87] Moreover, the picture of Paul's action is in accordance with his teaching, which verifies the teaching and adds weight to the corresponding prescriptions.[88] The

---

[83] Friendship is an important element in moral exhortation, especially that which is effected through letters, as seen above 12, 51, 55, 57, 63, 86-89, 94-95, 107, 117, 121-25, 130, 149-52, 158-59, 161. See also G. Bohnen- blust, *Beiträge zum Topos "peri philias"* (Berlin: Gustav Schade [Otto Francke], 1905); L. Dugas, *L'Amitié antique* (Paris: Librairie Félix Alcan, 1914); Fr. Hauck, *Die Freundschaft bei den griechen und im Neuen Testament* (Leipzig: A. Deichert [D. Werner Scholl], 1928); J. Kabiersch, *Untersuchungen zum Begriff der Philanthropia bei Kaiser Julian,* Klass.-Philol. Studien, 21 (Wiesbaden: Harrassowitz, 1960); S. Lorenz, "De progressio notionis *philanthropias*" (Diss. inaug. Leipzig, 1914); Spicq, *Epîtres,* 2:657-76 and "La Philanthropie hellénistique, vertu divine et royale," *ST* 12 (1958) 169-91.

[84] A corollary to friendship and another commonplace in the literature surveyed is spiritual kinship between teacher-father and pupil-child as noted in rhetorical theory, 34-35; Socratics, 122-23, 136, 149; as well as among members of the school, 152.

[85] The letter effects a surrogate presence of the sender. In this way the sender not only communicates his prescriptions, but also bolsters his exhortation by his own example, both explicit and implicit. In doing this, he provides himself as one of the good associates which he wants his addressee to seek out (see n. 74). The theme has been noted above, 11, 30, 55-57, 82-83, 87-89, 95, 105, 129, 235. For the dialogue character of the letter in its use by Paul and the early church see A.N. Wilder, *Early Christian Rhetoric: The Language of the Gospel* (Cambridge: Harvard University, 1971) 14-15, 31.

[86] Like the official letter (see 82-83) the hortatory letter expressed the author's teaching for a wide audience (see the principle on 85 and applications in Plutarch, 70; Socratics, 116, 124-26, 131-32, 144-46). Compare Isocrates' usage described on 46, 51, 53-54, 55-56, 59-62.

[87] It would be precipitous to conclude from this that the authority, whether of Paul or of his successors in the Pauline church of the Pastorals, was lost or in question (see n. 56). Rather, as in the appeal to Socrates and the long-standing tradition of mild Cynicism (see 116-21 above), the point is to reaffirm the commonly accepted line of tradition. See also n. 89.

[88] P. Trummer, "'Mantel und Schriften' (2 Tim 4,13). Zur Interpretation einer persönlichen Notiz in den Pastoralbriefen," *BZ* n.F. 18 (1974) 193-207, he finds in the personal request and references here and elsewhere a corroboration in exemplary deed of

audience enter into the dramatic situation alongside Timothy and Titus and feel themselves addressed and challenged by Paul,[89] who describes the model life practices for the whole church (*hina eidē$_i$s pōs dei en oikō$_i$ theou anastrephesthai, hētis estin ekklēsia theou zōntos* 1 Tim 3:15; *pantes hoi thelontes eusebōs zēn en Christō$_i$ Iēsou diōchthēsontai* 2 Tim 3:12;[90] *ēmen gar pote kai hēmeis anoētoi ktl.* Titus 3:3; *hina phrontizōsin kalōn ergōn proïstasthai hoi pepisteukotes theō$_i$* Titus 3:8-9; and cf. 1 Tim 1:16; 4:12).

Throughout the letters, Paul consistently exhibits the qualities which are outlined in the example sections, e.g., knowledge, 1 Tim 1:8; Titus 1:1; faith, 1 Tim 2:7; Titus 1:1, 4; toil and struggle, 1 Tim 4:10; attempt to reform others 1 Tim 1:20; *euseibia* 1 Tim 4:2; Titus 1:1; love, 1 Tim 2:7; suffering for the gospel and enduring on behalf of the elect, 2 Tim 2:9-10; forgiveness of those who abandon him, 2 Tim 4:16; feeling protected by God, 2 Tim 1:12; 4:16-18, and empowered by God, 2 Tim 4:17. At Titus 3:3 ff. he identifies himself with the vices which still plague the apostates but which the community of believers has left aside, e.g., *anoētoi, apeitheis, planōmenoi, douleuontes epithymiais kai hēdonais poikilais, en kakia$_i$ kai phthonō$_i$ diagontes, stygētoi, misountes allēlous.* This is enough to get an idea of the implicit example in the Pastorals. The picture will be filled out in the discussion below of the composite images of the examples in the letters.

There is a consistency throughout the letters between Paul's explicit and implicit examples.[91] A composite picture of the examples of Paul and the others

---

the principles laid down in the letters. See also C. Ritter, *Neue Untersuchungen über Platon* (Munich: C.H. Beck, 1910) 362-66 and contrast K. Erbes, "Zeit und Ziel der Grüsse Röm 16, 3-15 und der Mitteilungen 2 Tim 4, 9-21," *ZNW* 10 (1909) 128-47, 195-218. See also Trummer, *Paulustradition,* 74-85; N. Brox, "Zu den persönlichen Notizen der Pastoralbriefe," *BZ* n.F. 13 (1969) 76-94; and contrast B. Reicke, "Chronologie der Pastoralbriefe," *TLZ* 101 (1976) 81-94; S. de Lestapis, *L'Enigme des pastorales de St. Paul* (Paris: Gabalda, 1976).

[89] W. Stenger, "Timotheus und Titus als literarische Gestalten: Beobachtungen zur Form und Funktion der Pastoralbriefe," *Kairos* 16 (1974) 25-67, suggests that the letters are doubly fictitious, in both sender and receiver. The addressees are not, therefore, to be considered as the historical persons nor are they simply programmatic-typical personifications of a super-shepherd office (Brox, 257 ff.). They function in conjunction with the pseudonymity of Paul. The aim is not to stamp current ideas with Pauline authority, nor is it merely to confirm and pass on authentic apostolic tradition. Rather, it is to set out the living presence and perduring relevance of apostolic origins for the community in post-apostolic times. Like the letter itself as a form (see n. 85) the official representatives are means of establishing this perduring presence.

[90] Note the shift in reference from "you" to "all" in Titus 3 from "we" to "they."

[91] This consistency is to be expected from the letter "collection" in Paul's name which the Pastorals have always represented, a collection which promotes the Pauline example in a concerted way. See A.E. Barnett, *Paul Becomes a Literary Influence* (Chicago: University of Chicago, 1941) 183, 222, 251. H. Binder, "Die historische Situation der Pastoralbriefe," in *Geschichtswirklichkeit und Glaubensbewährung* (Fest. F. Müller, F.C. Fry, ed., [Stuttgart: Evangelisches Verlagswerk, 1967]) 71-72, offers arguments and evidence that the Pastorals

mentioned in the letters will reflect a similar consistency, on both the positive and the negative sides. Before the composite picture is drawn, however, it is important to see the paraenetic nature of the teaching in the letter. With this clearly indicated, the function of the examples in promoting it will be better appreciated.

V. The Paraenetic Teaching of the Pastorals

Paraenetic features abound in the letters.[92] There are numerous other indications that the teaching which preoccupies the attention of the Pastorals is largely paraenetic. To start with Paul, he was seen above to be a teacher who exhibits the moral improvement and the virtues toward which his teaching aims.[93] His instruction is better characterized as paraenetic than as didactic. First, in addition to the direct imperative prescriptions, note his use of *parakalō* (1 Tim 1:3; 2:1) and *parangellō* (1 Tim 6:13 and cf. 1 Tim 1:5, 18), *anamimnēskō* (2 Tim 1:6). These are paraenetic terms. Nowhere does he actually "teach" in the letters and he often accompanies his command to teach with a command to exhort (1 Tim 4:11, 13; 6:2; 2 Tim 4:2; Titus 2:15, and cf. 2 Tim 3:16; Titus 2:7).

Second, he calls attention to *parathēkē mou*,[94] which Timothy must safeguard (1 Tim 1:20; 2 Tim 1:14) and *to euangelion mou* (2 Tim 2:8), which some oppose (1 Tim 1:10-11) but along with which he suffers (2 Tim 1:8). This tradition one could also refer to as his *didaskalia*. But 2 Tim 3:10 ff. indicates that his own attitude

---

are reworked Pauline originals. See also P.N. Harrison, *The Problem of the Pastoral Epistles* (London: Oxford University [H. Milford], 1921); "The Authorship of the Pastoral Epistles," *ExpTim* 67 (1955) 77-81; *Paulines and Pastorals* (London: Villiers, 1964). For the Pastorals as a collection see W. Schmithals, "Zur Abfassung und ältesten Sammlung der paulinischen Hauptbriefe," *ZNW* 51 (1960) 244 and "Pastoralbriefe," *RGG*³ 5:147. The testamentary character of 2 Timothy has been discussed by J. Munck, "Discours d'adieu dans le Nouveau Testament et dans la littérature biblique," *in Aux Sources de la tradition chrétienne* (Fest. M. Goguel, O. Culmann, ed., [Neuchâtel: Delachaux & Niestlé, 1950]) 163; H.J. Michel, *Die Abschiedsrede des Paulus an die Kirche Apg 20.17-38,* SANT 25 (Munich: Kösel, 1973) 67; O. Knoch, *Die 'Testamente' des Petrus und Paulus: Die Sicherung der apostolischen Überlieferung in der spätneutestamentlichen Zeit,* SBS 62 (Stuttgart: KBW, 1973) 44-64; E. Cortès, *Los discorsos de adiós de Gn 49 a Jn 13-17; Pistas para la historia de un género literario en la antigua literatura judía* (Barcelona: Herder, 1976) 387-96. In this 2 Timothy is different from 1 Timothy and Titus, although the latter also contain some testamentary features; Michel, 67; Munck, 162; Cortès, 387-96; Knoch, 29-30. None of these studies makes use of the material from the philosophical traditions as applied above to the Socratic letters, and which will have to be done in a later study for the Pastorals. The character of 1 Timothy and Titus as community regulations and as church order documents has been noted above 3-6.

[92] See Chapter II.

[93] See above 198-200, 204-5, 207-8.

[94] See C. Spicq, "Saint Paul et la loi des dépôts," *RB* 40 (1931) 481-502; S. Cipriani, "La dottrina del 'depositum' nelle lettere pastorali," *AnBib* 17-18 (1963) 2:130-42; C. Mauer "*tithēmi*," *TDNT* 8 (1972) 152-68; and J. Roloff, 245 ff.

and actions occupy a place alongside the *didaskalia* as objects of Timothy's attention and that learning leads to wisdom, salvation, right conduct, and virtue (15-16).

Furthermore, 1 Tim 4:6 also commands Timothy's pursuit of good teaching and constrasts with false asceticism and other dissembling and false teachings. The alternative to this is specified (7b-10) in terms of spiritual *gymnasia* which leads to *eusebia*, not to knowledge (and cf. 14-16). Titus 2:1 ff. details *ha prepei tē_i hygiainousē_i didaskalia_i* in the actions and moral qualities to be acquired by the community members.[95]   In fact, at 3-5 the upright conduct of older women renders them *kalodidaskaloi* who, because their lives are in order, can teach or rather *sōphronizein* younger women and instil virtue in them.

As for *to euangelion,* even here the doctrinal statements have an exemplary and paraenetic twist to them.   At 1 Tim 1:15 the teaching that Jesus came to save sinners has observable effects in the *makrothymia* experienced by Paul, 16, and which he holds out for other believers.   The mystery of *eusebeia,* which was revealed by Christ, 1 Tim 3:16, is present and future spiritual well-being. Jesus witnessed this for his day, 1 Tim 2:4-6, iust as Paul in the letter proclaims it for his own, 1 Tim 4:8-9. This revelation is not just of a truth to be learned but of a condition to be acquired (by *gymnasia* at 1 Tim 4:8). Another reference to Jesus at 1 Tim 6:13 notes that he witnessed the good confession before Pilate and calls for (*parangellō*) an equally blameless observance of *tēn entolēn.* 2 Tim 1:8 ff. (cf. 2:8-13) and the example and corresponding call not to learn but to suffer with the gospel and Christ's witness has been discussed above. The appearance of God's grace in Christ, mentioned again at Titus 2:11 ff., has as a pedagogical object (*paideuousa hēmas*) not *didachē* but *parainesis* (*hina arnēsamenoi tēn eusebeian kai tas kosmikas epithymias sōphronōs kai dikaiōs kai eusebōs zēsōmen ktl.*). The same is true for the purpose of Christ's death, *hina lytrōsētái hēmas apo pasēs anomias kai katharisē_i heautō_i laon periousion, zēlōtēn kalōn ergōn.* At Titus 3:8 ff., after the statement about the appearance of divine kindness and philanthropy in Christ (3-7), comes the insistence that (*hina*)[96] the believing community take thought (*phrontizein*) about performing in good works (cf. 3:14 where good works are also the express object of learning).

---

[95] Sound teaching is directly linked with paraenesis at 1 Tim 1:10 where vices are said to be its opposite; at 1 Tim 6:13 ff. where, in addition to the vices, the contrast is drawn with *tē_i kat'eusebeian didaskalia_i* at 2 Tim 1:3 in Paul's example; at 2 Tim 4:3 in both the vice list and in the paraenetic features of the correct form of teaching (i.e., *elenchein, eptiman, parakalein*); at Titus 1:9 where the bishop's good character qualifies him *parakalein en tē_i didaskalia_i tē_i hygiainousē_i kai ... elenchein;* and cf. Titus 2:2 where moral virtue is listed alongside *hygiainōn* in faith, love, and patience; and Titus 2:8 where good works are a part of being above reproach. See also n. 33. See also K. Grayson "A Problem of Translation: The Meaning of Parakaleo, Paraklesis in the New Testament," *ScrB* 11 (1980) 29; H. von Lips, *Glaube—Gemeinde—Amt: Zum Verständnis der Ordination in den Pastoralbreifen,* FRLANT 122 (Göttingen: Vandenhoeck & Ruprecht, 1979) 45, 72-76.

[96] *hina* here gives the content of what is insisted on, not its purpose. See BAG 377; BDF 387 (3).

Third, the paraenetic nature of Paul's teaching in the Pastorals can also be seen in those passages contrasting it with foolish speculations of false teachers. Titus 3:8-9 urges good works which are here characterized as *kala* and *ōphelima* and later as responding to needs (*eis tas anankaias chreias* 14). Insistence on works in Paul's instruction (*peri toutōn boulomai se diabebaiousthai*) contrasts with the *mōras ... zētēseis kai genealogias kai ereis kai machas nomikas* which are *anōpheleis* and *mataioi* and should be avoided. 2 Tim 2:14 ff. sets up a similar contrast. Timothy is cautioned to avoid *logomachein, ep'ouden chrēsimon, epi katastrophē tōn akouontōn* and instead is to establish himself as a worthy and unashamed *ergatēs*. In this he will become a *skeuos eis timēn, hēgiasmenon, euchrēston ... eis pan ergon agathon hētoimasmenon*. The *logos tēs alētheias* is contrasted with *hai bebēloi kenophōniai*. The latter lead to *asebeia* and work like *gangraina*, while the former to salvation (2:10-13). The way to choose is through virtue (*dikaiosynē pistis agapē eirēnē ... ek katharas kardias*), and avoiding *mōrai kai apaideutoi zētēseis*, which provoke *machai*. It is a question of method here and not aim (*doulon de Kyriou ou dei machesthai alla ēpion einai pros pantas, didaktikon, anexikakon, en praÿtēti paideuonta*) and the virtue of the teacher should win a receptive audience but also be a demonstration of what is being taught. The inscription on God's foundation brings this out as well. The second insists that confession of God and wrongdoing (*adikia*) are incompatible, while the first warns that God is not deceived as to who really belong to him. In the hoped-for result, *metanoia*, two poles are present: *epignōsis alētheias* and *ananēpsōsis ek tēs tou diabolou pagidos;*[97] but inherent in the truthful teaching is the ethical behavior (cf. 1 Tim 2:2-4). The same point of the paraenetic nature of the teaching in contrast to mythical speculation and argumentative inquiries has already been observed for 1 Tim 1: 3 ff.[98] The traditional nature of the teaching as entrusted to Paul, safeguarded by him, passed on to his collaborators for safekeeping, and ultimately passed on by them as well is also a hallmark of its paraenetic character (1 Tim 1:11, 12, 14; 6:20; 2 Tim 1:12, 14; 2:2). This contrasts with the objects of fruitless inquiries into new areas and interpretations.[99]

The perversion of the truth by false teachers for the sake of profit is condemned at Titus 1:10 ff. The problem is Jewish myths and human commands drawn up by people with faulty minds and consciences. Their teaching is thus untrue and immoral. Moreover, their own actions are questionable. Their words

---

[97] Cf. 1 Tim 3:7.

[98] See above, 199-200.

[99] Both G.C. Fiske, *Lucilius and Horace: A study in the Classical Theory of Imitation* (Madison: University of Wisconsin, 1920) 27, 31, 39-40, and E. Hatch, *The Influence of Greek Ideas on Christianity* (New York: Harper & Brothers, 1957) 86 ff., note the inclination toward the traditional in the classical period, reinforced by the instruction in the rhetorical schools which grew to dominance in the "Augustan" and "Silver" ages. Both form and content were affected by this tendency and the Socratics' and Pastorals' uses of traditional personages of the past and commonplace exhortation are instances of this.

and works do not correspond. Indeed, because of their vice, they are *pros pan ergon adokimoi.*

The preceding observations have shown the paraenetic character of the teaching in the Pastorals. As Paul himself says at 1 Tim 3:14-15, *tauta soi graphō ... hina eidē̦s pōs dei en oikō̦ theou anastrephesthai.*[100] Since this is the case, the place of example is crucial to the letters' pedagogy. As a complement to the prescriptions, the examples offer an incarnation of the ideal way of life which the Christian teaching professes to inculcate.[101] They indicate which actions are acceptable and which are to be avoided. They reinforce the teacher's prescriptions by presenting his own life and works as conforming to them. They also back up the prohibitions by presenting the failure of those who follow another way.

As seen above, the letters describe the positive and negative examples in several distinct sections. The qualities which they comprise, however, overlap and form essentially uniform portraits, which this study will now attempt to summarize. As was case in the Socratic letters between the examples of Socrates and his followers, there are minor differences in the Pastorals between Paul's and his followers' examples, but agreement in the essential features. The composite picture of the positive and negative examples will now be put together.

VI. **The Positive Example of the Pastoral Epistles and its Contrast**

Paul is the apostle-teacher-herald, called by God, and obedient in service.[102] This service keeps him traveling and causes him persecution and suffering but God remains at his side throughout, even when all others abandon him (2 Tim 4:16-18). He meets suffering unashamed and he faces death with equanimity (2 Tim 4:8). While no one else can be an apostle, he calls upon his representatives to carry on his work of teaching, exhortation, and divine service (2 Tim 2:24; 3:17), assuring them of the same spiritual support (2 Tim 1:6 ff.; 1 Tim 4:14). He is faithful (1 Tim 1:12; 2:7; 2 Tim 1:3; 3:10; 4:7; Titus 1:1, 3) and pious (Titus 1:1; 2:12) and urges piety and faith on his addressees and the community (1 Tim 2:2, 10, 15; 3:9, 11, 13; 4:6, 7, 8, 12; 5:2, 4, 22; 6:6, 11, 12; 2 Tim 1:3, 5; 2:2, 22; 3:12, 15; Titus 2:2, 7, 10, 12; 3:15). He also calls on them to join in the suffering unashamed, and predicts this to be the plight common to all believers (2 Tim 3:12). But he assures them that God will save them in the end (1 Tim 1:1, 16; 2:4; 4:10, 16; 6:19; 2 Tim

---

[100] As seen above in both the theory and its applications, the nature of a paraenetic work is to provide a broad range of prescriptions for virtuous conduct which will be perennially applicable. In this regard, this phrase of 1 Timothy should be compared to the matters discussed and noted in rhetorical theory, 41, 46; Isocrates, 53-56, 59-62, 64; Plutarch, 70, 76; official letters, 82-83; Socratics *Eps.* 6.10; 27.2 ff.

[101] The universalizing (catholicizing) character of the Pastorals' exhortation was noted by E. von Dobschütz, *Die urchristlichen Gemeinden: Sittengeschichtliche Bilder* (Leipzig: J. Hinrichs, 1902) 193.

[102] See 1 Tim 1:1, 11, 12; 2:7-8; 2 Tim 1:1, 11: 3:10; 4:17; Titus 1:1, 3.

1:9-10; 2:10-13; 3:15; 4:8; Titus 1:3-4; 2:13-14; 3:4-7). He warns his associates of a coming time when both teachers and audience will fall away (2 Tim 4:3-5) and reject the true teaching.

The contrasting picture has false teachers with an eye for wealth (1 Tim 6:5; 2 Tim 3:2; Titus 1:11 and cf. 1 Tim 3:3, 8; Titus 1:7). Some of these even surreptitiously corrupt gullible women in their homes (2 Tim 3:6ff., 1 Tim 5:13). Though claiming to be teachers, they are ignorant (1Tim 1:6-7; 6:4, 20; 2 Tim 3:8-9; Titus 1:10, 15-16; 3:9 and cf. 1 Tim 1:13; Titus 3:3) and deceived (1 Tim 4:1; 2 Tim 3:13 and cf. Titus 3:3), faithless (1 Tim 1:19; 4:1; 6:10; 2 Tim 2:18; 3:8; Titus 1:13, 15 and cf. 1 Tim 1:13; Titus 3:3) and impious (1 Tim 1:9; 6:5; 2 Tim 2:16; 3:5). While they themselves are ruined (*diephtharmenoi ton noun* 1 Tim 6:5) and go from bad to worse (1 Tim 6:9; 2 Tim 3:13, as do their followers at 2 Tim 3:6-7), they cause trouble for Paul and his followers (2 Tim 4:14-15). Deception (1 Tim 4:2; 2 Tim 3:5; Titus 1:10, 16 and contrast 1 Tim 1:5) and flattery (2 Tim 4:3) are their pedagogical techniques.

As for Paul and his followers, they hope *sōthēnai kai eis epignōsin alētheias elthein*[103] 1 Tim 2:4 (contrast 1 Tim 6:5; 2 Tim 2:25; 3:7) as God designs. This knowledge of the truth is *kat'eusebeian* (Titus 1:1), with the instruction in it being both paraenetic and didactic. Hence the letters place an emphasis on virtue and exercise. Paul seeks no wealth from his teaching but finds riches in *eusebeia meta autarkeias* 1 Tim 6:6 and so counsels being satisfied with the necessities of life (*toutois arkesthēsometha* 1 Tim 6:7-8). In accord with this conviction, Paul insists that eternal life is the desired inheritance (*klēronomoi ... zōēs aiōniou* Titus 3:7) and that, for now, the Christians must be schooled in good works (*hina phrontizōsin kalōn ergōn proïstasthai* Titus 3:8; *manthanetōsan ... kalōn ergōn proïstasthai* 3:14; cf. Titus 2:14; 3:1; 1 Tim 2:10; 6:18; 5:10), following the example of their teachers (*typos kalōn ergōn* Titus 2:7; cf. 2 Tim 2:21; 3:17; 4:5; 1 Tim 3:1; 5:25; and contrast 2 Tim 4:14, 18; Titus 1:16).

In contrast to the high-mindedness of the rich (1 Tim 6:17, *hypsēlophronein*) and the ignorance of the heterodox, Paul acknowledges that he and all believers receive *pneuma ... dynameōs kai agapēs kai sōphronismou* 2 Tim 1:7 and are instructed to live *sōphronōs kai dikaiōs kai eusebōs en tō̧ nyn aiōni* Titus 2:12. Church officials and members are to display the quality of soundness of mind (1 Tim 2:9, 15; 3:2; Titus 1:8; 2:2, 5) and the young addressees are to instil this quality (Titus 2:6) in young men as the older women are to do in the younger women (Titus 2:4). This virtue is confirmed by the other references to the fact that the exemplary figures have been instructed and have learned, just as the community ought to do (*manthanein* 1 Tim 2:11; 5:4; 2 Tim 3:14; Titus 3:4; *paideuein* 2 Tim 2:25; Titus 2:12; *paideia* 2 Tim 3:16; *oida* 1 Tim 1:8, 9; 3:15; 2 Tim 1:12; 2:23; 3:14, 15).

---

[103] M. Dibelius, "*EPIGNOSIS ALETHEIAS*," in *Botschaft und Geschichte*, 2 vols. (Tübingen: J.C.B. Mohr [Paul Siebeck], 1956) 2:1-13, analyzes the phrase and finds it to be a technical expression in the Pastorals which includes both teaching and Christian life generally. In this connection, he interprets *hygiainousē didaskalia* as the teaching of Christianity. See also Lips, 80-84.

Sōphrosynē is but one of a host of virtues promoted by the example of the letters.[104]   Others include: *agapē* 1 Tim 1:5, 14; 2:15; 4:12; 6:11; 2 Tim 1:7, 13; 2:22; 3:10; Titus 2:2, 10; *dikaiosynē* 1 Tim 6:11; 2 Tim 2:22; 3:16; 4:8; Titus 2:12; 3:5; *pistis* noted above; *eusebeia* noted above; *hypomonē* 1 Tim 6:11; 2 Tim 2:10, 12; 3:10; Titus 2:2; and also 2 Tim 1:8; 2:3, 11; 3:12; *makrothymia* 1 Tim 1:16; 5:19; 2 Tim 2:24-26; 3:10; 4:2, 16; Titus 3:10; *praÿpathia* 1 Tim 6:11; 2 Tim 2:25; *epieikeia* 1 Tim 3:3; Titus 3:2.[105]

As in the examples, so also in the exhortation the accent rests on pursuit (*diōkein* 1 Tim 6:11; 2 Tim 2:22), movement toward (1 Tim 2:4), exercise (*gymnazein* 1 Tim 4:7), struggle (*agōnizein* 1 Tim 4:10; 6:12; 2 Tim 4:7), battle (*strateuesthai* 1 Tim 1:18 and cf. 2 Tim 2:3), persistence (*menein* 1 Tim 2:15; 4:16; 2 Tim 3:14), diligent practice (*meletan* 1 Tim 4:15), and progress (*prokopē* 1 Tim 4:15), rather than on a perfected state.[106]   The state of perfection is not really looked toward even at the end of the struggle, but only the reward for the struggle (2 Tim 2:11-13; cf. 2 Tim 4:8).   Balancing the pursuit of virtue is the rejection of pleasures (Titus 2:12).   Youthful pleasures are a particular problem for the young addressees to be aware of (2 Tim 2:22).

Before the hedonistic (*philēdonos* 2 Tim 3:4) and false teachers, who seek to be rich (*philargyroi* 2 Tim 3:2), pleasures and riches lie as a snare and lead them to destruction (1 Tim 6:9-10).   They are led astray from the faith to sin and vice (*apoplanan* 1 Tim 6:10; Titus 3:3) as are their followers (2 Tim 3:6), and their vain inquiries lead to disputes (2 Tim 2:23; contrast *chōris orgēs kai dialogismou* 1 Tim 2:8).   Moreover, they are lawless and unruly (*anomos, anypotaktos* 1 Tim 1:9; and cf. *hybristēs* 1 Tim 1:13; *anomia* Titus 2:14), arrogant and precipitate (*hyperēphanos, propetēs* 2 Tim 3:1-4).   Their ignorance has no outlet but their own destruction (1 Tim 6:9) and their progress toward the worst is inevitable now (2 Tim 2:16; 3:9, 13) and will be known to all (2 Tim 3:9; 1 Tim 5:24-25) as they come to eventual judgment (1 Tim 2:24).

For Paul useful (*ōphelimos*) is a decisive criterion, whether one is judging spiritual *gymnasia* (1 Tim 4:8), scripture (2 Tim 3:16) or good works (Titus 3:8). The needs of others are to be met as part of the fruitfulness of a Christian's good works (Titus 3:14).   On the contrary, *logomachein* is rejected because it is *ep' ouden chrēsimon* (2 Tim 2:14).   Paul himself claims to have done good works (Titus 3:4) and expects his addressees to do the same (2 Tim 3:17).[107]   He arranges for

---

[104] See B.S. Easton, "New Testament Ethical Lists," *JBL* 51 (1932) 1-12, and N.J. McEleney, "Vice Lists of the Pastorals," *CBQ* 26 (1974) 203-19 and above 73-75.

[105] The last two qualities do not appear in the example sections but they do come up where Paul speaks to Titus of the sinful past common to all Christians and the new conduct expected of the saved and renewed (Titus 3:3-11).

[106] Paul, at the end of his career, is confident that he has completed his task (2 Tim 4:6-8); others in the full vigor of life must engage in their task, as in a race or contest.

[107] See also Titus 2:7. Good works are required not just of his addressees but of the officials in the community (1 Tim 3:1; 5:10, 25; 2 Tim 2:21) as well as of the community

provisions for two travelers at Titus 3:13 and declares that he worked for the evangelization of *panta ta ethnē* (2 Tim 4:17).

Paul sees particular usefulness in his mode of teaching (1 Tim 1:20) and that urged on his representatives because it is not flattery (2 Tim 4:3) or pointless abuse (*loidoria* 1 Tim 5:14; *oneidismos* 1 Tim 3:7) but constructive criticism (*nouthesia* Titus 3:10), with the expectation of reform. The reform (1 Tim 1:20; 5:20; 2 Tim 2:25; Titus 1:13) makes the teaching and the criticism really useful, just as false teaching or *logomachia* is not but is actually destructive (*epi katastrophē$_i$ tōn akouontōn* 2 Tim 2:14).

A bond of affection and spiritual kinship has grown up between Paul and his associates (1 Tim 1:2, 18; 2 Tim 1:2, 4; 2:1; 4:9; Titus 1:4; 3:15) and he expects this to continue in his representatives (1 Tim 5:1-2). He also enjoys the support of his friends (2 Tim 1:15-17; 4:9 ff.) and lauds this support among the members of the community as well (2 Tim 1:18; 1 Tim 5:16). Paul's concern goes beyond the community to include prayers for kings and rulers (1 Tim 2:2-4; Titus 3:1), reflecting a desire for tranquil surroundings as well as the salvation of all people.[108] But his chief concern is the community's proper conduct, well-being and good order (1 Tim 3:15; Titus 1:5).

As mentioned above, the false teachers' inquiries and debates are useless and, in fact, harmful and destructive because of their ignorant and compromising stance on riches and the dangerous passions resulting from them (1 Tim 6:3-10). This is dramatized in the example of false teachers who dupe gullible women (2 Tim 3:6-7; cf. the threat for the future at 2 Tim 4:3-4). This ignorance, disobedience, deception, and enslavement to passions were once the condition common to all (Titus 3:3) until the salvation in Christ offered an alternative of life (Titus 2:11-13). The call to flee youthful passions (2 Tim 2:22) is backed up by the insistence on attention to one's personal growth in virtue (1 Tim 2:15; 4:14-16; 2 Tim 3:14). This insistence makes the use of personal example in the Pastorals particularly appropriate for the exhortation, offering as it does not just an abstract standard but the embodiment of the desired qualities in a figure who is well-known and important to the community.

The analysis undertaken thus far in this chapter has established the formal characteristics of the use of example in the Pastoral Epistles and has also laid out the content of the examples. In order to locate this usage in the tradition of epistolary exhortation, it is now appropriate to compare it to the uses of example in the Pauline homologoumena and the Socratic Epistles.

---

members generally (1 Tim 2:10; 6:18; Titus 2:14; 3:1, 8, 14). Works are of secondary importance to God's design and grace in the quotation of traditional material at 2 Tim 1:9, and to his mercy in the quotation at Titus 3:5. The bad works of the apostates and false teachers are referred to at 1 Tim 5:25; 2 Tim 4:14, 18; Titus 1:16.

[108] 1 Tim 2:7; 3:16. The command to pray for officials and for peace promotes civic responsibility for the "bourgeois" Christianity of the Pastorals, according to P. le Fort, "La Responsabilité politique de l'église d'après les épîtres pastorales," *ETR* 49 (1974) 1-14.

VII. Comparison of Example in the Pauline Homologoumena and in the Pastorals

These two groups of letters bear a general resemblance to each other from their common employment of traditional hortatory features. While this includes their use of example, closer scrutiny reveals important differences in their use of the device. First, the specific character of the occasions and persons provoking the homologoumena directs the examples toward specific problems rather than toward a generalized exhortation to Christian life and service as in the Pastorals.[109] Second, Paul, conscious of the prerogatives of his fatherhood, calls attention to himself and others, but the latter always in relation to himself.[110] The examples in the Pastorals exercise a paradigmatic role derived from Paul but distinctly their own.[111] Third, the urgency of the situations leads Paul to rely largely on explicit examples, while the Pastorals can employ more indirection with implicit examples.[112] Fourth, Paul's "opponents" are likewise specific and rarely the typical, negative models of the Pastorals.[113] Fifth, the homologoumena are not as consistent as the Pastorals in expanding the examples through lists and prescriptions.[114] Sixth, Paul includes the imitation of Christ's mind and attitudes but the Pastorals call attention only to Christ's exemplary witnessing.[115] Seventh, the variety of hortatory devices surrounding the examples in the homologoumena is more restricted and they stand in a different structure than in the Pastorals.[116]

In addition to these areas of direct contact and divergence, other characteristics of the two groups of letters confirm the distinction noted between them. First, the Pastorals stress the effect of good example both on the credibility of the community among outsiders[117] and on the community's own acceptance of their officials' admonitions.[118] Paul's examples look toward inner community edification[119] and toward bolstering his own beleaguered position.[120] Second, the tra-

---

[109] See 168-69, 172-75, 179-80, 183-86 on Paul and 198-99, 200-1, 205, 7, 211 on the PE. (Pastoral Epistles will be abbreviated PE in these notes). See also A. Oepke, *Die Missionspredigt des Apostels Paulus* (Leipzig: J.C. Hinrichs, 1920) 20, 31-33.

[110] See 176-81, and see J. Roloff, 118-19.

[111] See 170-71, 174-77, 180, 184-85, 189 on Paul and 202, 204, 209, 211-13 on the PE. Lips, 121-38, finds the PE official's role described with reference to his place as father of the household (1 Tim 3:5). In this, the focus is on direction and not begetting, which the homologoumena stress.

[112] See 188-89 on Paul and 197, 213-16.

[113] See 171, 175, 184, 188 on Paul and 196, 200-1, 207-8, 210-11 on the PE.

[114] See 179, 184, 188 on Paul and 196, 198, 206, 208, 211.

[115] See 181-82 on Paul and 203-4, 217.

[116] See 189-90 and 74 n. 42.

[117] See 212-13.

[118] See 214-151.

[119] See 169 179-80, 182-83, and note his call to imitate his striving, 178, 185.

[120] See 188-89. Like Paul's, Socrates' actions or attitudes are questioned (*Eps. 1 and 6)*

dition (*para-, diathēkē*) of Paul's teaching, attitude and action constitutes part of the paraenetic example in the Pastorals.[121] In the homologoumena, the tradition (*paradosis*) fills the same role but is spelled out less remotely in the *hodoi* and *peripateia* of which Paul reminds his addressees.[122]

As a result of this comparison, one can see more clearly that while example is an important device in the Pauline letters surveyed, its use in the homologoumena diverges noticeably from that in the Pastorals. The line of inquiry now turns to the Socratic Epistles and a comparison of example there and in the Pastoral Epistles.

VIII. Comparison of Example in the Socratic and the Pastoral Epistles

The Socratic Epistles resemble the Pastorals in a striking way and understanding the intent behind their creation casts light on the writing of the Pastorals as well. As for the resemblances, first, the analysis of the Socratic Epistles has uncovered the full range of hortatory language, devices and techniques [123] familiar from the other works surveyed above, including the Pastorals. Second, as in the Pastorals, the variety of devices sometimes falls into the arrangement proper to the development of the chria.[124] Third, the Socratic letters express and have been formulated on a concern to preserve a tradition of teaching and practice. Thus they stress the memorabilia form and biographical details about Socrates and his followers for their hortatory aims.[125] This is one aspect of their paraenetic character.

Fourth, the examples, as varied as they are in the Pastorals,[126] are often simple sketches,[127] elaborated in conjunction with virtue and vice lists and with pre-

---

and he and his followers find his imprisonment and execution a possible source of embarrassment or discredit (*Eps.* 14, 15, 16, 17, 21). Similar, though less direct, challenges to Paul's attitudes (1 Tim 1:3 ff.; Titus 1:10 ff.) and a similar shame and defection over Paul's imprisonment 2 Tim 1:8 ff.; 2:9 ff.; 4:9 ff.) are noted in the PE. Unlike the homologoumena, however, these epistles are less concerned to reaffirm the authority of either Socrates or Paul, and more to focus on his example of virtue and self-sacrificing and the exhortation derived from them.

[121] See 201-2, 216-19, and 1 Tim 6:20; 2 Tim 1:12, 14, 2:2.

[122] See 167-68, 178-82, 184-86.

[123] See 132-34, 201 n. 29 on the SE (The Socratic Epistles will be abbreviated SE in these notes.) and Chapter II on the PE.

[124] See 138-43 on the SE and 22-25 on the PE. See also 42 n. 63. This results in a literary structure which is not a logical one but proceeds by the association of ideas. See R. Coleman, "The Artful Moralist: A Study of Seneca's Epistolary Style," *CQ* n.s. 24 (1974) 285.

[125] See 124-25, 128-30, 150 on the SE and 201-2, 216-17, and n. 87 above on the PE.

[126] See 137 in the SE and 18-19 on the PE.

[127] See 134, 143 on the SE and 200, 205-7 on the PE.

cepts.[128]   Fifth, while the teacher-father Socratic, like Paul, is the principal example, others join him in fully exercising that function, as do Timothy, Titus and their associates.[129]   Sixth, the author of the Socratics chooses his examples to fit the traditional criteria that they be *oikeia kai gnōrima,* and noble and important, in effect the founding fathers of the Socratic and Cynic traditions.[130]   For the community of the Pastorals, the examples are largely of the same stature, i.e., Paul and his associates. Seventh, with most of the examples both the Socratics and the Pastorals hope to promote a particular mode of conduct.   As prototypes, they play a hortatory role.[131]

Eighth, offsetting these positive examples in both sets of letters are negative examples in antithetical relationship.[132]   Largely unnamed, indefinite or typical,[133] these teachers and companions propose goals beyond even their own reach, indulge in and flatter their disciples, and lead them to ruin.[134]   Ninth, both the Socratics and the Pastorals urge the same remedy: avoid the harmful associations[135] or criticize them in a constructive way.[136]   The first tactic, keeping oneself blameless and above reproach, actually provides a basis for the second, *parrēsia* or frank criticism.[137]   Tenth, the two letter groups emphasize assiduous attention to one's acquisition of virtue by the principles taught.[138]   In addition to the credibility this lends to one's criticism, it bears the positive effect of verifying by example the advantages and usefulness of the way of life being promoted.[139] In this connection, the letters reflect the typical theme of progress in virtue[140] and make use of athletic imagery to express it.[141]

Eleventh, as works in the paraenetic tradition with the life of virtue as their aim, both the Socratics and the Pastorals contain a broad range of perennially

---

[128] See 125-26, 133, 136, 142-43, 145 on the SE and 195-96, 199-200, 204-5, 209-11, 219.

[129] 105, 115-16, 135-43, 146-47 on the SE and 202, 204-5, 209-11 on the PE.

[130] See 105, 135-37.

[131] See 127, 136-37 on the SE and 202-3, 207-12, 214-15, 219 on the PE.

[132] See 134-43, 148-53 on the SE and 201, 205, 207-8, 210-11, 219-22 on the PE.

[133] See 138-42 on the SE and 200-1, 205, 207-8, 210-11, 218-21 on the PE.

[134] See 117-18, 135, 140, 148-50, 151-52 on the SE and 200-1, 207-8, 210-11, 222 on the PE.

[135] See 152 and *Eps.* 8, 9, 11 for the SE and 199, 208, 210-11, 218, and n. 74 above on the PE.

[136] See 150 on the SE and 201, 207, 211, 222 on the PE.

[137] See 121-22, 137, 150 and *Ep.* 1 for the SE and 209-14, 217 on the PE.

[138] See 150, 152 on the SE and 199, 207-8, 210-211, 217, 222 on the PE.

[139] See 124-25, 136, 139-40, 141, 144-45 for the SE and 209-10, 216 on the PE.

[140] See 153-4 on the SE and 208-10 on the PE.

[141] See 151, 160 on the SE and 206, 209 on the PE.

applicable teachings,[142] be they in word or in exemplary deed.[143] Their intended audiences are equally broad,[144] but the gap in time and space is bridged by the tone of friendship and even spiritual kinship between the stated correspondents.[145] Twelfth, without the occasion for direct dialogue among the Socratic and Pauline friends and spiritual family, the letters stand as the preferred substitute.[146] Thus, explicitly and implicity, the letters keep the teacher, the good example and helpful companion, always present, and they are a constant reminder of his program. Their uncomplimentary descriptions of the foolish teachers and harmful companions to be avoided [147] make the positive model seem all the more preferable. They also make the direct but corrective criticism appear more palatable in contrast to seductive flattery and pointless abuse, both of which are equally harmful.[148]

While some of these points of similarity also hold true for the Pastorals and the homologoumena, the resemblance between the use of example in the Socratic and Pastoral Epistles is more extensive in both the form, aim, and thematic content of their exhortation. Stepping back from these details of their paraenetic character, one will also find in the Socratic Epistles some help in appreciating the choice of the letter form in the Pastorals and the community of those letters.

While the letter form of the Pastorals evidences a natural and even necessary continuation of Paul's literary activity, it achieves an impact which exceeds that intended by the Apostle in the homologoumena. The similar literary enterprise in the Socratic Epistles brings this to light. In the first place, the creation there of a lively exchange of letters establishes a believable context for the ensuing development of the philosophical exhortation. Unable, and some apparently unwilling, to pursue their philosophical discussions together in one locale, the disciples of Socrates make themselves present and carry on their exchange by letter.[149] Timothy and Titus in the Pastorals do not share the contentiousness which surfaces among some of the Socratics, but they depend on the letters to keep in touch with the absent Paul.[150]

Second, the program of letter writing is ostensibly undertaken to keep a record of Socrates' teachings and virtue,[151] and the completed corpus actually incorporates some earlier letters under Socrates' name.[152] The full corpus, how-

---

[142] See 124-26, 134, 162, *Eps.* 6, 10, 27.2 ff. for the SE and 219 for the PE.
[143] See 128, 136-39, 145 on the SE and 216-17, 219 on the PE.
[144] See 116, 130, 145 on the SE and 214-15 on the PE.
[145] See 121-24, 130, 136, 149, 152 on the SE and 214 on the PE.
[146] See 105, 123, 129, 143-46 on the SE and 213-16, on the PE.
[147] See 135-43, 148-53 on the SE and 200-1, 210-11 on the PE.
[148] See 117-18, 150-52 on the SE and 201, 208 on the PE.
[149] See 118-21, 123-24, 128-30.
[150] See 1 Tim 1:3; 3:14-15; 4:13; 2 Tim 1:11; 4:9 ff., 21; Titus 1:5; 3:12.
[151] See 128-29.
[152] See 103, 106-7.

ever, accomplishes both less and more than its declared goal. Less, because Socrates is indeed the principal figure in the corpus and he is duly vindicated and praised for his teaching, way of life, and untimely death. On closer analysis, however, Socrates voices and embodies not necessarily his own teachings but those of mild Cynicism.[153] In fact, his Cynic depiction is largely consistent throughout the corpus, undergoing some modification in the letters of the Socratics further in the direction of mild Cynicism which the corpus wishes to propagate.[154] More, because not only Socrates but his disciples as well are marshalled forth as examples in deed and word of this brand of Cynicism. The anecdotal and doxographical traditions about the first-generation Socratics have supplied the framework for a letter corpus propagandizing a popular philosophical program in a later period.[155] The Pastoral Epistles, too, present a picture of Paul and his activity which echoes the tradition.[156] More closely observed, however, the Paul of the Pastoral Epistles is less the *kēryx kai apostolos...didaskalos ethnōn* (1 Tim 2:7) of the homologoumena (and even Acts) and more the paradigmatic church leader concerned for the stability and continuity of church life on the local level. Furthermore, his co-workers Timothy and Titus and their associates share his concern and exemplary function.[157]

Third, the letter form invites the latter-day Socratics, i.e., the followers of mild Cynicism in the early Empire, to enter the dialogue as friends in the philosophical association. Thus, the intended audience, as opposed to the fictitious correspondents, are engaged actively in the process of evaluating the interpretations and aims of the writers of the various letters. They are thereby drawn to react and, ideally, to take action themselves on the Cynic message of the corpus.[158] The device of implicit example expands the focus of the reader from any explicitly designated example to the way of life proposed by the details of the composite letter corpus. Even the apparently banal biographical details often fill in the details of the philosophical *bios* in which the Cynic author wants to stimulate interest and practice. No one figure in the letters is the all-encompassing paradigm, but rather the paradigm encompasses all the figures.[159] So, too, in the Pastoral Epistles a

---

[153] See 111-12, 114-15, 117-21. See 115-16 for a discussion of the choice of Socrates as exemplar.

[154] See 111-12, 120-21, 145-48.

[155] See 105-6, 145-46.

[156] See A.E. Barnett, *Literary Influence* and also "The Use of the Letters of Paul in Pre-Catholic Christian Literature" (Diss. University of Chicago, 1932) and Harrison, *Problem, Paulines,* and "Authorship."

[157] See 201, 204-5, 209-13. See also R.F. Collins, "The Image of Paul in the Pastorals," *Laval Théologique Philosophique* 31 (1975) 147-73; J. Wanke, "Der verkündigte Paulus der Pastoralbriefe," in *Dienst der Vermittlung,* Erfurter Theologische Studien 37 (Fest. zum 25. jährigen Bestehen des philosophisch-theologischen Studiums im Priesterseminar Erfurt, W. Ernst et al., eds., [Leipzig: St. Benno, 1977]) 165-89.

[158] See 131-32. Seneca's letters seem to aim at a similar reaction (see 87-92). Isocrates may paint his discourses in epistolary tones (see 56-57) for the same reasons.

[159] See 112, 132, 143-46.

variety of individuals exercise paradigmatic roles and the implicit example used in the letters requires the audience's attention, reaction, and commitment to details of attitude and conduct outside the explicit example sections.[160]

By harmonizing the relationships the first generation Socratics, even to their anticipated reunion in Athens (*Eps.* 16 and 17), the Socratic Epistles suggest something of a community or school setting for their exhortation to mild Cynicism. The rhetorical character of the letters moves toward the same observation.[161] As stated above, this, too, helps one understand the Pastoral Epistles. First, the link with Socrates and the first-generation Socratics confirms that the letters' exhortation makes Socrates' virtue and teaching present in the contemporary audience, just as it was among his first followers through similar hortatory efforts of theirs.[162] The Pastoral Epistles likewise call upon Paul and his associates and thereby confirm that the letters' exhortation makes present to the contemporary Church their founders' teaching and virtue. The reaction desired by both groups of letters is the same, namely, that the audience follow the example which embodies the desired way of life.[163]

Second, while the Socratic Epistles pursue a conciliatory path within their school, they mince no words in criticizing their adversaries.[164] The confrontation between mild and rigid Cynicism is real and the Socratic Epistles reflect long-standing tensions.[165] Nonetheless, the letters are essentially hortatory pieces, not polemical writings, and the criticized position stands as a foil to the proper way of life which the letter corpus promotes. Moreover, the letters play down and warn against dissension among the associates because of the damage this causes to the external image of the school.[166] The Pastoral Epistles also face those, some even one-time members of the community, who adhere to and spread another brand of Christianity.[167] These become the negative examples in the letters' exhortation, whose wrong-doing will sooner or later be clear to everyone (1 Tim 5:24 ff.; 2 Tim 3:9-13). In their concern for the image of the community among outsiders, the letters urge harmony and discourage controversy.[168] They want the community to set a good example, avoiding any occasion for criticism from outside.[169] And so, they urge proper conduct for the community (1 Tim 3:15) and even prayer and respect for secular authority (1 Tim 2:1 ff.; Titus 3:1-2). This tactic in the two sets

---

[160] See 213-16.
[161] See 105, 108-10, 115-16, 123-24.
[162] See 123-26.
[163] See 145 and 204 n. 39, 215 n. 89.
[164] See 106, 117-18, 121-23.
[165] See 153-61.
[166] See 121.
[167] See 1 Tim 1:3 ff.; 4:1 ff.; 6:3 ff.; 2 Tim 1:15-16; 2:16 ff.; 3:1-2; 4:14 ff., Titus 1:10 ff.; 3:9 ff.
[168] See 1 Tim 2:8; 3:3; 5:1-2; 6:4-5, 20; 2 Tim 2:14, 23 ff.; 3:2-3; Titus 3:2, 9.
[169] See 212-13.

of letters, that is, to teach and to urge select attitudes and actions, ultimately aims at verifying that the philosophy of life of the community or school is the correct and true one.[170]

Third, in the Socratic Epistles the narrowing of Socrates' oral ministry with its undefined borders to the limits of a school and an environment of literary activity matches the shift from making philosophical converts to inculcating and preserving the true philosophical tradition.[171] The philosopher's focus on a loose and mutually supportive group of friends takes on the coloring of a community physically present to each other and with concerns for continuity and leadership.[172] The Pastoral Epistles preserve the peripatetic nature of the ministry of Paul and his associates in the geographical notices,[173] but the concern in the rest of the letters, as seen in the *Haustafeln, Gemeindeordnungen,* the preoccupation with trust and the "deposit", and the innumerable prescriptions and recommendations, is for the establishment of well-ordered communities under responsible officials and faithful to the principles of their founding father.

Fourth, the rhetorical and hortatory features of the Socratic Epistles, in conjunction with their philosophical propagandizing, suggest a community setting in the school of a grammaticus or rhetor of the early Empire.[174] The Pastoral Epistles use many of the same rhetorical features, although they do not make theoretical observations as do the Socratic Epistles.[175] This is not enough to justify a claim that the community of the Pastoral Epistles is most like a scholastic community.[176] It does suggest, however, that at least the author was schooled in the manner of his educated contemporaries and that at least some of the audience would have been able to appreciate his work for its rhetorical merits.[177]

Fifth, to take the last observation in another direction, compare the composite descriptions of the examples in both the Socratic Epistles and the

---

[170] See 124-28 on the SE and 214-16 on the PE.

[171] See 145-46.

[172] See 115-16, 121-24, 128-30.

[173] See 1 Tim 1:3; 3:14-15; 2 Tim 1:15 ff.; 4:9 ff.; Titus 1:5; 3:12-13.

[174] See 108-10, 127-28, 129-30.

[175] See Chapter II and the material footnoted in this chapter. Note particularly the pattern of the development of the chria, the stress on *nouthesia* (or constructive criticism), the two types of letters (2 Timothy, a testament; and 1 Timothy and Titus, official letters of instruction), and the inclusion at 1 Tim 6:7-16 of instructional material previously formulated (like the diatribe in Socratic *Ep.* 6.7[236.6-14]), for which see also n. 35.

[176] Cf. E.A. Judge, "The Early Christians as a Scholastic Community," *JRH* 1 (1960-61) *passim.*

[177] The letters' exacting standards for its leadership (1 Tim 3:2 ff.; Titus 1:6 ff.) indicate a sufficiency of people of stature among to choose their officials. Other comments suggest the same, e.g., 1 Tim 5:8, 16; 6:2; 2 Tim 1:16 ff.; 4:19. Presumably, these people would share the educational opportunities of the well-to-do and would become acquainted there with the rhetorical theory and its application which would have been elucidated earlier in this study.

Pastoral Epistles.[178]   Despite their relative brevity and consequent lack of elaboration, the Pastoral Epistles nonetheless give their positive and negative examples the essential lines of those of the Socratic corpus. Admittedly there are facets of the examples which are peculiar to each set of letters. Socrates and his followers are joined in a free association of philosophical friends with generalized norms, informal leadership, and loose boundaries, but not the hierarchy and structural self-identity of the church of the Pastoral Epistles.[179]   The examples of the Socratic Epistles serve a philosophical aim: they focus on moral instruction, with the accent on youth and an eye on the political arena. This is not surprising because of Socrates' actual career and also because of the school setting of the letters with its training for public life. The religious community is the milieu for the examples of the Pastoral Epistles just as it was for Paul. God is not the marginal deity of the Socratics but is the inspiration and aim of the moral life, with Christ as the manifestation and witness to the divine love. While the Socratics work toward happiness in this life, the Pastoral Epistles enjoy salvation and forgiveness now and await a reward from God in the next.

Despite these differences, the two letter corpora face their challenges with a full panoply of hortatory devices and techniques, primary among which are personal examples of the ideal attitudes and conduct. The similarity of the example indicates an extensive dependence in the Pastoral Epistles on contemporary, popular philosophy in content as well as method.

Some of the traits of the good and bad examples in the Pastoral Epistles seem to come out of the, by then, age-old conflict between mild and rigorous Cynicism.[180]   Just how closely related the Pastorals' community and the contemporary followers of Cynicism were is a matter for another study.[181]   The analysis in the present study suggests that the Pastoral Epistles dissociate themselves from the extremes for which rigid Cynicism was criticized, even by other Cynics.

---

[178] See 146-53 on the SE and 219-23 on the PE.

[179] See Vögtle, 232. A Dihle, *Die Goldene Regel: Eine Einführung in die Geschichte der antiken und frühchristlichen Vulgärethik* (Göttingen: Vandenhoeck & Ruprecht, 1962) 75-76 suggests that the regulated community life goes beyond Paul himself, especially in its requirement to adopt commonly accepted and suprapersonal rules in practical-moral relations. Paul's relation to traditional paraenesis seems to be closer than Dihle allows, but his observation is helpful in depicting a community emphasis which seems untypical for Paul.

[180] See 117-18, 153-61.

[181] For suggestions along this line see E. Zeller, "Über eine Berührung des jüngeren Cynismus mit dem Christentum," in *Kleine Schriften* II, O. Leuze, ed. (Berlin: Georg Reimer, 1910) 41-45; Malherbe, "Gentle as a Nurse" and "Hellenistic Moralists and the New Testament," in *ANRW*, W. Hasse, ed. (Berlin: de Gruyter, forthcoming) II, 26; W.H.C. Frend, *Martyrdom and Persecution in the Early Church: A Study of a Conflict from the Maccabees to Donatus,* Anchor Books (Garden City: Doubleday, 1967) 203-5.

The comparison of the use of personal example in the Pastoral Epistles and the Socratic Epistles will now be brought to a close. The study has found the similarities to be wide ranging and the comparison has cast considerable light both on the Pastoral Epistles as letters with a hortatory program and on the community behind those letters.

IX. Concluding Remarks

The analysis of the Pastorals and the comparison with the other literature surveyed has confirmed the hortatory nature of the Pastorals as noted in a preliminary way in the heuristic analysis above. Moreover, the significant elements of their paraenetic technique have been identified and expanded upon. The particular contribution of the letter form to their hortatory end has also been highlighted. Over all, the place of personal example explicit and implicit, positive and negative, in the hortatory argument and in the epistolary form has received the attention it merits for its important role in the letters and their hortatory program.

Conclusion

This study has paid close attention to details of structure and form in the Pastoral Epistles. As a result, the question of the genre and purpose of the Pastoral Epistles, posed in the Introduction, has come a long way to being answered. As for their genre, this small collection of letters in the Pauline tradition are works of epistolary paraenesis, heirs to a long tradition of Greco-Roman exhortation literature and to the popular philosophical principles therein promoted. The Pastorals blend two particular paraenetic traditions: (1) hortatory instructions addressed to young officials on the conduct and attitudes expected of them and their constituencies; (2) epistolary exhortations to a way of life consistent with the traditions of a philosophical school.

From this determination of genre, conclusions can be drawn as to the purpose of the Pastoral Epistles. On the positive side, they encourage in the Christian community the adoption and practice of the highest moral standards of the community at large, with the addition of some properly Christian obligations and motivation. At the same time, they set standards of leadership within the Christian community, again largely along traditional lines. On the negative side, they call attention to exaggerations in practice and theoretical pursuits which are to be avoided. Again, these aberrations are largely common to the popular philosophical rivalries of the day, with some coloring peculiar to the context of early Christianity.

The particular focus of this study, example, has proven to be an important feature in the exhortation of the Pastoral Epistles and, to be sure, of the paraenetic tradition on which it draws. From a technical point of view, this standard element in the instruction to young officials and in philosophical exhortations is particularly well suited to the letter form. The letters serve as vehicles by which both explicit examples are referred to and implicit examples are detailed. In the latter capacity, the letter becomes the example, for all practical purposes. Moreover, examples act in consort with other hortatory features in a loosely structured hortatory development. With lists and prescriptions, such as those of the Pastorals, they have a close, complementary relationship. From a practical viewpoint, the Pastoral Epistles and the type of community members and leaders they hope to encourage present the outward face of the Christian community in the community at large. Thus, the exemplary behavior being urged looks to the Church's internal edification and external reputation.

The analysis of example and its place in the exhortation of the Pastorals revealed some divergence from the use of the device in the Pauline homologoumena.

While the issues of Christian pseudonymous works and the authorship of the Pastorals [1] are not the main concerns of this study, the analysis of form and content undertaken in this study lends support to those who hold pseudonymity of the Pastoral Epistles. [2] Furthermore, pseudonymity was seen to be a key device in the appeal to tradition in the Socratic Epistle corpus and played a part in the Isocratean corpus as well. In short, it is a device quite at home in paraenetic works to which the Pastorals are related and, more than an ornament or appeal to authority, the pseudonymity pushes the examples back to the roots of the tradition

---

[1] See K. Aland, "The Problem of Anonymity and Pseudonymity in Christian Literature of the First Two Centuries," *JTS* n.s. 12 (1961) 29-49; H. Balz, "Anonymität und Pseudepigraphie im Urchristentum: Überlegungen zum literarischen und theologischen Problem der urchristlichen und gemeinantiken Pseudepigraphie," *ZTK* 66 (1969) 403-36; G. Bardy, "Faux et fraudes littéraires dans l'antiquité chrétienne," *RHE* 32 (1936) 5-23, 275-302; L.H. Brockington, "The Problem of Pseudonymity," *JTS* n.s. 4 (1953) 15-22; N. Brox, *Falsche Verfasserangaben: Zur Erklärung der frühchristlichen Pseudepigraphie,* SBS 79 (Stuttgart: Katholisches Bibelwerk, 1975); "Zum Problemstand in der Erforschung der altchristlichen Pseudepigraphie," *Kairos* n.F. 15 (1973) 10-23; J.C. Fenton, "Pseudonymity in the New Testament," *Theology* 58 (1955) 51-56; E.J. Goodspeed, "Pseudonymity and Pseudepigraphy in Early Christian Literature," in *New Chapters in New Testament Study* (New York: Macmillan, 1937) 169-88; D. Guthrie, *New Testament Introduction: The Pauline Epistles,* Appendix C (London: Tyndale, 1965); "Acts and Epistles in Apocryphal Writings," in *Apostolic History and the Gospel* (Fest. F.F. Bruce, W.W. Gasque and R.P. Martin, eds., [Grand Rapids: Wm. B. Eerdmans, 1970]) 329-44; A.E. Haefner, "A Unique Source for the Study of Ancient Pseudepigraphy," *ATR* 16 (1934) 8-15; A. Mayer, "Religiöse Pseudepigraphie als ethisch-psychologisch Problem," *ZNW* 35 (1936) 262-79; B. Metzger, "Literary Forgeries and Canonical Pseudepigraphia," *JBL* 91 (1972) 3-24; M. Rist, "Pseudepigraphy and the Early Christians," in *Studies in New Testament and Early Christian Literature* (Fest. A.P. Wikgren, D.E. Aune, ed., [Leiden: Brill, 1972]) 75-91; W. Wrede, "Miscellen," *ZNW* 1 (1900) 66-85.

[2] C.K. Barrett, *The Pastoral Epistles in the New English Bible* (Oxford: Clarendon, 1963) 4-12; J.L. Houlden, *The Pastoral Epistles; I and II Timothy; Titus,* Pelican N.T. Commentaries (Harmondsworth: Penguin, 1976) 34; M. Dibelius and H. Conzelmann, *The Pastoral Epistles,* Hermeneia, P. Buttolph and A. Yarbro, trans. (Philadelphia: Fortress, 1972) 1-5; N. Brox, "Lukas als Verfasser der Pastoralbriefe?" *JAC* 13 (1970) 62-77; "Zu den persönlichen Notizen der Pastoralbriefe," *BZ* n.F. 13 (1969) 76-94; W. Nauck," Die Herkunft des Verfassers der Pastoralbriefe, ein Beitrag der Auslegung der Pastoralbriefe" (Diss. Göttingen, 1950); A. Lemaire, "Pastoral Epistles: Redaction and Theology," *BTB* 2 (1972) 25-42; P. Trummer, *Die Paulustradition der Pastoralbriefe,* BET 8 (Frankfurt am M.: Peter Lang, 1978) 161-72. For earlier discussions see J.A. Wegscheider, *Der erste Briefe des Apostels Paulus an den Timotheus, neu übersetzt und erklärt, mit Beziehung auf die neuesten Untersuchungen über die Authentie desselben* (Göttingen: Johann F. Röwer, 1810); M. Baumgarten, *Die Aechtheit der Pastoralbriefe, mit besonderer Rücksicht auf den neuesten Angriff von Herrn Dr. Baur, vertheidigt* (Berlin: L. Dehmigke, 1837); W. Michaelis, *Pastoralbriefe und Gefangenschaftsbriefe: Zur Echtheitsfrage der Pastoralbriefe,* Neutestamentliche Forschungen, Paulusstudien 1, 6 (Gütersloh: C. Bertelsmann, 1930).

which the paraenesis keeps alive and transmits. It also allows the author to choose details and to cast the letters in a way which best depicts those examples and the lesson which they incarnate.

The analysis of the genre and purpose of the letters also suggests the outlines of a likely historical situation for the letters, another of the issues raised in the Introduction. With their hortatory focus on official and community attitudes and actions and in view of the commonplace paraenetic roots for this, the Pastorals suggest a period of inner settling-in and outer window-dressing. The ready appeal to the example of the community's founder and his associates suggests an unbroken continuity with them. Difficulties are alluded to in some areas like abstinence, legalism, Jewish influence, and resurrection faith. These, however, do not appear to be gathered together into an opposing system nor are they viewed as a theoretical threat. The letters treat the problems as a matter of practice and not of theology and deal with them on that level. Furthermore, the letters characterize the problem of heresy as a perduring phenomenon for the Church, not as an immediate threat.[3] With this in mind, the letters would seem to fit well in the late first or early second century A.D., before the Gnostic alternative became fully articulated and before Paul himself became the chosen theologian of the heretics later in the second century.[4]

In the hortatory program devised by the Pastorals to respond to the circumstances of their day, the figures of Paul, Timothy, Titus, and the others mentioned in the letters are models for the Church officials and, by extension, for the Church in general. By and large, they are well-known from the homologoumena and the Acts of the Apostles and are important figures from the time of the community's foundations. As members of the first generation Christians, they represent the standard or source which determines the flow of present and future development in the community of the Pastoral Epistles.[5]

In his defense of Pauline authorship of the Pastorals, F.W. Maier[6] outlines his objections to the claims of their pseudonymity. While it is not the objective of this study to demonstrate the counter position, his objections are useful here in that they raise questions about the Pastoral Epistles for which this study has attempted to provide some answers. As such, they will serve as an organizing

---

[3] 2 Tim 2:20ff. and see Trummer, 161-72.

[4] E.H. Pagels, *The Gnostic Paul: Gnostic Exegesis of the Pauline Letters* (Philadephia: Fortress, 1975) 1-10.

[5] See J.D. Quinn, The Last Volume of Luke: The Relation of Luke-Acts to the Pastoral Epistles," in C.H. Talbert, ed., *Perspectives on Luke-Acts* (Edinburgh: T & T. Clark, Ltd., 1978) 62-75 for his theory on the relation of the Pastorals to Luke and his view of the Pastorals as an epistolary corpus.

[6] F.W. Maier, "Die Hauptprobleme der Pastoralbriefe Pauli," in *Biblische Zeitfragen gemeinverständlich erörtert,* J. Nikel and I. Rohr, eds. (Münster, i.W.: Aschendorff, 1910) 485-540.

principle for a final review and summary. He objects, first, that the aim of the pseudonymous writing is not sufficiently clear, i.e., neither sufficiently anti-heresy or pro-orthodoxy, nor consistently oriented to ecclesiastical hierarchy. This study has shown that the only sufficiently comprehensive aim for the letters is a paraenetic one, under which these other aspects can be included as secondary elements.

Second, he finds no literary precedent for the new *Gattung* Pastoral letter. This study has analyzed a parallel letter corpus, as well as other discourses and letters. While none of these is the same as the Pastorals, they are indeed literary precedents.

Third, he sees no reason for composing three letters of similar aim where one would have done nicely. This study has shown that there are really two types of letters in this "collection" and that the motivation is the same as that behind the composition of the Socratic letters, i.e., to promote a way of life with the aid of the method used and learned in the rhetorical schools and philosophical associations.

Fourth, he calls pointless the ecclesiastical regulations in 1 Timothy and Titus when Ignatius and 1 Clement had already advanced further in hierarchical theory. The regulations, however, are not pointless if seen, as this study has tried to view them, in light both of their paraenetic tradition and of their function in terms of the examples being delineated.

Fifth, he finds a contrast between 2 Timothy's epistolary ornament and its curtailment in 1 Timothy. This study sees not a contrast here but the creation of two letter types with different objectives.

Sixth, he finds it unlikely that so many historical details would be used in the second century which would easily be recognized as false or derived from the Acts of the Apostles or from Philippians. On the contrary, this study has found this to be part of the art of the authors of the Socratic letters and, most likely therefore, of the Pastorals in their depiction of examples to suit their exhortations. This was an art learned in the rhetorical schools.

Seventh, he considers it unlikely that churches in Crete, Ephesus-Asia-Minor, and Rome would not have caught the "deception". This study hoped to show that the critically trained Christians would indeed have caught the "deception" but with relish over its artfulness and ethical appropriateness.

Eighth, he asks what advantage there was to set the letter to Titus in the relatively insignificant Crete and to choose the two little known addressees, Timothy and Titus. This study has laid out the importance in example theory and practice of examples close to and significant for the community being exhorted, just as the two Pauline co-workers are. The setting on Crete would nicely "fill out" the background of Paul's mission as the Socratic letters "fill out" anecdotal and biographical notices.

Ninth and last, he asks who the anonymous author would have been who would compose with greater authority than Paul on questions of importance for Church life. This study has tried to set the letters in their paraenetic context, where continuity of tradition and not of authority is the key element. As such, any faithful follower could have created these letters so as to continue Paul's teaching and apply it to new situations. As to the matters covered, they are much more paraenetic commonplaces than instructions of a specifically Christian sort and attest the capacity of early Christianity to absorb the best of its surroundings in content as well as in form.

With these remarks, the study will be brought to a close. If it has led the reader to appreciate the learned, rhetorical skill of the Pastoral Epistles in making use of example within their hortatory program, then it has met its aim.

Bibliography

Encyclopedias and Dictionaries

Abbott-Smith, G. *A Manual Lexicon of the New Testament.* 3rd ed. New York: Charles Scribner's Sons, 1936.

Bauer, Walter. *A Greek-English Lexicon of the New Testament and Other Early Christian Literature.* 2nd rev. ed. from the 5th edition by F. Wilbur Gingrich and Frederick W. Danker. Chicago/London: University of Chicago, 1979.

Blass, F. and A. Debrunner. *A Greek Grammar of the New Testament and Other Early Christian Literature.* Rev. by Robert W. Funk. Chicago/London: University of Chicago, 1961.

Campenhausen, Hans F. von, Kurt Galling et al., eds. *Die Religion in Geschichte und Gegenwart: Handwörterbuch für Theologie und Religionswissenschaft.* 3rd rev. ed. Tübingen: J.C.B. Mohr, 1957-.

Dölger, Franz J., Hans Lietzmann et al., eds. *Reallexikon für Antike und Christentum: Sachwörterbuch zur Auseinandersetzung des Christentums mit der antiken Welt.* Stuttgart: K. W. Hiersemann, 1950-.

Ernesti, Johann C. G., ed. *Lexicon technologicae Graecorum rhetoricae.* Leipzig: Caspar Fritsch, 1795.

Estienne, Henri, ed. *Thesaurus Graecae Linguae.* Repr. ed. Graz: Akademische Druck-u. Verlagsanstalt, 1954.

Hammond, Nicholas G. and Howard H. Scullard, eds. *Oxford Classical Dictionary.* 2nd ed. Oxford: Oxford University, 1970.

Hastings, James, ed. *Encyclopedia of Religion and Ethics.* New York: Charles Scribner's Sons, 1928.

Kittel, Gerhard, ed. *Theological Dictionary of the New Testament.* Trans., ed. by G. N. Bromiley. Grand Rapids: Wm. B. Eerdmans, 1964-74.

Lausberg, Heinrich. *Handbuch der literarischen Rhetorik: Eine Grundlegung der Literaturwissenschaft.* Munich: Max Hüber, 1960.

Liddell, Henry G. and Robert Scott. *A Greek-English Lexicon.* Rev. by Henry S. Jones and Roderick McKenzie. 9th ed. Oxford: Clarendon, 1925-40.

Moulton, James H. and George Milligan. *The Vocabulary of the New Testament: Illustrated from the Papyri and Other Non-Literary Sources.* Repr. ed. Grand Rapids: Wm. B. Eerdmans, 1974.

Pauly, August F. von, ed. *Paulys Real-encyclopädie der classischen Altertumswissenschaft.* Ed. and rev. by Georg Wissowa, Wilhelm Kroll et al. Stuttgart: J. B. Metzler, 1894-.

Viller, Marcel et al., eds. *Dictionnaire de spiritualité, ascetique et mystique, doctrine et histoire.* Paris: Beauchesne et ses Fils, 1932-.

Zerwick, Max and Mary Grosvenor. *Grammatical Analysis of the Greek New Testament.* Vol. 2. Rome: Biblical Institute, 1979.

Ziegler, Konrat and Walther Sontheimer, eds. *Der Kleine Pauly: Lexikon der Antike.* Stuttgart: A. Druckenmüller, 1964-.

Texts and Translations

Alciphron, Aelian and Philostratus. *The Letters of Alciphron, Aelian and Philostratus.* Trans. by Allen R. Benner and Francis H. Fobes. LCL. Cambridge: Harvard University, 1949.

Aristippus. *Aristippi et Cyrenaicorum fragmenta.* Ed. by Erich Mannebach. Leiden/Cologne: E. J. Brill, 1961.

Aristotle. *The "Art" of Rhetoric.* Trans. by John H. Freese. LCL. London: W. Heinemann, 1927.

———. *Ars rhetorica.* Ed. by Rudolf Kassel. Berlin/New York: de Gruyter, 1976.

———. *Ars rhetorica quae vulgo fertur Aristotelis ad Alexandrum.* Ed. by M. Fuhrmann. Leipzig: B. G. Teubner, 1966.

———. *Problems and Rhetorica ad Alexandrum.* Trans. by H. Rackham and W. S. Hett. LCL. 2 vols. London: W. Heinemann, 1936.

Athenaeus. *The Deipnosophists.* Trans. by Charles B. Gulick. LCL. 7 vols. London: W. Heinemann, 1927.

The Babylonian Talmud. Ed. by I. Epstein, trans. by J. Schachter and H. Freedman. London: Soncino, 1935-53.

Cicero. *Ad C. Herennium Libri IV: De ratione dicendi.* Trans. by Harry Caplan. LCL. Cambridge: Harvard University, 1954.

———. *Brutus, orator.* Trans. by H. M. Hubbell. LCL. London: W. Heinemann, 1939.

———. *De inventione, de optimo genere oratorum, topica.* Trans. by Harry M. Hubbell. LCL. Cambridge: Harvard University, 1949.

———. *De natura deorum, academica.* Trans. by Harris R. Rackham. LCL. London: W. Heinemann, 1933.

———. *De officiis.* Trans. by Walter Miller. LCL. London: W. Heinemann, 1913.

———. *De oratore, de fato, paradoxa stoicorum, de partitione oratoria.* Trans. by E. W. Sutton and Harris R. Rackham. LCL. 2 vols. Cambridge: Harvard University, 1949.

———. *De republica, de legibus.* Trans. by Clinton W. Keyes. LCL. London: W. Heinemann, 1928.

———. *De senectute, de amicitia, de divinatione.* Trans. by William A. Falconer. LCL. London: W. Heinemann, 1923.

———. *The Letters to His Friends.* Trans. by William G. Williams. LCL. 4 vols. London: W. Heinemann, 1927-29.

———. *The Verrine Orations.* Trans. by L. H. G. Greenwood. LCL. 2 vols. London: W. Heinemann, 1928.

Clement of Alexandria. *Opera.* Ed. by Wilhelm Dindorf. 4 vols. Oxford: Clarendon, 1869.

The Cynic Epistles: A Study Edition. Ed. and intr. by Abraham J. Malherbe. SBLSBS 12, Wayne A. Meeks, ed. Missoula: Scholars Press for the SBL, 1977.

Demetrius of Phalerum. *Demetrii et Libanii qui feruntur TYPOI EPISTOLIKOI et EPISTOLIMAIOI CHARAKTERES.* Ed. by Valentine Weichert. Leipzig: B. G. Teubner, 1910.

———. *On Style.* Trans. by William Rhys Roberts. In the same volume with Aristotle's *The Poetics* and "Longinus'" *On the Sublime,* W. Hamilton Fyfe, trans. LCL. Rev. ed. London: W. Heinemann, 1932.

Cassius Dio. *Dio's Roman History*. Trans. by Ernest Cary. LCL. 9 vols. London: W. Heinemann, 1914.

Dio Chrysostom. *Discourses*. Trans. by James W. Cohoon and H. Lamar Crosby. LCL. 5 vols. London: W. Heinemann, 1932.

Diogenes Laertius. *Lives of Eminent Philosophers*. Trans. by Robert D. Hicks. LCL London: W. Heinemann, 1925.

Dionysius of Halicarnassus. *The Critical Essays*. Trans. by Stephen Usher. LCL. 2 vols. Cambridge: Harvard University, 1974.

————. *Dionysii Halicarnasei quae exstant*. Ed. by Hermann Usener and Ludwig Radermacher. 6 vols. Leipzig: B. G. Teubner, 1904-29.

Epictetus. *The Discourses as Reported by Arrian, the Manual, and Fragments*. Trans. by William A. Oldfather. LCL. London: W. Heinemann, 1926.

Epicurus. *Epicurea*. Ed. by Hermann K. Usener. Leipzig: B. G. Teubner, 1887.

Epistolographi Graeci. Ed. by Rudolf Hercher. Paris: A. Firmin Didot, 1873, repr. Amsterdam: A. M. Hakkert, 1965.

Aulus Gellius. *The Attic Nights*. Trans. by John C. Rolfe. LCL. 3 vols. London: W. Heinemann, 1927.

Gnomologium Vaticanum e codice vaticano graeco 743. Ed. by Leo Sternbach. Texte und Kommentare: Eine altertumswissenschaftliche Reihe 2. Berlin: de Gruyter, 1963.

Hermogenes. *Opera*. Ed. by Hugo Rabe. Leipzig: B. G. Teubner, 1913.

Horace. *Satires, Epistles and Ars Poetica*. Trans. by H. Rushton Fairclough. LCL. 2 vols. London: W. Heinemann, 1926.

Isocrates. *Discours*. Trans. by Emile Brémond and Georges Mathieu. Paris: Société d'édition "Les Belles Lettres," 1928.

————. *Isocrates*. Trans. by George Norlin. LCL. 3 vols. London: W. Heinemann, 1928.

————. *Opera*. Ed. by Engelbert Drerup. Leipzig: Dieterich (Theodor Weicher), 1906.

Julian. *The Works of the Emperor Julian*. Trans. by Wilmer C. Wright. LCL. 3 vols. London: W. Heinemann, 1913.

Juvenal. *Juvenal and Persius*. Trans. by G. G. Ramsay. LCL. London: W. Heinemann, 1918.

Libanius. *Demetrii et Libanii qui feruntur TYPOI EPISTOLIKOI et EPISTOLIMAIOI CHARAKTERES*. Ed. by Valentine Weichert. Leipzig: B. G. Teubner, 1910.

Livy. *Livy*. Trans. by B. O. Foster. LCL. 14 vols. London: W. Heinemann, 1919.

Lucian. *The Works of Lucian*. Trans. by Austin M. Harmon. LCL. 8 vols. London: W. Heinemann, 1913.

Lucretius. *De rerum natura libri sex*. Ed. by Cyril Bailey. 3 vols. Oxford: Clarendon, 1947.

Lysias. *Lysias*. Trans. by W. R. M. Lamb. LCL. London: W. Heinemann, 1930.

Maximus of Tyre. *Philosophoumena*. Ed. by Hermann Hobein. Leipzig: B. G. Teubner, 1910.

Cornelius Nepos. *Vitae*. Ed. by Peter K. Marshall. Leipzig: B. G. Teubner, 1977.

Novum Testamentum Graece. Ed. by Kurt Aland et al. 26 rev. ed. Stuttgart: Deutsche Bibelstiftung, 1979.

Ovid. *Metamorphoses*. Trans. by Frank J. Miller. LCL. 2 vols. London: W. Heinemann, 1928.

Philo. *Philo*. Trans. by Francis H. Colson and George H. Whitaker. LCL. 12 vols. London: W. Heinemann, 1929.

Philostratus. *Philostratus and Eunapius: The Lives of the Sophists*. Trans. by Wilmer C. Wright. LCL. London: W. Heinemann, 1922.

Plato. *Euthyphro, Apology, Crito, Phaedo, Phaedrus*. Trans. by Harold N. Fowler. LCL. London: W. Heinemann, 1914.

———. *Laches, Protagoras, Meno, Euthydemus*. Trans. by C. W. Lamb. LCL. London: W. Heinemann, 1924.

———. *Laws*. Trans. by R. G. Bury. LCL. 2 vols. London: W. Heinemann, 1926.

———. *Lysis, Symposium, Gorgias*. Trans. by C. W. Lamb. LCL. London: W. Heinemann, 1925.

———. *Republic*. Trans. by Paul Shorey. LCL. 2 vols. London: W. Heinemann, 1930-35.

———. *Timaeus, Critias, Cleitophon, Menexenus, Epistles*. Trans. by R. G. Bury. LCL. London: W. Heinemann, 1929.

Pliny, the Younger. *Letters, Panegyric*. Trans. by Betty Rice. LCL. 2 vols. Cambridge: Harvard University, 1969.

———. *Epistularum libri decem*. Ed. by Roger A. B. Mynors. Oxford: Clarendon, 1963.

Plutarch. *Moralia*. Trans. by Frank C. Babbitt and Harold N. Fowler. LCL. 15 vols. London: W. Heinemann, 1926; Cambridge: Harvard University, 1969.

———. *Moralia*. Ed. by Curt Hubert et al. Leipzig: B. G. Teubner, 1925.

Propertius. *The Elegies of Propertius*. Trans. by H. E. Butler. London: W. Heinemann, 1912.

Quintilian. *The Institutio Oratoria of Quintilian*. Trans. by Harold E. Butler. LCL. 4 vols. London: W. Heinemann, 1920.

———. *M. Fabi Quintiliani institutionis oratoriae libri XII*. Ed. by Ludwig Radermacher, rev. by Vincenz Buchheit. 2 vols. Leipzig: B. G. Teubner, 1965.

Rhetores Graeci. Ed. by Leonhard von Spengel. 3 vols. Leipzig: B. G. Teubner, 1853.

Rhetores Graeci. Ed. by Christian Walz. 9 vols. Stuttgart/Tübingen: J. G. Cotta, 1835.

Royal Correspondence in the Hellenistic Period: A Study in Greek Epigraphy. Ed. by Charles Bradford Welles. Chicago: Ares, 1974.

Seneca, the Elder. *Declamations*. Trans. by Michael Winterbottom. LCL. 2 vols. Cambridge: Harvard University, 1974.

Seneca, the Younger. *Ad Lucilium epistulae morales*. Trans. by Richard M. Gummere. LCL. 3 vols. London: W. Heinemann, 1917.

———. *Ad Lucilium epistulae morales*. Ed. by L. D. Reynolds. 2 vols. Oxford: Clarendon, 1965.

———. *Moral Essays*. Trans. by John W. Basore. LCL. 3 vols. London: W. Heinemann, 1928.

Stobaeus. *Anthologium*. Ed. by Kurt Wachsmuth and Otto Hense. Berlin: Weidmann, 1884-1919.

Suetonius. *Lives of the Caesars*. Trans. by John C. Rolfe. LCL. 2 vols. London: W. Heinemann, 1914.

Syrianus. *In Hermogenem commentaria*. Ed. by Hugo Rabe. 2 vols. Leipzig: B. G. Teubner, 1893.

The Tebtunis Papyri. Ed. by Bernard P. Grenfell et al. 4 vols. London: H. Frowde, 1902-38. Vol. 3, 1 ed. by Arthur S. Hunt, J. Gilbart Smyly et al. London: Humphrey Milford, 1933.

Teles. *Teletis Reliquiae*. Ed. by Otto Hense. Tübingen: J. C. B. Mohr, 1909.

Terence. *Terence*. Trans. by John Sargeaunt. LCL. 2 vols. London: W. Heinemann, 1912.

Valerius Maximus. *Factorum et dictorum memorabilium libri novem*. Ed. by Karl Kempf. Stuttgart: B. G. Teubner, 1888.

Velleius Paterculus. *Compendium of Roman History and Res Gestae Divi Augusti*. Trans. by
Frederick W. Shipley. LCL. London: W. Heinemann, 1924.
Xenophon. *Anabasis, Symposium and Apology*. Trans. by Carleton L. Brownson and O. J.
Todd. LCL. 2 vols. London: W. Heinemann, 1922.
———. *Memorabilia, oeconomicus*. Trans. by E. C. Marchant. LCL. London: W.
Heinemann, 1923.

Commentaries and Studies

Aland, Kurt. "The Problem of Anonymity and Pseudonymity in Christian Literature of the
First Two Centuries." *JTS* n.s. 12 (1961) 39-49.
Albertini, Eugène. *La Composition dans les ouvrages philosophiques de Sénèque*. Bibliothè-
que des Ecoles Françaises d'Athènes et de Rome 127. Paris: Thorin et Fontemoing,
1923.
Albertz, Martin. *Die Botschaft des Neuen Testaments: I Die Entstehung der Botschaft: II Die
Entstehung des apostolischen Schriftkanons*. 2 vols. in 4. Zollikon/Zürich: Evan-
gelischer Verlag, 1952.
Albrecht, Emil. "Zu Pseudoisokrates *Pros Dēmonikon*." *Philol*. 43 (1884) 244-48.
Alewell, Karl. *Über das rhetorische PARADEIGMA: Theorie, Beispielsammlungen, Verwen-
dung in der römischen Literatur der Kaiserzeit*. Leipzig: A. Hoffmann, 1913.
Allazzis, Leon. *Socratis, Antisthenis et aliorum Socraticorum epistolae*. Paris: Sebastian
Cramoisy, 1637.
Andrews, Alfred C. "Did Seneca Practise the Ethics of His Epistles?" *CJ* 25 (1929-30) 611-25.
Arnim, Hans F. A. von *Ein altgriechisches Königsideal*. Frankfurter Universitätsreden 4.
Frankfurt am M., 1916.
———. *Leben und Weise des Dio von Prusa*. Berlin: Weidmann, 1898.
Arullani, Mario, *Ricerche intorno all'opuscolo Plutarcheo EI PRESBYTEROI
POLITEUTEON*. Scuola di Filologia Classica dell'Università di Roma I,1. Rome:
L'Universale, 1928.
Babut, D. *La Religion des philosophes grecs de Thalès aux stoiciens*. Littératures Anciennes
4. Paris: Presses Universitaires, 1974.
Baldwin, Charles S. *Medieval Rhetoric and Poetic (to 1400) Interpreted from Representative
Works*. New York: Macmillan, 1928.
Balz, Horst R. "Anonymität und Pseudepigraphie im Urchristentum: Überlegungen zum
literarischen und theologischen Problem der urchristlichen und gemeinantiken Pseu-
depigraphie." *ZKT* 66 (1969) 403-36.
Bardy, Gustave. "Faux et fraudes littéraires dans l'antiquité chrétienne." *RHE* 32 (1936)
5-23, 275-302.
Barnett, Albert E. *Paul Becomes a Literary Influence*. Chicago: University of Chicago, 1941.
———. "The Use of the Letters of Paul in pre-Catholic Christian Literature." Diss. Uni-
versity of Chicago, 1932.
Barrett, C. K. *The Pastoral Epistles in the New English Bible*. Oxford: Clarendon, 1963.
Barton, John M. T. "Bonum certamen certavi ... fidem servavi." *Bib*. 40 (1959) 878-84.
Bassler, Jouette. "Lois and Eunice: Women in the Pastorals, a Functional Approach."
unpublished study, Yale 1976.
Bauernfeind, Otto. "*strateuomai*." *TDNT* 7 (1971) 701-13.
Baumgarten, Michael. *Die Aechtheit der Pastoralbriefe, mit besonderer Rücksicht auf den
neuesten Angriff von Herrn Dr. Baur, vertheidigt*. Berlin: L. Dehmigke, 1837.

Baur, Ferdinand C. *Die sogennanten Pastoralbriefe des Apostels Paulus.* Stuttgart/Tübingen: J. C. Cotta, 1835.

Bentley, Richard. *Dissertations upon the Epistles of Phalaris, Themistocles, Socrates, Euripedes, and upon the Fables of Aesop.* London: J. H. for H. Mortlock and J. Hartley, 1699; repr. ed. with intr. and notes by Wilhelm Wagner. Berlin: S. Calvary, 1874.

Bernays, Jacob. *Lucian und die Kyniker.* Berlin: Wilhelm Hertz, 1879.

———. *Phokion und seine neueren Beurteiler: Ein Beitrag zur Geschichte der Philosophie und Politik.* Berlin: Wilhelm Hertz, 1881.

Betz, Hans D. *Lukian von Samosata und das Neue Testament: Religionsgeschichtliche und paränetische Parallelen.* Corpus Hellenisticum Novi Testamenti. Berlin: Akademie, 1961.

———. *Nachfolge und Nachahmung Jesu Christi im Neuen Testament.* Tübingen: J. C. B. Mohr (Paul Siebeck), 1967.

Betz, O. "Die Geburt der Gemeinde durch den Lehrer." *NTS* 3 (1956-57) 314-26.

Bevan, Edwyn. "Hellenistic Popular Philosophy," in *The Hellenistic Age,* J. B. Bury, ed. Cambridge: Cambridge University, 1923.

Bickermann, E. and J. Sykutris. "Speusipps Brief an König Philipp." *Berichte über die Verhandlungen der sächsischen Akademie der Wissenschaften.* Phil-hist. Kl. 80,3 (Leipzig, 1928) 1-86.

Bignone, Ettore, trans., intr., comm. *Epicuro: Opere, frammenti, testimonianze sulla sua vita.* Studia Philologica 4. Rome: "L'Erma" di Bretschneider, 1964.

Billerbeck, Margarethe. *Epiktet von Kynismus.* Leiden: E. J. Brill, 1978.

———. *Der Kyniker Demetrius.* Philosophia Antiqua 36. Leiden: E. J. Brill, 1979.

Binder, Hermann. "Die historische Situation der Pastoralbriefe," in *Geschichtswirklichkeit und Glaubensbewährung* (Fest. Bischof D. Dr. h.c. Friedrich Müller), Franklin C. Fry, ed. Stuttgart: Evangelisches Verlagswerk, 1967.

Bjerkelund, Carl J. *Parakalô: Form, Funktion und Sinn der parakalô-Sätze in den paulinischen Briefen.* Bibliotheca theologica Norvegica 1. Oslo: Universitetsforlaget, 1967.

Blumenthal, Albrecht von. "TYPOS und *PARADEIGMA.*" *Hermes* 63 (1928) 391-414.

Boehnecke, Karl G. *Demosthenes, Lykurgus, Hyperides und ihr Zeitalter.* Berlin: Georg Reimer, 1864.

Boer, Willis P. de. *The Imitation of Paul: An Exegetical Study.* Amsterdam/Kampen: J. H. Kok, 1962.

Bohnenblust, Gottfried. *Beiträge zum Topos "peri philias."* Berlin: Gustav Schade (Otto Francke), 1905.

Born, Lester K. "The Perfect Prince According to the Latin Panegyrists." *AJP* 55 (1934) 20-35.

Bover, José M. "Fidelis Sermo." *Bib.* 19 (1938) 74-79.

———. "Imaginis notio apud B. Paulum." *Bib.* 4 (1923) 174-79.

Brockington, L. H. "The Problem of Pseudonymity." *JTS* n.s. 4 (1953) 15-22.

Brokate, Carl. *De aliquot Plutarchi libellis.* Göttingen: Robert Noske, 1913.

Brown, E. F. "Note on 2 Tim ii, 15." *JTS* 24 (1923) 317.

Brox, Norbert. *Falsche Verfasserangaben: Zur Erklärung der früchchristlichen Pseudepigraphie.* SBS 79. Stuttgart: KBW, 1975.

———. "Lukas als Verfasser der Pastoralbriefe?" *JAC* 13 (1970) 62-77.

———. *Die Pastoralbriefe.* 4 ed. RNT 7. O. Kuss, ed. Regensburg: Friedrich Pustet, 1969.

———. "Zu den persönlichen Notizen der Pastoralbriefe." *BZ* n. F. 13 (1969) 76-94.

———. "Zum Problemstand in der Erforschung der altchristlichen Pseudepigraphie." *Kairos* n. F. 15 (1973) 10-23.

Bruck, E. Fr. *Totenteil und Seelgerät im griechischen Recht.* Munich: C. H. Beck, 1926.

Bruns, Carl G. "Die Testamente der griechischen Philosophen," in *Kleine Schriften II.* Weimar: Hermann Böhlau, 1882, 192-237.

Bruns, Ivo. *Das literarische porträt der Griechen im fünften und vierten Jahrhundert vor Christi Geburt.* Berlin: Wilhelm Hertz, 1896.

Bultmann, Rudolf. *Der Stil der paulinischen Predigt und die kynisch-stoische Diatribe.* Göttingen: Vandenhoeck & Ruprecht, 1910.

Bunn, Leslie H. "2 Timothy ii.23-26." *Exp. Tim.* 41 (1929-30) 235-37.

Burgess, Theodore C. *Epideictic Literature.* Studies in Classical Philology. Chicago: University of Chicago, 1902.

Burk, August. *Die Pädagogik des Isokrates als Grundlegung des humanistischen Bildungsideals im Vergleich mit den zeitgenössischen und den modernen Theorien dargestellt.* Studien zur Geschichte und Kultur des Altertums 12, 3/4, E. Drerup, ed. Würzburg, 1923.

Campenhausen, Hans F. von. *Ecclesiastical Authority and Spiritual Power in the Church of the First Three Centuries.* Trans. by J. A. Baker. Beiträge zur historischen Theologie 14, G. Ebeling, ed. Stanford: Stanford University, 1969.

————. "Polykarp von Smyrna und die Pastoralbriefe," in *Aus der Frühzeit des Christentums: Studien zur Kirchengeschichte des ersten und zweiten Jahrhunderts.* Tübingen: J. C. B. Mohr (Paul Siebeck), 1963, 197-252.

Cancik, Hildegard. *Untersuchungen zu Senecas epistulae morales.* Spudasmata: Studien zur klassischen Philologie und ihren Grenzgebieten 18, Hildebrecht Hommel and Ernst Zinn, eds. Hildesheim: Georg Olms, 1967.

Capelle, Wilhelm. "De Cynicorum epistulis." Diss. Göttingen, 1896.

Carcopino, Jerome. *Cicero: The Secrets of His Correspondence.* London: Routledge & Kegan Paul, 1951; repr. Westport, CT: Greenwood, 1969.

Caster, M. *Lucien et la pensée religieuse de son temps.* Paris: Société d'édition "Les Belles Lettres," 1937.

Cecchi, Sergio. *La paideia ateniese dalle orazioni di Isocrate.* Turin: Loescher, 1961.

Chalon, Gérard. *L'Édit de Tiberius Julius Alexander.* Olten/Lausanne: Urs Graf, 1964.

Cipriani, Settimo. "La dottrina del 'depositum' nelle lettere pastorali." *An. Bib.* 17-18 (1963) II:127-42.

Clark, Donald L. *Rhetoric in Greco-Roman Education.* New York/London: Columbia University, 1957.

Clift, Evelyn H. *Latin Pseudepigraphy: A Study in Literary Attributions.* Baltimore: J. H. Furst, 1945.

Coleman, Robert. "The Artful Moralist: A Study of Seneca's Epistolary Style." *CQ* n.s. 24 (1974) 276/89.

Collins, Raymond F. "The Image of Paul in the Pastorals." *Laval Théologique Philosophique* 31 (1975) 147-73.

Collomp, P. "La lettre à plusieurs destinataires," in *Atti del IV Congresso Internazionale di Papirologia - Firenze 1935.* Milan: Società Editrice "Vita e Pensiero," 1936, 199-207.

Colson, F. H. *M. Fabii Quintiliani institutionis oratoriae liber I.* Cambridge: Cambridge University, 1924.

————. "'Myths and Genealogies' — A Note on the Polemic of the Pastoral Epistles." *JTS* 19 (1917-18) 265-71.

————. "Quintilian I.9 and the 'Chria' in Ancient Education." *CR* 35 (1921) 150-54.

Constable, Giles. *Letters and Letters Collections.* Turnhout, Belgium: Brepols, 1976.

Conzelmann, Hans. *I Corinthians.* Trans. by James W. Leitch. Hermeneia. Philadelphia: Fortress, 1975.

Cortès, Enric. *Los discorsos de adiòs de Gn 49 a Jn 13-17: Pistas para la historia de un género literario en la antigua literatura judia.* Barcelona: Herder, 1976.

Crönert, Wilhelm. *Kolotes und Menedemos.* Studien zur Palaeographie und Papyruskunde 6, C. Wessely, ed. Leipzig: Eduard Avenarius, 1906.

——. Review of Sykutris' edition of the Socratic letters. *Gnomon* 12 (1936) 146-52.

Dahl, Nils. "Paul and the Church at Corinth According to 1 Corinthians 1:10-4:21," in *Studies in Paul.* Minneapolis: Augsburg, 1977, 40-61.

Deissner, Kurt. *Paulus und Seneca.* Beiträge zur Förderung christlicher Theologie 21, 2, D. A. Schlatter and D. W. Lütgert, eds. Gütersloh: C. Bertelsmann, 1917.

Delatte, A. "Le Sage-témoin dans la philosophie stoico-cynicienne." *Academie Royale de Belgique. Bulletin de la classe des lettres et des sciences morales et politiques,* 5 sér., 39 (1953) 166-86.

Dibelius, Martin. *"EPIGNOSIS ALETHEIAS,"* in *Botschaft und Geschichte,* col. 2. Tübingen: J. C. B. Mohr (Paul Siebeck), 1956, 1-13.

——. *A Fresh Approach to the New Testament and Early Christian Literature.* New York: Charles Scribner's Sons, 1936; repr. Westport, CT: Greenwood, 1979.

——. *From Tradition to Gospel.* Trans. By Beltram L. Woolf. New York: Scribner, 1935.

Dibelius, Martin and Hans Conzelmann. *The Pastoral Epistles.* Trans. by Philip Buttolph and Adela Yarbro. Hermeneia. Philadelphia: Fortress, 1972.

Dibelius, Martin and Heinrich Greeven. *James.* Trans. by Michael A. Williams. Hermeneia. Philadelphia: Fortress, 1976.

Dihle, Albrecht. *Die goldene Regel: Eine Einführung in die Geschichte der antiken und frühchristlichen Vulgärethik.* Göttingen: Vandenhoeck & Ruprecht, 1962.

——. "Posidonius' System of Moral Philosophy." *JHS* 93 (1973) 50-57.

Dittmar, Heinrich. *Aischenes von Sphettos: Studien zur Literaturgeschichte der Sokratiker, Untersuchungen und Fragmente.* Philologische Untersuchungen 21. Berlin: Weidmann, 1912.

Dobschütz, Ernst von. *Die urchristlichen Gemeinden: Sittengeschichtliche Bilder.* Leipzig: J. C. Hinrichs, 1902.

Döring, Klaus. *Exemplum Socratis: Studien zur Sokratesnachwirkung in der kynisch-stoischen Popularphilosophie der frühen Kaiserzeit und im frühen Christentum.* Hermes Einzelschriften 42, J. Bleiken et al. eds. Wiesbaden: Franz Steiner, 1979.

Dornseiff, Franz. "Literarische Verwendungen des Beispiels." *Bibliothek Warburg* 4 (1924-25) 206-28.

Dörrie, H. "Sokratiker-Briefe." *Kl. Pauly* 5 (1975) 257-58.

Doty, William G. *Letters in Primitive Christianity.* New Testament Series, Dan O. Via, ed. Philadelphia: Fortress, 1973.

Dudley, Donald R. *A History of Cynicism, from Diogenes to the 6th Century A. D.* Hildesheim: Georg Olms, 1967.

Dümmler, Ferdinand. *Akademika: Beiträge zur Literaturgeschichte der sokratischen Schule.* Giessen: J. Ricker, 1889.

Dugas, Ludovic. *L'Amitié antique.* Paris: Librairie Félix Alcan, 1914.

Duncan, J. Garrow. *"pistos ho logos."* *Exp. Tim.* 35 (1923-24) 141.

Easton, Burton S. "New Testament Ethical Lists." *JBL* 51 (1932) 1-12.

——. *The Pastoral Epistles.* New York: Charles Scribner's Sons, 1947.

Edelstein, Emma. "Xenophontisches und platonisches Bild des Sokrates." Diss. Heidelberg. Berlin: Dr. Emil Ebering, 1933.

Ellicott, Charles J. *The Pastoral Epistles of St. Paul: With a Critical and Grammatical Commentary and a Revised Translation.* 4 rev. ed. London: Longmans, Green, 1869.

Emeljanow, Victor E. "The Letters of Diogenes." Diss. Stanford University, 1967.

———. "A Note on the Cynic Short-Cut to Happiness." *Mnemos.* 4 ser. 18 (1965) 182-84.

Emminger, Kurt. "Ps-Isokrates *pros Dēmonikon* (1)." *Jahrbücher für Philologie und Pädagogik.* suppl. B. 27 (1902) 373-442.

Erbes, K. "Zeit und Ziel der Grüsse Röm 16, 3-15 und der Mitteilungen 2 Tim 4, 9-21." *ZNW* 10 (1909) 128-47, 195-218.

Ernesti, Johann C. "*schēmatizein,*" in *Lexicon technologiae Graecorum rhetoricae.* Leipzig: Caspar Fritsch, 1795, 341.

Farrer, James A. *Literary Forgeries.* London: Longmans, Green, 1907.

Feldman, Louis, H. "Abraham the Greek Philosopher in Josephus," *TAPA* 99 (1968) 145-56.

———. "Josephus" Portrait of Saul," *HUCA* 53 (1982) 45-99.

Fenton, J. C. "Pseudonymity in the New Testament." *Theology* 58 (1955) 51-56.

Field, Guy C. "Aristippus." *OCD,* 111.

Fiske, George C. *Lucilius and Horace: A Study in the Classical Theory of Imitation.* Madison: University of Wisconsin, 1920.

Foerster, Werner. "*eusebeia.*" *TDNT* 7 (1971) 175-85.

———. "*EUSEBEIA* in den Pastoralbriefen." *NTS* 5 (1958-59) 213-18.

Ford, J. Massyngberd. "Proto-Montanism in the Pastoral Epistles." *NTS* 17 (1970-71) 338-46.

Fort, Pierre le. "La Responsabilité politique de l'église d'après les épîtres pastorales." *ETR* 49 (1974) 1-14.

Frend, W. H. C. *Martyrdom and Persecution in the Early Church: A Study of a Conflict from the Maccabees to Donatus.* Anchor Books, Garden City: Doubleday, 1967.

Frey, Josef. "Studien zur dritten Rede des Isokrates." Diss. Freiburg in d.S., 1946.

Fritz, Kurt von. "Phaidon von Elis und der 12. und 13 Sokratikerbrief." *Philol.* 90 (1935) 240-44.

Funk, K. "Untersuchungen über die lucianische Vita Demonactis." *Philol.* suppl. B. 10 (1905-07) 559-674.

Funk, Robert W. "The Apostolic 'parousia': Form and Significance," in *Christian History and Interpretation. Studies Presented to John Knox,* W. R. Farmer et al., eds. Cambridge: Cambridge University, 1967, 246-68.

Ganss, Wilhelm. *Das Bild des Weisen bei Seneca.* Freiburg i.d.S.: W. Theiler, 1951.

Geffcken, Johannes. "Antiplatonica." *Hermes* 64 (1929) 87-109.

———. *Kynika und verwandtes.* Heidelberg: Carl Winters, 1909.

Gerhard, Gustav A. *Phoinix von Kolophon: Texte und Untersuchungen.* Leipzig/Berlin: B. G. Teubner, 1909.

———. "Untersuchungen zur Geschichte der griechischen Briefes." *Philol.* 64 (1905) 27-65.

———. "Zur Legende vom Kyniker Diogenes." *Archiv für Religionswissenschaft* 15 (1912) 388-408.

Gerhardsson, Birger. *Memory and Manuscript: Oral Tradition and Written Transmission in Rabbinic Judaism and Early Christianity.* Acta Seminarii neotestamentici Upsaliensis 22. Uppsala: Almqvist & Wiksell, 1961.

Giannantoni, Gabriele. *Scuole socratiche minori e filosofia ellenistica.* Consiglio Nazionale delle Ricerche. Centro di Studio per la Storia della Storiografia Filosofica 4. Bologna: Il Mulino, 1977.

Gigon, Olof. *Sokrates: Sein Bild in Dichtung und Geschichte.* Bern: A. Francke, 1947.

Gomme, Arnold W. and F. H. Sandbach. *Menander: A Commentary.* Oxford: Oxford University, 1973.

Goodenough, Erwin R. "The Political Philosophy of Hellenistic Kingship." *YCS* 1 (1928) 55-102.

Goodspeed, Edgar J. "Pseudonymity and Pseudepigraphy in Early Christian Literature," in *New Chapters in New Testament Study.* New York: Macmillan, 1937, 169-88.

Goppelt, Leonhard. *"typos." TDNT* 8 (1972) 246-59.

Grayson, Kenneth. "A Problem of Translation: The Meaning of Parakaleo, Paraklesis in the New Testament." *ScrB* 11 (1980) 27-31.

Grube, Georges M. A. *A Greek Critic: Demetrius on Style.* Toronto: University of Toronto, 1961.

Gudeman, Alfred. "Literary Frauds Among the Greeks." *TAPA* 25 (1894) 140-64; also in *Classical Studies in Honour of Henry Drisler.* New York: Macmillan, 1894, 52-74.

Guillemin, Anne Marie. *Pline et la vie littéraire de son temps.* Collection d'études latines 4, J. Marouzeau, ed. Paris: Societé d'édition "Les Belles Lettres," 1929.

Guthrie, Donald. *New Testament Introduction: The Pauline Epistles.* Appendix C. London: Tyndale, 1965.

———. "Acts and Epistles in Apocryphal Writings," in *Apostolic History and the Gospel: Biblical and Historical Essays Presented to F. F. Bruce,* W. Ward Gasque and Ralph P. Martin, eds. Grand Rapids: Wm. B. Eerdmans, 1970, 329-44.

Gutierrez, Pedro. *La Paternité spirituelle selon S. Paul.* Paris: Gabalda, 1968.

Hadot, Ilsetraut. *Seneca und die griechisch-römische Tradition der Seelenleitung.* Berlin: de Gruyter, 1969.

Haefner, Alfred E. "A Unique Source for the Study of Ancient Pseudepigraphy." *ATR* 16 (1934) 8-15.

Harrison, Percy N. "The Authorship of the Pastoral Epistles." *Exp. Tim.* 67 (1955) 77-81.

———. *Paulines and Pastorals.* London: Villiers, 1964.

———. *The Problem of the Pastoral Epistles.* London: Oxford University (H. Milford), 1921.

Hartlich, Paulus. *De exhortationum a Graecis Romanisque scriptarum historia et indole. Leipz. Stud.* 11 (1889) 207-336; also Leipzig: S. Hirzel, 1889.

Hatch, Edwin. *The Influence of Greek Ideas on Christianity.* New York: Harper and Brothers, 1957.

Hauck, Friedrich. *Die Freundschaft bei den griechen und im Neuen Testament.* Leipzig: A Deichert (D. Werner Scholl), 1928.

Hengel, Martin. "Anonymität, Pseudepigrpahie und 'literarische Fälschung' in der jüdisch-hellenistischen Literatur," in *Pseudepigrapha I,* Kurt von Fritz, ed. Fondation Hardt 18. Geneva: Vandoeuvres, 1971, 229-308.

Hense, Otto. "Eine Menippea des Varro." *RhM* 61 (1906) 1-18.

Hercher, Rudolf. "Zu den griechischen Epistolographen." *Hermes* 4 (1870) 427-28.

———. "Zu den griechischen Prosaikern." *Hermes* 6 (1872) 55-56.

Hijmans, Benjamin L., Jr. *ASKESIS: Notes on Epictetus' Educational System.* Assen: Van Gorcum, 1959.

———. *Inlaboratus et Facilis: Aspects of Structure in Some Letters of Seneca.* Mnemos. suppl. 38, W. den Boer, ed. Leiden: E. J. Brill, 1976.

Höistad, Ragnar. *Cynic Hero and Cynic King: Studies in the Cynic Conception of Man.* Lund: Carl Blom, 1948.

Holl, Karl. "Die Schriftstellerische Form des griechischen Heiligenlebens." *Neue Jahrbuch für das klassische Altertum, Geschichte und Deutsche Literatur* 29 (1912) 406-27.

Holladay, Carl H. *"Theos Aner"* in Hellenistic Judaism: A Critique of the Use of This Category in New Testament Christology. SBL Dissertation Series 40. Missoula: Scholars, 1968.

Hollerbach, Hans R. "Zur Bedeutung des Wortes *chreia.*" Diss. Cologne, 1964.

Holmberg, Arne. *Studien zur Terminologie und Technik der rhetorischen Beweisführung bei lateinischen Schriftstellern.* Uppsala: Almqvist & Wiksell, 1913.

Holtzmann, Heinrich J. *Die Pastoralbriefe.* Leipzig: Wilhelm Engelmann, 1880.

Horna, K. "Gnome, Gnomendichtung, Gnomologien." *PW* suppl. 6, 74-90.

Hornsby, H. M. "The Cynicism of Peregrinus Proteus." *Hermathena* 48 (1933) 65-84.

Houlden, James L. *The Pastoral Epistles: I and II Timothy; Titus.* Pelican New Testament Commentaries. Harmondsworth: Penguin, 1976.

Humbert, Jean. *Socrate et les petits socratiques.* Paris: Presses Universitaires, 1967.

Ingenkamp, Heinz G. *Plutarchs Schriften über die Heilung der Seele.* Göttingen: Vandenhoeck & Ruprecht, 1971.

Jaeger, Werner. *Paideia: The Ideals of Greek Culture.* Trans. by Gilbert Highet. 3 vols. New York: Oxford University, 1939.

Javierre, Antonio. "Pistoi Anthropoi 2 T 2.2: Episcopad y sucesión apostolica en el nuevo testamento." *An. Bib.* 17-18 (1969) 2:109-18.

Jebb, Richard C. *The Attic Orators from Antiphon to Isaeos.* 2 vols. London: Macmillan and Co., 1893.

Jeuckens, Robert P. *Plutarch von Chaeronea und die Rhetorik.* Dissertationes Philologicae Argentoratenses Selectae 12, 4, B. Keil and R. Reitzenstein, eds. Strassburg: Karl J. Trübner, 1907.

Johnson, Luke T. "II Timothy and the Polemic Against False Teachers: A Reexamination." *Ohio Journal of Religious Studies* 6-7 (1978-79) 1-26.

Joly, Henri. *De cynica institutione sub imperatoribus Romanis.* Paris: Ernest Thorin, 1869.

Jost, Karl T. *Das Beispiel und Vorbild der Vorfahren bei den attischen Rednern und Geschichtschreibern bis Demosthenes.* Rhetorische Studien 19, E. Drerup, ed. Paderborn: F. Schöningh, 1936.

Judge, E. A. "The Early Christians as a Scholastic Community." *JRH* 1 (1960-61) 4-15, 125-37.

Kabiersch, J. *Untersuchungen zum Begriff der Philanthropia bei Kaiser Julian.* Klass-philol. Studien 21. Wiesbaden: Harrassowitz, 1960.

Käsemann, Ernst. "Das Formular einer neutestamentlichen Ordinationsparänese," in *Neutestamentliche Studien für Rudolf Bultmann,* W. Eltester, ed. BZNW 21. Berlin: Alfred Töpelmann, 1954, 261-68.

Kamlah, Ehrhard. *Die Form der katalogischen Paränese im Neuen Testament.* WUNT 7, J. Jeremias and O. Michel, eds. Tübingen: J. C. B. Mohr (Paul Siebeck), 1964.

Karris, Robert A. "The Background and Significance of the Polemic of the Pastoral Epistles." *JBL* 92 (1973) 549-64.

———. "The Function and Sitz-im-Leben of the Paraenetic Elements in the Pastoral Epistles." Diss. Harvard University, 1971.

Kelly, John N. D. *A Commentary on the Pastoral Epistles: I Timothy, II Timothy, Titus.* Black's New Testament Commentaries. London: Adam and Charles Black, 1963.

Kennedy, George. *The Art of Rhetoric in the Roman World*. Princeton: Princeton University, 1972.

Kindstrand, Jan F. *Bion of Borysthenes*. Stockholm: J. F. Kindstrand/Almqvist and Wiksell Distributors, 1976.

————. "Demetrius the Cynic." *Philol.* 124 (1980) 83-98.

Kittel, Gerhard. "*akolouthein.*" *TDNT* 1 (1964) 210-16.

————. "Die *genealogiai* der Pastoralbriefe." *ZNW* 20 (1920-21) 49-69.

————. "*eikōn.*" *TDNT* 2 (1964) 246-56.

Kleck, Joseph. *Symbouleutici qui dicitur sermonis historiam criticam per quattuor saecula continuatam*. Rhetorische Studien 8, E. Drerup, ed. Paderborn: Ferdinand Schöningh, 1919.

Klotz, Alfred. "Zur Literatur der exempla und zur Epitome Livii." *Hermes* 44 (1909) 198-214.

Knight, George W. *The Faithful Sayings in the Pastoral Letters*. Repr. Grand Rapids: Baker, 1979.

Knoch, Otto. *Die 'Testamente' des Petrus und Paulus: Die Sicherung der apostolischen Überlieferung in der spätneutestamentlichen Zeit*. SBS 62, H. Haag et al., eds. Stuttgart: KBW, 1973.

Köhler, Liselotte. *Die Briefe des Sokrates und der Sokratiker herausgegeben, übersetzt und kommentiert*. Philologus suppl. B. 20,2. Leipzig: Dieterich, 1928.

Koelling, Heinrich. *Der erste Brief Pauli an Timotheus*. Berlin: Hugo Rother, 1882.

Kornhardt, Hildegard. *Exemplum: Eine bedetungsgeschichtliche Studie*. Göttingen: Robert Noske, 1936.

Koskenniemi, Heikki. *Studien zur Idee und Phraseologie des griechischen Briefes bis 400 n. Chr*. Annales Academiae Scientiarum Fennicae, ser. B, 102.2. Helsinki: Finnischen Akademie der Wissenschaften, 1956.

Lee, E. Kenneth. "Words Denoting 'Pattern' in the N. T." *NTS* 8 (1961-62) 166-73.

Lemaire, André. "Pastoral Epistles: Redaction and Theology." *BTB* 2 (1972) 25-42.

Leo, Friedrich. "Diogenes bei Plautus," *Ausgewählte kleine Schriften: I, Zur römischen Literatur des Zeitalters der Republik*, Eduard Fraenkel, ed. Rome: Edizione di Storia e Letteratura, 1960, 185-90; originally in *Hermes* 41 (1906) 441-46.

Lesky, Albin. *A History of Greek Literature*. Trans. by James Willis and Cornelis de Heer. New York: Thomas Y. Crowell, 1966.

Lestapis, Stanislas de. *L'Enigme des pastorales de St. Paul*. Paris: Gabalda, 1976.

Lévêque, Ch. "La Vie socratique et la vie cynique." *Académie des Sciences Morales et Politiques, Séances et Travaux*. n.s. 27 (1887) 199-221.

Lippert, Peter. *Leben als Zeugnis: Die werbende Kraft christlicher Lebensführung nach dem Kirchenverständnis neutestamentlicher Briefe*. Stuttgart: KBW, 1968.

Lips, Hermann von. *Glaube—Gemeinde—Amt: Zum Verständnis der Ordination in den Pastoralbriefen*. FRLANT 122. Göttingen: Vandenhoeck & Ruprecht, 1979.

Litchfield, Henry W. "National *Exempla Virtutis* in Roman Literature." *HSPh* 25 (1914) 1-71.

Lofthouse, W. "Imitatio Christi." *Exp. Tim.* 65 (1953-54) 338-42.

Lohse, Eduard. *Die Ordination im Spätjudentum und im Neuen Testament*. Göttingen: Vandenhoeck & Ruprecht, 1951.

Loisy, Alfred. *Les Livres du Nouveau Testament*. Paris: Emile Nourry, 1922.

————. *The Origins of the New Testament*. Trans. by L. P. Jacks. New York: Macmillan, 1950.

————. *Remarques sur la littérature épistolaire du Nouveau Testament*. Paris: Emile Nourry (J. Thiébaud), 1935.

Lorenz, S. "De progressio notionis *philanthrōpias*." Diss. Leipzig, 1914.

Lührmann, D. "Epiphaneia: Zur Bedeutungsgeschichte eines griechischen Wortes," in *Tradition und Glaube* (Fest. Karl G. Kuhn), G. Jeremias et al., eds. Göttingen: Vandenhoeck & Ruprecht, 1971, 185-99.

Lütgert, Wilhelm. *Die Irrlehrer der Pastoralbriefe*. Beiträge zur Förderung christlicher Theologie 8. Gütersloh: C. Bertelsmann, 1909.

Lumpe, A, "Exemplum." *RAC* (1966) 6:1229-57.

McEleney, Neil J. "Vice Lists of the Pastorals." *CBQ* 36 (1974) 203-19.

Maehlum, Helge. *Die Vollmacht des Timotheus nach den Pastoralbriefen*. Theologische Dissertationen 1, Bo Reike, ed. Basel: Friedrich Reinhardt, 1969.

Maier, Friedrich W. "Die Hauptprobleme der Pastoralbriefe Pauli," in *Biblische Zeitfragen gemeinverständlich erörtert*, J. Nikel and I. Rohr, eds. Münster i.W.: Aschendorff, 1910, 485-540.

Malherbe, Abraham J. "Ancient Epistolary Theorists." *Ohio Journal of Religious Studies* 5 (1977) 3-27.

———. "The Beasts at Ephesus." *JBL* 87 (1968) 71-80.

———. "First Thessalonians as a Paraenetic Letter." (Paper delivered at the 1972 SBL Seminar on the Form and Function of the Pauline Letters.) Rev. version "Exhortation in First Thessalonians," *NovT* 25 (1983) 238-56.

———. " 'Gentle as a Nurse'; The Cynic Background to I Thess ii." *NovT* 12 (1970) 203-17.

———. "Hellenistic Moralists and the New Testament," in *ANRW*, W. Haase, ed. Berlin: de Gruyter, forthcoming, II.

———. "Medical Imagery in the Pastoral Epistles," in *Texts and Testaments: Critical Essays in Honor of Stuart D. Currie*, W. E. March, ed. San Antonio: Trinity University, 1980, 19-35.

———. "Pseudo-Heraclitus, Epistle 4: The Divinization of the Wise Man." *JAC* 21 (1978) 42-64.

———. "Self-Definition Among Epicureans and Cynics," in *Self-Definition in the Graeco-Roman World*, Ben F. Meyer, ed. Philadelphia: Fortress, 1982.

Mangold, Wilhelm. *Die Irrelehren der Pastoralbriefe*. Marburg: Elwert, 1856.

Marrou, Henri I. *A History of Education in Antiquity*. Trans. by George Lamb. New York: New American Library, 1964.

Martin, Josef. *Antike Rhetorik: Technik und Methode*. Handbuch der Altertumswissenschaft 2,3, H. Bengston, ed. Munich: C. H. Beck, 1974.

Maurer, Christian. "*tithēmi.*" *TDNT* 8 (1972) 156-68.

Mauersberger, Arno. "Plato und Aristipp." *Hermes* 61 (1926) 208-30, 304-28.

Mayer, Arnold. "Die religiöse Pseudepigraphie als ethisch-psychologisches Problem." *ZNW* 35 (1936) 262-79; and in *Archiv für die gesamte Psychologie* 86 (1932).

Mayer, Hans H. *Über die Pastoralbriefe*. FRLANT n.F. 3. Göttingen: Vandenhoeck & Ruprecht, 1913.

Merk, Otto. *Handeln aus Glauben: Die Motivierung der paulinischen Ethik*. Marburger theologische Studien 5. Marburg: N. G. Elwert, 1968.

Merlan, O. "Minor Socratics." *JHPh* 10 (1972) 143-52.

Metzger, Bruce M. "Literary Forgeries and Canonical Pseudepigrapha." *JBL* 91 (1972) 3-24.

Metzger, Hubert. "Zur Stellung der liturgischen Beamten Ägyptens in frührömischer Zeit." *MH* 2 (1945) 54-62.

Metzger, Wolfgang. "Die neoterikà épithumíae in 2 Tim 2,22." *TZ* 33 (1977) 129-36.

Meyer, Eduard. *Ursprung und Anfänge des Christentums: III, Die Apostelgeschichte und die Anfänge des Christentums.* Stuttgart/Berlin: J. G. Cotta, 1921-23.

Meyer, Heinrich A. W. *Critical and Exegetical Hand-Book to the Epistles to the Corinthians.* Trans. by D. Douglas Bannerman. New York: Funk and Wagnalls, 1884.

Michaelis, Wilhelm. "*mimeomai.*" *TDNT* 4 (1967) 666-73.

————. *Pastoralbriefe und Gefangenschaftsbriefe: Zur Echtheitsfrage der Pastoralbriefe.* Neutestamentliche Forschungen 1, Paulusstudien 6, Otto Schmitz, ed. Gütersloh: C. Bertelsmann, 1930.

Michel, Hans Joachim. *Die Abschiedsrede des Paulus an die Kirche Apg 20:17-38.* SANT 25. Munich: Kösel, 1973.

Mikkola, Eino. *Isokrates: Seine Anschauungen im Lichte seiner Schriften.* Annales Akademiae Scientiarum Fennicae ser. B, 89. Helsinki: Finnischen Akademie der Wissenschaften, 1954.

Misch, Georg. *Geschichte der Autobiographie: Das Altertum.* 2 ed. Leipzig: B. G. Teubner, 1931.

Misener, Geneva. "Iconistic Portraits." *CPH* 19 (1924) 97-123.

Mittelhaus, Karl. "De Plutarchi praeceptis gerendae reipublicae." Diss. Friederich Wilhelm University, Berlin, 1911.

Moffatt, James. *The First Epistle of Paul to the Corinthians.* London: Hodder and Stoughton, 1951.

Müller, Ulrich B. *Zur frühchristlichen Theologiegeschichte: Judenchristentum und Paulinismus an der Wende vom ersten zum zweiten Jahrhundert nach Christus.* Gütersloh: Gerd Mohn, 1976.

Munck, Johannes. "Discours d'adieu dans le Nouveau Testament et dans littérature biblique," in *Aux Sources de la littérature biblique* (Fest. M. Goguel), O. Cullmann, ed. Neuchâtel: Delachaux & Niestlé, 1950, 155-70.

Nauck, W. "Die Herkunft des Verfassers der Pastoralbriefe: Ein Beitrag der Auslegung der Pastoralbriefe." Diss. Göttingen, 1950.

Nieder, Lorenz. *Die Motive der religiös-sittlichen Paränese in den Paulinischen Gemeindebriefen: Ein Beitrag zur paulinischen Ethik.* Münchener theologische Studien I, historische Abteilung 12. Munich: K. Zink, 1956.

Nock, Arthur D. "Notes on the Ruler Cult." *JHS* 48 (1928) 21-43.

Norden, Eduard. "Beiträge zur Geschichte der griechischen Philosophie." *Jahr. f. cl. Phil.* 19 suppl. B. (1893) 365-462.

"Note on 2 Timothy iii.10." *Expositor* 9 ser. 1 (1924) 456-57.

Obens, Wilhelm. *Qua aetate Socratis et Socraticorum epistulae, quae dicuntur, scriptae sunt.* Münster i.W. Aschendorff, 1912.

Oberlinner, Lorenz. "Die 'Epiphaneia' des Heilswillens Gottes in Christus Jesus: Zur Grundstruktur der Christologie der Pastoralbriefe." *ZNW* 71 (1980) 192-213.

Oepke, Albrecht. *Die Missionspredigt des Apostels Paulus: Eine biblisch-theologische und religionsgeschichtliche Untersuchung.* Leipzig, J. C. Hinrichs, 1920.

Oltramare, André. *Les Origins de la diatribe romaine.* Lausanne: Librairie Payot, 1926.

Orelli, Johann C. *Socratis et Socraticorum, Pythagorae et Pythagoreorum quae feruntur epistolae. Dissertationes et iudicia de epistolis Socraticis et indicem adiecit.* Leipzig: Weidmann, 1815.

Pagels, Elaine. *The Gnostic Paul: Gnostic Exegesis of the Pauline Letters.* Philadelphia: Fortress, 1975.

Paquet, Léonce. *Les Cyniques grecs: Fragments et témoignages.* Collection Philosophica 4. Ottawa: University of Ottawa, 1975.

Parry, Reginald St. J. *The First Epistle of Paul the Apostle to the Corinthians.* Cambridge: Cambridge University, 1916.

Pax, Elpidius. *EPIPHANEIA: Ein religionsgeschichtlicher Beitrag zur biblischen Theologie.* Münchener theologische Studien 1,10. Munich: K. Zink, 1955.

Peter, Hermann. *Der Brief in der römischen Literatur: Literargeschichtliche Untersuchungen und Zusammenfassungen. Abh. sächs. Ges. Wiss.* 47, Philol-hist. Kl. 20,3. Leipzig: B. G. Teubner, 1901.

Peterson, Erik. "Zur Bedeutungsgeschichte von *parrēsia,*" in *Zur Theorie des Christentums* (Fest. Reinhold Seeberg), vol. 1, Wilhelm Koepp, ed. Leipzig: A. Deichert (D. Werner Scholl), 1929, 283-97.

Pétré, Hélène. "Exemplum," *Dictionnaire de Spiritualité,* IV, 2, 1885-92.

Pfitzner, Victor C. *Paul and the Agon Motif: Traditional Athletic Imagery in the Pauline Literature.* NovTSup. 16, W. C. van Unnik, ed. Leiden: E. J. Brill, 1967.

Pflugmacher, Ernest. *Locorum communium specimen.* Greifswald: Hans Adler, 1909.

Picard, Roger. *Artifices et mystifications littéraires.* Montreal: Dussault et Péledeau, 1945.

Praechter, Karl, ed. *Friedrich Überwegs Grundriss der Geschichte der Philosophie: I, Die Philosophie des Altertums.* 12 rev. ed. Berlin: E. S. Mittler & Sohn, 1926.

Préaux, Claire. "L'Image du roi de l'époque hellénistique," in *Images of Man in Ancient and Medieval Thought* (Fest. G. Verbeke), F. Boissier, ed. Louvain: University of Louvain, 1976, 53-76.

Price, Bennet J. "Paradeigma and Exemplum in Ancient Rhetorical Theory." Diss. University of California at Berkeley, 1975.

Quinn, Jerome D. "On the Terminology for Faith, Truth, Teaching, and the Spirit in the Pastoral Epistles: A Summary," in *Teaching Authority and Infallibility in the Church: Lutherans and Catholics in Dialogue VI,* P. Empie et al. eds. Minneapolis: Augsburg, 1980.

———. "The Last Volume of Luke: The Relation of Luke-Acts to the Pastoral Epistles," in *Perspectives on Luke-Acts,* C. H. Talbert, ed. Edinburgh: T. & T. Clark, Ltd, 1978, 62-75.

Rabe, Hugo. "Aus Rhetoren-Handschriften." *RhM* n.F. 64 (1909) 284-309.

Rahn, Helmut, "Die Frömmigkeit der Kyniker." *Paideuma* 7 (1960) 280-92.

Reichel, Georg. *Quaestiones progymnasticae.* Leipzig: Robert Noske, 1909.

Reicke, Bo. "Chronologie der Pastoralbriefe." *TLZ* 101 (1976) 81-94.

Reiff, Arno. "Interpretatio, imitatio, aemulatio: Begriff und Vorstellung literarischer Abhängigkeit bei den Römern." Diss. Cologne, 1959.

Rendall, Frederick. "Faithful Is the Word." *Expositor* 53 n.s. (1887) 314-20.

Renoirte, Thérése. *Les "Conseils politiques" de Plutarque: Une lettre ouverte aux grecs à l'époque de Trajan.* Recueil de Travaux d'Histoire et de Philologie 3,40. Louvain: University of Louvain, 1951.

Rich, Audrey N. "The Cynic Conception of *autarkeia.*" *Mnemos.* 9 (1956) 23-29.

Riewald, Paul. "De imperatorum Romanorum cum certis dis et comparatione et aequatione." Diss. Halle, 1912.

Rist, Martin. "Pseudepigraphic Refutations of Marcionism." *JR* 22 (1942) 39-62.

———. "Pseudepigraphy and the Early Christians," in *Studies in New Testament and Early Christian Literature* (Fest. A. P. Wikgren), David E. Aune, ed. Leiden: E. J. Brill, 1972, 75-91.

Ritter, Constantin. *Neue Untersuchungen über Platon.* Munich: C. H. Beck, 1910.

Roloff, Jürgen. *Apostolat—Verkundigung—Kirche. Ursprung, Inhalt und Funktion des kirchlichen Apostelamtes nach Paulus, Lukas und den Pastoralbriefen.* Gütersloh: Gerd Mohn, 1965.

Ronconi, Alessandro. "Introduzione alla letteratura pseudoepigrafa." *Studi Classici e Orientali* 5 (1955) 15-37.

Rosenkranz, Bernhard. "Die Struktur der Ps-Isokrateischen Demonicea." *Emerita* 34 (1966) 95-129.

Rudberg, Gunnar. "Die Diogenes-Tradition und das Neue Testament." *ConNT* 2 (1936) 36-43.

———. "Zu den literarischen Formen der Sokratiker: Eine Skizze," in *DRAGMA* (Fest. Martin P. Nilsson), Gustaf Adolf, ed. Lund: Håkan Ohlsson, 1939, 419-29.

———. "Zum Diogenes-Typus." *Symbolae Osloensis* 15 (1936) 1-18.

———. "Zur Diogenes-Tradition." *Symbolae Osloensis* 14 1935) 22-43.

Sand, Alexander. "Anfänge einer Koordinierung verschiedener Gemeindeordnungen nach den Pastoralbriefen," in *Kirche im Werden: Studien zum Thema Amt und Gemeinde im Neuen Testament,* Josef Hainz, ed. Munich: Ferdinand Schöningh, 1976, 215-37.

Sayre, Farrand. *Diogenes of Sinope: A Study of Greek Cynicism.* Baltimore: J. H. Furst, 1938.

Scarpat, Giuseppe. *Parrhesia: Storia del termine e delle sue traduzioni in latino.* Brescia: Paideia, 1964.

Schenkeveld, Dirk M. *Studies in Demetrius on Style.* Amsterdam: A. M. Hakkert, 1964.

Schering, Otto. *Symbola ad Socratis et Socraticorum epistulas explicandas.* Greifswald: Hans Adler, 1917.

Schlier, Heinrich. "hypodeigma." *TDNT* 2 (1964) 32-33.

———. *Die Zeit der Kirche: Exegetische Aufsätze und Vorträge.* Freiburg: Herder, 1956.

Schmid, W. "Das Sokratesbild der Wolken." *Philol.* 97 (1948) 209-28.

Schmid, Wilhelm and O. Stählin. *Geschichte der griechischen Literatur. I, Klassische Periode der griechischen Literatur.* 6th ed. 3 vols. Munich: C. H. Beck (Oskar Beck), 1912.

Schmithals, Walter. "Pastoralbriefe." *RGG*[3] 5:144-48.

———. "Zur Abfassung und ältesten Sammlung der paulinischen Hauptbriefe." *ZNW* 51 (1960) 225-45.

Scheneider, Otto. *Isocrates. Ausgewählte Reden für den Schulgebrauch erklärt, I.* Leipzig: B. G. Teubner, 1874.

Schroeter, Friderich. *De regum hellenisticorum epistulis in lapidibus servatis quaestiones stilisticae.* Leipzig: B. G. Teubner, 1931.

Schubart, Wilhelm. "Das Gesetz und der Kaiser in griechischen Urkunden." *Klio* 13 (1937) 54-69.

———. "Das hellenistische Königsideal nach Inschriften und Papyri." *APF* 12 (1937) 1-26.

———. "Das Königsbild des Hellenismus." *Die Antike* 13 (1937) 272-88.

Schulz, Anselm. *Nachfolge und Nachahmen: Studien über das Verhältnis der neutestamentlichen Jüngerschaft zur urchristlichen Vorbildethik.* Munich: Kösel, 1962.

Schwarz, Roland. *Bürgerliches Christentum im Neuen Testament? Eine Studie zu Ethik, Amt und Recht in den Pastoralbriefen.* Österreichische Biblische Studien 4. Klosterneuburg: Österreichisches Katholisches Bibelwerk, 1983.

Scott, Ernest F. *The Pastoral Epistles.* London: Hodder and Stoughton, 1936.

Scott, Kenneth. "Plutarch and the Ruler Cult." *TAPA* 60 (1929) 117-35.

Seck, Friedrich. "Untersuchungen zum Isokratestext mit einer Ausgabe des Rede an Nikokles." Diss. Hamburg, 1965.

Sheehan, Michael. "De fide artis rhetoricae Isocrati tributae." Diss. Bonn 1901.

Sint, Josef A. *Pseudonymität im Altertum: ihre Formen und ihre Gründe.* Commentationes Aenipontanae 15. Innsbruck: Wagner, 1960.

Sipple, Anton. *Der Staatsmann und Dichter Seneca als politischer Erzieher.* Würzburg: Konrad Triltsch, 1938.

Smith, Morton. "Pseudepigraphy in the Israelite Literary Tradition," in *Pseudepigrapha I,* Kurt von Fritz, ed. Fondation Hardt 18. Geneva: Vandoeuvres, 1971, 189-214.

Soffel, Joachim. *Die Regeln Menanders für die Leichenrede: In ihrer Tradition/dargestellt, herausgestellt, übersetz, und kommentiert.* Beiträge zur Klassischen Philologie 57. Meisenheim am Glan: A. Hain, 1974.

Speyer, Wolfang. *Bücherfunde in der Glaubenswerbung der Antike mit einem Ausblick auf Mittelalter und Neuzeit.* Hypomnemata 24. Göttingen: Vandenhoeck & Ruprecht, 1970.

————. "Fälschung, pseudepigraphische freie Erfindung und echte religiöse Pseudepigraphie," in *Pseudepigrapha I,* Kurt von Fritz, ed. Geneva: Vandoeuvres, 1971, 331-66.

————. *Die literarische Fälschung im heidnischen und christlichen Altertum: Ein Versuch ihrer Deutung.* Handbuch der Alterumswissenschaft 1,2, Hermann Bengston, ed. Munich: C. H. Beck, 1971.

Spicq, Ceslas. "Gymnastique et morale, d'après 1 Tim IV, 7-8." *RB* 54 (1947) 229-42.

————. "La Philanthropie hellénistique, vertu divine et royale." *ST* 12 (1958) 169-91.

————. "Saint Paul et la loi des dépots." *RB* 40 (1931) 481-502.

————. *Saint Paul: Les Epîtres pastorales.* 4 rev. ed. 2 vols. Paris: Gabalda, 1969.

Stanley, David M. "'Become Imitators of Me': The Pauline Conception of Apostolic Tradition." *Bib.* 40 (1959) 859-77.

Steidle, Wolfgang. "Redekunst und Bildung bei Isokrates." *Hermes* 80 (1952) 257-96.

Stemplinger, Eduard. *Das Plagiat in der griechischen Literatur.* Leipzig/Berlin: B. G. Teubner, 1912.

Stenger, Werner. "Timotheus und Titus als literarische Gestalten: Beobachtungen zur Form und Funktion der Pastoralbriefe." *Kairos* 16 (1974) 252-57.

Straub, Johannes A. *Vom Herrscherideal in der Spätantike.* Forschungen zur Kirchen- u. Geistesgeschichte 18. Stuttgart: W. Kohlhammer, 1939.

Stuart, Duane R. *Epochs of Greek and Roman Biography.* Sather Classical Lectures 4. Berkeley, University of California, 1928.

Süpfle, Gottfried. "Zur Geschichte der cynischen Secte. Erster Teil." *Archiv für Geschichte der Philosophie* 4 (1891) 414-24.

Susemihl, Franz. *Geschichte der griechischen Literatur in der Alexandrinerzeit.* 2 vols. Leipzig, 1892; repr. Hildesheim: Georg Olms, 1965.

Swift Riginos, Alice. *Platonica: The Anecdotes Concerning the Life and Writings of Plato.* Columbia Studies in the Classical Tradition 3. Leiden: E. J. Brill, 1976.

Sykutris, Johannes. *Die Briefe des Sokrates und der Sokratiker.* Studien zur Geschichte und Kultur des Altertums 18,2. Paderborn: Ferdinand Schöningh, 1933.

————. "Mitteilungen: Die Handschriftliche Überlieferung der Sokratikerbriefe." *Philologische Wochenschrift* 48 (1928) 1284-95.

————. "Sokratikerbriefe." *PW* suppl. B. 5, 981-87.

Syme, Ronald. "Fraud and Imposture," in *Psedepigraphia I*. Fondation Hardt 18, Kurt von Fritz, ed. Geneva: Vandoeuvres, 1971.

Tarrant, Dorothy. "The Tradition of Socrates." *G & R* 1 (1931) 151-57.

Theissen, Gerd. "Soziale Schichtung in der Korinthischen Gemeinde." *ZNW* 65 (1974) 332-72.

Thomas, Ernst. *Quaestiones Dioneae*. Leipzig: Dr. Seele and Co., 1909.

Thraede, Klaus. *Grundzüge griechisch-römischer Brieftopik*. Zetemata: Monographien zur klassischen Altertumswissenschaft 48, Erich Burk and Hans Diller, eds. Munich: C. H. Beck, 1970.

Thurén, Jukka. "Die Struktur der Schlussparänese 1 Tim 6,3-21." *TZ* 26 (1970) 241-53.

Thyen, Hartwig. *Der Stil der jüdisch-hellenistischen Homilie*. Forschungen zur Religion und Literatur des Alten und Neuen Testaments n.F. 47, R. Bultmann, ed. Göttingen: Vandenhoeck & Ruprecht, 1955.

Trillitzsch, Winfried. *Senecas Beweisführung*. Berlin: Akademie, 1962.

Trummer, Peter. " 'Mantel und Schriften' (2 Tim 4,13). Zur Interpretation einer persönlichen Notiz in den Pastoralbriefen." *BZ* n.F. 18 (1974) 193-207.

———. *Die Paulustradition der Pastoralbriefe*. BEvT 8, J. Becker and H. G. Reventlow, eds. Frankfurt am M.: Peter Lang, 1978.

Tzaneteas, Peter. "The Symbolic Heracles in Dio Chrysostom's Orations 'On Kingship.' " Diss. Columbia University, 1972.

Vetschera, Rudolf. *Zur griechischen Paränese*. Smichow/Prague: Rohliček and Sievers, 1911-12.

Vielhauer, Philipp. *Geschichte der urchristlichen Literatur: Einleitung in das Neue Testament, die Apokryphen und die apostolischen Väter*. Berlin: de Gruyter, 1975.

Vögtle, Anton. *Die Tugend- und Lasterkataloge im Neuen Testament: Exegetisch, religions- und formgeschichtlich untersucht*. Neutestamentliche Abhandlungen 16,4/5. Münster i.W.: Aschendorff, 1936.

Wagenmann, Julius. *Die Stellung des Apostles Paulus neben den Zwölf in den ersten zwei Jahrhunderten*. BZNW 3. Giessen: A. Töpelmann, 1926.

Wallis, P. "Ein neuer Auslegungsversuch des Stelle 1 Cor 4,6," *TLZ* 75 (1950) 506-8.

Wanke, Joachim. "Der verkündigte Paulus der Pastoralbriefe," in *Dienst der Vermittlung* (Fest. zum 25-jährigen Bestehen des philosophisch-theologischen Studiums im Priesterseminar Erfurt), W. Ernst et al., eds. Erfurter Theologische Studien 37. Leipzig: St. Benno, 1977, 165-89.

Weber, Ernst. *De Dione Chrysostomo Cynicorum sectatore. Leipz. Stud.* 9-10 (1886-87) 77-268.

Wefelmeier, Carl. *Die Sentenzensammlung der Demonicea*. Athens: John Rossolatos, 1962.

Wegener, E. P. "The *ENTOLAI* of Mettius Rufus (pVindob G Inv 25824 V-VI 7)," in *Symbola Raphaeli Taubenschlag dedicatae* (Bratislava: Ossolineum, 1956) and also *Eos* 48 (1956) 331-53.

Wegscheider, Julius A. *Der erste Brief des Apostels Paulus an den Timotheus neu übersetzt und erklärt, mit Beziehung auf die neuesten Untersuchungen über die Authentie desselben*. Göttingen: Johann F. Röwer, 1810.

Weidinger, Karl. *Die Haustafeln: Ein Stuck urchristlicher Paränese*. UNT 14, H. Windisch, ed. Leipzig: J. C. Hinrichs, 1928.

Weiss, Johannes. *Die Briefe Pauli an Timotheus und Titus*. Kristisch-exegetischer Kommentar über das Neue Testament 11, H. Meyer, ed. Göttingen: Vandenhoeck & Ruprecht, 1894.

Wendland, Heinz D. *Die Briefe an die Korinther*. Göttingen: Vandenhoeck & Ruprecht, 1968.

Wendland, Paul. "Betrogene Betrüger." *RhM* 49 (1984) 309-10.

———. *Die hellenistisch-römische Kultur in ihren Beziehungen zu Judentum und Christentum*. HNT 1,2/3. Tübingen: J. C. B. Mohr (Paul Siebeck), 1912.

———. *Philo und die kynisch-stoische Diatribe*. Beiträge zur Geschichte der griechischen Philosophie und Religion (Fest. Hermann Diels), P. Wendland and O. Kern, eds. Berlin: Georg Reimer, 1895.

———. "Die Rede an Demonikos," in *Anaximenes von Lampsakos: Studien zur ältesten Geschichte der Rhetorik*. Berlin: Weidmann, 1905.

Wenley, Robert M. "Neo-Cynicism," in *Encyclopedia of Religion and Ethics* 9:298-300.

Wersdörfer, Hans. *Die PHILOSOPHIA des Isokrates im Spiegel ihrer Terminologie: Untersuchungen zur frühattischen Rhetorik und Stillehre*. Klassisch-philologische Studien 13, E. Bickel, ed. Leipzig: O. Harrassowitz, 1940.

Wette, Wilhelm M. L. de. *Kurze Erklärung der Briefe an Titus, Timotheus und die Hebräer*. Leipzig: Weidmann, 1847.

Whitaker, G. H. "2 Timothy III.10." *Expositor* 8 ser. 18 (1919) 342-44.

Wibbing, Siegfried. *Die Tugend- und Lasterkataloge im Neuen Testament und ihre Traditionsgeschichte unter besonderer Berücksichtigung der Qumran-texte*. BZNW 25. Berlin: A. Töpelmann, 1959.

Wilamowitz-Möllendorff, Hans U. von. "Phaidon von Elis." *Hermes*. 14 (1879) 187-93.

———. "Unechte Briefe." *Hermes* 33 (1898) 492-98.

Wilcken, Ulrich. "Urkunden Referat." *APF* 11 (1935) 148-49.

Wilder, Amos. *Early Christian Rhetoric: The Language of the Gospel*. Cambridge: Harvard University, 1971.

Willms, Hans. *EIKON: Eine begriffsgeschichtliche Untersuchung zum Platonismus. I Teil: Philon von Alexandria mit einer Einleitung über Platon und die Zwischenzeit*. Münster i.W.: Aschendorff, 1935.

Wohlenberg, G. *Die Pastoralbriefe (der erste Timotheus-, der Titus-, und der zweite Timotheusbrief)*. Kommentar zum Neuen Testament 13, T. Zahn, ed. Leipzig: A. Deichert (Georg Böhme), 1906.

Woolcombe, K. J. "Le Sens de 'type' chez les Pères." *La Vie Spirituelle* suppl. 16 (1941) 84-100.

Wrede, Wilhelm. "Miscellen." *ZNW* 1 (1900) 66-85.

Zahn, Theodor von. *Introduction to the New Testament*. Trans. by John M. Trout et al. 3 vols. New York: Charles Scribner's Sons, 1909.

Zeller, Eduard. *Socrates and the Socratic Schools*. Trans. by Oswald J. Reichel. New York: Russell and Russell, 1962.

———. "Über eine Berührung des jüngeren Cynismus mit dem Christentum," in *Kleine Schriften II: Zur Geschichte der antiken Philosophie*, Otto Leuze, ed. Berlin: Georg Reimer, 1910, 41-45.

———. "Wie entstehen ungeschichtliche Ueberlieferungen?" in *Kleine Schriften II: Zur Geschichte der antiken Philosophie*, Otto Leuze, ed. Berlin: Georg Reimer, 1910, 46-90; originally in *Deutsch Rundschau* 74 (1893) 189-219.

Ziegler, Konrat. "Plagiat." *PW* Halbb. 40: 1956-97.

Zucker, F. "Verbundenheit von Erkenntnis und Wille in griechischen Sprachbewusstsein beleuchtet durch Erscheinungen aus der Bedeutungsentwicklung von *AGNOIA, AGNOEIN, AGNOEMA*," in *Studies Presented to D. M. Robinson II*, G. E. Mylonas and D. Raymond, eds. St. Louis: Eden, 1953, 1063-72.

Index of Modern Authors

Subject Index

Index to the Pauline Epistles

Index to Ancient Authors